THE USDF GUIDE TO Dressage

THE USDF GUIDE TO Dressage

JENNIFER O. BRYANT

WITH A FOREWORD BY GEORGE WILLIAMS

 Storey Publishing

The mission of Storey Publishing is to serve our customers by publishing practical information that encourages personal independence in harmony with the environment.

Edited by Deborah Burns and Marie Salter

Cover design by Kent Lew

Text design by Vicky Vaughn

Text production by Liseann Karandisecky

Production assistance by Jennie Jepson Smith

Front cover and spine: U.S. competitor Guenter Seidel aboard Graf George, owned by Dick and Jane Brown, at the 1996 Olympic Games in Atlanta. Photograph by © Bob Langrish.

Back cover photographs: © Arnd Bronkhorst/www.arnd.nl, lower right; © Bob Langrish, top four; © SusanJStickle.com, lower left

Frontispiece: Guenter Seidel aboard Nikolaus 7, owned by Dick and Jane Brown, at the 2002 World Equestrian Games in Jerez de la Frontera, Spain. Photograph by © Bob Langrish.

Complete photography credits are provided on page 331.

Illustrations by Joanna Rissanen; arena diagrams by Chuck Galey

Indexed by Susan Olason/Indexes & Knowledge Maps

The information in this book is true and complete to the best of our knowledge. All recommendations are made without guarantee on the part of the author or Storey Publishing. The author and publisher disclaim any liability in connection with the use of this information. For additional information please contact Storey Publishing, 210 MASS MoCA Way, North Adams, MA 01247.

Storey books are available for special premium and promotional uses and for customized editions. For further information, please call 1-800-793-9396.

Printed in Hong Kong by Elegance

10 9 8 7 6 5 4 3 2 1

LIBRARY OF CONGRESS CATALOGING-IN-PUBLICATION DATA

Bryant, Jennifer O. (Jennifer Olson)
    The USDF guide to dressage / by Jennifer O. Bryant ; with a foreword by George Williams.
        p. cm.
    Includes index.
    ISBN-13: 978-1-58017-529-6; ISBN-10: 1-58017-529-5 (hardcover : alk. paper) 1. Dressage. I. United States Dressage Federation. II. Title.

SF309.5.B79 2006
798.2′3—dc22   2005032239

R-E-S-P-E-C-T: U.S. competitors Debbie McDonald and Brentina bring the house down with their Motown-themed freestyle at the 2005 FEI Offield Farms Dressage World Cup in Las Vegas.

CONTENTS

Foreword .... *ix*

Preface .... *x*

Acknowledgments .... *xi*

PART I. Preliminaries   1

    Chapter 1. Origins and History 2

    Chapter 2. Are You Dressage Material? 14

    Chapter 3. Dress for Success 18

    Chapter 4. Outfitting Your Horse 28

PART II. Basic Training   53

    Chapter 5. Selecting an Instructor 54

    Chapter 6. Your First Dressage Lessons 65

    Chapter 7. The Training Scale 88

    Chapter 8. The Walk 97

    Chapter 9. The Trot 112

    Chapter 10. The Canter 130

    Chapter 11. Basic Dressage Movements 147

    Chapter 12. Training and Cross-Training 190

PART III. Showtime!   201

Chapter 13. Letters and Levels 202

Chapter 14. Know before You Show 210

Chapter 15. Show-Ring Attire and Turnout .. 224

Chapter 16. Show-Day Pointers 238

PART IV. Physical Education   251

Chapter 17. The Fit Dressage Rider 252

Chapter 18. Your Dressage Partner 268

Chapter 19. Keeping Your Horse Sound
and Healthy 274

PART V. Fun Extras   289

Chapter 20. Dressage with a Twist 290

Chapter 21. Learning Outside the Arena 296

Chapter 22. Must-See Shows and Events ... 304

PART VI. Appendixes   311

Appendix A. All about the USDF 313

Appendix B. Dressage-Related Associations .. 317

Appendix C. Resources 319

Appendix D. Outfitters 325

Glossary 326

Photography Credits 331

Index 332

FOREWORD

ven to those of us who grew up trying to do it, dressage has always seemed mysterious. Over the years, a few books have been published that have helped to demystify this intriguing and addicting sport; Jennifer Bryant has written such a book.

When I was a small boy, I remember my father saying that it takes a better teacher to explain something complex, such as Einstein's theory of relativity, in an understandable manner at the elementary school level than it does to explain it at the college level. Although dressage is not rocket science, in *The USDF Guide to Dressage* Jennifer Bryant tackles a complex topic by breaking it down into concepts understandable to the uninitiated. In clear, concise language, she simplifies dressage, making it accessible to everyone. She guides aspiring dressage enthusiasts through the crucial process of finding the right instructor and explains the terminology, fundamentals, and principles of dressage. The book covers the basics in detail, enabling readers to understand them, to appreciate their importance, and therefore to progress in their dressage training. Also included are exercises for the continual improvement of both horse and rider.

This wonderful book "opens the door," allowing many to enter and experience the world of dressage, a sport that at times can be both frustrating and delightful. The frustration sometimes originates from a lack of knowledge or a lack of a clear path to follow through the challenges presented during the course of daily

training; the delight comes from the relationships we forge with our horses when we are successful in our daily training.

The key to training success is our understanding of the principles of dressage as developed over the centuries. Dressage has its base in the teachings of the Greek master Xenophon, whose teachings were expanded on by many subsequent expert horsemen and continue to evolve to this day. As our understanding of equine biomechanics, physiology, and psychology continues to advance with each successive generation of experts in horsemanship, we become more enlightened. When we gain the proper education, historical perspective, and practical knowledge, along with equestrian skill, our horses benefit, and we benefit through the joy that comes from the bond we share with our horses.

Books like *The USDF Guide to Dressage* help us feel the joy and delight that come with the study of dressage and make the journey more rewarding.

—George Williams
Vice President, USDF, and international
Grand Prix–level dressage competitor

◄ **DRESSAGE DIVA:** The Grand Prix mare Rocher, owned by Chuck and Joann Smith, and George Williams.

PREFACE

I am the perfect person to write this book, not because I'm a great dressage rider or trainer, which I'm not, or because I edit *USDF Connection,* the member magazine of the United States Dressage Federation (USDF), which I do. No, I'm the perfect choice because when I began studying dressage back in the 1980s, I had no "feel" whatsoever, no natural seat, no innate gift. I am blessed with good hand-eye coordination, mediocre athletic ability, and decent posture. That was about it for me in the "suitable for dressage" category. If I'd been a sport-horse candidate, I probably wouldn't have passed the breed registries' inspection tests.

I give you this background to explain that everything I've learned about dressage has been hard earned. I now ride at a fairly advanced level, but nothing has come easily. I have struggled with my riding position until the unforgiving saddle drew blood. I have read countless books and magazine articles, many of which I didn't understand because they seemed to be written for people who already know what a half-halt is and don't bat an eye when told mysterious things like, "Your horse is behind your leg." Huh? Fortunately, dressage is a sport in which dedication and hard work can overcome many obstacles, so if you don't consider yourself a natural athlete or a natural rider, don't let that deter you.

Dressage is classical horsemanship. Just as a gymnast or dancer learns to combine athleticism with grace to create a performance that delights our senses, so does a dressage rider teach the horse to develop his own innate gifts and movement in accordance with his natural tendencies and expressions. When it is done well, the horse appears to be dancing of his own accord and the rider appears just to sit there. It looks simple, joyful, and effortless. And those moments of perfection

— as fleeting as they can be, especially when starting out — are what get riders hooked.

My goal in writing this book was to produce the resource I wish I'd had when I first took up dressage. When I was a newbie, I yearned for a book that translated the jargon and explained the fundamentals in easy-to-understand terms; that didn't assume that my horse and I already had some dressage basics under our belts; that detailed common stumbling blocks and how to fix them and didn't assume that all horses are textbook-perfect, programmed always to give "desired response A" when cued with "correct rider aid A"; and that presented classical, humane, trustworthy advice and training expertise.

The USDF Guide to Dressage is the first on the subject to be fully endorsed by the USDF, the only national organization in the United States dedicated to, in the words of its mission statement, "education, the recognition of achievement, and the promotion of the sport of dressage." USDF, an umbrella organization comprising approximately 130 local, state, and regional dressage associations nationwide, spearheads the education and certification of dressage instructors and the training of fledgling dressage judges, to name just two of its major programs. Many of the most respected and accomplished dressage riders, instructors, trainers, and judges in the United States help to administer these programs and to further the sport of dressage domestically. The information presented in this book has been reviewed by USDF experts to help ensure that what you read is doable, practical, time-tested advice. (Any errors are solely the fault of yours truly, however.)

Dressage is a challenging discipline, but it holds many rewards. There is nothing like the warm greeting and trusting eyes of a horse who enjoys being your partner and who looks forward to the day's session. It is exhilarating to feel, even if just for a moment, the power and grace of a horse you are controlling as he dances with you. Dressage engages both the mind and the body, and its practice develops mental and physical discipline, challenging and calming the mind and spirit. Participation in dressage will make you stand taller, feel stronger, and move more gracefully when you're out of the saddle. You'll feel proud to be part of a centuries-old tradition of classical horsemanship. Dressage makes you a better rider and your horse a better horse. You'll discover things about yourself that other people probably pay therapists to discover for them. And, last but not least, it's incredibly fun! Let's begin.

Acknowledgments

Grateful thanks to the following: the USDF Executive Board and staff, for their faith in me and for their enthusiasm for this project; Karen Solem, agent, fellow dressage rider, and friend; Storey Publishing, for believing in this book; dressage experts Lisa Gorretta, Marilyn Heath, Janine Malone, Melanie Tenney, and George and Roberta Williams, for their careful review and excellent comments and suggestions; photo models Christopher Hickey, Emily Gershberg, Meghan Jackson, and Bonnie Olie, for their patience and cheerful cooperation; Gemma Gatti and Richard and Char-An Ireland, for the use of their beautiful dressage facilities in Loxahatchee, Florida, and East Fallowfield, Pennsylvania; Meghan Jackson, for the use of her Pilates Body Center in West Chester, Pennsylvania; Chris Hickey, for the use of his horse Levin in the photographs, and these other generous horse owners: Emily Gershberg (Pancratius), Brenna Kucinski (Regent), and Char-An Ireland (Otelo and Sultan); Bob Langrish and Amy Dragoo, for their top-notch work and good company during long photo shoots; Todd Flettrich, for teaching me a lot of what's in this book; everyone at The Dressage Center, East Fallowfield, Pennsylvania, for putting up with me during this project; that last point goes double or triple for my mom and for my husband, Michael. Semper Fi.

PART I

PRELIMINARIES

Perhaps you've seen dressage in photographs or in performance, and you were captivated. You think you'd like to try this sport with the horse you have, sturdy soul that he is. Beyond that, you're not sure what to do or how to begin.

Not to worry: I'll lead you through the getting-started process, step by step. In the chapters that follow, you'll become acquainted with the rich history of dressage, and you'll learn what you need to know to outfit yourself and your horse so that you're comfortably, correctly, and safely prepared to begin your dressage studies.

◄ Nicola McGivern on Active Walero at Aachen 2004.

CHAPTER 1

ORIGINS AND HISTORY

s the saying goes, if you want to know where you're going, you need to know where you've been. So let's begin our study of modern dressage by exploring its rich history and traditions, then move on to a discussion of dressage in the United States. We'll delve into the sport's military origins and follow its evolution from royal pastime to modern-day athletic pursuit.

A Tradition of Classical Horsemanship

The oldest surviving work of equestrian literature is *The Art of Horsemanship,* by the Greek historian Xenophon, who died in approximately 350 BC. The equestrian writings of Xenophon, which mainly concern training warhorses for long journeys and to be nimble partners in battle, are significant because they advocate a humane and patient approach to training, which was something of a novelty at the time.

In the first century AD, Lucius Flavius Arrianus (also known as Arrian) was born. He wrote the Roman cavalry manual *Ars Tactica* (The Art of Horsemanship), which is the only book of its kind to have survived from that era. *Ars Tactica* presents a number of important dressage-training concepts, each with success in battle as its goal.

After the collapse of the Roman Empire, the development of humane, gymnastic means of training horses as athletes for various purposes (generally referred to as *classical horsemanship*) waned. In the Middle Ages, horses were used primarily for transportation and for war, and little or no equestrian literature was produced. But with the Renaissance came a resurgence of interest in equine studies and the founding of several notable schools.

Going for Baroque

During the Renaissance, noblemen enjoyed riding and training horses to rarefied levels of athleticism, including various spectacular gymnastic feats. This was

THE FAMED LIPIZZAN STALLIONS of Vienna's Spanish Riding School half-pass in unison during a performance.

referred to as *manège riding* (horsemanship) and was generally pursued in an enclosed indoor arena or "school." This pursuit, also known as *haute école* (high school) equitation, was considered a refined, genteel pastime, similar to art and music. Noblemen enrolled in newly created schools of classical horsemanship (also known as *schools of equestrian art*) and enjoyed attending performances of *haute école* dressage.

The Royal Academy of Equestrian Art, founded in 1420 by King Duarte in Lisbon, Portugal (where, after the wartime destruction of its riding hall and a lengthy cessation of operation, it was reestablished in 1979), was the world's first school of classical horsemanship. It was followed in the mid-1500s by the School of Naples in Italy, founded by Federico Grisone, author of *Gli Ordini di Cavalcare* (Orders of Riding). Although today Grisone is largely frowned on for his endorsement of severe bits and other training methods considered inhumane by modern standards, his book is acknowledged as the first to set down a system for training a horse to the highest levels of dressage. The Duke of

Hapsburg brought Iberian horses (Spanish and Portuguese horses bred for *haute école* work) to his stud in Lipizza, and in 1580 the famed Lipizzan breed was born. The Spanish Riding School of Vienna, so named because of the Lipizzan's Spanish origin, was founded in 1572 and today is still home to the Lipizzan stallions. The "dancing white stallions" of Disney-movie fame are dressage's best-known ambassadors; and the chandelier-bedecked riding hall in Vienna, in which the stallions regularly school and perform, is a perennial tourist favorite.

Parlez-vous Français?

Dressage is French for "training." In the United States, most people pronounce it "dreh-SAZH." The ubiquitous British show announcers at U.S. dressage competitions seem to prefer "DREH-sazh." Whichever you choose, be aware that the common mispronunciation "DREH-sidge" will brand you as among the uninitiated.

TWO LESSER-KNOWN "AIRS," the *croupade* and the *ballotade*, as depicted in the equestrian classic *École de Cavalerie* by La Guérinière (Paris, 1733). (Courtesy National Sporting Library Collection, Middleburg, Virginia.)

In the late 1600s, Louis XIII of France and his son, "Sun King" Louis XIV, built the palaces of Versailles into world-renowned splendor. Never known for doing things halfway, Louis XIV made his École de Versailles into the finest equestrian center in all of Europe. For entertainment, he held *quadrilles* (choreographed rides featuring four horses and riders), dressage extravaganzas known as *carousels* (hence the name of the modern merry-go-round), and staged mock battles and other over-the-top equestrian amusements.

Most significant, at least as far as modern dressage is concerned, Versailles was home to *écuyer* (riding master) François Robichon de La Guérinière. Known as the father of modern horsemanship, La Guérinière developed and refined several noteworthy dressage movements and concepts and in 1733 penned his masterpiece, *École de Cavalerie* (School of Horsemanship), which many modern dressage enthusiasts consider to be the most important work of equestrian literature ever written.

Equestrian teachings spread throughout Europe and eventually made their way to England, where in 1743 William Cavendish, the Duke of Newcastle, wrote *A General System of Horsemanship,* which sums up much of the theory of the Baroque period, when horsemanship, like art, was pursued for its own sake.

Today, several renowned schools of horsemanship exist, in addition to the Spanish Riding School and the Royal Academy of Equestrian Art. In France, the École Nationale d'Équitation (National Riding School) in Saumur, founded in the late 1500s and home of the famed Cadre Noir and the former French Cavalry School, has supplanted Versailles as the headquarters of classical riding. The Royal Andalusian School of Equestrian Art, in Jerez, Spain, was founded in 1973, building on a tradition of *haute école* exhibitions that dates back to the 1600s. The German Olympic Training Center in Warendorf, run by the German National Equestrian Federation, is a mecca to many of today's top dressage competitors. Sweden's Equestrian Educational Center in Strömsholm also enjoys a reputation as a top-flight training center.

The Cavalry Connection

Cavalry warfare is the basis for much of modern dressage. As we've already learned, *dressage* is French for "training." Elementary dressage training teaches a horse to respond promptly and obediently to a rider's commands, to travel well in both directions, and to be compliant (easy to handle and guide) — all desirable traits for a horse whose rider is faced with swords, arrows, or bullets. A cavalry mount doesn't do his rider much good if he's disobedient, unresponsive, and difficult to maneuver. Basic horsemanship was required training in military schools, such as the celebrated French Cavalry School at Saumur.

At some point, clever cavalrymen discovered that they could make their horses even more useful by teaching them special movements that would give them a strategic advantage in battle. A swordsman, for instance, could literally rise above the enemy — mounted or unmounted — by cuing his horse to do a *levade,* a low, controlled rear on command. He could scatter foot soldiers by asking his horse to do a *courbette,* a movement in which the horse rears up, then, towering from a fearsome height, hops forward on his hind legs. And he could inflict some serious damage by wheeling around in a graceful pirouette and then having his horse perform a *capriole,* a vertical leap with a backward, full-force kick of the hind legs at its apex. These and other elevated *airs above the ground,* as they are known, are still practiced today by a few keepers of the flame, most notably the famed Spanish Riding School of Vienna.

The cavalry needed mounts with excellent endurance that could negotiate varying terrain and obstacles. To help select the best all-around horses and to test horses' fitness, obedience, and athleticism, a three-phase, four-day test called the *Military* was devised. The first phase assessed dressage. The second was a speed-and-endurance test comprising a steeplechase course and a cross-country jumping course over natural obstacles. The third was a show-jumping course over manmade obstacles designed to test jumping ability, speed, and fitness, coming as it did on the heels of the arduous cross-country course. When swords were replaced with guns, there was little need for horses that could capriole and courbette, so cavalry mounts in the late nineteenth and early twentieth centuries were trained in dressage on a more basic level. The jumping and dressage competitions in today's equestrian triathlon (known as *three-day eventing* or simply *eventing*) are direct offshoots of the Military.

Art Meets Sport

Much of the popularity of modern dressage can be attributed to the efforts of Count Clarence von Rosen, "master of the horse" to the king of Sweden.

THE LEVADE: The horse sinks on his haunches to a 45-degree angle and raises his forehand off the ground, holding the position for several seconds.

THE COURBETTE: The horse hops forward several times on his hind legs — a supreme feat of balance and strength.

A NOBLEMAN executes a capriole *(left)* while another rides piaffe between pillars *(right)* in this illustration from *École de Cavalerie.* (Courtesy National Sporting Library Collection, Middleburg, Virginia.)

Baron Pierre de Coubertin of France founded the International Olympic Committee (IOC) in 1894, with the goal of reviving the Olympic Games as a modern international sporting competition. The first modern Olympiad took place in Athens in 1896. Von Rosen believed that including equestrian competition in the Olympics would stimulate interest in horse sports among the general public, so he established the International Horse Show Committee, which presented the idea to the IOC. The IOC approved the measure for the 1908 London Olympics, but the public waited four more years for its first glimpse of equestrian competition. In 1912, the Stockholm Olympics featured three equestrian disciplines — a three-day event for military personnel, an individual dressage competition, and individual and team show-jumping competitions — all of which today remain part of the Olympic program.

During the first five decades of modern Olympic equestrian competition, only military men were eligible to compete, so the predetermined dressage patterns, or *tests,* were tailored to suit their horses' level of training. Olympic competition set the standard for other international equestrian competitions and for competitions within the various participating nations. For this reason, dressage tests do not include the levade

and capriole (which became obsolete with the advent of modern weaponry) but do include the *piaffe,* a challenging "trot on the spot," and *passage,* an elevated trot with a moment of hesitation between footfalls — two movements that are generally considered the ne plus ultra of the modern dressage horse and are the most collected movements in modern dressage competition.

THE PASSAGE (executed here by Farbenfroh and Germany's Nadine Cappellmann) is one of the most advanced movements in modern dressage competition.

THE 1932 U.S. ARMY OLYMPIC EQUESTRIAN TEAM. Through the 1948 Olympics, only military officers competed in international equestrian competition for the United States.

In 1921, the International Horse Show Committee was replaced by the Fédération Equestre Internationale (FEI, or International Equestrian Federation), which continues to govern the three Olympic equestrian disciplines as well as endurance riding and combined driving at the international level. Headquartered in Lausanne, Switzerland, since 1991, the FEI regulates and sanctions international competitions. (International dressage competitions are known as *Concours Dressage Internationale,* or CDI). The FEI comprises 130-plus member nations, and today there are numerous international-level competitions in addition to the Olympic Games. Each FEI member country has an equestrian national governing body that regulates and sanctions national competitions.

The Advent of Judging

The evolution of dressage from military activity to sport introduced a critical element never before associated with dressage: judging. At a dressage show, a judge (or panel of judges) awards a score for each *movement,* or required element, in the test. Scores range from 0 (not performed) to 10 (excellent). Each test has a maximum number of possible points. The actual points earned divided by the maximum number of available points results in a percentage (e.g., 68.215 percent), which is how a score is usually expressed.

Judges undergo extensive training to earn their licenses, and most strive to evaluate rides fairly and objectively. Still, judging can be contentious. Judges are human and have preferences and pet peeves, just like the rest of us. One judge's score of 7 might be another's 6. Predictably, the winner of a *class* (a group of competitors at a specified level) usually feels that the judging was fair and accurate; the also-rans may feel less so. Fortunately, many quality judges are committed to improving the sport of dressage and regularly participate in educational forums and other means of professional

SPANISH RIDING SCHOOL *Oberbereiter* (chief rider) Klaus Krizisch and the Lipizzan stallion Siglavy Mantua I in an exemplary piaffe.

The Biggies

There are many international equestrian competitions. Here are a few of the biggest. (See chapter 22 for more premier dressage events.)

- Dressage World Cup Final: six international "leagues" vie to qualify riders for this annual competition.
- World Equestrian Games (formerly World Championship competitions): held two years after each Summer Olympics.
- Continental championships: held the year before the Summer Olympics; the Americas participate in the Pan American Games.

development. (See page 315 for the role of the U.S. Dressage Federation in judge education.)

Dressage in America

In the United States, much of our dressage knowledge has been imported from Europe. Little is known about the history of dressage in the United States prior to the 1912 Olympic Games. From that time until the mechanization of the cavalry in the 1950s, dressage in the United States was the province of the U.S. Army, with several officers earning medals in Olympic and other international equestrian competition. Some, such as Maj. Gen. Guy V. Henry Jr. and Capt. Hiram Tuttle, now claim a place in the USDF Hall of Fame. Henry's protégé, Harry D. Chamberlin, himself an Olympic equestrian gold medalist, penned the U.S. Cavalry School's *Manual of Horsemanship* (1927) and also wrote the classic equestrian texts *Riding and Schooling Horses* (1934) and *Training Hunters, Jumpers and Hacks* (1937).

Henry and a number of other former cavalrymen were instrumental in helping U.S. equestrian sports gain a foothold in the civilian world after horses became obsolete for war and the means of preparing U.S. equestrian teams for international competition disappeared. Many military titles grace the list of founders of the United States Equestrian Team, which was established in 1950 to fill the void left by the cavalry's abandonment of equestrian pursuits.

With the transformation of the equestrian world from military to civilian, it was only a matter of time

MAJ. GEN. GUY V. HENRY JR. (pictured on Grey Falcon) competed in all three Olympic equestrian disciplines and was the first American president of the FEI.

CAPT. HIRAM TUTTLE and his 1936 Olympic dressage mount, Si Murray. The pair won team bronze in 1932, America's first medal in Olympic dressage. Tuttle is the first U.S. rider known to have specialized in dressage and was largely self-taught.

before nonmilitary folks became interested in eventing, dressage, and jumping as sport. Former cavalrymen continued to pass along their riding and training know-how, but the burgeoning class of equestrian sportsmen and sportswomen, thirsty for knowledge, were eager to benefit from the wisdom of those with centuries of equestrian experience.

With the world's top trainers and schools located in Europe, U.S. dressage enthusiasts sought to improve their knowledge by importing that expertise. This yearning to learn from the best and to raise the caliber of American dressage was the impetus for the founding of two important organizations: the American Dressage Institute and later the U.S. Dressage Federation.

The American Dressage Institute

To date, the founding of the American Dressage Institute (ADI) is the closest the United States has come to launching a national dressage school. The ADI was the brainchild of a few common-minded folks who wanted to help educate U.S. dressage riders and trainers. These New England–area dressage enthusiasts gathered at the Ox Ridge Hunt Club in Darien, Connecticut, in the early 1960s to swap ideas. Several, including Grand Prix–level rider Margarita "Migi" Serrell and Swiss émigré Max Gahwyler, began spending summers working together, with their horses, in Saratoga Springs, New York, a well-known racing and resort town. There they met such cultural notables as the late Lincoln Kirstein, founding president of the School of American Ballet and former general director of the New York City Ballet, and Broadway producer Chandler Cowles.

In 1967, the group held an informal dressage seminar in Saratoga. Kirstein, Cowles, and Olympic show-jumping gold medalist William Steinkraus (whose wife, Helen, a dressage judge, went on to become an ADI director) cosponsored the program. Bolstered by the success of the event, the group decided to offer a formal

DR. MAX GAHWYLER, author, dressage judge, and former ADI president, aboard Dresden, age 26 in this photo.

three-week educational program; Migi Serrell organized the effort.

In 1968, the newly formed ADI, with Serrell as president, began what would become a long-standing American tradition of importing top European trainers to teach clinics. Then-director of the Spanish Riding School, Col. Hans Handler, a friend of Gahwyler and his wife, came from Austria to lead the first program. Subsequent visiting clinicians included Swedish Col. Bengt Ljungquist, who went on to teach ADI-sponsored clinics at the U.S. Equestrian Team headquarters in Gladstone, New Jersey, and became coach of the U.S. dressage team.

Interest in ADI spread by word of mouth, and soon its program attracted riders from the mid-Atlantic states, the Midwest, and the West Coast, as well as New England. It looked as if the ADI might become a permanent school of dressage in 1971, when Skidmore College opened its equestrian facilities in Saratoga. The college reserved an office, ten stalls, and student housing for the ADI. ADI representatives and several veterans of the Spanish Riding School attended the grand opening in July 1971, and the audience was treated to dressage exhibitions in the new indoor arena.

Max Gahwyler became the ADI's final president in 1974. Several well-known riders, trainers, and judges attended the ADI. However, the group's crowning achievement was perhaps training and fielding the dressage team that won a bronze medal at the 1976 Montreal Olympics. Team members Hilda Gurney (on Keen), Dorothy Morkis (on Monaco), and Edith Master (on Dahlwitz) were ADI graduates, and the ADI spent $20,000 to send them to Montreal. Thinking back on the 1976 bronze medal, Gahwyler says the team's accomplishment was especially impressive because the United States hadn't won a medal since 1948, and the team did not train and compete in Europe beforehand to gain international exposure, the way most top U.S. dressage riders do today.

In 1973, a new organization, the U.S. Dressage Federation (USDF), was founded and soon eclipsed the ADI in terms of membership and financial resources; the ADI was dissolved in 1978.

THE LEGENDARY THOROUGHBRED KEEN and Hilda Gurney, who won team bronze at the Montreal Olympics in 1976.

The U.S. Dressage Federation

Until the 1970s in the United States, only two major groups were involved with dressage: the American Horse Shows Association (AHSA, later known as USA Equestrian and now as the U.S. Equestrian Federation) and the U.S. Equestrian Team (USET, now the USET Foundation).

Dressage competition was around in the late 1960s and early 1970s, but enthusiasts weren't happy with what they perceived to be a lack of attention from the AHSA, which governed dressage at the time. Some complained that dressage judges needed more education and preparation before earning their licenses. Riders and trainers fretted because in the United States, unlike in Europe, instructors of dressage and other disciplines weren't required to earn certification or licensing. Still others were concerned about the apparent lack of standards in dressage education. Dressage in the United States as it then existed was a ragtag assortment of local and regional clubs with no established means of communication or interaction. The time had come for a national organization whose sole focus would be to further dressage in the United States.

Handfuls of dressage supporters had been meeting in various locations (at the American Dressage Institute in Saratoga Springs, for one) where pockets of activity and interest existed. Lowell Boomer, founder

USDF FOUNDER LOWELL BOOMER. For many years, USDF was headquartered in his hometown, Lincoln, Nebraska.

The U.S. Equestrian Federation

In 2003, USA Equestrian and the USET merged, becoming the U.S. Equestrian Federation, the national governing body of equestrian sport under the U.S. Olympic Committee. The new organization carries on all of the duties and responsibilities that the two factions (which for some years prior to the merger were infamously warring) previously conducted separately. They include:

- writing the rules for competitions (everything from what kinds of equipment and attire are permitted to how long a judge's rest break must be)
- establishing and enforcing rules banning the use of potentially performance-altering drugs and medications in show horses
- licensing judges who officiate at national-level competitions
- sanctioning (or "licensing") national-level competitions
- for dressage, writing the national-level tests (patterns) used in competition
- fielding and funding U.S. teams for international equestrian competition
- establishing the selection procedures for U.S. equestrian teams in FEI competitions, including the Olympic Games, the World Equestrian Games, and the Pan American Games, among others
- providing promising riders and horses with opportunities to train and compete abroad, as a means of affording them desired international exposure to top trainers and judges

In addition to dressage, the USEF oversees hunters, jumping, driving, and endurance, among other disciplines. According to current USEF membership demographics, dressage is second in numbers behind hunters and jumpers.

U.S. BRONZE-MEDAL DRESSAGE TEAM, 1976 Montreal Olympics. Hilda Gurney on Keen, Edith Master on Dahlwitz, and Dorothy Morkis on Monaco.

of the Nebraska Dressage Association, decided that it was time to back up all the talk with some action. He placed an advertisement in *The Chronicle of the Horse,* the weekly news magazine of English horse sports, bidding that "all those who are interested in the advancement of Dressage" come to Lincoln, Nebraska, in February 1973 to found a national organization.

Seventy people answered Boomer's call. In attendance were a number of equestrian VIPs, including representatives from the AHSA Dressage Committee and the USET. Their presence, although welcome and necessary, brought up a thorny question: how could an organization be founded with the collective blessing of the establishment when dissatisfaction with the establishment was the impetus for founding the new organization?

Dressage enthusiasts are a passionate bunch given to exhaustive discourse about their favorite topic and eminently willing to engage in heated debate should the occasion arise. To help keep a lid on the pot, someone wisely requested the services of Capt. John "Jack" Fritz, a college history professor who also happened to be a retired cavalryman, a member of the AHSA Dressage Committee, and a USET official. As one attendee later recounted, Fritz put his skills at managing boisterous college students to work, and with a dose of his trademark humor, aided by a few of Boomer's own stunts (such as having the University of Nebraska

THE LATE, GREAT GIFTED, now a member of the USDF Hall of Fame, carried U.S. owner and rider Carol Lavell to team bronze in the 1992 Barcelona Olympics.

ROBERT DOVER (with FBW Kennedy, owned by Jane Forbes Clark, at the 2004 Athens Games) has competed on more Olympic dressage squads than any other rider.

marching band troop through the proceedings to break the tension), kept the group on track for two long days until consensus could be reached and the USDF established.

In November 1973, the USDF held its first official business meeting, during which it elected a slate of officers, approved bylaws, launched committees, and wrote a mission statement. These core elements, although since expanded and embellished, have endured for more than thirty years. (For more on the mission and programs of the USDF, see appendix A.)

The Challenges We Face

Because the United States is a vast geographic area, we don't have the benefit of a centrally located national equestrian training center. It's simply not feasible for most riders to load Dobbin in the trailer and drive several hours to train, the way riders do in Germany and other European countries. Many people rely primarily on books, magazines, and videos for dressage instruction and information, particularly if they live in remote areas. Through instructor certification and its other educational programs, however, the USDF helps to promote correct, quality dressage instruction and training.

There is a great diversity of horse breeds in the United States. In addition to the warmblood breeds, we have such famous American breeds as the Morgan, the Appaloosa, and the Quarter Horse. All are different from the European warmblood and have certain broad differences of conformation, movement, temperament, and ability as it relates to dressage. Compounding this, each horse is an individual and has his own set of strengths, weaknesses, and peculiarities. Some are talented for dressage, but all pose slightly different training challenges for the dressage rider. (See chapter 18 for more on breeds, conformation, and movement.)

What's Their Secret?

Germany dominated international dressage for the latter half of the twentieth century and continues to be an international powerhouse in the sport. Its national system of dressage training gives the country a distinct advantage. German riding instructors are licensed, the German National Equestrian Federation operates a national dressage school, and set criteria (such as minimum scores in competition and previous placements) dictate the levels at which horses and riders are permitted to compete and when they may advance. In addition, horse breeds in Europe tend to be more homogeneous than those in the United States. Most are warmbloods, thereby posing less of a challenge to dressage judges. In the United States, dressage judges have to compare "apples to oranges" in terms of the varied ways of going seen among the more numerous breeds used in competition.

NOT MANY HORSES compete in multiple Olympics. USDF Hall of Famer Graf George went twice, in 1992 (under Mike Poulin) and 1996 (under Guenter Seidel, pictured); he won team bronze both times.

CHAPTER 2

ARE YOU DRESSAGE MATERIAL?

I'll answer my own question. If you're reading this book, you probably are dressage material. But let's make sure. I love horses. Still, there are plenty of equestrian sports that simply don't interest me, perhaps because their emphasis and objectives don't suit my personality. Before we delve any deeper, let's do a little sport psychology.

Time for a quick quiz. Don't panic; there are no right or wrong answers. Just be honest with yourself. True or false:

- Deep down, you wouldn't miss never jumping again. *true/false*
- Your current equestrian activities are fun, but you're a bit bored. You have a sense of "Is this all there is?" *true/false*
- You're somewhat turned off by horse sports in which the animal appears to be little more than a tool, the way a bicycle or a football is. *true/false*
- You find yourself yearning for a more meaningful partnership with your horse. *true/false*
- Your busy lifestyle leaves you with little time for contemplation and reflection. *true/false*
- You wish your horse were a more willing and obedient partner. *true/false*
- Your horse's movement is lovely to watch when he's at liberty, but all of that grace and balance seems to disappear when you get on his back. *true/false*
- Speaking of grace and balance, you think you could use a little more of that yourself. *true/false*
- You're a traditionalist: you prefer the time-tested to the trendy. *true/false*
- You like to have fun as much as the next person, but you're not a thrill seeker — at this point in your life, anyway. *true/false*

Now tally the number of true and false responses. The more trues, the more likely you are to find the study of dressage an absorbing and rewarding pastime. Of course, every round hole is bound to have a few square pegs, but generally this quiz is a good assessment tool. Folks who gravitate toward extreme activities, such as bungee jumping and skydiving, tend not to be able to tolerate endless hours of trotting in circles, perfecting myriad subtleties.

Most dressage riders juggle job and family commitments with a compulsion to spend most of their disposable income on horses and dressage education. You'll find us at the barn early in the morning and late at night, sporting our best grubbies, while our horses luxuriate in color-coordinated blankets and pricey tack.

Common Traits

Those of us who have been bitten by the dressage bug tend to share certain characteristics. These attributes include:

● *A penchant for perfectionism.* OK isn't enough in a sport in which details are everything. If you don't hold yourself to a high standard and are not at least a little nitpicky by nature, then you might find dressage monotonous.

● *Patience, patience, patience.* Do you give up easily? Then consider abandoning ship now, because dressage is a sport that will test the limits of your patience like no other. Imagine fleeting moments of transcendent bliss and planet-aligning harmony between horse and rider interspersed amid a vast expanse of tedium, occasional frustration, and a generous helping of I-know-it's-not-quite-right-but-I-can't-seem-to-fix-it.

If right now you lack Zen-like serenity and endurance, that's OK. Once you've tried dressage, it tends to make you want to keep going. It's human nature to hang in there an incredibly long time for the occasional payoff — a phenomenon, well-known by players of slot machines, called *partial reinforcement.*

● *Willingness to "just do it."* No athlete — and believe me, that's how you'll have to regard yourself if you take up dressage — improves without training both body and mind. Thankfully, you don't have to be marathon-fit to get started in this sport. But if you've ever wondered how much the dressage rider does because "it looks like she's doing nothing up there," you'll soon find out. It takes a great deal of balance, endurance, and overall strength to sit the trot for a few minutes without looking and feeling like a sack of potatoes.

At some point in their pursuit of dressage perfection, many riders discover the benefits — both in and out of the saddle — of augmenting their riding time with aerobic exercise and strength and flexibility training. The health benefits of such activities are well documented. (See chapter 17 for specifics about how to start and maintain a fitness routine.)

● *Sensitivity and introspection.* Dressage is not all physical, of course. Developing a deep and satisfying relationship with a horse requires a surprising amount of introspection and self-examination. U.S. Olympic dressage veteran Michael Poulin once said that the horse-rider relationship is not unlike a marriage: for better or for worse, for richer or for poorer (OK, usually for poorer), in sickness and in health.

A marriage takes work. To sustain the relationship and to grow together, spouses may occasionally need to take a long, hard look at their behavior patterns and then grapple with how to change entrenched habits and automatic responses. Likewise, the dedicated dressage rider is willing to do a little self-examination — particularly during those "stuck" times, when the rewards seem few and far between — to determine whether ego and other issues are obstructing the path to progress.

Some people are so intent on branding themselves upper-level riders that they push their nice young horses too far, too soon. A poorly built foundation is weak, and the same is true in dressage training. Lots of young horses have been ruined because riders' egos got in the way. A good rider and horseman always puts the horse's welfare first.

Problems in other areas of your life have an uncanny way of coloring your riding. Someone who feels unrewarded and frustrated at work, for example, may subconsciously use riding as a means of gaining respect and a sense of accomplishment. Such a person may be inclined to place a great deal of importance on winning in competition, which ultimately may not be the best thing for the horse.

TEAMWORK: Dressage is all about developing a partnership with your horse.

Classic sport-psychology performance issues also come into play: fear of failure, show-day nerves, and so on. If you're willing to examine and address these issues as they arise, you'll be rewarded with greater satisfaction in your riding and a happier horse. Isn't that what it's all about?

● ***Enjoyment of a solitary pursuit.*** You and your horse are a team. In a way, dressage is the ultimate team sport, but it is also the antithesis of traditional team sports. There is no banter with fellow players (not counting time spent chatting with barn buddies in the tack room), no one else to help share the blame or take the credit, and no cheering crowd. Ultimately, it's you, your horse, and a lonely expanse of arena. Your instructor, your significant other, and your mom may administer pregame encouragement and postgame pep talks, but that's it.

In dressage, you compete against a standard of perfection, not the other riders. Your ribbon, if you're fortunate enough to win one, is evidence of how well your performance stacked up against the others in your class — all measured individually by the judge against the "perfect 10" standard.

The upshot is that dressage can be a competitive sport, and there are certainly many riders with competitive personalities. But dressage is not really about winning and losing; it's about the pursuit of perfection.

Prerequisites

Even if you think you fit the dressage "psychological profile" to a T, I'd be remiss if I didn't discuss the basic riding skills and abilities that you'll need to use this book successfully and to get started in this sport.

● ***You're a reasonably healthy person, without any conditions that would preclude your delving into the world of dressage.*** If you are pregnant or have any health issues that might affect your ability to ride

DRESSAGE IS A SOLITARY PURSUIT, but that would be no problem if you had access to this beautiful arena, would it? Here, Olympian Guenter Seidel schools at home in California — perfect, but we wish he were wearing protective headgear.

dressage, check with your doctor before you begin. (Riding and pregnancy don't always mix; see chapter 17 for more on this topic.) People with bad backs need to be especially careful when it comes to dressage.

● **You have a grasp of the basics of horse care (grooming and tacking up, for example).** If you don't, I highly recommend a good comprehensive introduction (see the suggested readings on page 319).

● **You put your horse's health and well-being — and your own safety — first.** Dressage training is supposed to build you up, not tear you down. If ever you're unsure about your horse's physical or mental health or you get that nagging feeling that you're treading on dangerous ground, you are astute enough to heed your intuition and seek guidance from your veterinarian or a knowledgeable trainer.

● **You have attained at least an elementary skill level in the saddle.** You can "go and whoa" and turn and circle safely at the walk, trot, and canter (that's walk, jog, and lope for you Western types).

● **You have a reasonably independent seat,** meaning that you don't require a death grip on the reins to stay on. Losing a stirrup isn't the end of the world.

● **You possess the coordination needed to operate various body parts independently of one another.** (You'll find this quite useful when someone says things like "*Left* rein! *Right* leg!")

● **You may be interested in competing in dressage someday, but the show ring isn't necessarily your goal.** I offer advice on riding a dressage test (a pattern of movements, as prescribed for competition) in chapter 16, but how to win in dressage isn't the primary aim of this book.

If everything I've described sounds good, then it's time to take the next step.

CHAPTER 3

DRESS FOR SUCCESS

*S*afety, comfort, and practicality are essential when it comes to choosing the proper attire for dressage. For everyday schooling, you'll need a few basic items. As you progress, you may want to add some extras that will enhance your riding experience. I'll review them here. (Show attire is discussed separately in chapter 15.)

Must-Haves

For your safety and comfort, don't climb into the saddle without these items.

Helmet

Yes, you'll see plenty of bareheaded dressage riders. Even the requirements for show attire don't currently specify the wearing of safety headgear, except in a couple of specific instances. But please buy yourself a quality, good-fitting equestrian helmet, and strap it on every time you put a foot in the stirrup. I won't belabor the point here except to say that even skilled and experienced dressage riders have been seriously injured and even killed when riding without helmets. Most riding accidents don't happen during jumping and other, seemingly riskier, pursuits: they happen during trail rides, hacks around the farm, and innocuous flatwork sessions.

Quality safety headgear is easy to find and very affordable. If you can afford to ride, you can afford a helmet, and even if you can't afford to ride, you can afford a helmet! Today's equestrian safety helmets are lightweight (less than a pound), ventilated, and comfortable; many have removable washable liners. Only helmets that carry certification as equestrian headgear from the American Society for Testing and Materials (ASTM) and the Safety Equipment Institute (SEI) have proved to meet minimum standards for protection in the event of a fall. Don't buy anything that isn't ASTM/ SEI-certified. If an item is billed as "apparel only," then it's just for looks, even if it looks much like its certified cousins.

USDF-CERTIFIED INSTRUC-TOR Christopher Hickey models one of the many approved safety equestrian helmets available today. A properly fit helmet sits down evenly on the forehead, with the visor approximately at eyebrow height.

SIDE VIEW of the safety helmet. If the helmet fits well, it will sit level on the head, as Chris's does. It will not shift forward or backward — or fall off — as the wearer moves or bends over; however, the helmet is not considered secured unless the chin strap is fastened as snugly as is tolerable.

If you're a cyclist, you may wonder whether your bike helmet can do double duty. Unfortunately, it can't. Bike helmets are designed and shaped differently than equestrian helmets and do not meet the standards for head protection in equine sports.

Virtually all tack shops and equestrian-supply catalogs offer safety headgear (see appendix C for a list of resources). If you've never been fitted for a helmet before, buy it in person and not online or through a catalog. Visit your local tack shop and ask to be fitted by an experienced salesperson. He or she will ensure that the helmet you choose is snug enough that it won't rock back and forth when you move your head but not so tight as to induce an instant headache. The salesperson should also show you how to adjust the chin strap so that it's sufficiently snug without cutting into your windpipe. And do I have to say this? Riding with the chin strap undone is like driving without a seat belt; don't do it.

Boots

Although you might think otherwise if you've ever tried to break in a pair of new ones, snug-fitting, knee-high riding boots weren't designed as instruments of torture. They're actually very helpful in protecting your legs from rubbing against the saddle flaps and stirrup leathers. Certain types can even aid your leg position.

Most important, though, is the low heel (about half an inch) that every standard-issue riding boot has. That heel can help save your life in the event that your foot ever gets shoved deep into the stirrup iron. The heel prevents your foot from passing all the way through; if it did, your foot would probably become caught in the iron. If you should be unlucky enough to fall off the horse as this is happening, you might become "hung up" in the stirrup — unable to free your foot — and could be dragged and seriously injured or even killed if your frightened mount bolts. *Never* get on a horse without first donning a pair of low-heeled riding shoes or boots.

Now, if you're coming to dressage from the hunter/jumper ranks, you know that lots of folks never don boots and breeches outside the show ring. They prefer to school in jeans, "English-style" chaps, and so-called paddock boots (ankle-high, heeled riding boots). For Western riders, of course, boot-cut jeans, chaps, and cowboy boots are *de rigueur*. But you'll rarely see a dressage rider in anything other than tall boots and breeches or riding tights. (The exception might be a young child, who would tend to don jodhpurs — ankle-length, cuffed riding pants — and the aforementioned paddock boots.) My own introduction to dressage came via the world of eventing. A convert from the hunter/jumper/equitation ranks, I had neither fashion sense

SAFE AND APPROPRIATE ATTIRE for dressage schooling, as worn by USDF-certified instructor Emily Gershberg: approved safety helmet, breeches, dress boots, and gloves.

WHAT'S WRONG WITH THIS PICTURE? It demonstrates what not to wear for schooling. Conspicuously missing are helmet and gloves; she's wearing jeans (can you say *rubbed spots?*); and her sneakers have no heels, making them vulnerable to slipping through the stirrup irons and catching her feet. Correct riding attire is safe and comfortable.

nor, apparently, common sense when it came to riding attire. One day, while observing me prepare for a ride by wrapping my jean-clad calves with horse leg bandages — a cheap, cooler version of chaps among some of the hunter/jumper crowd — my eventing instructor said gently, "You really should wear boots and breeches when you school. It'll help your position."

Actually, I think it helped her sensibility most, by not having her student look like a complete yokel and slob. Chastened, I donned my seldom-worn correct attire and soon discovered that she was right. The breeches didn't bind or rub, and they allowed complete freedom of movement. And the boots afforded protection that a length of fabric just couldn't match.

If you're just starting out in dressage, there is no reason for you to run out and spend an inordinate amount of money on a pair of expensive custom or semicustom imported dressage boots. Affordable, relatively inexpensive alternatives are available that will be quite serviceable. So which to choose? Here's a guide to the most common options.

DRESSAGE BOOTS VERSUS EVERYTHING ELSE

Visit a tack shop that carries both dressage and hunter/ jumper or eventing attire. Ask to see a dressage boot and a typical boot that, say, a hunter rider would wear. Compare the thickness and feel of the leather. You'll notice that the dressage boot is noticeably thicker, heavier, and stiffer than the other boot. That's because we dressage riders don't need quite the mobility that our fence-jumping counterparts require, and we want our legs to stay in place (more or less) and look quiet and elegant.

The first time I slipped on (OK, pulled on, with considerable effort) my first pair of real dressage boots and threw an unbending leg over the saddle, I was shocked at how much the boots aided my leg position. They actually helped keep my legs quiet!

Dressage boots generally have two other helpful features. Most have stiffeners sewn into the back of the boot, running from the top to just above the ankle. The purpose of the stiffeners is to prevent the boot tops from dropping and wrinkling, thereby spoiling the desired long, elegant look. Unlike a hunter rider's boot, which typically is so wrinkled that it looks as if it could use a face-lift, a dressage boot's only wrinkles after break-in are around the ankle. This, plus the fact that most riders want their boots as tall as possible to make their legs look as long as possible, means that it is almost impossible to bend at the knee in new boots, which can make for some funny moments when mounting. Even today, in my six-year-old Königs dressage boots, I cannot squat.

The other ubiquitous dressage-boot feature is the so-called Spanish top. In the Spanish top, the outside of the boot is cut markedly higher than the inside — again, all in pursuit of that coveted long, lean look.

DRESS BOOTS VERSUS FIELD BOOTS

Most dressage boots are *dress* style, meaning that they are closed pull-ons. Hunter riders lean toward the field boot, which has laces across the instep and usually a useless little flap of leather (called a *swagger tab*) dangling from the outside cuff. The laces make field boots much easier to get in and out of and offer the ability to obtain a more custom fit through the foot and ankle. (As for the swagger tab, I think it's the equestrian equivalent of equine splint bones — a vestigial remnant, no longer useful but not yet evolved into extinction.)

If you like field boots, by all means buy them. You can school in anything you please, and you won't get kicked out of the show ring, either. Just realize that, past a certain point in your dressage education (and you'll know it when you get there), you'll feel a smidge awkward in anything other than a dress boot.

ZIPPERS AND GUSSETS

Putting zippers and gussets in dressage boots was probably the brainchild of some desperate dressage rider who got tired of throwing out her back every time she wedged her feet in a bootjack and tried to pull off her boots. These clever modifications — now standard features in some boots — speed the on/off process and can save quite a bit of uncomfortable pulling.

Zippers are inserted into the boots so that they won't interfere with your riding. A flap of leather conceals the zipper and snaps closed at the top of the boot. Even though zippers can be the first thing in a boot to break, they are a favorite of many riders, especially

A. The classic dress boot: closed instep and Spanish top. B. Field boots lace through the instep. This model lacks swagger tabs.

A

B

busy trainers, who have to get in and out of their boots all day long.

Gussets are discreet elastic inserts in the upper inside part of the boots, so they're invisible when you're mounted. They allow just enough give to ease the on/off process. My boots are fitted such that there's no room for error, so to speak. My gussets "forgive" the couple of pounds gained over the holidays and allow me to ride in comfort. And if you've ever worn a too-tight boot, with that awful, pulse-pounding, cramping feeling in your calves, you won't be in a hurry to repeat the experience.

Like zippers, gussets are generally less sturdy than the rest of the boot. I think they're worth the tradeoff, though; and they're replaceable.

HOW TO BUY BOOTS

Just as in shoe shopping, get fitted, or measure yourself, for riding boots at the end of the day, when your feet and legs are at their most swollen. Wear a typical pair of breeches (the thickest pair, if you have a choice) and the type of socks you'll ride in. If it gets cold where you live, wear the heaviest sock you'll wear while riding. You may not be able to get a super-thick hiking sock

under your boots, but trust me, when the mercury drops, you'll want to wear something more substantial than knee-high hose or flimsy trouser socks.

Most tack catalogs that offer riding boots include descriptive diagrams and instructions on how to measure your feet and legs for boots. A tack-shop employee who's knowledgeable about boot fit and the differences among brands can be an invaluable resource. Even economy-priced riding boots aren't inexpensive, so take the time to get your measurements right.

Breeches

If you've never tried to sit the trot, it won't be long before you appreciate the need for riding pants that don't shift, bind, rub, pinch, or twist (plus, other kinds of pants don't slip easily into riding boots).

Riders have a love-hate relationship with breeches. On the plus side, today's breeches are stretchy and comfortable. Some casual styles can even do double duty as fitness tights or leggings for street wear. And a stylish pair can flatter the figure. But if you are somewhat self-conscious, you may not relish the thought of parading around in a pair of tight pants. The sport of dressage compounds this concern with its unofficial

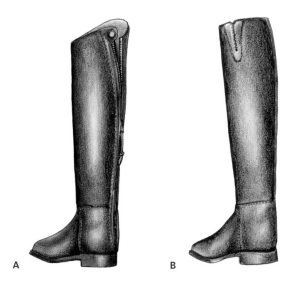

A. A zipper is a boon to the busy trainer who's on and off various mounts all day and needs a boot that's easy to get in and out of. B. Gussets (elastic inserts) can't be seen when the rider is mounted and give riding boots a more forgiving fit.

Boot-Care Basics

Take care of your riding boots, and they should give good service for quite a few years. My six-year-old boots need new elastic gussets and a little patching but are otherwise sound, and they still look great.

Here are some tips for keeping your boots looking and feeling their best:

- *Minimize exposure to moisture, sweat, and dirt.* Take off your boots before you hose down your horse. Don't wear them to clomp through the muddy pasture to catch him. Remove the after-ride buildup of horse sweat and grime with a clean, damp sponge. If you must ride in the rain or walk or stand in wet conditions, pop a pair of galoshes (available from tack shops and equine-supply catalogs) over the feet of your boots.
- *Don't overdo the cleaners and conditioners.* Although I cleaned my first pair of boots religiously, eventually they refused to shine up, no matter what kind of boot polish I tried. A shoe repairer told me that my diligent use of saddle soap and leather conditioners had gunked up the leather's pores to the extent that polish no longer did its thing.

Now the only part of my boots that conditioner or soap ever touches is the inside of the ankle and calf, where contact with the saddle and my horse's sides has worn off the finish. The rest of the gleaming black surface gets a daily buffing with a clean, soft cloth and a weekly application of a good-quality polish.

- *Keep them treed.* Help maintain your boots' shape by inserting shoe and boot trees when you're not wearing them. Cedar trees are more expensive than plastic ones, but the wood helps to absorb moisture and also reduces odors.

---

rule that only white or light-colored breeches are appropriate for the show ring. Not only do white breeches show every trace of dust and horse snuffle like a road map, but they also magnify any roundness in the thigh area.

The bottom line is that, besides serving as an occasional unplanned weight-loss incentive, breeches or riding tights are really the only sensible garment option for your lower half when you're in the saddle. These duds come in almost endless price ranges, colors, and options. Here are the main ones you'll have to be concerned about.

BREECH VERSUS TIGHT

I refer to all my riding pants as *breeches,* a generalization sure to horrify the equestrian trade industry. In broad terms, *breeches* are the more formal of the two main types of riding pants used in dressage. They usually have either a front or a side zipper with a snap or hook at the top, a defined waistband, and belt loops. Most close at the ankle with hook-and-loop fasteners. Some have slash or zip pockets. Breeches are made from a variety of fabrics, with different weights to suit different seasons and climates; today's materials, unlike the "peg leg" versions of yesteryear, have two- or four-way built-in stretch.

A *riding tight,* as you might imagine, is similar to a pair of leggings or exercise tights. Most are strictly pull-on in style, with minimal extras. Most lack belt loops and exterior pockets, though many have small coin pockets — big enough for a key or a couple of coins, and not much else — hidden beneath the waistbands.

Because breeches are tailored more like slacks than tights, they're considered the dressier of the two types of riding pants. They can also be a tad more forgiving to the less-than-perfect body because they're not necessarily skintight. Some popular styles feature comfy

Breeches and Tights

Schooling ring or show ring, casual or tailored, hot weather or cold, adult or child — whatever your needs, there's a breech for you.

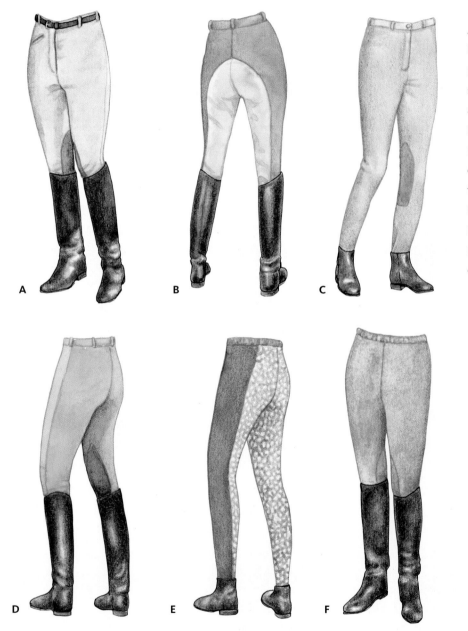

A. The classic breech has a front zipper, belt loops, one or more pockets, and knee patches. **B.** Many dressage riders favor full-seat models because of the added grip for a deep, secure seat. **C.** Another view of a knee-patch breech.

D. "Extended patch" or "dressage patch" combines grip with freedom of movement through the seat. **E.** Riding tights with rubber appliqués are funky, fun, and cool in hot weather. **F.** Most riding tights are simply styled pull-ons and come in a variety of colors, grip options, and fabrics.

front pleats. Others have high waistbands, which look nice on some body types. In a throwback to the "peg leg" look, a few even have an eased fit through the thigh, which is nice if you don't happen to enjoy your legs' feeling as if they're in sausage casings.

Many riders' wardrobes contain a mixture of breeches and riding tights. Breech fabric tends to be a bit sturdier than that of the lightest riding tight, which is why I like the thinnest, unfussiest type of tight for those dog days of summer. When winter rolls around, you'll find me in a high-tech riding tight made of a windproof outer layer of heavy, stretchy fabric fused to a fleece interior. Such super-duper cold-weather riding apparel usually comes in the form of tights — and, frankly, when it's really cold, I don't care what I look like.

As a rule, breeches cost more than riding tights — especially if they're imported from Europe, as so many dressage brands are. It is when you begin to shop for riding apparel that you learn the apparent unwritten rule that everything related to dressage is priced assuming that all riders are independently wealthy. No wonder so many of us descend like cicadas on tack shops' sales and hound the bargain sections of our favorite Web sites and catalogs!

GET A GRIP

As you become familiar with English-riding apparel, you'll soon notice that most breeches and riding tights marketed for dressage have what's known as full seats. These are overlays or inserts of leather or faux suede that extend from derriere to midcalf, so that every part of the garment that touches the saddle is covered. The purpose of the full seat is to provide a surface that grips for an extra-secure seat, with minimal slippage.

Although full seats are all the rage, there's no rule that says you have to wear them. Some dressage riders prefer the traditional knee patch, which covers the insides of the knees only. Others like the so-called dressage patch (also known as the extended knee patch), a harder-to-find option that extends the length of the leg but doesn't cover the seat.

Because the full seat requires more material, it's more expensive than the knee patch or the dressage patch. Depending on the material, it can also be hotter in the summertime. I have a mixture of full seats and knee patches in my own wardrobe. A couple of my knee-patch models are great in warm, sticky weather but can be a tad slipperier than I'd like when it's cold and dry out.

Some clever manufacturers offer an option that combines the coolness of a tight with the security of a full seat: rubberized patterns applied to a tight where the full seat would be. The patterns, which are available in many designs and colors, are not quite as good at gripping as a real full seat but are quite adequate for general schooling. They're cool in warm weather and fun to wear, although during quick dashes to the grocery store, I've drawn a chuckle or two at the sight of bright purple horses galloping across my backside.

Whatever you choose to wear, get in the habit of tucking your shirt in, at least for lessons and clinics. You'll give your instructor a much better view of your upper-body posture, and subtle flaws won't be hidden beneath a billowing shirt.

Gloves

Strictly speaking, gloves aren't required for schooling (although they are customary in the show ring, so you might as well get accustomed to riding in them). However, I consider them an indispensable part of my riding wardrobe. Here's why.

Riding can be tough on the hands. Rubs and blisters tend to come with the territory, and gloves do a lot to prevent chafing.

Reins can get pretty slippery when they're wet with sweat. Even gloves won't eliminate slipping entirely, but they're a thousand times better than bare hands. One of the mantras of dressage training is "steady, even contact" with the reins. That's tough to achieve in the best of circumstances, but add a pair of slippery reins and, well, just forget about it. You don't need to master a death grip, but you do need to be able to keep the reins at an even length — and that's not as easy as it sounds. Gloves help.

It may go without saying, but you'll appreciate gloves even more when it's cold outside. There are many cold-weather riding gloves to choose from, and today's models manage to be both cozy and lightweight.

You can school in any type of glove you please, but I advise against choosing one that's not designed for equestrian use. Riding gloves are reinforced in the areas that get the hardest wear — especially the area between the pinky and ring fingers, where the rein lies — and are made of materials that stand up to hard use and horse sweat.

Special Extras

Some dressage riders give as much thought to what's under their attire as they do to the schooling outfit itself. The right undergarment can make the difference between a pleasant day in the saddle and an equestrian

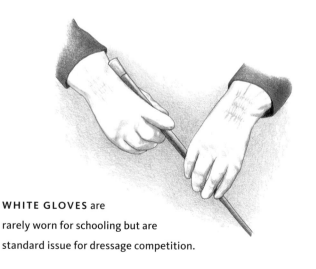

WHITE GLOVES are rarely worn for schooling but are standard issue for dressage competition.

| TIP | **Remove Rings** |

For safety's sake, remove any rings before you ride or work around horses. Rings can catch on halter edges, reins, and other objects and could potentially cause injury. They also tend to get bumped and bashed, so it's wise to leave your valuable jewelry at home in order to keep it — and your hands — looking good.

For the Ladies

Gals, you may want to consider investing in a few good sport bras. Sitting the trot is uncomfortable if you need a sport bra and aren't wearing one. The average bra designed for daily wear doesn't offer enough support. Buy a bra specially designed for high-impact activity. You'll look better, and you'll feel better and more confident in the saddle.

Padded Underwear

You've heard of padded bicycle shorts? Well, they make similar garments for riders, padded in the appropriate areas. Some riders swear by them. Personally, although I've suffered from my fair share of saddle rubs and abrasions, I've always found that either the saddle or my position was to blame. Ultimately, if padded underwear helps make your time in the saddle more enjoyable, by all means wear it.

Spurs and Whips

Ride dressage for a little while and you're bound to want spurs or whips. Both encourage horses to go forward. The sport's governing bodies set strict rules as to the sizes and types that are permitted. You won't find a cat-o'-nine tails in dressage, nor will you find wickedly pointy spurs such as you see in Westerns.

It's important that you understand that neither whips nor spurs are intended as — or should be used as — instruments of torture. Horses can be quite lazy and thick-skinned (kind of like the rest of us) at times, and occasionally they need something a bit stronger than the whisper of a calf to get them going. Used properly, a spur is like a nudge with an elbow, and a whip is a precise tap. To use either in anger or roughly is inhumane and unacceptable.

Beginning riders don't wear spurs because they haven't yet gained the balance and body control needed to ensure that they'll never jab their horses unintentionally. Later, when your legs become more "educated," the spur can serve as a sophisticated amplification.

Perhaps the greatest challenge in learning to use the whip is gaining sufficient ambidexterity to deliver precise, well-timed taps where you want them with either hand. As a southpaw, I had to practice for years before I felt as comfortable with my whip in my right hand as in my left. In dressage, it matters which hand the whip is in, so you need to learn to switch hands with equanimity.

If you're new to dressage, don't rush out to equip yourself with spurs and whips from the get-go. Your instructor will tell you when you're ready for one or both and can help steer you toward the types that are most appropriate for your needs and for those of your horse.

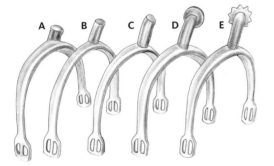

Spurs and Whips

SPURS ARE ONLY FOR riders who have sufficient leg control to ensure they won't goose their horses accidentally. U.S. Equestrian Federation rules govern everything from bits to spurs. These five spur types, all currently legal, are the most common for dressage. Left to right, from mildest to harshest: Tom Thumb spur (A), short straight-neck (B), long straight-neck (C), dime or disk rowel (D), pointed rowel (E).

DRESSAGE WHIPS come in various lengths and degrees of stiffness. Pictured are four typical examples: whip with metal cap and leather-wrapped handle (A), "balance" whip with two-part handle (B), whip with knob-topped handle (C), and grippy, rubber-covered handle (D). Be aware that only one whip no longer than 43.3 inches (110 cm), including lash, may be carried while schooling or showing at a recognized dressage competition. Handle styles are largely matters of personal taste and comfort.

CHAPTER 4

OUTFITTING YOUR HORSE

*K*eep two things in mind as you read this chapter: tack and equipment for dressage, more so than for other equestrian disciplines, is tightly regulated by the organizations that govern dressage competition; and, like most of the other English-riding disciplines, dressage is a conservative sport. Subtle trends come and go, but traditional, time-tested items tend to endure.

Requirements for tack and dressage equipment are spelled out in painstaking detail in the various rule books (see chapter 14 for more information). You might be thinking, "So what? I have no interest in showing. Why should I try to comply with rule-book legalities?" Good point, if indeed you never set hoof on a show ground. However, beyond the stipulations about what your horse can and cannot wear in the show ring, the spirit of the rules helps to ensure the humane treatment of horses and upholds a correct, classical standard of training. There's usually a good reason that one type of bit is legal for competition and another is not, for example. By following the spirit of the law, you demonstrate your commitment to learning to ride and train dressage with your horse's welfare foremost in your mind.

You may see riders in some wild getups in their home arenas, but come show day they're all in the same basic outfit. Tack and saddlery in dressage is likewise conservative. Most dressage experts believe that the simplest, most classic, and least gimmicky types of equipment are best; they don't chase the latest fads.

With these points in mind, let's take a look at the main categories of dressage tack and equipment, and how they differ from the items used in other equestrian disciplines.

Saddles

Saddles help to cushion and protect a horse's back and also offer a rider security and position assistance that would be much harder to achieve bareback. To serve a horse well, a saddle must properly fit the shape and contours of the horse's back. If it doesn't, like an ill-fitting pair of shoes, a saddle can cause pinching, rubbing, and muscle spasms, among other problems — all of which can lead to discomfort and poor performance and behavior. To serve a rider well, a saddle must be comfortable and its design must facilitate the type of activity that the rider is undertaking.

Saddle Fit

Saddle fit is always a topic of interest. It never fails to draw eager learners (even experienced riders and horse owners) to clinics and seminars, and it's a perennial favorite in the horse magazines. Why? A horse can't tell us how his saddle feels. Instead, he shows us. We notice any of a long list of vague equine behaviors — from "kicks when I tighten the girth" and "bucks when I get on" to "seems reluctant to go forward" and "hard to get him to pick up the left-lead canter" — and wonder what the problem is. Am I doing something wrong? Does his back hurt? Is he lame? Muscle sore? Lazy? Just plain naughty? We don't know for sure, but we're taught, correctly, to evaluate and eliminate any possible physical causes of resistance or disobedience first, before assuming that he's a rotten apple in need of correction. One of those possible physical causes is improper saddle fit.

When a saddle fits correctly, the seat is level on the horse's back, thereby enabling the rider to maintain a balanced position, and remains in position when properly girthed; it does not creep forward onto the withers or slide backward. The *pommel,* the front of the saddle, does not press down on the horse's withers, and the *channel* or *gullet* of the saddle (the "tunnel" that runs along his spine) is sufficiently high and wide that no part of the saddle touches the sensitive spinal area. Instead, the rider's weight is distributed evenly along the length and breadth of the *panels,* the padded areas under the rider's seat and on either side of the saddle

gullet. Likewise, the contours of the panels fit the horse's back conformation so the pressure is evenly distributed. Finally, the *saddle tree* — the saddle's skeleton, a structure of metal, fiberglass, or other materials that gives the saddle seat its shape — is as wide as the horse, and the *tree points* (the parts of the tree that lie under your upper legs when you're mounted) are wide enough to accommodate his shoulders without pinching, yet not so wide that the saddle rocks from side to side like a tipsy sailboat.

An experienced saddle fitter can help you find a saddle that's comfortable for both you and your horse. Saddle fit can be adjusted to a limited extent by *reflocking* — adjusting the amount and placement of the saddle's stuffing to make it fit your horse's back better. Some saddles have adjustable trees that permit a certain amount of width modification. Still, a saddle cannot be redone to fit completely differently from its original basic design and contours. Take it from one who's suffered the consequences of an ill-fitting saddle: it's less aggravating and more economical in the long run to replace an ill-fitting saddle than it is to deal with performance issues, lameness, and lost training time.

What Makes It a Dressage Saddle?

Take a look at the photographs on page 32. Each depicts a horse and rider engaged in a different equestrian sport and the appropriate saddle for the job. When it comes to saddles, function dictates form.

WESTERN SADDLE

A Western saddle is utilitarian. Its wide, deep, padded seat is designed to allow the rider to sit in comfort for hours on end — after all, this is the saddle of the cowboys who roamed the wide-open range. The *fenders* (the pieces of the leather that hang down from the seat, beneath the rider's legs) help protect the rider's legs. The saddle horn is not a handgrip but a home for the lariat.

Choosing a saddle that fits horse and rider correctly can be a challenge for any rider. What's more, even the right saddle can be made to fit incorrectly if it's not positioned properly on the horse's back. Here's a pictorial how-to primer.

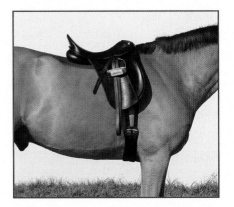

CORRECT SADDLE FIT AND POSITION *(left)*. When a saddle fits your horse correctly and is positioned properly the deepest point of the seat is in the center, and the saddle sits level, as it does here. **VIEWED FROM BEHIND** *(right)*. There is ample clearance between his spine and the saddle's gullet or channel, which ensures that there will be no painful pressure.

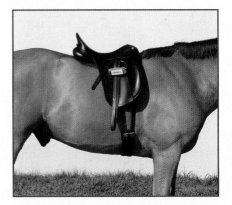

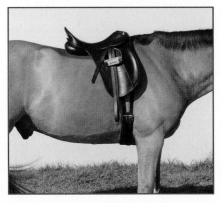

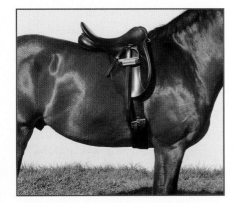

TOO FAR BACK. Here's the same saddle positioned too far back. The seat tilts forward and the girth is behind the natural hollow where it should rest.

TOO FAR FORWARD. Even a good-fitting saddle can be made to fit improperly if it is not positioned correctly on the horse's back. This saddle is too far forward. The seat slopes to the rear, the flaps rest against his shoulders, and the girth is wedged behind his elbows.

TOO HIGH IN FRONT. Saddle sizes and makes vary in cut and fit. This saddle is positioned correctly but sits too high in front. The pommel is higher than the cantle, and the deepest point of the seat is too far back. If you were to ride this horse in this saddle, you'd be forced into a "chair seat," with your legs out in front of you.

RACING SADDLE

A racing saddle is the polar opposite of the Western saddle. Astonishingly lightweight (especially if you've ever hefted a Western saddle), this tiny scrap of leather with the barely-there seat gives a jockey maximum mobility aboard a thousand pounds of thundering horseflesh, his only purchase, his feet anchored in the saddle's jacked-up aluminum stirrup irons. To keep saddle weight to a minimum, this type of saddle offers practically no security for the rider.

JUMPING SADDLE

Somewhat more substantial but still considered a "postage stamp" by most Western riders is the jumping, or forward-seat, saddle. This type, ubiquitous in the hunter ring and in all kinds of jumping competitions, has a relatively shallow seat to enable the rider to lift up off the horse's back quickly and easily while clearing fences. The *flap* (the large piece of leather under the rider's upper leg) is cut with a forward angle to accommodate the rider's bent knee. The forward-seat saddle isn't as extreme as the racing saddle, but it too is built for mobility, not security. Still, many models feature padded flaps (for a little extra grip and comfort) and knee rolls (padded, wedge-shaped pieces under the flaps at the forward edges of the saddle, which help to stabilize the rider's legs). The seats of these saddles are mostly flat; some "serious" jumping models feature slightly deeper seats for a tad more security over the big fences.

DRESSAGE SADDLE

Now we come to the dressage saddle. A glance at the photographs shows that it's a cousin of the forward-seat saddle, which it most closely resembles. A closer look, however, reveals several important differences.

Compare the photos of the dressage rider and the hunter/jumper rider. The dressage rider has a longer

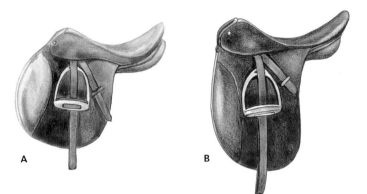

A   **B**

JUMPING VS. DRESSAGE SADDLE. Put a jumping saddle (A) next to a dressage saddle (B), and notice several important differences. The flaps of the jumping saddle are short and cut forward to accommodate the rider's short stirrups and greater hip and knee angles. The seat is shallow to permit more freedom of movement. The deeper-seated dressage saddle is cut for a long leg and greater security.

stirrup for a longer leg and more open hip, knee, and heel angles. Therefore, the dressage saddle features a longer, straighter flap.

SEAT DEPTH Next, let's look at the seats of the two saddles. The dressage saddle has a deeper seat than its forward-seat counterpart. Its *pommel* (the arch at the forward point of the seat) and *cantle* (the rearmost point of the seat) are higher, and the seat of the saddle is correspondingly deeper. This is a saddle that you can move in somewhat — you're not quite as planted as you are in a Western saddle — but not too much. Dressage riders prize a deep, quiet seat, one that gives the impression of being immobile, so dressage saddles are designed to aid riders in achieving this goal.

PADDED FLAPS AND KNEE ROLLS Dressage riders want their legs to be quiet — no inadvertent flapping or shifting — so most dressage saddles have padded flaps as well as knee rolls of varying thicknesses

Comparing Saddles

When it comes to saddles, form and function are intertwined. Designed to help riders achieve the goals of various equestrian disciplines, saddles and the accompanying stirrup length and placement facilitate the position that best enables riders to get the job done.

THE WESTERN SADDLE *(left)*, designed for comfort and utility, is the tool of working cowboys as well as many pleasure riders.

THE FORWARD-SEAT ENGLISH SADDLE *(right)* combines a measure of security with a relatively flat seat that enables the rider to get up out of the saddle over fences; it is a favorite of hunter and jumper riders. The flaps are cut forward to accommodate the angle of the rider's legs in stirrups that are short enough to provide good support for galloping and jumping.

THE RACING SADDLE *(left)* is the polar opposite of the Western saddle. It's miniscule, lightweight, and provides little more than a place to hang the super-short stirrup leathers.

THE DRESSAGE SADDLE *(right)* has a deeper seat and a longer, straighter flap than a forward-seat English saddle, thereby enabling the rider to sit erect and fairly still, with a long leg that does not rely much on the stirrup irons for support.

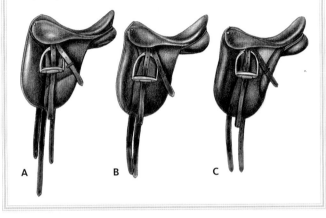
resulting outline resembling a person sitting in a chair. Many such riders appreciate saddles with super-thick knee rolls and other leg-stabilizing features. Other riders feel inhibited by such saddle designs and prefer a flatter model that enables them to position their legs where they want.

SEAT PADDING Likewise, opinions differ on seat padding. Of course, there is some padding beneath the seat of every saddle. However, some designs are relatively hard — on the rider, not on the horse's back — while others are lushly padded expressly for rider comfort. Some riders find a harder seat uncomfortable or even painful and appreciate soft-seat models. Other riders complain that a cushy seat, while comfortable, diminishes the desired feel of the horse's back: "It's like sitting on an overstuffed sofa."

STRAPS (BILLETING SYSTEM) One other obvious difference between most dressage saddles and other types of saddles are the *billet straps,* those two curiously long straps to which the girth buckles on either side of the horse. All English saddles have billet straps, but most don't hang low, dangling a good foot or so beneath the bottoms of the flaps.

Why the difference? Because with a conventional girthing arrangement (with shorter billet straps and a girth whose buckles sit beneath the saddle flaps) and longer stirrup leathers, your legs would tend to lie right on top of the buckles. The usual solution — typical for almost all of today's dressage saddles — is long billets and a short girth. This way, the girth buckles lie in front of your legs instead of underneath them. The design works well and is comfortable for both rider and horse. The only challenge is that it's a bit more of a gymnastic exercise to tighten a short girth while mounted. If you have a bad back, after you've mounted you may want to enlist the aid of a helper on the ground to snug the girth.

and prominence. If you lift a dressage saddle's flap, however, you'll notice that there's very little leather under the leg. That absence of bulk is designed to enhance your ability to feel the horse's sides with your legs. Unlike riding Western, of which it is sometimes said that the rider "rides the saddle and not the horse," a dressage saddle should not place unwanted bulk between you and your horse, for it would inhibit your ability to discern your horse's every movement.

SECURITY FEATURES The design element in which dressage saddles vary the most is in the amount of "security features" they offer. Some riders struggle to keep their legs in the desired position: shoulders, hips, and heels in alignment (see page 67 for a discussion of this position). A common nemesis is the "chair seat," in which the rider's legs creep forward, with the

How to Choose?

The saddle that is right for you is the one that fits you and your horse comfortably and that enables you to sit in balance with minimal effort. Sure, you may have a crookedness issue or struggle to sit the trot, but you shouldn't have to fight your saddle, too. A good choice is the saddle that's comfortable and supportive in the right places and otherwise feels as if it stays out of your way. When you're riding, you're able to forget about it. It's not constantly bothering you or causing you to readjust your position or to engage in contortions in order to avoid pain or discomfort.

The *billeting system,* as some saddle manufacturers refer to it, varies from model to model. The billet straps of some saddles lie parallel, which is the traditional positioning. Increasingly popular in recent years, however, is the so-called triangle arrangement, in which the front billet angles backward and the rear billet is straight or angled slightly forward. This system purportedly renders the saddle more secure on the horse's back and less likely to creep forward as you ride. The angled front billet is said to help hold the saddle in place and can help eliminate the need for a *foregirth,* which is a device that fits snugly against the front of the saddle and serves as a barrier that prevents the saddle from sliding forward as the horse moves. (Horses with very low withers are especially prone to this problem.)

As with the basic saddle design, and despite manufacturers' claims, one billeting system is not inherently superior to another. The trick is to find a combination that fits horse and rider well and doesn't slip, creep, twist, roll from side to side, or frustrate you or your horse. How will you know if it's frustrating him? If he's always been good about saddling and mounting but lately has begun making ugly faces — or worse — or if his normally free movement has inexplicably shortened, something's wrong. If the changes coincide with a switch to different tack or equipment, the culprit may be easy to identify. Go back to using your old stuff and see what happens. If, however, nothing external has changed, then call your veterinarian.

On some dressage saddles, you'll see a *flap strap,* a third, thinner leather strap dangling from each flap, with a buckle on one end. It purportedly holds down the flaps and thus prevents them from bunching under the rider's legs. I've ridden in saddles with and without flap straps, and I didn't notice much difference. If your saddle has a flap strap, simply snug it up as you tighten the girth, but don't worry about making it as tight as the girth itself, as it isn't meant to keep the entire saddle in place.

"You Can Have Any Color You Want, as Long as It's Black"

So said assembly line–automobile pioneer Henry Ford about the Model T, according to legend. A glance at any catalog or tack shop might well convince you that the same is true in the sport of dressage.

The majority of dressage tack is black, but brown has been making quiet inroads over the past several years, and now a number of manufacturers offer both black and brown. Both colors are absolutely correct for the show ring, so it's a matter of personal taste. Most riders choose the tack color they feel is most flattering to their horse's color. Some people find brown especially handsome on a chestnut horse, for instance. Many riders agree that a black or dark-bay horse would look odd in brown tack, although there's no rule that says you can't use it if you happen to like the way it looks.

Whichever saddle color you choose, you'll want to pick a girth of the same color for the sake of continuity. It's advisable to select a bridle of the same color, as well. (See page 41 for more on bridles.)

Leather or Synthetic?

Leather remains the material of choice and the industry standard for dressage saddles. However, saddles crafted of synthetic materials — such as the well-known Wintec brand, with a model endorsed by German Olympic dressage gold medalist Isabell Werth — have established a foothold in the English-riding world. Synthetics are attractive for two reasons: price and ease of care.

Leather, as you know, is skin. Most leather dressage saddles are made of cowhide, but some high-end manufacturers craft models from such exotic hides as elk and buffalo. Whatever the animal origin, the fact remains that leather tack, just like your own skin, requires regular cleaning and conditioning to remain soft and supple. Good care is also necessary to help preserve the stitching. The time that you spend cleaning your tack is an excellent opportunity to inspect for rips, badly worn areas, or weakened stitching that, if left unrepaired, could lead to a dangerous equipment failure. (See below for a primer on leather care.)

I'm a tack junkie who enjoys the daily cleaning ritual, but not all riders share this passion. Even the finest leather will dry and crack and the stitching will rot if sweat and grime are not removed faithfully and the appropriate type of cleaning or preservative product applied. If you're not meticulous about keeping things clean, then by all means consider a saddle made of synthetic materials. Bear in mind, however, that a synthetic will not "break in" and conform to your and your horse's contours the way that leather does. Leather is still unsurpassed for its durability and "conformability," and these qualities make it worth the price for many riders.

Leather-Care Basics

Caring for your leather tack is easy and adds just a few minutes to your daily riding and horse-care regimen. Here are the basic steps:

- Remove sweat and grime with a clean, lightly dampened sponge or cloth.
- Apply a light coat of a cleaner or a combination cleaner/conditioner with a clean sponge or cloth. A good saddle soap (I'm partial to Tattersall) is my top choice for daily use.
- Every once in a while, or when leather seems particularly dry (such as in the winter or in dry climates), give the leather an extra helping of moisture by applying a light coat of a good conditioning product. Use oils sparingly, if at all; they can make leather soggy, and some types can cause stitching to deteriorate. Some conditioning products, such as Passier's Lederbalsam, are beeswax-based solids that go on as a thin film and "soak in" overnight. These products do a good job of deep-conditioning leather, but go easy or your leather will get goopy. If extra conditioning is needed, multiple thin coats are better than one thick coat.
- After each ride, dunk your horse's bit in clean water or wipe it with a clean, dampened rag or sponge to remove saliva and feed particles.
- To get bits and stirrup irons super clean, run them through the dishwasher on the top rack.
- Every few months or so, unbuckle or unhook all tack pieces, and give every square inch a going-over. Doing so helps to preserve the leather and also serves as a visual safety inspection for cracks that may indicate a piece is on the verge of breaking.
- For that show-ring shine, polish irons, bit rings (but never the mouthpiece), buckles, nameplates, and any other metal trim with a good metal polish.

Girths

Saddles are generally sold "less fittings," that is, they come without girths and stirrup leathers and irons. Most saddle manufacturers sell girths that complement their saddles. However, as long as you're pairing long billets with a short girth or short billets with a long girth, any brand should do. (If you're not sure, ask a salesperson for help.)

Dressage girths come in an even wider variety of materials than saddles. As with saddles, the most expensive girth material is leather. Leather girths require regular care and cleaning. A dirty, crud-encrusted girth can irritate your horse's skin and can even cause sores, so at the very least wipe it off every time you ride.

Girths made of synthetic materials abound. I happily paired my leather saddle with a girth made of a soft neoprene that doesn't slip yet cushions my horse's tender tummy. The only care it requires is a daily wipe with clean water. There are also girths made of string, cotton webbing, or cotton-synthetic blends. Some girths incorporate a short length of elastic for additional comfort for your horse.

Girths are available in a variety of shapes, from straight to assorted contours designed to reduce rubbing and chafing. And if you decide that your horse needs a little extra comfort, you can slip on a girth cover made of sheepskin, neoprene, or many other materials.

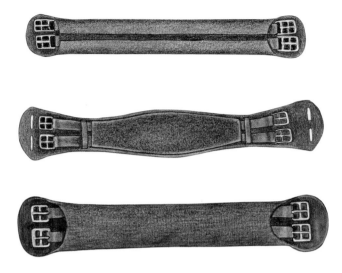

THREE TYPES OF SHORT DRESSAGE GIRTHS, all for use on saddles with long billet straps. Girths are available in leather and synthetics and in straight and contoured styles, as shown here.

Girth Caution

If you choose an elastic girth, remember this: elastic can be overtightened, and it can be tricky to get an elastic girth sufficiently snug without causing it to resemble a tourniquet. If you're not sure how tight is too tight, then choose another kind of girth or ask a knowledgeable trainer to show you.

Stirrup Leathers and Irons

Girths, billet straps, reins, and stirrup leathers are subjected to regular stress. If a piece of tack breaks, it's likely to be one of these four. So choose quality brands and don't try to economize on these items.

Stirrup Leathers

Quality stirrup leathers look like good saddle or bridle leather, with sturdy, even stitching and hefty buckles. (A few models feature an adjusting mechanism at the bottom of the leather instead of the traditional buckle at the top, supposedly to eliminate that annoying lump under your thigh. The standard arrangement works fine for most riders, but it's a matter of personal choice.) Good leathers tend to retain their shape and are less likely to stretch than those of lesser quality.

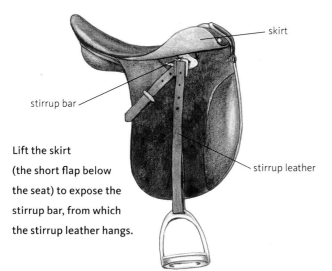

skirt

stirrup bar

stirrup leather

Lift the skirt (the short flap below the seat) to expose the stirrup bar, from which the stirrup leather hangs.

A correctly adjusted dressage stirrup leather allows the rider to lift the toe and lower the heel slightly without losing the stirrup iron.

How long should stirrup leathers be? With the leathers properly adjusted, you should be able to lift your toes and lower your heels slightly without losing your stirrups. At most, your foot should be parallel to the ground. If you have to draw your heels up, then you're sacrificing effectiveness for security. Also be aware that in their quest for that lovely long leg, many dressage riders ride with the leathers too long. If you're constantly losing your stirrups or if you have to point your toe down to keep your stirrups, you're riding too long. Shorten the leathers so the irons are level with, or just slightly below, your anklebones. Punch "half-holes" in the leathers if needed to get the irons where you want them.

In dressage, evenness and balance are everything. Make sure you don't inadvertently cause your horse (and yourself) to become crooked by riding with one stirrup leather longer than the other. Every so often, switch the leathers from one side of the saddle to the other to even things out. Also, avoid mounting from the ground. Doing so puts added stress on the left leather and may stretch it, and the pulling and twisting action is bad for your horse's back. Instead, use a sturdy mounting block.

Stirrup Irons

For decades, most English riders used the same style of stirrup iron: the Fillis type, which features a weighted bottom that keeps the irons from flapping if you lose a stirrup, and therefore is easier to catch while riding. (The only variation you were likely to see was on children's mounts, whose saddles often sported "safety stirrups" with special quick-release designs to prevent feet from becoming hung up in the event of a fall.) Like all irons, Fillis models come in different widths to accommodate various foot sizes.

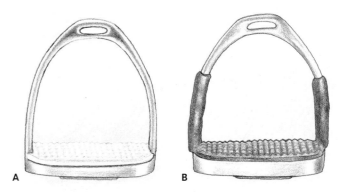

A   B

Both the classic weighted Fillis stirrup iron (A) and its modern cousin, the jointed iron (B), are legal for dressage competition.

Now that's all changed. Today, jointed or "flex" irons are all the rage. Many riders say that these models, which look distinctive with their partially black-rubber-covered shafts, are more comfortable than traditional irons and facilitate a better heels-down leg position. Jointed irons are permitted in dressage competition, but some models are quite a bit more expensive than standard Fillis irons.

Material can also hike the price of your irons, particularly if you choose German silver over ordinary stainless steel. German silver, which is not silver at all but rather a silver-hued amalgam of metals, is pricey. It and a few related metals are popular choices for bits because their taste stimulates salivation and mouthing by horses. But in stirrup irons, cost is really the bottom line. I've had the same pair of stainless-steel Fillis irons for about 25 years, and with regular care they're holding up just fine.

Stirrup pads (the rubbery, grippy inserts that line the feet of stirrup irons) wear out and must be replaced from time to time. White, treaded rubber pads are standard. If you like more grip, try models with inserts of a sandpapery or bristle-brush texture.

Saddle Pads

When it comes to things equestrian, many aspects of *turnout,* or horse and rider attire and appearance, are dictated by tradition. In dressage, the white, so-called square saddle pad, which is actually a rectangle, rules.

Why? I have no idea, except to say that dressage enthusiasts are absolutely mad for the color white — the most impractical color imaginable for use around horses. In addition, the uncovered expanse of pad behind the saddle flap allows for a nice, snowy accent. It also happens to be a convenient spot for sponsor logos, which adorn the saddle pads of some lucky riders, or warmblood-breed logos or national flags or emblems.

Most dressage saddle pads are white, although square pads intended specifically for schooling are available in a riot of colors, prints, and plaids. Some white pads have tasteful piping or edging in black and other colors.

Riders on gray mounts are sometimes inspired to reverse the contrast by choosing black pads with black or white piping.

Stirrup Safety

Stirrup leathers hang suspended from sturdy metal bars that lie beneath the *saddle skirts* (the little flaps that lie under your upper legs when you're mounted). These stirrup bars are hinged, and the rearmost inch or so can be moved (usually with some difficulty) into either a locked (perpendicular) or unlocked (open) position.

This mechanism is the safety catch, and it's designed to unlock under pressure to allow the leather to pull off the saddle in the event of an entanglement. However, if you've ever tried to remove your leathers, you know that the latches can be mighty tough to budge. For this reason, most experts recommend always leaving safety catches in the open (unlocked) position.

Unlocked stirrup-bar safety catch: the recommended position for safety.

The upright and locked position.

Most dressage saddle pads consist of two sides of tough cotton-blend material, quilted with a thin layer of foam in between. Some high-end "show pads" are made of velour or other lush materials — how big is your budget? Pads usually have *keeper straps* of nylon webbing through which the girth and the billet straps pass. Not all billeting systems work with billet keeper straps, but the straps can be easily removed with a seam ripper. I cut the billet keeper straps off my pads and have never noticed significant slippage as a result.

One innovation in saddle pads that's worth looking for is the *contoured wither*. This cut features a back seam that rises gently to accommodate the horse's withers, thereby eliminating any potentially painful pressure. Even with this design, when you tack up your horse, be sure to pull the saddle pad up into the saddle's channel or gullet, at the withers and at the cantle, so your horse has room to move. Most "square" pads are actually gently rounded at the edges. A fancier design is the *swallowtail pad,* which swoops down to a little point at the back edges. Swallowtail pads are acceptable for competition but can look a bit out of place on a small or plain Jane-type horse. Whatever style of saddle pad you choose, be certain that it's proportioned correctly for your horse and your saddle. A saddle pad should extend in front of and below the saddle flaps and behind the cantle by a couple of inches. If the saddle pad is too small, your horse will look as if he's wearing a tutu. If it's too big, he'll look like he's swathed in a blanket.

Specialty Pads

Dressage riders will do anything to make their horses more comfortable, relaxed, and happy. Our sport has almost single-handedly supported the thriving specialty and therapeutic saddle-pad industry.

Auxiliary pads, most of which nestle between the saddle and the regulation square pad, serve a variety of purposes. They were originally created because not all saddles fit perfectly. If you've ever used a shoe insert or an arch support, then you understand what a big difference a little pad can make. By taking up any extra room, a pad can help a too-wide saddle fit better. Special pads can lift the pommels or cantles of saddles that don't sit level. And then there's an entire category of pads with high-tech gel inserts and space-age materials designed to cushion a horse's back and thereby encourage him to move forward freely.

Saddle-fitting experts caution riders and horse owners that, although specialty pads can help correct minor fit flaws, they cannot make a truly ill-fitting saddle fit like a glove. They cannot compensate for lumpy and uneven *flocking* (the stuffing inside the saddle's panels); only a good restuffing can do that, and it can even correct some levelness issues. Specialty pads cannot counteract the effects of a rider whose position is crooked, resulting in an uneven distribution of weight. And they most certainly can't make up for a saddle with a crooked or broken tree. Used indiscriminately, specialty pads, by altering the way the saddle sits on the horse's back, can change a once correctly fitted saddle into an ill-fitting one. Finally, gel and other cushioning pads are meant to benefit the horse, not the rider.

Ideally, you will use a simple pad with a well-fitted saddle. In such a case, the pad's job is to keep the underside of the saddle clean, not to adjust the fit. If you can easily see that a saddle is causing your horse discomfort — say, it presses on his withers when you mount — ask a saddle fitter or a knowledgeable trainer whether use of a specialty pad might help. It's possible that a restuffing will solve the problem. It's also possible that you need a different saddle. Take it from one who's had a horse that developed a sore back as he matured because of a change in the fit of his saddle: you don't want to have to deal with an easily preventable back problem. But you also don't want to rush to throw extra pads under your saddle if there's no compelling reason to use them.

Saddle Pads

On the most basic level, a saddle pad protects the underside of the saddle from sweat and dirt. Different equestrian disciplines favor different styles and materials, and some pads help improve a so-so saddle fit. Here are some styles popular in dressage.

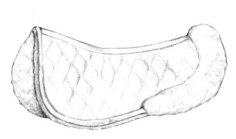

THE CLASSIC WHITE SQUARE dressage saddle pad *(left)* has the desirable contoured-wither shape for a neat fit under the saddle and no pressure on the withers, which can cause discomfort to the horse.

A SHEEPSKIN-LINED HALF-PAD *(right)* provides a little extra cushioning and lift under a standard saddle pad.

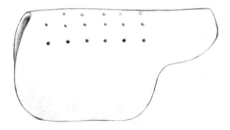

A THIN HALF-PAD of durable synthetic material, also used for extra cushioning.

A HALF-PAD WITH GEL INSERTS offers shock absorption and also takes up room under the saddle panels — helpful if the saddle is a tad too wide.

GEL INSERTS slip out so that the pad can be washed.

Bridles

Two types of bridles are used in dressage: the double bridle and the snaffle bridle.

The Double Bridle

At the higher levels of the sport, horses are shown in the full or double bridle, so called because the bridle has two bits and the rider holds two sets of reins. A double bridle is like a surgical instrument. In skilled, educated hands, it has tremendous power and can be used with delicate precision and incredible finesse. In uneducated hands, it can damage the horse's mouth, make him permanently afraid of contact with the bit, and even cause him to rear or engage in other dangerous behavior.

Proper use of the double bridle requires tact and training. The rider must learn how to use it skillfully and correctly, and the horse must learn to accept its two bits. For these reasons, the double bridle is not permitted in lower-level dressage. At the lower levels, the horse is shown in what is generally accepted as the most basic and humane bit ever created: the snaffle.

The Snaffle Bridle

The snaffle bridle features a single bit and one set of reins. There are many kinds of snaffle bits, but in dressage all feature a single mouthpiece that acts on the corners of the horse's mouth when pressure is applied via the reins. This is considered the gentlest type of bit action. (Some other types of bits, in contrast, have *shanks,* metal pieces that extend down on either side of the mouthpiece, to which the reins are attached. The shanks create leverage when the reins are pulled. As a result, the bit action is down, against the sensitive *bars,* the naturally toothless spaces on either side of the horse's lower jaw. Western bridles usually have shanked bits, and their severity is one reason Western riders keep their reins loose.)

Dressage is predicated on a horse's moving into and accepting what we call *contact,* an ever-present yet nonrestrictive seeking of and connection with the bit, which can't be achieved with loose reins. It makes sense, then, that a young horse would be introduced to the concept of contact with the mildest bit possible. That's why the snaffle bit is required for basic dressage training. (See page 45 for more on snaffle bits.)

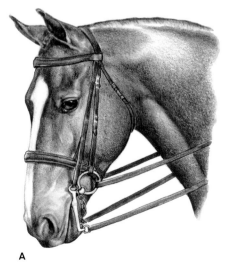

A. The double bridle, with two bits and two sets of reins, is used only by more advanced dressage riders and horses.

B. The snaffle bridle is standard at the lower levels of dressage, and even advanced horses school regularly in snaffles.

A

B

Snaffle Bridle Adjustment

After you've bought the correct size bit and bridle for your horse, you still need to adjust them properly. Here's how.

A TYPICAL DRESSAGE SNAFFLE BRIDLE with correctly adjusted flash noseband and loose-ring bit, as modeled by Pancratius ("Paul"), a Dutch Warmblood gelding owned by Emily Gershberg. The main cavesson rests below his cheekbones yet is not so low that it presses against his sensitive nasal cavities. The flash is snug but not tight. The cheekpieces to which the bit rings attach is adjusted such that the bit hangs properly in Paul's mouth, with one wrinkle in each corner.

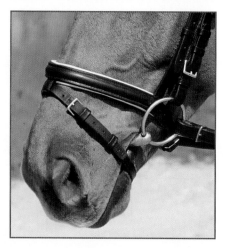

NOSEBAND TOO LOW. The cavesson and flash are pressing against Paul's nasal cavities.

BIT TOO LOW. We've removed the flash attachment from the bridle to give you a clearer look at the bit, which is too low in his mouth. The bit rings are sagging, and there is no wrinkle in the corners of his mouth.

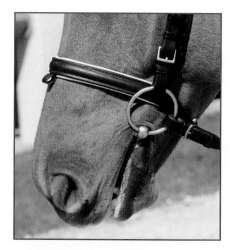

BIT TOO HIGH. Now the bit is too high. The mouthpiece is straining against the corners of Paul's mouth, and he's opening his mouth in discomfort.

Identifying a Dressage Bridle

The color of the bridle will be your first clue that it's intended for dressage. If a bridle is advertised as a dressage snaffle bridle, chances are good that it's black. Snaffle bridles aimed at the hunter/jumper set, in contrast, tend to be brown and often feature decorative stitching on the browbands and cavessons (nosebands).

The second clue that it's a dressage bridle will be the accents. If the browband or cavesson is lined with white leather for a piping effect or if there's a white insert on the browband, it's probably a dressage bridle. The same is true if the browband is adorned with a subtle metallic chain-type insert, a row of crystals, or something similar. If you see gaudy colors or patterns, such as polka dots, move on; it's probably a bridle for a different discipline.

The third and most definitive clue that a bridle is intended for dressage, however, is the cavesson style.

FLASH NOSEBAND

Nearly all dressage snaffle bridles currently sold in the United States feature a *flash noseband,* a sort of double noseband. First, there's the regular noseband that fits around the horse's jaw below his cheekbones and above the bit. Then, passing through a little loop attached to the regular noseband smack-dab in the middle of the horse's nose, there's the *flash attachment:* a strip of plain leather with holes punched in one end and a buckle on the other. The flash wraps under the horse's chin, in front of the bit rings, and buckles on the side of his nose. The flash attachment is meant to help keep his mouth closed and quiet.

Dressage training and competition place great importance on what's called acceptance of the bit, meaning a willingness to go forward into an elastic and unrestrictive contact with the bit. Such actions as tossing the head, opening the mouth, and sticking the tongue out the side of the mouth indicate a lack of acceptance of the bit and of the contact. This can be caused by myriad training problems, or it may be the horse's reaction to mouth pain. Whatever the cause, it needs to be identified and rectified.

Tightening the flash attachment will not address the problem. When adjusted correctly, there should be room to slip a finger or two between the flash strap and the horse's jaw, which allows the flash to gently encourage the horse to keep his mouth quiet, without discouraging him from lightly mouthing and chewing the bit mouthpiece. (This may sound like a contradiction, but it isn't. A horse that accepts bit contact often shows it through gentle mouthing, which stimulates his salivary glands and produces anywhere from a dribble to a copious amount of white foam. In a dressage horse, this foam is desirable — albeit messy. A dressage horse that's nicely "foamed up" isn't angry or ill; he's content.)

Savvy students of dressage usually recognize the apparent paradox of using a mouth-closing gizmo in a sport that prizes slow, patient, take-no-shortcuts training. But take comfort in the fact that no piece of equipment can mask genuine pain, discomfort, or resistance.

THE FLASH NOSEBAND is the most common dressage cavesson in the United States. This model features subtle white accents.

DROP NOSEBAND

In Europe and the United Kingdom, you're more likely to see a lower-level dressage horse in a *drop noseband,* a single noseband that accomplishes the same thing as a flash noseband. As its name suggests, the drop noseband is designed to sit lower than a standard cavesson, with the under-the-chin portion encircling the chin and lower jaw.

The drop noseband is a bit trickier to adjust than the flash noseband because if it's too low it can press on the horse's sensitive nasal bones. Before using a drop-noseband snaffle, ask a qualified instructor to check to be sure that it's adjusted properly and won't interfere with the horse's breathing.

FIGURE-EIGHT NOSEBAND

A third type of noseband that accomplishes the same thing as the flash and the drop is the figure eight. It tends to be seen on eventers and sometimes on jumpers. This noseband style looks like a figure eight, with the top loop fastening around the upper jaw and the lower loop fastening under the chin. The loops cross over the bridge of the horse's nose, where they're held together by a circular piece of leather that's often padded for comfort.

CRESCENT NOSEBAND

Legal for recognized dressage competition at the U.S. national levels, this relatively uncommon design features a metal crescent-shaped piece on each side that arches over and out of the way of the bit rings. The upper and lower leather pieces of the noseband, as well as its cheekpieces, attach to the metal pieces.

The crescent noseband can be useful on horses that tend to tilt or twist their heads in an attempt to evade bit contact. The metal pieces help to keep the horse's nose straight. If he tries to yaw to one side or to "run through" the bit on one side, the crescent-shaped piece serves as a barrier of sorts. Most horses don't need a crescent noseband, but it can sometimes be a valuable tool. It is also less likely than other cavesson styles to chafe, because the chin strap cannot rub against the edge of the bit.

CRANK NOSEBAND

If you've ever taken a bridle apart, you know that they have lots of little straps and pieces. On dressage bridles, those pieces may fasten with standard buckles or with hooks. For years, most dressage cavessons closed with standard buckles. In recent years, tack manufacturers

DROP NOSEBAND. This single noseband sits lower on the bridge of the nose and secures behind the chin, thereby helping to keep the horse's mouth closed. Take care not to make it too low.

NOSEBAND TOO LOW. Now the drop noseband is adjusted too low. If it is tight, it will put painful pressure on the horse's nasal bones and can interfere with his breathing.

CORRECTLY FITTED FIGURE-EIGHT NOSEBAND on an event horse. The straps are adjusted so they do not press against the cheekbones or the nasal cavities.

THE CRESCENT NOSEBAND, named for the piece of metal to which the noseband and cheekpieces attach, helps to keep the horse's nose straight.

CRANK NOSEBAND WITH FLASH ATTACHMENT. At first glance, this looks like a standard flash noseband. Look closer at the main noseband's attachment under Paul's jawbone, however, and you'll see that the strap passes through a metal loop and doubles back on itself, which enables the noseband to be tightened down more securely than with a standard buckle closure.

introduced a second type of noseband closure: the crank noseband (spelled *krank* by some).

The crank style of noseband loops back on itself and then buckles, thereby allowing the attachment to be tightened more through the use of leverage. To help ensure that the cavesson remains comfortable for the horse, most cranks are wide and thickly padded.

Used properly, a crank noseband is no more or less humane (or advantageous to one's training) than a standard buckle cavesson. Overtightened, a crank could essentially put your horse's jaw in a vise.

Snaffle Bits

Have you ever looked in a tack shop or catalog and been overwhelmed by the sheer number of bit designs and options? Well, take comfort. The styles and subtleties are so difficult to keep track of that even people who work at dressage competitions have a hard time keeping them straight. A perennial topic of discussion at shows is whether certain bits are legal in the show ring; like so many things pertaining to the law, the decision may be based on one individual's interpretation.

Following is a discussion of the most common, legal variations found in dressage snaffle bits.

Rings

The rings of a snaffle bit serve as attachment points for the cheekpieces and the reins. They also prevent the bit from sliding or being pulled through the horse's mouth.

The *loose ring*, as shown in the illustration, is presently the most common type of snaffle-bit ring. Loose rings run through holes bored in the ends of the mouthpiece and therefore can slide freely. Most horses do just fine in loose rings, although the odd individual may get a lip pinched if a bit of skin gets caught between a ring and a mouthpiece hole.

The mouthpiece on an *eggbutt snaffle* attaches to fixed points on the ends of the rings, so there is no play in the rings as there is with a loose-ring snaffle. The fixed ends are slightly convex in shape — thinner on the ends and fatter in the middle, next to the mouthpiece attachment — thus the name of this ring design. There is no risk of the horse's lips pinching with an eggbutt snaffle, but some riders still prefer the loose-ring because they find that the "play" discourages the horse from leaning on the bit and encourages the desired mouthing and chewing of the bit.

The rings of an eggbutt snaffle bit may be round or D-shaped. The difference is mostly cosmetic. D-ring snaffles are seen more frequently on racehorses and on hunters and jumpers than on dressage horses, perhaps because the straight piece exerts pressure on the side of the horse's nose and helps the rider turn.

Snaffle bits with *cheeks* (vertical pieces extending above or below the level of the mouthpiece) also are permitted in dressage, although they're relatively uncommon. Like the crescent noseband, bit cheeks push the horse's nose in the direction the rider wants him to turn and aid straightness. A *Baucher* (bo-SHAY) *snaffle* has upper cheeks only and little rings on the ends to which the cheekpieces attach. If the bit has both upper and lower cheeks, it's called a *full-cheek snaffle*. The cheeks of a full-cheek snaffle are often held upright by means of small leather loops that affix to the cheekpieces. A *Fulmer* is similar to a full-cheek snaffle, except that the bit rings are loose rings and are not attached to the cheeks themselves.

Mouthpieces

Here's where snaffle bits get interesting and dressage technical delegates (gurus of official competition rules) get frustrated. Manufacturers love to make improvements, and bit mouthpieces are no exception. New snaffle mouthpieces are introduced quite frequently. Dressage-rules committees must evaluate them and decide whether they should be permitted in competition. Currently, there are six established, legal snaffle mouthpieces: single-jointed, double-jointed, Dr. Bristol (but not in FEI tests), French-link, rotating, and mullen-mouth.

A bit is granted legal status if it is deemed humane and "essentially classical" in terms of its effects and its purpose within the *scale of training,* a generally accepted progression of dressage training (see chapter 7). Almost all horses do just fine in some version of the styles discussed in this section.

SINGLE-JOINTED MOUTHPIECE

Say "snaffle," and most people think of the traditional single-jointed mouthpiece. If you've ever picked up one of these bits, you know that it folds in half, much as a handheld nutcracker closes on a nut. In fact, a single-jointed snaffle is said to have nutcracker action on the horse's tongue, although it is modified somewhat because the bit can't fold in half while in the horse's mouth. Still, some horses find this action objectionable, and riders need to know that single-jointed snaffles, while mild, are not as innocuous as their widespread

Snaffle Bits

Do you think snaffles are all the same? Think again. Although the differences may look subtle, they can dramatically affect your horse's comfort and acceptance of the bit. Also, they're not all legal for use in dressage competition. Check the current *United States Equestrian Federation Rule Book* for illustrations and descriptions of all bits currently legal in dressage competition.

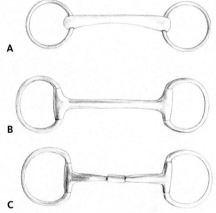

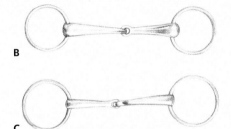

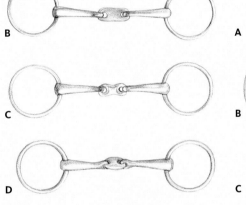

THREE COMMON TYPES OF SNAFFLE BITS, all with conventional jointed mouthpieces and all legal for dressage competition: eggbutt (A), medium-mouth loose ring (B), and thin-mouth loose ring (C).

THE TRADITIONAL JOINTED SNAFFLE BIT has one joint (A), but other models have two, including the Dr. Bristol (B), the loose-ring French-link snaffle (C), and the loose-ring KK snaffle (D). All are USEF competition legal. Some horses seem more comfortable in a double-jointed snaffle, which lessens the "nutcracker" effect that single-jointed bits can have.

THESE LEGAL SNAFFLE MOUTH-PIECES are used less commonly but work well with some horses: a plastic "happy mouth" mouthpiece (A); unjointed mullen mouth (B); and a legal Myler bit, featuring a curved mouthpiece and a center coupling (C). Many "roller-mouth" and some "happy mouth" bits are not legal for competition, so check their status before you buy.

BALKENHOL SNAFFLE. Named for its designer, German Olympic gold medalist Klaus Balkenhol, this snaffle's curved mouthpiece is very comfortable for some horses and also is legal in the show ring.

use might otherwise suggest. My horse has a thick tongue and a low palate, and he can't tolerate single-jointed snaffles. He dislikes the tongue pressure, and the joint of the mouthpiece pokes the roof of his mouth.

DOUBLE-JOINTED MOUTHPIECE

A milder version of the single-jointed mouthpiece is the double-jointed variety. This mouthpiece consists of three sections: two longer outer sections and a short middle section that resembles a football. Marketed as the KK and KK Ultra designs, these mouthpieces drape across the tongue and don't fold with nutcracker action when the reins are tightened. Horses with low palates may be more accepting of this type of bit.

DR. BRISTOL AND FRENCH-LINK MOUTHPIECES

Two other mouthpiece designs are also double-jointed but are classified as distinct types. The *Dr. Bristol mouthpiece* has a flat, oval-shaped center section that is suspended, edge down, between the outer mouthpiece sections. Subtly different is the *French-link mouthpiece,* whose flat center section has a "waist" on both sides. The French-link is considered milder than the Dr. Bristol because its contoured middle piece places less pressure on the tongue.

ROTATING MOUTHPIECE

A relative newcomer to the list of approved mouthpieces is the *rotating mouthpiece* design, which features a center coupling. Be careful if you choose this type of bit, as many versions are not permitted in the show ring. So-called roller-mouth bits, for instance, are generally not permitted in competition.

MULLEN-MOUTH MOUTHPIECE

The Mullen-mouth is a legal, unjointed mouthpiece. Although many riders seem to be under the impression that the Mullen-mouth is more severe than its jointed counterparts, the opposite is true in many cases. Some unjointed mouthpieces have a slight arch that allows the horse's tongue more room but does not bump the palate.

MATERIALS

No matter the style of bit you choose, make sure it's smooth. Twisted-mouths, wrapped-wires, "slow twists," and the like are forbidden. The same goes for mouthpieces with dangling "keys" attached. And there must be only one mouthpiece — no double twisted wires.

Most bit mouthpieces are made of metal, but rubber- and leather-covered versions are also acceptable.

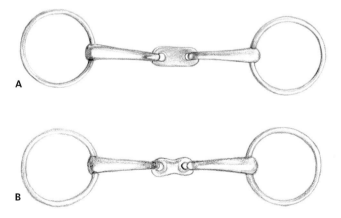

Dr. Bristol (A) and French-link (B) mouthpieces.

Mouthpieces made of rigid plastic ("happy mouth" bits) are OK, too; flexible rubber is permitted in national tests.

Stainless steel is the old standby as a bit metal. It has a nice silver color, needs no polishing, resists corrosion, and is neutral in terms of taste and odor.

During the past few decades, bit manufacturers have developed new alloys that stimulate salivation and, it is hoped, the desired mouthing of the bit. The German manufacturer Herm. Sprenger pioneered the technology with the development of "German silver," which is not silver at all but rather a blend of copper, nickel, and zinc. German silver's high copper content (60 percent) gives the metal a slight "warm" cast when compared to stainless steel. The copper's oxidation stimulates the flow of saliva in the horse's mouth.

Following the successful introduction of German silver, Sprenger came up with Aurigan, which contains even more copper (85 percent) than German silver, plus silicon and zinc. Aurigan has a distinct gold color and oxidizes more rapidly than German silver, thus stimulating even more salivation. All of these metals are legal in the show ring. Which you choose depends on how much you are willing to spend and on how much difference you believe the choice of metal makes in your horse's acceptance of the bit. Stainless steel is the least expensive but also may stimulate salivation the least. There's a sizeable price jump up to German silver, and yet another increase for Aurigan. Sprenger's metals have been imitated by other manufacturers, whose offerings tend to be less costly than the originals.

Whichever brand and type of bit you choose, look and feel before you buy. A cheaply made bit with rough edges and a poor finish is no bargain.

SIZING

Most bits come in several mouthpiece sizes, measured from inside edge to inside edge. A bit is properly sized when you can't slide it from side to side in your horse's mouth and when the ends of the rings aren't partially inside his mouth.

Mouthpieces come in varying thicknesses, as well. You may have been taught that a thick mouthpiece is milder than a thinner one, and to a certain extent that's true. However, some horses don't like having a lot of bulk in their mouths. With my horse's thick tongue and low palate, the less I put in his mouth, the better. So for him, the kindest choice is actually a fairly thin mouthpiece.

Beyond measuring, there is no science to finding the right bit for your horse. The correct bit is the one in which he goes the most quietly and willingly, preferably with some mouthing and salivation, and with the least amount of fussing with his mouth and head. If my horse doesn't like a bit, he puts his tongue out the side of his mouth and leaves it there. He opens his mouth and generally acts busy with his mouth until the offending bit is removed. Your horse may react differently. Know what's normal for him and how he expresses discomfort or displeasure. If you pay attention to his body language, he'll tell you which bit he likes best.

A CORRECTLY FITTED AND ADJUSTED snaffle bit creates one wrinkle in each corner of the horse's mouth.

Applying a Polo Wrap

Many dressage riders wrap their horses' legs with fleece polo wraps for schooling — but know that leg wraps or boots of any kind are illegal in the show ring. Here, Emily Gershberg shows one method of polo-wrap application.

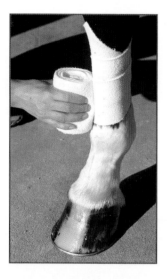

1. Leaving a short extra length of material at the top of the leg, she begins wrapping from front to back (clockwise on right legs, as shown here; counterclockwise on left legs) and from top to bottom, overlapping with each turn. Wrap snugly but not tightly, applying tension at the front of the leg, against the cannon bone, instead of at the back of the leg, against the tendon.

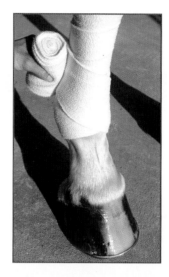

2. At the bottom of the leg, she makes an angled turn around each side of the fetlock, producing a shallow inverted V at the front of the leg.

3. Back at the top of the leg, she folds down the extra material and wraps over it.

4. When she reaches the end of the material, she snugs the hook-and-loop closures into place. The result is a smooth, secure wrap with no unevenness of tension or gaps, lumps, or bulges.

Leg Protection

Many dressage riders protect their horses' legs from cuts and other injuries during schooling sessions and show warm-ups. (Leg bandages or boots of any kind are illegal in the show ring.) The classic dressage look is the white polo wrap, which offers a modest amount of protection. Other riders favor easy-to-apply fleece-lined leg boots made of sturdy leather or vinyl with elasticized hook-and-loop closures. Still others prefer so-called support boots, which cradle the horse's fetlock and feature a fetlock "sling strap" purported to help support tendons and ligaments during movement. White is always a good choice.

Be a Legal Eagle

What does a French-link snaffle look like? Can I show in that new type of snaffle I saw advertised in a magazine? Does it matter what kind of metal the bit is made of?

You'll find the answers to these and practically every other dressage-equipment-related question in the rule book of the U.S. Equestrian Federation, the national governing body of dressage and many other equestrian sports in the United States.

The *United States Equestrian Federation Rule Book* contains helpful illustrations, including those of many dressage movements, as well as the official descriptions and criteria used in training and judging dressage. It's dry reading, but it actually contains a lot of valuable training information and competition dos and don'ts. USEF members are entitled to receive printed copies (available on request) of the rule book, which is updated annually, although so-called extraordinary rule changes can and do go into effect throughout the year. The rule book and updates are also available online at the USEF Web site (see page 318).

Applying a Leg Boot

Easy-to-apply leg boots are another popular method of leg protection that also can be used for turnout. (Don't turn out in polo wraps, as they can be hazardous if they come undone.) Dressage riders favor white models, such as the one pictured below.

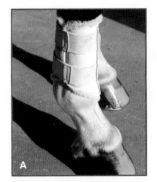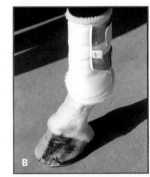

This front-leg boot is lined with fleece and secures with two elastic-end straps that have hook-and-loop closures (A). Make straps snug but not overly tight. On the insides of the boots are tough pieces of vinyl material that help protect horses' legs from blows (B). Hind-leg models may have three straps.

SUPPORT BOOT with a sling strap across the fetlock joint.

BASIC TRAINING

ow we delve into the good stuff: riding and training. You'll learn how to find a qualified instructor and what to expect from your first dressage lessons. Then you'll become familiar with the training scale, the gaits, and the basic figures and movements. These chapters represent several years' worth of systematic training, so remember that there are no shortcuts and no quick fixes.

Although the gaits are discussed separately, don't think that you must master one gait before moving on to the next or that your schooling sessions should focus on only one gait at a time. Mixing it up is actually better for you and your horse.

◄ **BEATING THE HEAT:** U.S. competitors Carol Lavell and Gifted withstood the Barcelona temperatures to win team bronze at the 1992 Olympics.

CHAPTER 5

SELECTING AN INSTRUCTOR

*Y*ou can teach yourself typing and maybe even basic dance steps, but don't go it alone in your riding. You need the benefit of a knowledgeable teacher who can serve as an objective observer and provide regular, quality instruction. Even the best riders need a good "eye on the ground" to help them bridge the occasional gap between how the horse feels and how he looks.

We humans have a remarkable capacity for becoming accustomed to things. From a kinesthetic perspective, this means that our physical crookedness, imbalance, and other quirks feel normal to us, even if they are immediately noticeable to others. Because we may not be aware of these problems, they are nearly impossible to self-correct. A common example is the rider whose instructor continually implores her to sit up straight and not lean forward. The rider feels perfectly straight and so does not alter her position. The frustrated instructor tells the student to bring her upper body back. The student then inches back toward the vertical position, and the instructor cries, "There! *Now* you're straight!" The dismayed student says she feels as if she's lying on her horse's back and protests, "But now it feels wrong!"

That's what's challenging about breaking bad habits: wrong feels right, and right feels weird, uncomfortable, and hard. Believe me, it's difficult to maintain proper position even with an instructor's constant reminders. Most of us don't have sufficient body awareness to identify and correct everything that's wrong with our equitation without outside feedback. Even a mirrored arena isn't a ticket to do-it-yourself riding, but it's certainly a valuable tool.

The way your horse's body feels as you ride can also be misleading or elusive. A pleasant feeling is not always synonymous with correctness. For example, a horse whose neck is overbent and who is mincing forward in a constrained trot may be comfortable and easy to sit; I used to ride this way. But the first time my instructor got me to wind my horse up in a big, forward, free-moving trot, I was dismayed: I bounced all over the place! My horse's movement became far less comfortable, and suddenly I wasn't sitting the trot as well. I had to revise my definition of a good trot, push myself out of my comfort zone, and learn to sit this new big trot, all the while resisting the impulse to take back on the reins to restore the previous, smaller, "safer" trot. These improvements might not have come if I didn't have someone on the ground to nudge me forward.

A good instructor wants you to learn and to have fun but also wants to safeguard your well-being and that of your horse. An instructor's mastery of horsemanship, coupled with his understanding of your skills, makes him uniquely qualified to match you with a suitable mount. If you heed the good advice you're bound to hear, you may save yourself untold frustration, disappointment, and even possible injury by not making the classic "green horse with a green rider" mistake. A good instructor will also intervene if a situation threatens to get out of control.

Even a decent horse-rider match can and will hit some rough spots during the training process, and even the nicest horses seem to go through resistant or uncooperative phases. An experienced trainer can stage an intervention of sorts and may be able to get Dobbin back on the straight and narrow so that you can again ride safely and confidently. If the problem you encounter is more technical than terrifying in nature, there's no substitute for having an experienced professional throw a leg over the horse to feel what's going on. How things look may not reflect how they feel, and vice versa. The eye can observe much of the picture, but time on the horse fills in the details.

What Makes a Good Instructor?

Having ability and skill in a particular area — riding, playing the violin, painting — does not qualify someone to teach that subject to others. Not all "doers" have a solid theoretical grounding in the subject matter, for one, and some find themselves unable to articulate concepts and steps. Especially-gifted performers sometimes make the worst teachers because they don't know how they do things. Their abilities are so innate and their actions so intuitive that they're unable to describe in detail what they're doing and why. Ideally, the dressage instructor you choose will prize safety and humane training methods and will have years of riding experience, in-depth theoretical knowledge, and the desire and ability to teach and mentor you.

DRESSAGE JUDGE AXEL STEINER instructs U.S. FEI-level competitor Jan Ebeling during a clinic.

Safety First

The safety and well-being of you and your horse must be your instructor's top priority. Safety-consciousness takes many forms: ensuring that students are not over-mounted on horses that are too strong, "hot," or strong-willed for them to manage safely; insisting on safe prac-tices, both on the ground and in the saddle; stepping in if a horse appears unsound; and maintaining safe facil-ities (buildings and footing) or insisting on such, to name a few. The instructor should also have basic knowledge of first aid for horses and humans, in case of accidents.

Humane Methods

In any equine sport, the horse's health and welfare should come first. Training as an equine athlete requires considerable effort by the horse and may result in muscle soreness, but it should never involve outright pain, intimidation, or fear.

There is a saying in dressage that art ends where force begins. A tense, uncomfortable, unhappy horse being compelled to execute movements and "tricks" is not a pretty sight. Take time to watch your prospective instructor ride horses and teach some lessons. Do the horses look mostly willing, relaxed, and content; or do you see signs of discomfort or tension, such as tail wringing, pinned ears, and kicking out?

There's a big difference between unemotional, appropriate correction for naughty behavior and abuse. Repeated whipping, spurring, and jerking of the reins are red flags. Shouting, cursing, and any other signs of impatience and temper should also set off alarm bells.

A humane approach to training involves giving a horse the benefit of the doubt. A friend recently told me that her normally placid Appaloosa had suddenly begun rearing and generally being difficult to handle. Although she certainly wasn't going to reward the horse for the undesirable behavior, my friend didn't immediately engage in a battle with the unruly mare. She asked her instructor for help, and the trainer deter-mined the source of the problem: a combination of too much grain, too little exercise, and the departure of a stablemate. A responsible owner and instructor look for possible physical and environmental causes of problems and don't automatically assume that willful disobedience is to blame.

Riding Experience

There's no substitute for mileage. An instructor who's been there and done that has hard-won insights about the challenges and training issues that you and your horse will face. A professional who has ridden to a level higher than the one you're currently learning under-stands not only where you are but also where you're headed. Such perspective gives a rider a valuable understanding of the through-the-levels progression of dressage training that no textbook can impart quite as clearly or as well.

If your aspirations include competition, an instruc-tor who's had lots of show-ring experience under-stands the complexities of learning and riding dressage tests (predetermined patterns), dealing with nerves, handling horses that suddenly don't behave the way they do at home, and the myriad other challenges unique to showing. An experienced professional will get you to the church on time, properly attired and pre-pared for what lies ahead.

Theoretical Knowledge

An understanding of the concepts, goals, stages, and elements of dressage riding and training is the frame-work on which a good instructor hangs her hard-earned experience and occasional "aha" flashes of insight. Imparting this knowledge to you is key. With-out a solid foundation in theory, you won't know how to interpret your experiences and observations. You also will have difficulty understanding and assessing what your instructor knows and doesn't know. A good dressage instructor is a deep well of such knowledge. In her theoretical hip pocket should reside the following.

● **Understanding of the training scale, a pyramidal representation of the stages of dressage training** (see chapter 7 for more on the training scale). The U.S. Dressage Federation and the German National Equestrian Federation base their training and education programs on this progression and believe that it accurately represents the qualities that a horse must possess in order to advance properly in his dressage training, in accordance with classical principles that help to ensure correct gymnastic development.

● **Theoretical and biomechanical understanding of the horse's gaits and paces.** I'll discuss these in detail in chapters 8, 9, and 10. Briefly, dressage training is based on the three basic gaits: the walk, the trot, and the canter. Within any gait, the horse can lengthen and shorten his stride by varying amounts, just as you can when you walk or run. Dressage training and competition categorize and qualify these paces as *collected*, *working*, *medium*, *extended*, and *free*, depending on the particular gait.

● **Ability to lunge horse and rider, and an understanding of the benefits of lungeing.** Lungeing can help the horse to develop balance and an understanding of contact. Lungeing the rider helps to develop an independent, effective seat.

● **Understanding of correct rider position and why it is essential to effective riding, and the ability to develop it in students.** Through lunge lessons and other instruction, a good instructor emphasizes the importance of equitation.

● **Understanding of the aids (the use of one's weight, legs, hands, and occasionally voice to cue the horse) and their application.** A good instructor must be able to explain how and when to use the aids.

● **Knowledge of equine conformation (physical structure), movement, and temperament and awareness of which characteristics are desirable and undesirable in dressage.** Because instructors are often called on to help students find horses, they need to know how to select mounts that are suitable to students' skill levels and likely to be able to reach the students' training or competitive goals.

● **Horse-management knowledge and skills.** Understanding of care, grooming, trimming and shoeing, lameness and illness, feeding, stable management, and all other aspects of keeping the equine athlete sound and healthy. The instructor may be entrusted with the care of the student's horse. If the horse develops a health or soundness problem, the instructor likely will be the first line of defense.

● **Ability to select and correctly fit dressage tack and equipment.** The instructor must be able to guide the student in purchasing competition-legal, correctly sized, appropriate tack, and equipment and must be able to adjust it correctly to fit the horse.

● **Understanding of the equine psyche: horse behavior and why horses act (and react) the way they do.** Much of training is psychological. If the instructor does not understand why horses do the things they do, she cannot react appropriately to behaviors or advise students how to address various training issues.

● **Teaching skills.** Recognition of people's various learning styles, and the ability to adapt accordingly; ability to articulate concepts and to give clear directions; understanding of students' frustrations and challenges; professionalism and respect for students; ability to address issues logically.

Given that lengthy list of requirements, it's easy to understand why gifted and well-trained instructors are in such demand. It's also easy to understand why,

UNDER HER INSTRUCTOR'S watchful eye, a young competitor warms up.

despite the fact that anyone in the United States can hang out a shingle and proclaim himself to be a professional trainer or instructor, there may be a sizeable gap between some instructors' level of preparedness and the ideal. Unfortunately, the horse world is filled with "professionals" who know more than their novice clients, but not as much as they should. Finding a skilled instructor can sometimes be challenging. Following are some helpful strategies.

The Hunt

Before you can decide which instructor best suits your needs, you need to locate some instructors in your area. If you know where to look, this is a fairly easy task. Here are some good sources.

Specialty Publications

National dressage magazines — in the United States, *USDF Connection* and *Dressage Today* — occasionally carry advertisements for dressage trainers and instructors. Of course, they also feature articles by or about prominent professionals. The editorial mention can generally be construed as a vote of confidence in the person's skills and reputation, especially if the expert is featured in an article about training or teaching. If a featured pro happens to live in your area, you can try contacting his or her facility and asking whether new students are being accepted, in the same way you'd ask whether a physician is taking new patients.

Regional Publications

Virtually every corner of the United States is served by at least one regional all-breed, all-discipline equine publication. Some of these are full-fledged magazines, complete with interesting and informative articles; others are advertisement-only "shoppers"; still others carry some editorial, but mostly in the form of press releases and stories about businesses advertising in the issue.

You'll find your area's "nag mags" at most tack shops and feed stores. They may also turn up at horse shows and equine expositions. Some are free; others aren't. All carry ads for local and regional training facilities and instructors of all sorts. These publications feature lots of other types of ads, as well, which may serve as valuable leads.

Dressage Clubs

The U.S. Dressage Federation is an aggregate of approximately 130 dressage and eventing organizations around the country. Each of these group-member organizations (GMOs) operates more or less independently but adheres to certain procedures that qualify it for the benefits of USDF affiliation (see appendix A for more on USDF).

If you join your local GMO, you'll receive its newsletter and notices of upcoming events. You'll probably read about area trainers and facilities, and some may advertise in the newsletters, as well. Attend club-sponsored events and you'll meet fellow dressage enthusiasts who will be happy to tell you whom they train with and where.

Local Dressage Shows

Being a spectator at a dressage show is one of the best ways to observe the fruits of a dressage instructor's labor: her students and horses in action. You'll want to spend some time at the competition arena, of course, but the best way to see what's cooking between instructor and student is to observe the warm-up arena.

This busy and somewhat harried place is where numerous anxious riders (and some anxious horses) prepare to enter the show ring. Leaning against the rail are instructors, grooms, friends, and assorted hangers-on. You'll recognize the instructors because they'll be saying things like, "More leg. *More* leg!" to the riders.

Being sure to keep away from the in-gate and out of the general traffic pattern, find a good vantage point along the rail and hang out for a while. Observe how the instructors interact with their students. Is there calm and methodical preparation, or is there lots of yelling and confusion? If a horse misbehaves, how is the behav-

ior dealt with? If the student seems exceptionally nervous or upset, how does the instructor handle it? Is the instructor focused on the student (and there may be more than one in the warm-up ring at any given time), or does she seem more interested in chatting with the people lining the rail? Does the instructor's communication style appeal to you?

Take a look at the competitors' turnout, too. Sloppily attired riders and poorly groomed horses with bad braid jobs are not good advertisements for an instructor, because in dressage details count. Even the lowest-level horse and the most inexperienced rider can and should appear spick-and-span neat, with a gleaming coat, neat braids, clean tack, and polished boots.

Next, look at the horses. A crew of workmanlike, healthy-looking animals is a credit to an instructor. They don't all have to look like they're going to the Olympics, but they should seem comfortable with what's being asked of them. One nervous or naughty Nellie isn't sufficient reason to remove a name from your list of prospects, but a ringful of misbehavior is cause for concern. Wander over to the show office (ask someone for directions if there's no signage) and look for the lists of posted show results; usually, a cluster of anxious riders and instructors will be crowded around it. The show secretary or another volunteer will post competitors' scores on the list as they're received by the show office and will record the final placings after a class has concluded. Although students of top instructors don't win or even place well all of the time, as a whole they generally do better than average.

If you spot a horse-and-rider combination that impresses you, wait for a moment of relative quiet (even if it means following them back to the stabling area) and ask the rider if she'll tell you whom she trains with. Most riders are flattered to be singled out, and the trainer may be there, as well — a perfect opportunity for you to introduce yourself.

Clinics

Clinics are lessons with guest instructors. Some clinics are one-day affairs, while others last for two or even three days, usually over a weekend. Look for notices of upcoming events in regional publications and GMO newsletters.

Most clinics welcome auditors (spectators). There may be a nominal fee, but many clinics are free to auditors; call the clinic organizer beforehand to find out and to learn what you need to do. Watching a clinician teach seven or eight lessons in a single day is an excellent way to learn how that person works with horses and riders at various skill levels and with various issues. It's more relaxed than the competition environment and is focused on training rather than show-ring readiness.

Clinics with top-level instructors are worthwhile opportunities to learn from trainers who live elsewhere. Of course, a clinician who resides in another state probably isn't the best choice for your primary instructor, but some travel a regional circuit and visit an area facility on a regular basis.

The Internet

There is plenty of dressage on the information superhighway. Dressage riders are an exceptionally analytical group on the whole, and many love nothing better than to read, discuss, and chat about their passion. You'll get opinions on everything you ask for (and on some things you didn't) on the message boards of various dressage-themed sites. For a list of sites, see appendix C.

Are Certified Instructors Better?

It depends where you live. In some countries — Germany being the most often-cited example — dressage trainers and instructors are required to pass tests and earn licenses before they can practice their craft. It's similar to the way aviation is regulated in the United States. A pilot must hold one or more licenses before he will be permitted to fly. To become a flight instructor, additional tests must be passed and licenses obtained, and so on up the ladder.

CHECK OUT A PROSPECTIVE INSTRUCTOR by auditing a clinic (pictured: rider Lisa Blackmon during a USDF National Dressage Symposium). You'll get a good feel for the instructor's methods and personality.

In the United States, however, there are no such requirements for riding instructors and horse trainers. The certifications available to U.S. dressage professionals are purely voluntary. Following is an overview of the major certifying organizations, the levels of certification offered, and the qualifications for each. You'll find contact information for each in appendix C.

American Riding Instructors Association

Established in 1984, the mission of the American Riding Instructors Association (ARIA) is to promote safe, quality riding instruction. Its certification program (ARICP) certifies instructors of riders at three levels:

- *Level I:* instructor in training
- *Level II:* instructor of beginner through intermediate
- *Level III:* instructor of beginner through advanced

Instructors may earn certification in up to fourteen specialty areas that encompass most of the equestrian world: from stock seat and recreational riding to hunter seat and driving. The levels of ARICP certification correspond to the following dressage levels:

- *Levels I and II:* through First Level, including knowledge of U.S. Equestrian Federation rules (for a discussion of the levels, see chapter 13)
- *Level III:* through Third Level

Level I tests are a series of written examinations that evaluate candidates' knowledge of the subject matter. To earn Level II and Level III certification, candidates must have a minimum of three and six years of teaching experience, respectively, and must submit videotaped footage of themselves teaching a lesson in the appropriate specialty, in addition to passing written exams.

The ARIA Web site contains a directory of instructors, searchable by state. The certified teachers represent a variety of disciplines, with dressage a minority.

There are several prominent master instructors on the ARICP roster, which means they are qualified to conduct instructor-certification tests. Among them are Olympian and hunter-seat legend George Morris, Centered Riding instructor Susan Harris, famed hunter-seat trainer Judy Richter, and Olympic eventer Michael Page. In dressage, among the best-known and most-recognized names are Olympian Lendon Gray, an ARICP master instructor who is also a USDF certification examiner; and Olympian Robert Dover, an ARICP master instructor.

Certified Horsemanship Association

The mission of the Certified Horsemanship Association (CHA) is broader than that of ARIA. CHA exists to promote safety and education, not only in riding lessons but also in riding camps, youth associations, clubs, college riding programs, and group riding programs. It offers more diverse certifications than ARIA, including trail guide, riders with disabilities, and seasonal equestrian staff, in addition to instructor. The eight levels of instructor certification (assistant instructor through clinic instructor) stipulate expertise in English or Western riding; no dressage specialty is offered.

U.S. Dressage Federation

The USDF maintains an instructor certification program, the first of its kind in the United States to evaluate and certify dressage instructors based on the German system, including the training scale. Not surprisingly, the USDF program is the most dressage-focused of the instructor certification programs offered in the United States.

It began in 1990 with a pilot "mock testing" session, the culmination of eleven years of USDF-run seminars for dressage instructors, which today continue as the USDF National Dressage Symposium, an annual educational event for a general audience; and the USDF

Fédération Equestre Internationale (FEI)–Level and National-Level Trainers' Conferences, intensive weekend seminars aimed at dressage professionals. Currently, ten certification examiners assess candidates' skills in lungeing the horse, lungeing the rider, riding, and teaching. To attain certain levels of certification, candidates also must pass written examinations, hold American Red Cross first-aid certification, submit written references, and submit minimum scores, earned at designated levels in recognized dressage competition, from both students and themselves. They must also be USDF participating members.

For years, USDF offered only two levels of certification: Training through Second Level, and Training through Fourth Level. The certification program has been expanded considerably, and today the following levels of certification are offered:

- **Associate instructor.** This category recognizes dressage instructors who have participated in at least three USDF instructor workshops: a minimum of one each in lungeing, riding, and teaching.
- **Certified instructor/trainer, Training through Second Level.** The instructor/trainer designation refers to a professional who has demonstrated the skills and experience necessary to teach riders and to train and ride horses.
- **Recognized teacher, Training through Second Level.** The teacher designation refers to a professional who has demonstrated expertise in teaching riders but not in training and riding horses. The teacher examination does not include a riding portion.
- **Recognized teacher, Third and Fourth Levels.** Same as above, but expanded to include the teaching of students who are riding at Third and Fourth Levels.
- **Certified instructor/trainer, Third and Fourth Levels.** The certified instructor/trainer at this level has demonstrated expertise in teaching riders and in training and riding horses through Fourth Level dressage.

FEI-level certification (for upper-level instructors and trainers) is currently being developed by the USDF Instructor/Trainer Council. Realize, however, that many USDF-certified instructors have trained riders and horses past the levels through which they are certified, so don't assume that an instructor certified through Second Level can't do a competent job teaching a Fourth Level pair, for example.

The core of the USDF Instructor Certification Program is an extensive series of instructor workshops held at various locations around the country, each focusing on a different aspect of riding, teaching, and training, and taught by a faculty of selected trainers. These workshops, which feature demonstration riders and horses, can be audited and are excellent for riders at all levels. The certification testing sessions are closed to observers. You can find the complete calendar of instructor workshops and testings in *USDF Connection,* the monthly USDF member magazine, and online.

Making a Decision

Now that you know about the available types of instructor certification, it's time to decide whether you want a certified instructor or one who's uncredentialed. In the United States, certification of riding instructors is voluntary. It's a rigorous, time-consuming, and expensive process. Many excellent instructors and trainers choose not to pursue certification. Their credentials consist of their achievements in competition, their students' achievements, and the achievements of horses they've trained. Many dedicated instructors regularly pursue continuing education with respected trainers in the form of clinics and symposia. Our recent U.S. Olympic dressage squads, for example, have consisted mostly of individuals who are not USDF-certified, but that hasn't affected their popularity as instructors. Participating in the Olympics clearly distinguishes them as being among the dressage elite.

Although the number of USDF-certified instructors continues to increase, it's possible you may not have access to a local dressage instructor who is certified. If there isn't one in your area, then you'll need to use the instructor-sleuthing techniques explained on page 58. But if you're fortunate enough to have a choice between a certified and uncertified instructor, your decision may come down to references, location, availability, price, and a dose of gut feeling. The really big names tend to be booked solid, with no time for new students. Their lessons are usually more expensive, too. Some prefer to focus on the elite and don't teach low-level dressage riders. Although they have much to offer, big-name trainers may be more than you need at this point in your riding.

Understand the Fine Print

Unlike most other sports, taking dressage lessons can be a bit more complicated than getting in the car and driving to the practice area. There's the matter of the horse, and so the $64,000 question may become: who will travel, the horse or the instructor?

Many instructors are based at facilities (their own or sometimes ones at which they have contracts to work or lease stalls) and do not travel to clients' barns and boarding facilities, except for special occasions, such as clinics. So if Jane Instructor is based at Green Acres and only teaches there, you'll have to board your horse there if you want to take lessons with Jane.

If you can't board at Jane's farm but you really want to train with her, your only other option is to trailer in for lessons — if Jane and the farm owner permit, and if you have access to a truck and trailer. This can be a good solution if you keep your horse at home or have a horse-keeping arrangement that you don't want to change. Just factor in the added time and expense of trailering: figure an extra two hours on top of your lesson for loading and unloading, not to mention the drive time itself. Don't be surprised if you get charged extra for the "privilege" of trailering in. Some farms assess haul-in fees to cover the extra wear and tear on the facilities.

Some instructors — particularly those just starting out — are willing to travel to their clients, which makes life easy for you. If you board your horse, however, make sure that outside instructors are permitted to

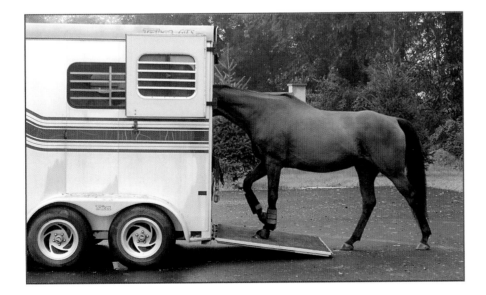

ON THE ROAD AGAIN: Many dressage students haul their horses to lessons with off-site instructors.

teach on the property. Some facilities don't allow it because of potential insurance liability. Others don't allow it because the resident instructors don't want outside competition or the hassle of having to share the ring.

Training facilities with resident instructors on-site charge for lessons and training in one of two ways. The first is the à la carte method: you sign up for as many or as few lessons as you want, and you pay as you go. The second is the training-board method, in which boarders pay a flat fee (much higher than regular board would be) that includes a certain number of lessons, rides, or both. For instance, training board might include two lessons a week plus the trainer riding your horse three additional days per week. There's no bargaining and no discounts for fewer lessons or rides, unless perhaps in cases of illness or injury. Training board serves two purposes: it's a convenient all-in-one monthly fee instead of the client's having to write multiple checks, and it discourages the not-so-serious rider or horse owner from boarding at the facility. Facilities with a training-board policy cater to dedicated, well-heeled riders and horse owners who want to make a *lot* of progress and are willing to invest substantial time and money to achieve their goals.

Satisfy Your Needs

The greatest instructor in the world won't do you any good if she has a personality or a teaching style that drives you crazy. Some instructors are incredibly enthusiastic and lavish praise on their students. This may seem fine, but too much praise can sound hollow after a while if what you want is constructive criticism. Other instructors find fault after fault after fault. If you have a tough ego and respect the person's opinions, go for it; if you need a lot of stroking, you may find yourself flattened under such an approach.

Interview your prospective instructor. Talk to him frankly about your goals and your and your horse's level of training. Don't try to mislead him about what level you've ridden to; any instructor worth his salt will know the truth as soon as he sees you ride.

Your instructor doesn't have to be your buddy, but you should get along well with her and feel comfortable talking with her. The instructor should be able to explain concepts clearly (clearly to *you,* that is) and should be willing to try a different approach if she isn't getting through to you. The same goes for your horse. Horses are individuals. Anyone who uses a one-size-fits-all training approach isn't doing her job. (How will you know? Watch some lessons.)

It's a big plus if the instructor likes (or at least refrains from complaining about) your horse. Most of us need to work with the horses we have and can't just trade up at the drop of a hat. Most important, the instructor should feel that you and your horse are a decent match, at least from a safety standpoint. If a professional warns you that "he's too much horse for you" or something similar, and especially if you've heard that sentiment before, you may want to take that opinion seriously because the pro may see that you're risking injury. But beware of a trainer who says your horse is unsuitable and just happens to have the perfect mount in his barn. That's a horse dealer, not an instructor.

Even if you're brand-new to dressage, you're not new to people. Trust your instincts. I've met trainers who were slick, dishonest, flaky, disorganized, self-absorbed, gossipy, lazy, rough, and a host of other unprofessional attributes. I've also met instructors who were straightforward, hardworking, humane, caring, attentive, and encouraging. Spend some time with the instructor and his entourage (clients, employees, friends, horses, pets) and you'll get a pretty good feeling for the operation. Then ask yourself whether you and your horse will fit in.

CHAPTER 6

YOUR FIRST DRESSAGE LESSONS

I remember my first dressage lesson as if it were yesterday. I had been taking hunter-seat lessons for about six years and had done my share of equitation classes, mostly on a motley assortment of school horses. I had acquired my first horse, an off-the-track Thoroughbred mare, about a year earlier, and quickly became frustrated at our failure to communicate.

The endless trotting and cantering around and the repeated jumps over cross-rails and low verticals seemed so superficial. I wondered if there was a way to connect with my horse on a deeper level. Then I met a local eventing trainer who assured me that there was a way to subtly influence a horse's entire body, to create lightness and roundness and gymnastic ability, and for me to feel more connected with my horse. I was hooked just on principle.

In my first dressage lesson, my instructor explained that I could use my legs in time with the rhythm of my mare's gaits to influence her movement. This was a new concept to me. I knew how to make my mare walk, trot, canter, stop, and turn; but it had never occurred to me

that I could or should be doing anything while she was cruising along. I had no idea that I could actually change her tendency (common in most horses) to canter through corners with her head and neck cocked to the outside and her haunches to the inside. I didn't know that the length and loft of a horse's strides are so adjustable. And I certainly didn't know how to sit the trot correctly!

If I Could Do It Over . . .

If I could go back in time to the beginning of my riding career, right from the start I'd spend lots more time working on my seat and position. One lesson that I've had to learn, over and over, is that my horse's body can be no more balanced, even, strong, supple, or straight than my own. And there's simply no better way to learn correct position than at the end of a lunge, or longe, line.

Round and Round You Go

You know the old chestnut about the difficulty some people have walking and chewing gum at the same time? Well, just imagine attempting to make your horse letter-perfect while simultaneously trying to learn to sit the trot. Sitting correctly requires an enormous amount of total-body control. Particularly when you're first starting out, you need to focus so completely on your seat that precious few brain cells are left over to think about what your horse is doing.

That's where lunge lessons come in. Even though dressage books, magazines, and USDF literature all tout the value of lunge lessons in developing correct rider position, few dressage instructors actually give lunge lessons. This is partly because good lunge horses — solid, sound individuals who walk, trot, and canter quietly and obediently at the end of a line — are in short supply. And many people don't want to subject their precious horses to lots of work on the lunge, the repetitious nature of which can be tough on the feet and legs. (If your horse lunges well, by all means ask whether you can volunteer Dobbin for your private use.)

I suspect that there are two other reasons many instructors don't give lunge lessons. First, they simply may not think of it. The standard 45-minute instructor-sits-on-the-sidelines-and-coaches lesson is so automatic that the whole lungeing rigmarole may seem like a lot of extra work. Second, many riders don't enjoy lunge lessons. They're hard work and tedious, and, let's face it, it's more fun practicing the movements than going around in circles, sitting the trot with no stirrups. Plus, once they've reached a certain level, riders may think they're past the point of needing lunge lessons. Wrong, wrong, wrong!

I find lunge lessons liberating. I enjoy the luxury of being able to concentrate only on myself and my position and not feeling responsible if my horse doesn't bend or pick up his canter lead. Yes, lunge lessons are hard work, but I finish feeling proud for having done what the books say I should, happy to be able to check *work out* off my to-do list for the day, and usually pleased at some new discovery I've made. Any rider at any level can benefit from work on the lunge. I've been riding for close to thirty years, but I'd sign up for a lunge lesson tomorrow if someone would give me one.

Do you still need convincing about the virtues of lunge-line work? Consider this: At the famed Spanish Riding School of Vienna, new riders are worked exclusively on the lunge for up to two years. That's right: no reins and no independent riding until they develop an *independent seat* — the ability to remain balanced atop the horse at all times, no matter what, without relying on the reins, and the ability to use the hands, legs, and seat independently of one another (no inadvertent "I used my right rein so I automatically tightened my right leg, too").

LUNGE LESSONS can benefit all riders.

If you can, find an instructor who's experienced at lungeing horses and riders, and invest in as many lunge lessons as you can afford, before or during your horse's introduction to dressage. (USDF-certified teachers and instructor/trainers are proficient in lunge-line work, so consider that when choosing an instructor.)

Position Primer

In the hunter/jumper world, junior riders talk about "equitating" — perching in the saddle and looking pretty on the flat and over fences. Coming from that background, I believed that rider position was simply an aesthetic consideration: *good position* meant "pretty position." Only later did it begin to dawn on me that *good position* really means "effective position."

As I explained in chapter 4, different saddles put riders in different positions, with different leg lengths and hip and knee angles, depending on the chosen activity. In dressage, the object is to use every inch of one's body to control every inch of the horse's body. It stands to reason, therefore, that a dressage rider would want as much contact with the horse as possible, thus the desired long legs and deep seat.

The hallmarks of the classical rider position share many of the same qualities that we seek to develop in our horses. They are:

- **Balance:** the ability to keep your center of gravity over your horse's center of gravity
- **Alignment:** the ability to keep your body parts "lined up" on both the vertical and the horizontal plane
- **Strength:** sufficient muscle tone to maintain proper position, to absorb the horse's movement with your seat without bouncing or slipping, and to influence the horse's body with your own
- **Suppleness:** flexibility in muscles and joints to enable you to softly absorb the shock of the horse's strides, to move parts of your body independently without inadvertently affecting others, and to move easily and gracefully
- **Evenness:** equal measures of alignment, strength, and suppleness on the left and right sides of your body

Let's start by picturing how these principles of good position look. Here is a photo of a rider sitting correctly. What is he doing right, and why?

GOOD RIDER POSITION AT THE HALT, as demonstrated by Chris Hickey. Chris's upper body is erect in the saddle, and he is looking straight ahead. He is sitting balanced with his weight over his heels, and his legs are lying quietly at his horse's sides. His elbows are in, and his hands are together over the horse's withers, with his thumbs up. He looks balanced and ready for anything.

ALIGNMENT CHECK: When seated on your horse, would an imaginary line pass through your ear, shoulder, hip, and heel — hallmarks of a balanced position?

Chris is clearly sitting in balance. If his horse were to vanish from beneath him, he'd land standing with ease. How can we tell he's in balance? By using the old ear-shoulder-hip-heel test. Draw an imaginary line from the rider's ear, through his shoulder, through his hip joint, and through his ankle joint. Ideally, the line will be straight and perpendicular to the ground. If the line leans forward or backward or if it angles this way and that on its way down, then some part of the rider's body is out of alignment.

There is an exception to every rule, and there are cases in which the aforementioned perfect body alignment is not possible. In most of these cases, the rider's conformation is such that achieving textbook alignment is difficult or impossible. As famed hunter/ jumper trainer George Morris has observed, the ideal riding body is tall, slim, and long-limbed, with a relatively short torso. That's good news for all the supermodels out there, but the rest of us may have to make some concessions. Still, the ear-shoulder-hip-heel test is a good guide and most riders can achieve a fairly close approximation, even allowing for any conformational quirks.

Now let's look closely at each aspect of Chris's good position.

Head and Neck

Chris is gazing straight ahead, his chin is level, and he is carrying his head and neck erect and aligned with his torso. Simple? Sure. After all, these are nothing more than fundamentals of good posture, which you probably already know. In practice, however, it's surprising how many riders fail to look up and keep their heads and necks in line with their upper bodies.

Your head weighs approximately eight to ten pounds. If it tips forward or downward, as it does when you look down, you throw your body and your horse's body out of balance. Yes, your horse really is that sensitive!

Looking down serves no purpose, anyway, because only feel tells you what you need to know to improve your horse. The occasional glance down — eyeballs only, no craning — to confirm that you're on the correct diagonal or lead, or to confirm that you can see your horse's inside eye during a lateral flexing or bending movement, is OK. That's it. I tend to look down, so I know how tough this habit can be to break. Work on it. Be disciplined and resist that impulse.

The other reason that you must learn to control where you look is that it becomes part of your aiding system. When riding, we tend to go where we look, just as when driving a car. Simply looking to the left can change our balance and posture enough to influence the horse's movement. If you're trotting straight ahead and you look to the left, he will probably begin to turn left or will at least drift a few steps in that direction.

Shoulders and Upper Torso

Many riders get so caught up in trying to perfect the dressage seat that they overlook the importance of the upper body in influencing the horse. Your upper body has a lot of leverage. Where your upper body is directly affects your horse's position and balance.

Looking at the photo of Chris on his horse, you'd probably say that his upper body is not particularly affected by the fact that he is mounted; that is, he's sitting straight and tall, just as you'd expect if you saw a photo of him sitting properly in a chair or walking down the street. The truth is that your upper body has to *work* to look that way when you're in the saddle.

For years, instructors told me, "Shoulders back! Shoulders back!" Actually, they should have been saying, "Shoulders *down* and back." If you merely yank your shoulders back, your shoulder blades will "wing" out behind you, your chest will stick out, and your back will hollow. The large muscles of your back (the latissimus dorsi) will not be engaged, and therefore you will not be using the full complement of muscles to stabilize your torso and lift your chest.

Try this simple exercise. Rotate your shoulders forward, up, back, and down a few times until you feel loose and relaxed. Then, the next time you move your shoulders back and down, hold them there for a few moments. You should feel as if your collarbones are spreading apart and the space between your shoulders and your ears has increased. Now, keeping your shoulders back and down, lift your sternum (that place right in the middle of your chest, about where the point of a

V-neck shirt falls) and gaze straight ahead. Look in a mirror and admire your tall, elegant posture.

All the regal posture in the world won't do you much good if you lean forward over your horse's neck. This tendency is strongly ingrained in many former hunter/jumper riders, who lean forward and perch over the front of the saddle, never bringing their upper bodies to vertical. (Eventers do this, too, although they're more susceptible to the cross-country upper-body hunch.) Western riders and saddle-seat riders may have an edge here, as they're accustomed to sitting tall in the saddle.

Your weight strongly affects your horse's balance, so leaning forward is a problem. A key object of dres-

AN ERECT, BALANCED, RELAXED POSTURE will benefit your riding and your overall health and well-being; demonstrated by Pilates instructor Meghan Jackson.

sage training, as I'll explore in more detail in the coming chapters, is to teach your horse to shift his center of gravity rearward, so he bears more weight on his hindquarters and less on his forehand (head, neck, shoulders, and front legs). Horses naturally carry 60 percent of their weight on the forehand and only 40 percent on their hindquarters. If you lean forward, you force the horse to carry more weight on the forehand and make it more difficult for him to balance the way you want him to.

Dressage horses are trained to go forward from what's called a *driving seat,* a component of which is the rider's upper body positioned at, or sometimes even slightly behind, the vertical. This response is the opposite of what many horses are trained to do, which is to go faster when the rider leans forward. (For an extreme example, think jockeys and racehorses.) Advanced dressage horses become so sensitive to their riders' position that an unexpected forward weight shift makes them feel "blocked" and reluctant to go forward. An inexperienced rider once rode my horse and kept losing her balance and tipping forward at the waist. Imagine her embarrassment as my horse halted suddenly each time she did it. It may seem counterintuitive to sit back in order to go forward, but it's something you'll need to master as you progress in your dressage training.

Arms and Elbows

In the photo, Chris's arms are at his sides; his elbows are bent but are not held rigidly. There is a straight line between his elbows and his horse's mouth.

As a rider who has engaged in a colorful variety of arm positions over the years, I can tell you that developing an arm that "hangs" from the socket and remains next to the body and an elbow joint that bends smoothly to accommodate the movement of the horse's head and neck with each stride sounds simple yet can be incred-

There should be a straight line between the rider's elbows and the horse's mouth.

ibly difficult. For years, I hiked up my shoulders somewhere around my ears in an attempt to stabilize my torso, while simultaneously doing my best chicken-wing imitation with my elbows, especially the left one. Years later, I realized that my position flaws, like most people's, were the result of attempts to compensate for weaknesses. In my case, I had strong biceps and pectoral (chest) muscles but weak triceps, and my postural and back muscles were practically nonexistent.

Yes, even the position of your elbows influences your horse. In dressage, your goal is to "organize" your horse's body so that it is balanced and aligned. Dressage trainers occasionally speak of "the box": the horse's body and limbs should remain within an imaginary box drawn around him, with no hind legs or shoulders poking out. If your arms do not rest quietly at your sides, the flapping and bouncing actually opens a door through which a part of the horse's body can escape. It may sound weird, but it's true.

When I described Chris's good arm position, I mentioned that there is a straight line between his elbow and his horse's mouth. This straight line is important because the reins serve as an extension of your horse's mouth. If all goes well, you actually get the feeling that your hands are "talking" directly to his mouth via the bit. In her seminal right-brain approach to riding, *Centered Riding,* Sally Swift put it better than I ever could, so I'll borrow her imagery. The holy grail, as it were, is the feeling that you have developed super-long arms that reach all the way from your elbows to the bit. Therefore, if you hold your hands so low or so high that you break the line from your elbows to the bit, you're breaking the connection, literally and figuratively. There are occasions that call for raising or lowering the hands temporarily, but when and if this is advisable requires more advanced judgment.

Using Your Seat

Your biggest and strongest muscles are in your core or trunk — the region from your navel to your knees — and this area is your center of gravity. Movement originates here, and at the same time your core stabilizes every other part of your body, just as a tree's trunk stabilizes its limbs and branches.

In riding, your seat is in constant contact with your horse. Therefore, this aid has the potential to have the greatest influence over your horse's body.

Of all the directives you'll hear during your dressage education, "use your seat" is one of the most universally mystifying to beginner and even intermediate riders. To explain what "use your seat" means, let me begin by telling you what it is not.

● "Use your seat" does not involve rhythmic clenching and unclenching of the gluteus maximus muscles. My glutes are definitely doing something when I sit the trot, but I don't use them the way I would when doing squats with weights, for example.

● It does not refer to a pelvic thrust or any other movement that would raise eyebrows in polite company.

● It does not involve maintaining a death grip on the horse with the thighs, although learning to contract and relax the thigh muscles is an important element of using the seat.

"Use your seat" means using your core muscles to distribute your weight as desired over your seat bones in order to influence your horse to go forward, to slow down or halt, to go sideways, to bend, and to make transitions from gait to gait. Your seat is the most mobile part of your body and is the primary means of shock absorption when you're in the saddle. If a good rider appears to be sitting quite still, she's matching the movement of her hips, abdominal muscles, and lower back to that of her horse so effectively that you can't see it.

Much has been written about correct and incorrect pelvic angles as they pertain to the dressage seat. Illustrations that attempt to explain these notions tend to confuse me, so instead I'll sum up the important points.

● When you sit properly, you can feel two distinct bony points, one under each buttock. These are your *seat bones.* Through weighting, unweighting, and positioning these bones, you communicate *weight aids* to your horse that influence his balance, positioning, direction, and gait. It all starts there, folks.

● If you slouch in the saddle as if you were relaxing on a couch, you'll feel pressure on your tailbone. You need to sit more erect.

● If you arch and tighten your lower back — which will cause your buttocks to poke out behind you and your chest to stick out — you'll wind up in the so-called fork seat, with your weight distributed in a triangular area between your pubic bone and your seat bones. To remedy this, relax your lower back while tucking your pelvis until your weight is over your seat bones.

Common Position Faults

Emily demonstrates several common faults in rider position. All can be improved by work on the lunge line and through diligent training, both in and out of the saddle.

LEFT HIP COLLAPSED *(left).* In this rear view, her left hip is collapsed. This has caused her weight to be uneven over both seat bones and her upper body to become crooked.

RIGHT HIP COLLAPSED *(right).* Now Emily has collapsed her right hip. Not only has her upper body become crooked as a result, but her left lower leg has pulled away from her horse's side.

PERCHED SEAT. This position is common in former hunter/jumper riders, among others, when they first take up dressage. Emily's lower leg is drawn back and her upper body is hunched over. This position inevitably puts the horse on his forehand because all of the rider's weight is thrown forward over the horse's withers.

CHAIR SEAT. This "chair seat" is common in riders who formerly rode Western, or who lack core strength in their lower abdominal muscles and upper legs. Emily is slumped back on her tailbone instead of erect on her two seat bones. Her legs are out in front of her instead of being underneath her body weight. If her horse were to make a sudden move, her unbalanced position would make her more vulnerable to a fall.

LEGS DRAWN UP. When they begin learning to sit the trot, many riders do what Emily is doing here: drawing the legs up, instead of relaxing them down around the horse's sides, and clamping with the thighs in order to stay on. It takes practice to learn to stay on through balance and not through sheer physical effort.

COMMON CAUSES OF POSITION FAULTS

Many problems can cause a rider to sit incorrectly. One of them is an uncomfortable saddle. My first dressage saddle had a pommel that was like an instrument of torture. If I sat up straight, I got rubbed raw. Assuming that I and not the saddle was the problem, I developed the habit of tucking my pelvis too far under while slouching down and away from the pommel. I managed to keep my upper body fairly erect while I was doing this, so riding instructors had a hard time picking up the flaw. The result was that I developed a strong-in-the-wrong-places, "shove-y" seat that was able to absorb the horse's movement but over which I had no fine-motor control. Oh, and I still got rubbed raw — just in different places.

A second possible cause of poor seat position is "too much horse." A surprising number of amateur riders make the mistake of buying a big, fancy-moving warmblood, only to discover that they can't sit all that big movement. They resort to any number of incorrect gyrations in a desperate attempt not to bounce around in the saddle.

The third and most common cause of poor seat position is weakness. Dressage riding requires a fair amount of general strength and endurance (unfit riders huff and puff after just a few minutes of sitting trot), but even the most aerobically fit person would have a tough time in our sport if she lacked strong core muscles.

Working in concert, the muscles of your trunk anchor you deep in the saddle while allowing you to follow your horse's motion with your lower back and to weight your seat bones as desired to influence your horse. The core muscles stabilize your body in the saddle, absorbing your horse's movement and preventing unwanted bouncing. Insufficient core strength, often coupled with lack of flexibility, inevitably results in unsightly (and undesirable) movement elsewhere: unsteady lower legs, bouncing hands and arms, and even that peculiar head bob that some riders do when they sit the trot. Worse, in an attempt to compensate for core weakness, some riders resort to drawing back their lower legs (which influences the horse incorrectly), maintaining a death grip with their thighs (which effectively kills the horse's free movement and desire to go forward), or "water-skiing" by leaning back and balancing on the reins (so much for going forward).

All of what I've just described may sound simple and straightforward, and it is — in theory, anyway. If you're nodding in agreement, then you've learned the first fundamental truth about dressage: its principles are simple. What you will soon discover, however, is that proper execution of these principles is maddeningly complex. You can know precisely how a rider is supposed to look when she's sitting correctly, while being painfully aware that no one will volunteer you as the textbook example. But there can be a huge disconnect between point A (the image of perfection) and point B (you, reflected in the arena mirror or on camera). How to get from point A to point B quite often is unclear, no matter how book-smart a rider is. And that's why a knowledgeable instructor must help guide you.

Using Your Legs

From your hips to your knees, your legs act as part of your seat, stabilizing the rest of your body in the saddle and playing a role in communicating weight aids to your horse. Your thigh muscles may relax and allow the horse to go forward, or they may close against the saddle as your abdominal muscles tighten to slow him, halt him, or bring him "together" (known as half-halting) in preparation for a new movement or gait. Your thighs also influence your horse's shoulders and therefore his straightness. One thigh closing against the saddle creates a barrier of sorts and, in conjunction with the appropriate weight aids, can be used to help turn your horse's shoulders away from the closed thigh.

Have you ever seen an inflatable stand-up punching bag? Its bottom is weighted, and it tips and bobs when you sock it but always snaps upright, no matter how hard the punch. In the saddle, your thigh muscles, and the rest of your core, create the same weighted-bottom effect. Your position is so stable that no matter what your upper body does, you remain deep and balanced, with your center of gravity low so you're not easily dislodged. (Dressage instructors sometimes tell students to "sit in." This rock-solid, I'm-part-of-my-horse feeling is what they're talking about.)

From the knees down, your legs function as shock absorbers and precise aid-givers. Your horse's motion is transmitted through your hip, knee, and ankle joints, all of which flex and relax softly with each step. Your stirrup leathers are adjusted to a length that allows you to lift your toes slightly, thereby allowing your weight to sink into your heels. Note that I did not say "put your heels down." Jamming the heels down locks the ankle joints, which prevents them from absorbing shock.

Your lower legs — more precisely, the insides of your calves and ankles — ask your horse to go forward and also can be positioned to direct him in lateral movements, to pick up a desired canter lead, and (later in your training) even to ask him to execute a flying change of lead in the canter. A momentary squeeze and release at the girth, timed such that the squeeze happens just as one or both hind legs are set to leave the ground, can be an aid for the walk, trot, or canter. A lower leg positioned slightly behind the girth can help hold the hindquarters in a desired position or tell your horse which canter lead you want him to pick up.

To allow the inside of your lower leg to come into contact with your horse's side, your entire leg (from the hip down) must drape against the saddle — "like a piece of limp bacon," as some wags put it. Conformation (both yours and your horse's) permitting, this means that, when viewed from the front, your toes will point almost straight forward instead of turning out to the sides. (A sharply turned-out toe belies improper gripping with the ankles and knees and is usually accompanied by telltale daylight between the saddle and the rider's knees. Decreased contact with the saddle means decreased effectiveness and an erratic pattern of contact.)

It's only natural, particularly when you're learning to sit the trot, to attempt to brace against the stirrup irons. Another common problem is an inability to keep your stirrup irons and that annoying fishing around with your toes to find them again once they've been lost. The latter often is caused by a drawing-up of the legs in an attempt to stay on, balance, minimize bouncing at the sitting trot, or a combination of all three. All are considered position flaws and greatly diminish your effectiveness in the saddle.

Happily, there is something you can do to avoid and fix these problems. Unfortunately, it is neither easy nor instantaneous. Do the time now, however, and you'll reap great rewards later. The road to riding enlightenment, my friends, is paved with lunge lessons.

GOOD DRESSAGE LEG POSITION is turned in from the hip and draped (not clamped) around the horse's side, toes slightly lifted and pointing straight ahead. The inside of the thigh and calf, not the back of the leg, contacts the horse's side.

On the Lunge

On page 66, I explained the benefits of lunge lessons. Here's what you can expect.

The lunge horse should be outfitted in a dressage saddle, snaffle bridle, side reins (see page 78), and leg protection. The reins are twisted and looped through the throatlatch of the bridle, and the long lunge line is run through the bit rings and attached to the bit (see page 80). A short grab strap is attached to the front of the saddle, either to the D-rings on either side of the pommel or, if the saddle lacks D-rings, via a pair of stir-rup-buckle attachments with rings on the ends (see page 81). You will wear standard schooling attire: breeches, boots (no spurs), gloves, and safety helmet.

With the lunge line looped or coiled safely so it can't get tangled around a leg, your instructor holds your horse so that you can mount safely. With your stirrup leathers adjusted to an appropriate length, you start out riding with both stirrups and reins. The ends of the reins are knotted and looped securely through the grab strap, and you hold the reins in front of the strap as you

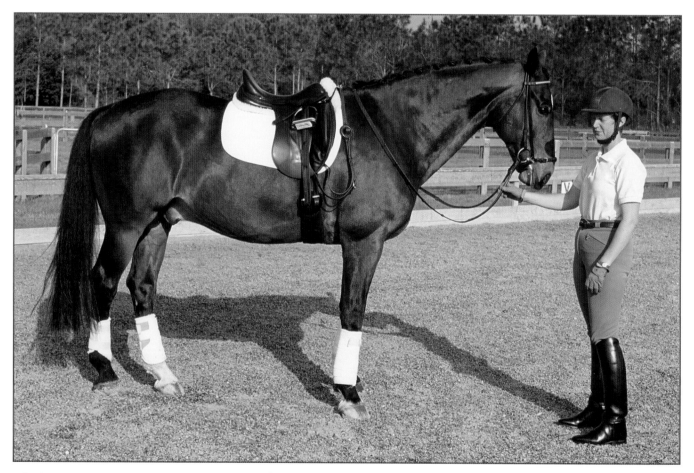

HORSE AND RIDER CORRECTLY TURNED OUT for a lunge lesson — an important step in developing an effective and independent seat. Chris Hickey's Grand Prix horse Levin, a Dutch Warm-blood by Ferro, cheerfully accepts his temporary role as lunge horse. Emily is wearing boots without spurs, an approved safety helmet, breeches, and gloves.

normally would: thumbs upright, with each rein passing between your pinky and ring fingers and then between your thumb and forefinger. After you're situated, your instructor will guide your mount into a large (20 meters or so) circle in one direction. The instructor stands in the middle of the circle; the lunge line at the horse's head and the lunge whip pointed at the ground near the horse's hindquarters "frame" him. Thanks to the line and the whip, you don't have to steer and you always have backup if you have trouble getting your mount to trot or canter.

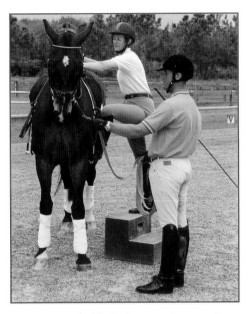

The instructor holds the horse at the mounting block while the student climbs on.

Chris is dressed properly for lungeing, with boots, gloves, and a safety helmet. The unused end of the lunge line is looped neatly and held in one hand.

Ready to lunge, Chris correctly holds the line in one hand and the looped excess along with the lunge whip in the other.

Side Reins

The lunge horse wears a piece of equipment not used in regular riding. The leather lines that run from the bit rings to the billet straps are called side reins because of their place at the horse's sides. Their purpose is not to force the horse's head and neck into a frame, but to serve as a substitute of sorts for the reins and a rider's legs. The side reins serve as a gentle boundary and prevent the horse from poking his nose into the air; their tension eases as soon as he gives in the poll and jaw. Side reins also help to contain the horse's shoulders and to channel his body in the desired direction. For these reasons, the side reins must be adjusted to a length that permits sufficient freedom of movement: not so short that the horse's head and neck are forced into a tight position, and not so long that they're ineffective at best and potentially hazardous at worst (he could catch a leg).

Chris shows where on the saddle billet straps to attach the end loops of the side reins.

Chris shows how the side reins are clipped up out of the way for safety before and after the lungeing session.

SIDE REINS ADJUSTED CORRECTLY. Chris has adjusted Levin's side reins correctly for a lunge lesson. The horse has freedom of movement on a gentle contact with these side reins, which give like a rider's hands, courtesy of the rubber doughnut inserts.

SIDE REINS TOO SHORT. Levin's side reins are too short in this photo — so much so that his nose has been pulled way behind the vertical.

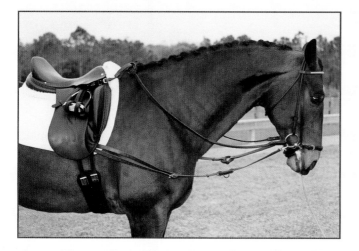

SIDE REINS TOO LONG. Here, Levin's side reins are too long. Dangling in this way, they will be ineffective at best and dangerous at worst, as the horse could catch a leg in them as he moves.

Attaching the Lunge Line

There are two ways to attach a lunge line. It can be attached to the center ring of a special lungeing cavesson, which is the preferred method (method 1). If you don't have access to a lungeing cavesson, however, or if your horse runs through it, you'll have to attach the lunge line directly to the bit rings (method 2).

METHOD 1

Levin models the lungeing cavesson, with the lunge line attached to the center ring on the cavesson.

METHOD 2

1. Chris passes the snap at the end of the lunge line through the inside bit ring, going from outside to inside.

2. He loops the line around the bit ring.

3. He passes the line through the bit ring a second time.

This rear view shows the line passed through both bit rings.

Reins and Grab Strap

In lunge lessons, you focus on balance and position. Because the instructor controls the horse, reins take a back seat; many exercises even require riding "no hands." These images show how you can safely tuck the reins out of the way and give yourself something to grab if you need it.

REINS KNOTTED PROPERLY. This close-up shows the reins knotted properly for the lunge lesson and a grab strap attached to the saddle — a much better handhold than the horse's mouth, should the rider lose her balance.

REIN ENDS LOOPED THROUGH GRAB STRAP. The instructor has looped the ends of the reins through the grab strap so that they can't slip off to one side.

SADDLE ATTACHMENT ACCESSORY. If your saddle lacks built-in D-rings to which the grab strap can be attached, don't worry: this handy accessory, available from tack shops and specialty catalogs, attaches to the stirrup-leather buckles instead.

The Lunge Lesson

You'll start by walking, trotting, and cantering on the line to get a feel for your mount. After you feel comfortable with the gaits and trust that Dobbin will indeed obey the person on the other end of the line, you'll be asked to drop your reins. This can be an unsettling moment, especially if you've inadvertently been using the reins to help you balance. Any upper-body wobbliness will suddenly become evident!

With your arms at your sides or resting against your thighs, you'll ride in all three gaits, getting the feeling for balancing by using your core muscles instead of your hands and arms. After this will come any number of balance and flexibility exercises, including arm "windmills," extending your arms overhead, and placing your hands on your head. You'll ride each exercise in the walk first and then progress to the trot and the canter as your comfort level increases. Because you and your horse must develop balance and flexibility in both directions, your instructor will halt him, switch the line to the other side, and reverse directions at least once during your lesson (see page 84 for lunge exercises).

For some real seat development, you'll eventually be asked to drop your stirrups, and your instructor will cross the leathers over the front of the saddle so they don't bang your mount's sides. You'll walk, trot, and canter in both directions without stirrups; eventually, you'll repeat the arm exercises without stirrups, as well. You may be asked to lift your legs up alongside the saddle, quasi-jockey fashion, as a balance exercise and to help you feel your seat bones in the saddle.

Some exercises may well give you that pat-your-head-and-rub-your-stomach coordination confusion, and that's the idea. It's important for you to develop your ability to use the parts of your body independently of one another, and to learn to sit your horse's movement well, even when your upper body is busy doing other things (see page 86 for exercises you'll do without stirrups).

As you ride on the lunge line, expect your instructor to correct your position frequently. You can also

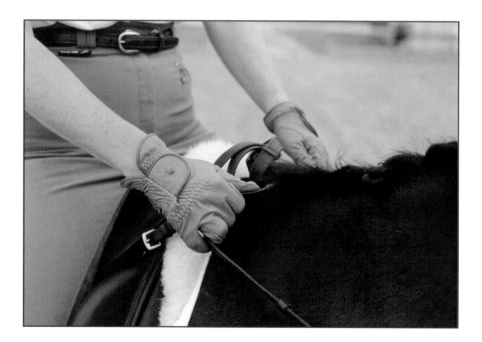

STARTING OUT. To help the student feel comfortable and secure, the instructor allows her to start off with stirrups and holding the reins. Emily holds the reins as she normally would, with the knotted excess between her hands.

expect to feel like a completely ineffective rider, at least sometimes. The first time an instructor told me to halt my horse on the lunge line without the benefit of reins, I reacted as if she'd just told me to fly to the moon — "Yeah, right!" I sucked in my stomach for all I was worth, and my horse continued trotting merrily around the circle. Finally, my instructor took pity on me and said *whoa*. The mere notion that one could slow or stop a horse without reins was baffling, as I hadn't yet learned how to still the motion of my seat, legs, and upper body. As would continue to happen in my dressage education, the mystery deepened. I was learning just how much I didn't know — and that's an important step in the journey.

If I could do it over, I'd like for someone to put me on the lunge line exclusively for at least a month. Doing so would have forced me to confront the issues related to an independent seat early on, and with luck I would have begun to discern some subtleties that it's taken me years of conventional riding lessons to learn. Ideally, even after I went off the lunge, I would have continued my lunge-line work, say, in weekly lessons. If I had done so, I would have progressed in my riding much more quickly.

Off the Lunge

Regardless of whether your introduction to dressage was at the end of a lunge line, it's a safe bet that your first regular dressage lessons will emphasize the basics: lots of walk, trot, canter, and halt. Expect much of the work to take place on the ubiquitous 20-meter circle, which is the largest *figure* (geometrical component of a dressage test) called for in dressage competition. Even young, inexperienced horses can usually manage the 20-meter circle without too much trouble. (The smaller the circle the bigger the strength and balance challenges it poses to your horse).

You and your instructor will soon be scrutinizing not only what you do but how you do it. In fact, as you'll soon learn, especially in the beginning, *how* your horse executes a movement — say, a transition from walk to trot — is more important than where he does it. In other words, you start by focusing on quality, and later you strive to attain both quality and precision.

In chapters 8 through 10, I'll discuss the walk, the trot, and the canter in detail. Before that, however, I need to give you the bigger picture: the goals and stepping-stones of dressage training.

Lunge-Lesson Exercises

After you've warmed up and feel comfortable riding on the lunge without reins, your instructor will lead you through a series of exercises designed to improve your seat and to teach you not to rely on the reins for balance. The exercises on these pages can be done with or without stirrups. Using the stirrups assists balance and improves security.

ARMS TO THE SIDE. Here Emily extends both arms out to the sides to challenge her balance and help her find an erect, centered position in the saddle.

ARMS OVERHEAD. Extending the arms overhead can help correct a slumping posture.

WORKING THE WAIST. Emily uses her obliques to twist to one side, arms extended. It's important to learn how to keep your seat bones down even while rotating your upper body, especially when you ride lateral or bending lines or movements.

HANDS ON HEAD. Putting the hands on the head helps give the rider the feeling of sitting straight and even in the upper body.

TOUCHING TOES. With Levin at a halt, Emily develops her flexibility by touching her toes with the fingers of her opposite hand.

An Extra Challenge: Riding without Stirrups

When your instructor feels you've acquired sufficient balance and strength, he'll have you drop your stirrups and try exercises like these.

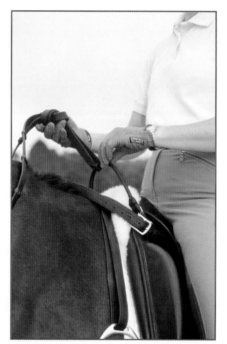

SAFETY PRELIMINARIES *(left)*. Chris helps cross Emily's stirrups over the front of the saddle so they'll be safely out of the way and won't bang against Levin's sides as he moves.

THE REINS ARE LOOPED *(right)* and secured through the grab strap so they can't flap around or catch on anything when Emily rides without reins and stirrups.

RIDING WITHOUT STIRRUPS. Even the best riders practice riding without stirrups periodically to improve their balance, position, and overall fitness.

BALANCE AND STABILITY CHALLENGE. Emily pulls up her lower legs to develop flexibility and to improve her balance.

MAKE LIKE A JOCKEY. Another useful lunge-lesson exercise for developing balance and flexibility is to practice drawing up the legs and then releasing them down. Doing so also helps the rider learn to feel her seat bones.

CHAPTER 7

THE TRAINING SCALE

*D*ressage riders tend to categorize their skills in terms of levels: "What level are you riding?" "I showed Second Level last weekend." "I'm an FEI-level rider." *Level,* in these instances, refers to the official national and international competition dressage tests, which require certain skill sets and movements that increase in difficulty as horse and rider progress.

It is not surprising, then, that many dressage riders focus on perfecting test movements, and thus they measure their horses' progress against what's called for at the various levels. But there is another — different although related — progression of levels that depicts the qualities that dressage training seeks to develop and enhance in our horses. It is called the *training scale* or, because of the way that it is commonly pictured, the *pyramid of training.*

In this chapter, I'll explain how the training scale was developed. Then I'll walk you through the various levels, to give you an understanding of why they are arranged the way they are, how they are interconnected, and why they serve as touchstones that guide all training decisions in the classical development of the dressage horse.

Background

The training scale is used by the USDF in its educational programs, including the Instructor Certification Program and the "L" Education Program for Judge Training (see page 315). Developed by the German cavalry, the training scale was written in its modern form in 1912. The German National Equestrian Federation uses the training scale to this day — and the Germans have led the world in dressage excellence for nearly a century.

The German FN, as the federation is known, bases its training methods on the training scale, which is widely acknowledged as depicting the classical progression of the horse up through the levels. Dressage tests are written using the training scale as a reference

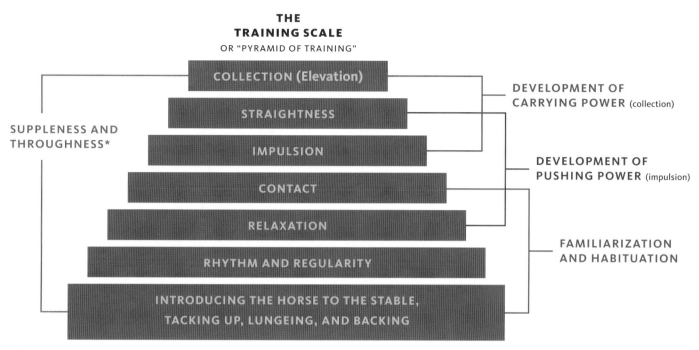

**THE
TRAINING SCALE**
OR "PYRAMID OF TRAINING"

COLLECTION (Elevation)

STRAIGHTNESS

IMPULSION

CONTACT

RELAXATION

RHYTHM AND REGULARITY

INTRODUCING THE HORSE TO THE STABLE,
TACKING UP, LUNGEING, AND BACKING

SUPPLENESS AND
THROUGHNESS*

DEVELOPMENT OF
CARRYING POWER (collection)

DEVELOPMENT OF
PUSHING POWER (impulsion)

FAMILIARIZATION
AND HABITUATION

*The supple, unblocked, connected state of the horse's musculature, such
that the rider's aids can go freely "through" to all parts of the horse.

to ensure that the tests are appropriate for horses at various stages in their training and to help make clear to competitors the qualities they need to develop in their horses.

Understanding the Training Scale

As you can see, the terms used in the training scale describe qualities, not competition levels or movements. There is an introductory sublevel that is not part of the training scale proper, and then there are six official steps. Together, the steps can be grouped into three stages: familiarization and habitation, development of pushing power (impulsion), and development of carrying power (collection). Let's take a look at each stage in detail.

First Things First

Before you can begin riding and training a young horse in dressage, he must become comfortable with all of the preliminaries: being groomed and handled, wearing tack, being lunged, and accepting a rider. Recognizing that careful introduction to these fundamentals is essential in creating a trusting youngster that does not fear humans or the training work. The German FN and the USDF use this stage as kindergarten for the horse. This stage, therefore, is expressed by the phrase *familiarization and habituation*.

Rhythm and Regularity

It is easy to get so caught up in "tricks" and movements that the importance of the three basic gaits is overlooked. This first rung of the training scale proper shows that purity of the gaits is paramount.

Music has rhythm. Your heartbeat has a rhythm. Your horse's gaits have distinct rhythms, too. Simply put, the first goal of dressage training is to find your horse's natural rhythms and to ensure that those rhythms — which are different for the walk, trot, and canter — stay regular throughout the work.

This sounds simple, but it's not as easy to achieve as you might think. For instance, it's more difficult for a horse to maintain his balance on turns and curved lines, and so he probably has a natural tendency to either speed up or slow down, or both, depending on the situation. His *rhythm* may remain the same, but his *tempo* may increase or decrease.

Tension and fatigue are notorious rhythm killers, especially in the walk and the canter. It can be surprisingly easy to disrupt your horse's rhythm through bad riding.

In the course of your horse's career, as he changes and develops, his tempos may also change. That's fine. What's important is that you find the pace at which he moves most easily and naturally, and then strive to maintain that tempo, metronome-like, for as long as he's in that gait.

Relaxation

Your horse shouldn't be in a stupor when you ride him, but he needs to be relaxed and comfortable.

Relaxation has a number of elements. Think about a time when you were particularly tense. Your muscles locked, shoulders and neck rigid, jaw clenched; you may have even unwittingly held your breath. Soon, voilà! Stiffness, tension headache, pounding temples, churning stomach — classic signs of stress. If someone had asked you to dance at that moment, you probably would have looked more like a jerky puppet on a string than a person of grace.

Your horse's body reacts the same way to tension. If he's worried, confused, afraid, or uncomfortable, he tenses his muscles in self-protection. On his back, you're likely to feel that tension as a stiff-as-a-board back that's uncomfortable to sit on, a rigid neck, and a stiff and unyielding jaw. His strides may feel short and choppy. He may hold his breath, too, which exacerbates the feeling that he's made of wood.

A tense horse is physically and mentally unable to do what you're asking him to do, because you can't fight millions of years of evolution. Horses are prey animals. As such, they'd rather flee danger than fight it. When they feel threatened, the fight-or-flight response kicks in. Equines have survived for millennia by getting out of Dodge first and asking questions later. So if your horse is scared or overwhelmed by something in the training, he's thinking, "How do I get out of here?" and not "Gee, I wonder what she wants me to do?" Only after his comfort level has been restored and he takes a deep breath (often literally) can you broach the subject again with any hope of success, or at least a rational response.

Relaxation also implies a level of confidence and happiness. Content horses understand what's being asked of them, are physically able to execute the demands of the job, and enjoy the work — most of the time. We all have days when we don't feel like working, and your horse is no exception. But if you tune in to your horse's signals, you'll find that he lets you know pretty clearly what he likes and doesn't like in life. My event horse, for instance, adored galloping and jumping, but found dressage dull. How did I know? He acted bored at first and then got cranky if we did too much drilling. Some of the eagerness went out of his expression and carriage when I led him into the dressage ring. My current dressage horse is just the opposite. A timid fellow at heart, he spooks and trembles if he finds himself in the Great Big World Out There. He's happiest in the arena, where he knows the routine and feels safe. Very different situations made these two horses feel safe or stressed. One's relaxation technique was the other's recipe for upset.

A horse — or you, for that matter — can be working very hard yet be relaxed. In fact, tension prevents a muscle from working optimally because the muscle fibers need to be able to fire — to contract and then relax — regularly and rhythmically. (Ah, that suggestion of rhythm again. Are you beginning to sense that these training-scale elements are intertwined?) A tense muscle is stuck in contraction and cannot relax, like an on switch with no corresponding off. It cannot work to its greatest potential.

Contact

The concept of contact baffles many riders, dressage and otherwise. Watch some other horse sports and you will quickly see that contact as it's practiced in dressage is *not* followed in most other disciplines. An obvious example is in Western riding, in which there is no contact with the horse's mouth whatsoever: the horse travels on loose reins. In many disciplines, the object is for the horse to carry himself in a desired manner (or *frame*) without the rider's assistance, thus making him a no-fuss, no-muss kind of ride.

We in dressage are not content to simply go along for the ride like a glorified passenger. Instead, we seek to cause the horse to develop his body as a gymnast or a ballet dancer does, and to move with balance, grace, coordination, and precision for the most beautiful and harmonious effect possible. This maximal effort can be achieved only by riding "on contact," meaning with the horse willingly stringing himself between the bit and the rider's hands, like an arrow in a bow, ready to fly.

Contact is one of the easiest dressage concepts to get wrong because, although it would appear to be taken by the rider, it is actually taken by the horse. Let me explain.

One of the maxims that you will encounter many times during your dressage education is "Ride back to front, not front to back." What this means is that you cannot put a horse together by pulling back on the reins. Instead, the horse must be taught to seek the contact by reaching forward and downward with his head and neck. Your job as the rider is to maintain a steady yet hospitable "handshake" (a pleasantly firm, relaxed feel) as he does this, by maintaining a steady yet elastic contact with the reins.

What does correct contact feel like? First of all, feel is difficult to describe because, well, you have to feel it for yourself. I'll do my best, however. Some of the equestrian literature describes correct contact as feeling as if the horse is a strung bow beneath your seat and hands. Correct contact is alive. The reins seem to sing with energy. Contrary to what some people believe, lightness is not the ne plus ultra of dressage; the reins are not supposed to feel weightless in your hands. Your horse is definitely there in front of you. At the same time, you don't feel as if you're holding him up or that his jaw is bearing down on the bit like a one-ton weight suspended from a pulley. Nor do you feel as if you're doing a triceps exercise to prevent him from sticking his head in the air.

Correct contact feels even — not as if you have a hundred pounds in one hand and ten in the other. As your horse turns, bends, and flexes laterally, the amount of contact may shift a bit between the two reins, but there is always a feeling of balance and evenness — of having his head, neck, and shoulders steadily between both reins. You do not seesaw the bit back and forth in his mouth, and he does not wag his head from side to side with each stride.

Your horse takes the contact, but he's not allowed to grab it or root against it. Just as you're supposed to maintain a steady and pleasing contact on your end of the reins, he also is supposed to be polite about it. Pulling, jerking, ducking down, and tossing his head skyward are not attempts to seek contact; they're attempts to get rid of it.

Impulsion

When you start to work on developing impulsion, you're ascending to the second major phase of your horse's dressage training: the development of pushing power, or thrust.

Your horse's hindquarters are his "engine." The energy that his engine generates can be channeled in different ways. In racing, for example, the energy is forward, forward, forward — speed is the only thing that matters. The opposite extreme might be a Saddlebred "park horse," with his distinctive high-stepping movement. His energy is up and down, with relatively little forward movement ("like a sewing machine," some dressage aficionados say, in criticizing a dressage horse whose manner of travel is similar).

If you're wondering whether these two examples mean that the dressage horse's energy falls somewhere in the spectrum between the racehorse and the Saddlebred, go to the head of the class. As your horse progresses in his dressage training, he develops *impulsion,* or pushing power. This means that the "engine" of his hindquarters finds a new and more powerful gear; his hind legs push more strongly off the ground and then reach energetically forward and upward beneath his body as he strides forward.

A horse moving with impulsion gives you the feeling that he's "taking" you. When you ask him to trot from a walk, for example, you'll actually feel the area behind the saddle rise up beneath you as his engine kicks in. With sufficient impulsion, you never get the feeling that you have to nag or cajole to keep him moving energetically forward.

A well-known dressage trainer and clinician once told me that most of the horses she sees when she travels to give clinics are not sufficiently forward and responsive to their riders' legs. In other words, they lack impulsion. Most of us are a little bit lazy by nature, and the same holds true for our horses. If your horse is "hot" (ultraresponsive) to your leg and you never have to ask him twice, then impulsion is probably not a problem for him. But if your horse is like mine, he'll happily tune you out and meander about the arena at his own leisurely pace, seemingly afflicted with delayed-reaction-time syndrome. His impulsion is purely man-made: it consists of my reminding him — usually dozens of times during a single training session — that anything less than a prompt "Yes, ma'am!" reaction to my light leg aid will be met with a quick box with my inner calves or a tap with the whip. If any hesitation or feeling of halfheartedness follows my aid, that's a red flag to me that impulsion is lacking.

Straightness

The concept of straightness would seem to be the most easily understood of the elements of the training scale, right? To some extent, yes, but when applied to horses, straightness is a bit complex.

In dressage, *straightness* refers to the axis of the horse's spine. At the most basic level, then, a horse moving in a straight line is said to be straight if his poll, spine, and tail all align.

IMPULSION IN ACTION. Pancratius ("Paul"), a Dutch Warmblood gelding owned by Emily Gershberg, shows good impulsion (pushing power) in this medium trot.

A horse can also be straight on a curved line, such as on a circle. In this instance, *straight* means "aligned." When traveling on a circle or through a corner, if you were to view the horse's outline from above, it should conform to the arc of the curved line that his feet are traveling on. When his body does this, he is moving in optimal balance.

When starting out, horses generally find it somewhat difficult to remain in this ideal state of alignment on curved lines and turns. Left to their own devices, one or more body parts are likely to bulge inward or outward. The haunches may swing slightly to the inside of the line, for instance, or the outside shoulder may "pop" slightly to the outside. These misalignments reflect a horse's natural crookedness and corresponding strengths and weaknesses.

No horse is born with perfect straightness and alignment, and neither is any human. We are right- or left-handed, and horses likewise have a dominant and a nondominant side. Muscles that control the dominant side tend to become strong, while those on the nondominant side are used less and are therefore weaker. Strong muscles pull structures in their direction and also may shorten and become less flexible, with less range of motion. Weaker muscles may be quite supple (because the stronger muscles cause them to stretch much of the time) but can't counterbalance the strong muscles. The result is crookedness.

If you've ever engaged in a form of exercise or bodywork that heightens body awareness, you probably know exactly where your stiff, weak, and crooked areas are. Dressage training is bodywork for your horse. Through schooling, you will discover all of the little idiosyncrasies in your horse's body. Through systematic gymnastic training, you will work to develop his strength and suppleness evenly on both sides so that he can remain comfortably aligned on straight lines, in turns, on circles, and, later, in movements that require him to move his body both forward and sideways (lateral movements).

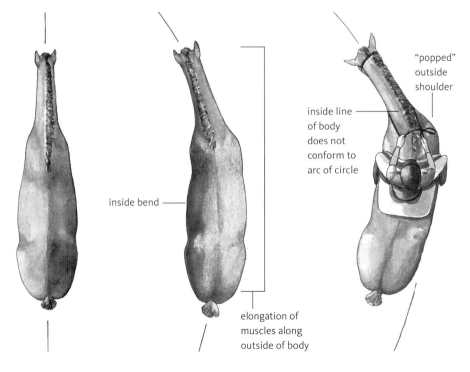

inside bend

"popped" outside shoulder

inside line of body does not conform to arc of circle

elongation of muscles along outside of body

STRAIGHT ON A STRAIGHT LINE *(left)*. You can draw a straight line from poll to tail.

STRAIGHT ON A CIRCLE OR TURN *(middle)*. The horse's body appears to be bent such that it is aligned with the arc of the curved path of travel.

"FALLING OUT" ON A CIRCLE *(right)*. The horse has "run through" the rider's outside (here, the right) rein and leg. He is crooked: his body does not appear to conform to the line of travel.

In dressage, the terms *inside* and *outside* are used to indicate the way your horse's body is positioned. Let's say that you're riding your horse in a circle to the right (clockwise), as shown in the illustration. To be aligned correctly, the outline of his body from poll to tail should appear to conform to the arc of the circle. His neck will flex laterally, slightly to the right. In this movement, he is said to be *bent* slightly to the right.

As you continue to ride in a clockwise direction, you can see the inside of the circle to your right, while everything to your left is outside the circle. But what really determines which side is inside and which is outside is the direction in which your horse is bent or flexed. In this case, he's bent to the right, and so right is inside while left is outside.

And this is where the concepts of inside and outside can get confusing. Let's say you're riding around the perimeter of your ring to the right (clockwise). Ordinarily, you'd expect that your horse would be flexed laterally and bent slightly to the right, especially as he travels through the corners of the ring. In this case, as in the circle example at right, *inside* is his right side and *outside* is his left side. However, there are some dressage movements in which you'd actually position him to the left, with his neck flexed and his body bent slightly to the left, as shown in the far-right illustration. In this case, *inside* and *outside* are the exact opposite. *Inside* is now the left and *outside* the right. So if you were doing this exercise and were told to shorten your inside rein, you would shorten the left rein.

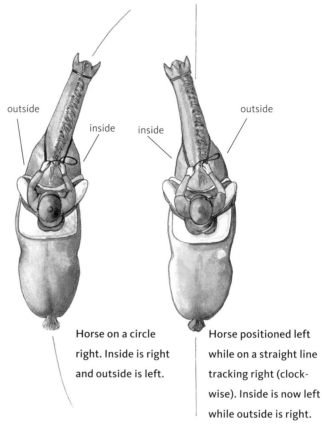

outside

inside inside

outside

Horse on a circle right. Inside is right and outside is left.

Horse positioned left while on a straight line tracking right (clockwise). Inside is now left while outside is right.

Your horse always has an inside and an outside, no matter where he is relative to the arena rail — and even when there's no rail at all, such as in an open field. The appropriate designation is determined not by his placement in space but by the way you position his body.

As you can see from the illustration, horses are not perfectly square. They're slightly wedge-shaped, with their hindquarters wider than their shoulders and their hind legs set wider than their front legs. Imagine taking this wider-behind equine and putting him next to a solid wall. What would happen? To accommodate his wide hindquarters and to keep from pressing up against the wall, he would probably shift his haunches away from the wall. In practice, that's precisely what happens: horses frequently travel with their hindquarters slightly to the inside of the line of travel.

Now imagine what you'd have to do to give his hindquarters room to move while keeping his body aligned: you'd shift his front end over until it is again lined up in front of his haunches. That's exactly what dressage riders do to straighten their horses: they bring their horses' shoulders in line with (or even slightly to the inside of) their haunches. *Straightness,* therefore, can be a relative term.

Collection, the sixth and highest level of the training pyramid, involves teaching the horse to redistribute his weight so he carries more over his hindquarters and less over his forehand. This is accomplished in part by teaching the horse to bring his hind legs a little closer together and to set them farther under his center of gravity as he travels. Exercises in which you bring his shoulders in front of his hindquarters, such as the shoulder-in, encourage this hind-leg positioning because of where they cause him to bear weight. Such exercises are frequently referred to as *straightening exercises* because the gymnastic efforts they require help to remedy the crookedness that crops up when the horse travels in a straight line.

In sum, you'll work on straight lines to improve your work on curved lines, and you'll work on curved lines or lateral movements to improve your work on straight lines. Think of this as the yin and yang of dressage training.

Collection

Ah, collection — the crowning achievement, the highest level of the training scale. A horse that is collected has achieved a state of total balance over all four legs. He has shifted weight off his forehand and onto his hindquarters, which have developed what's known as *carrying power.* The joints of his hind legs bend to a greater degree to accept the weight and to produce increased propulsion. The result is a horse that looks and feels as if he is traveling uphill, even when he is on flat ground. Because he has partially unweighted his forelegs, a collected horse can move with more freedom through his shoulders.

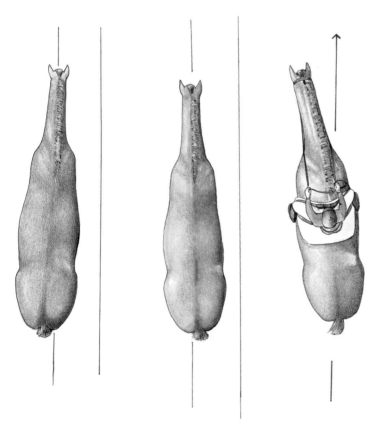

THE WEDGE-SHAPED HORSE *(left).* Horses' haunches are wider than their forehands, meaning that the inside line of their bodies is crooked (haunches-in) when the outside line is parallel to the rail or the line of travel.

STRAIGHTENING THE HORSE *(middle).* To bring the inside line of the horse's body parallel to the track, the rider must bring the horse's shoulders slightly in front of (to the inside of) his haunches.

SHOULDER-FORE *(right),* in which the horse's shoulders are brought slightly to the inside, is an excellent straightening exercise that can be done in all three gaits.

A collected horse's strides are shorter than his natural gait. Don't let the fact that he's covering less ground fool you into thinking that *collected* is synonymous with *slower,* however. A collected horse moves with just as much energy as his more forward-going counterpart. But in collection, some of that energy goes into the movement itself, making the strides loftier and more expressive. At the trot and the canter, the horse spends more time airborne than he does at the walk. (In the walk, one leg is on the ground at all times, meaning that there is no moment of suspension.) "He springs off the ground like a bouncing ball" is one common description.

Because the strides of a horse moving in collection at the trot and canter have more air time, they take on a certain measured and stately quality known as *cadence.* A correctly trained horse moving in collection is beautiful to watch. His cadenced strides are majestic and lofty. His raised head and neck give him a proud and noble look. His "bouncing ball" appearance belies the amount of contained energy in his strides — energy that at times can appear barely contained. Best of all, he maintains this state of balance and energy without depending on the rider to hold him together, a state known as *self-carriage.*

Stepping-stones, Not Steps

Although the training scale is rendered in a way that suggests you must achieve a level before ascending to the next, the actual progression is much more interrelated. Each level builds on what's come before; the levels cannot be achieved in isolation. For instance, a horse without sufficient impulsion cannot be straight. Good rhythm and regularity go hand in hand with correct acceptance of the contact. Improved straightness enhances relaxation. And so on.

The training scale isn't a progression with an identifiable end. Even at Grand Prix — the highest level of dressage competition — horses continue to show at the level for years, continually maturing and improving. The horses' skills are honed by their riders and trainers each day as they revisit the training scale, using it as a touchstone to identify, prioritize, and address any elements that could use strengthening. It is for this reason that a firm grasp of the training scale — the basics of all dressage training — is so important and why careful observation of and adherence to its principles will help keep you focused as you progress.

Ultimately, use of the training scale is a journey with no end. Knowing that you and your horse can always improve is what makes dressage so stimulating and challenging.

COLLECTED CANTER. Chris Hickey has Brenna Kucinski's Regent, a Dutch Warmblood gelding by Flemmingh, in a pleasant collected canter. *Collection* refers to elevation, and the gelding is coming up off the ground with good "jump" in his stride.

CHAPTER 8

THE WALK

"You can relax when you get off." So says Austrian trainer Ernst Hoyos, twenty-nine-year veteran of the celebrated Spanish Riding School of Vienna and coach of numerous international dressage competitors, including 2004 U.S. Olympic dressage team bronze medalist Lisa Wilcox. Every minute that you spend with your horse, you are training him — for better or for worse. If when you walk under saddle you allow him to shuffle aimlessly on a loose rein, don't be surprised if someday you go to a show and earn less than stellar marks for your walk work.

This "school is in session" mind-set does not mean that you should pick at your horse at every stride. If you do, you'll annoy him and will eventually cause him to tune you out in self-defense. It does mean, however, that you should expect a certain level of snap-to-it-ness whenever you're aboard, even at the walk. Walk breaks can still be walk breaks, but your horse should march briskly forward and not drag his toes through the dirt, even on a long rein. He should also "keep his eyes in the boat," as they say in the navy, focusing on the job at hand and not gazing dreamily about the countryside.

The walk is the easiest gait to ruin and the hardest to fix once its quality and purity erode. Some riders consider the walk a throwaway gait used mainly for moseying around and taking breaks from the "real work," but a lack of diligence with the walk now might hinder your training later. Dressage demands constant discipline.

In this chapter, we'll look at the biomechanics of the walk, and then we'll move on to some important basic principles that will govern the way you give the aids for all three gaits. We'll also look at some related concepts and issues: the various aids and how and when to use them, and what it means to get a horse "on the bit." In addition, I'll explain why various head and neck positions are considered faults and show you how to tell one from another.

The Walk Defined

The walk is a four-beat gait, meaning that each leg is lifted separately during the course of a *stride* (a complete cycle of limb movements). Moving from the halt, the horse begins the walk stride with a front leg. If he begins the walk stride with the right front leg, then the pattern of footfalls is right front, left hind, left front, right hind.

A look at the footfall sequence helps us see why the walk is so easily disrupted. In the walk, the footfalls occur in what biomechanics experts call *lateral couplets:* two legs on the same side, followed by two legs on the opposite side. In the walk, each leg is supposed to lift and lower in turn. If the horse becomes tense or his natural rhythm or tempo is disrupted, the lateral couplets are inclined to move in unison. A two-beat gait in which lateral pairs of legs, rather than diagonal pairs of

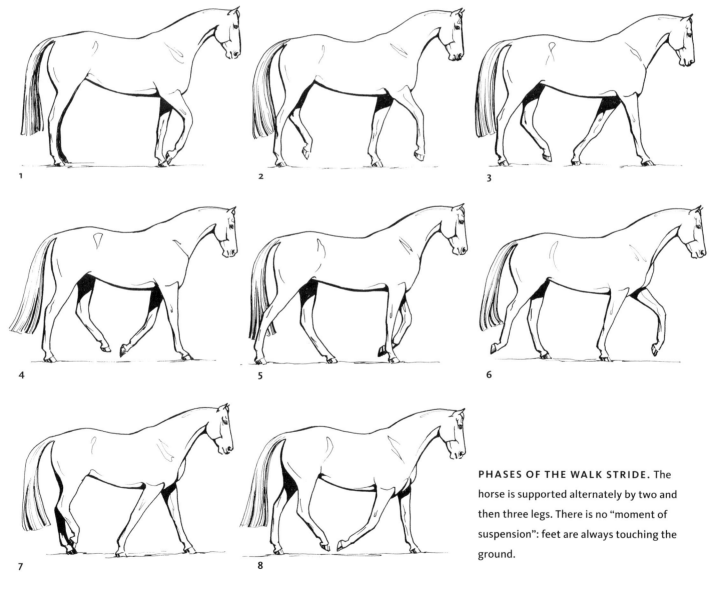

PHASES OF THE WALK STRIDE. The horse is supported alternately by two and then three legs. There is no "moment of suspension": feet are always touching the ground.

legs, move in synchrony is called a *pace*. Pacing is not a gait used in dressage and is considered a serious fault.

Of the three basic gaits (walk, trot, canter), the walk is the only one that lacks *suspension,* a moment in the stride during which all four feet are off the ground. In the walk, one or two hooves are always touching the ground, depending on the phase of the stride.

Before You Begin

Before you mount, you should be correctly attired for schooling, as described in chapter 3, and your horse should be tacked up in a regulation dressage saddle and snaffle bridle, as described in chapter 4. For now, leave off the spurs; you'll earn those later, after you've learned to give the aids correctly and are secure enough in your own body position to know that your legs won't flap and inadvertently jab your horse's sides. (A knowledgeable instructor can tell you when you're ready to don spurs.)

Walk This Way

At the halt, adjust the length of your reins until you have a light and steady feel of your horse's mouth, with your hands held about a fist's width apart and in front of his withers, elbows at your sides. Each rein should pass between your pinky and ring fingers and exit between your forefinger and thumb. Close your thumb atop the rein (not a death grip, but firmly enough that

A Word about the Whip

If your horse is whip-shy, seek the help of a professional trainer. Otherwise, most riders carry a regulation dressage whip. When not using the whip, hold it quietly against your thigh.

To apply the whip, give your wrist a quick flick and tap your horse so the whip touches his side in the area behind your leg. Learn your horse's level of sensitivity to the whip. My current dressage horse barely bats an eyelash when I tap him on the flank, but my previous mount would cow-kick or even buck in response. Never strike your horse around his head and neck, or you'll make him afraid of the whip.

A tap with the whip can range from a featherlight touch to a sharp rap. The whip should never be used in anger or to beat your horse. The whip is an aid — a forward driving aid, an extension of the leg aids — so your horse should never fear it. If your horse reacts sluggishly to your leg aid, a tap with the whip says, "Hey! I'm talking to you!"

THE DRESSAGE WHIP, when not in use, rests quietly against the rider's thigh.

TO APPLY THE WHIP, twist your wrist to the outside so the whip touches your horse's side.

the rein won't slip through your fingers). Let the *bight* (the ends of the reins, where they buckle together) hang down on whichever side you prefer.

Position your wrists so they're aligned with your forearms, your thumbs up. "Breaking" your wrists outward or curling them inward disrupts the all-important line of connection between your horse's mouth and your hands, as does turning the wrists so the knuckles are on top ("piano hands").

Make sure that you're sitting straight and balanced in the saddle with your weight distributed evenly over both seat bones. It shouldn't take much to get your horse to walk on. Look up (always gaze out between your horse's ears; looking down throws your entire body out of balance) and give a light squeeze with your inner calves. Concentrate on keeping your upper body erect and your upper legs in contact with the saddle. Don't turn your toes out or engage in other contortions

THE AREA FROM your hips to your knees is called *the seat*.

to give an aid. Ideally, your legs will remain draped around your horse's sides at all times, with your toes pointing straight ahead or fairly close to it. (Your toe position depends on your conformation as well as that of your horse.) Your goal should be to keep your inner calves, not the back seams of your boots, in contact with the sides of your horse.

A *leg aid* is a light touch of the legs, immediately followed by a release of the squeezing action. Getting the hang of the release of the aid — whether leg or rein — can be more challenging than learning to give the aid. A prolonged leg aid easily turns into a clamping leg, and before long you'll find yourself having to squeeze, or even kick, harder and harder to get a response. Your horse becomes duller, you become exhausted from all that squeezing, and any sense of timing — which you'll need when the pace picks up and you have to give a series of light and precise aids — goes right out the window.

A prolonged rein aid is the equivalent of hanging onto your horse's mouth and, as you might expect, effectively extinguishes his desire to go forward. It blocks his freedom of movement, creates tension, and can lead to persistent attempts to avoid the contact, a problem that can be devilishly difficult to overcome.

Believe me, your horse can feel your light leg aid. He twitches his skin at the mere suggestion of a fly, doesn't he? If he does not walk off promptly at a light calf squeeze, squeeze a little more strongly, then relax your leg pressure. If you still get a "huh?" response, give a little kick with both legs. If there's still nobody home, tap him with the whip.

When you're forced to engage in this progression of escalating aids — and you will be from time to time — keep in mind that your goal is to teach your horse to respond to a light aid. Many riders ask with a light aid, get no response, and give a hearty kick; the horse moves, and that's the end of the exchange. This approach teaches the horse that he can safely ignore the rider until she pulls out the big guns. Instead, and this can try your patience, after he responds, immediately begin again by asking him to respond to a light aid. If he again fails to respond promptly, start escalating the aids until he responds, always trying again with a light aid until Dobbin understands that you're serious and he'd better move out smartly the first time you ask.

How often will you have to repeat this lesson? Possibly forever, particularly if your horse tends to be lazy. As you progress in your dressage training, you will continually strive to fine-tune your aids and your horse's responses, because the more advanced you become, the more quickly the movements and sequences of movements come up. The work you do now to make your horse responsive to light aids will serve you both well later.

If you ask your horse for a forward response and you get more than you bargained for — say, you ask him to walk on and he picks up a trot — never punish him or yank back with the reins to stop him. Instead, let him trot for a few strides, then calmly bring him back to the halt and try again. Unless he's bolting or exploding outright (another case for a professional trainer), don't discourage an overeager response. Instead, regard it as feedback telling you that your aids were too strong, then turn down the intensity a notch or two.

You will make plenty of mistakes as you work to hone your dressage skills, but you shouldn't be punished for them, should you? The same holds true for your horse. Horses make mistakes when they're learning, often because we didn't communicate our wishes clearly or consistently. Dressage can be a humbling pursuit because, more often than not, problems begin with the rider. Horses, especially young ones, test us from time to time, but they do not have the capacity for premeditated malice. Undesired behavior, even when it's aggressive, usually is rooted in fear or pain.

Sequencing of Aids

Even if you're a slight, ninety-pound woman aboard a fifteen hundred–pound warmblood, those ninety pounds are your most important aid and, therefore, are used before leg and rein aids. Your weight and how you position it over your horse's back is important because your balance affects his balance.

Simply put, a horse is inclined to shift his weight in order to keep your weight balanced comfortably over his center of gravity. So if you sit a little heavier over

The Role of the Voice Aid

People vocalize to their horses all the time: clucking, soothing, encouraging, rewarding, scolding. So why didn't I mention the voice in the discussion of the walk aids? In dressage competition, voice aids are not permitted. As such, most instructors and trainers believe that it's best not to get into the habit of relying on an aid that's not available to you in the show ring.

Even if you're not interested in competing, it's a good idea not to vocalize too much when you ride. Some riders get so cluck-happy that they sound like chickens as they trot around the ring. After a while, they probably don't realize they're doing it — and neither do their horses. The cluck, which can be useful when used judiciously, when overused loses its effectiveness and becomes just so much white noise.

There's nothing wrong with saying "good boy" when delivering a well-deserved pat when your horse does something right. Horses seem to find that tongue-trill noise (*brrrrup*) soothing, as well. Most of us enjoy chattering to our horses as we groom and care for them. Just remember that talk becomes part of your horse's landscape, and that your aids and body language make a bigger impression than voice when you are training and riding.

your right seat bone, eventually he'll drift or turn right, even if you don't consciously use any other aids. (The same thing will happen if you simply direct your gaze to the right.)

The proper sequence of aids, then, is weight, legs, reins. Your weight and body position set the stage, your legs ask for the forward response and also help to position the horse's body, and your reins guide him and channel his energy.

As You Walk Along

You've asked your horse to walk on, and he's done so. Now what? For starters, concentrate on feeling each walk step and how the movement of his body causes your hips and lower back to undulate slightly in rhythm. Note that he's moving you, not the other way around. You really don't have to do anything; instead, you're simply following the motion — no hulalike gyrations are necessary. *Following the motion* means going with the horse's movement as opposed to actively

engaging the muscles of your seat (the muscles of your core and upper legs) to influence his movement — either to increase or decrease the pace or to ask for a transition to a different gait.

If you're lucky enough to have access to an arena with a mirror, watch your horse as he walks past it and pay attention to how each step corresponds to the movement you're feeling beneath your seat. (If you don't have a mirror, watch his shadow or ask someone to videotape you.) His hips lift and sink beneath you. His shoulders move forward and back in front of your upper legs and knees. You may even feel a slight swinging and pulsating directly underneath the saddle as the muscles of his back contract and relax with each stride. A swinging back is very good because it means that your horse is relaxed, his muscles are comfortably loose and warmed up, and he's using his whole body as he moves. A tight or hollow back feels rigid, and it is rather like sitting on a board. There's a mincing feeling, as if the horse isn't going anywhere (which he isn't, because his strides are usually correspondingly short). At the

THE HEAD NOD. The horse alternately raises and lowers his head during the walk stride. Here are Sultan and Bonnie Olie. Sultan has raised his head and neck slightly in the first part of the walk's characteristic head nod.

THE FOLLOWING HAND. Later in the stride, Sultan has lowered and extended his head and neck. Bonnie is giving with her elbows in order to maintain a steady and elastic rein contact that adapts to the horse's head and neck position.

faster gaits, a horse with a tight back is an uncomfortably jarring ride.

Can you feel the four-beat rhythm as your horse walks? Are the steps even (one, two, three, four), or is there any irregularity (one, two-three, four)?

What about the tempo (the rate of repetition of the steps)? Could you set a metronome to the beats of your horse's walk, or does his tempo vary, alternately becoming quicker and slower?

Remember the training scale from the last chapter? (See page 89.) You have just assessed the first element of the scale: rhythm and relaxation.

Now let's go back and watch your horse's walk again, either in a mirror or via shadows or videotape. You'll note that his head and neck nod rhythmically as he walks along. This action is part of the movement of the gait, and as such it's your job to allow and follow this movement with your arms. As when following the motion with your seat, this movement is subtle: your shoulder and elbow joints extend and bend slightly as your horse's head nods forward and then returns to its starting position. Meanwhile, your wrists remain steady but not rigid. Rowing isn't necessary.

Stop and Go

At some point, you'll want to bring your horse from the walk back to the halt. Here's how the sequence of aids works for this down transition.

First, make sure that your horse is marching along alertly in a rhythmic four-beat walk. (Yes, the quality of the gait affects everything — even transitions.) Next, instead of continuing to follow the motion with your seat, think of stilling your seat by firming your upper legs against the saddle and engaging your lower abdominal muscles. (Think "navel to spine": draw your lower belly inward and upward, an action that some refer to as "zipping up the abdominals"; don't merely suck in your gut.)

As you still your seat, close your fingers around the reins by tightening your grip, as if you are squeezing the water out of a sponge. This increases the pressure on your horse's mouth slightly but subtly. This is the basic rein aid and involves no pulling.

Perhaps most important, as you give the aids for the transition to halt, think *halt*. You already know that if you look to the right, your horse will drift to the right, because simply shifting your gaze affects your body position. The same holds true for the transition to the halt. Thinking about halting causes your body to still itself, even if you're not consciously trying to do so. In fact, as you and your horse become more experienced in dressage, you'll become increasingly attuned to each other's movements. Later, the most basic aids will become so automatic that you will only have to think *halt* and your horse will halt. The first time he reads your thoughts and responds this way is exciting. It will give you just a taste of how deep and profound the horse-rider connection can be, and how beautiful and harmonious it feels when horse and rider move as one.

After your horse has halted, practice walking on again. Repeat this exercise in different places in your arena or riding area and on both reins (moving to the left and to the right). Vary the amount of time spent in the halt. Some horses don't like standing still and fidget or fuss with their heads if they're asked to remain halted for more than a split second. These impatient individuals need to gradually learn to tolerate standing quietly for longer intervals, as dressage tests call for a five-second halt. Time yourself by counting "one-Mississippi, two-Mississippi" for the desired number of seconds.

Lazy horses like mine have the opposite problem: they go to sleep in the halt. In fact, my horse enjoys not moving so much that he tends to halt too abruptly, with his hind end sprawled out somewhere behind him. These placid creatures need to be ridden into the halt a bit more vigorously, with the rider's legs creating forward impulsion until the final split second before the halt, when the legs relax and the seat and hands create a wall of sorts, before which he stops. The horse's hindquarters are ridden underneath his body and center of gravity in the same way that an accordion can be compressed by holding one hand steady and bringing the other toward it.

Even at the halt, the horse must remain alert and ready to move off instantly at the rider's command. My horse's brain seems to be equipped with a gear that easily disengages. If I don't keep his attention at the halt, I'm greeted with a "Huh? Did you say something?" response when I ask him to walk or trot. I sharpen his responses by doing lots of transitions so he remains alert for whatever's coming next and can't go to sleep.

The Goldilocks Principle

In the children's tale, Goldilocks finds the extremes in oatmeal temperature and mattress firmness not to her liking but pronounces the middle-of-the-road examples of each "just right." "Not too hard, not too soft" can apply to dressage, as well, and finding the just-right response and tempo takes feel, experience, and a healthy dose of experimentation.

For example, let's look at a transition that we'll discuss in more detail in the next chapter: trot to halt. In a trot-halt transition, there should be no walk steps. Ridden too sluggishly and drawn out, or with insufficient balance, your horse will almost certainly take at least one or two walk steps before he comes to a full stop. Ridden too abruptly, the tires will screech and he'll do an imitation of a reining horse sliding to a stop. The goal: the just-right transition that is neither too indistinct nor too sudden.

The same principle holds true in finding your horse's ideal tempos. A pony's short legs will produce faster tempos than those of a big-striding warmblood. Just right for the pony would be a frantic pace for the big guy. The tempo is right when your horse can move in optimum balance. Too slow, and he'll lack energy and impulsion. Too fast, and he'll lose his balance and will run on his forehand (with his front end overly weighted and earthbound).

Don't Walk This Way

Some problem walks are inherent; others are rider created. Here's a rundown of three common faulty walks and what you can do to fix them.

Lateral Walk

A lateral walk occurs when the legs move in lateral pairs instead of separately. It is usually the result of tension created by pushing too strongly with the seat and legs, using the legs alternately in an exaggerated right-left fashion, holding too tightly with the reins (actually a form of pulling back with the reins), or a combination of all four.

LATERAL WALK. The horse's legs move in lateral pairs instead of separately. Often signifying tension, it is considered a major fault.

To correct a lateral walk, reestablish relaxation and free forward movement. This is sometimes easier said than done because a lateral walk can be difficult to eradicate once your horse has developed the habit. My horse's walk had a lateral tendency for a while because I rode him forward too aggressively, and thereby disrupted his rhythm, in a misguided attempt to liven up the gait and make him walk more energetically. Whenever his tempo got too quick, his walk became lateral. After I realized that his natural walk rhythm was more measured than what I'd been aiming for, I relaxed my driving aids and allowed him to settle into a slower tempo. The lateral walk disappeared, but, having created it, I must now be ever vigilant against its return.

Failure to Track Up

A reliable sign that your horse's strides at the walk are sufficiently forward and free-moving is *tracking up:* stepping into the prints of the forefeet with the hind feet. The medium and the extended walk should show *overtracking:* stepping at least partially in front of the prints of the forefeet. Overtracking is generally seen in naturally big-strided horses, such as some warmbloods, which are bred for free and expressive movement. (Some big movement is good but more is not always better: the hugest-striding horses, which may take spectators' and judges' breath away at the lower levels, sometimes have trouble compressing that movement later, when the dressage work becomes more advanced.)

If you lack access to a mirrored arena, the best way to find out whether your horse is tracking up or overtracking is to check your trail, preferably in freshly groomed footing so that you don't have to sort through other horses' hoofprints. Ride your horse at his normal walk; then circle back and look at the pattern of hoofprints. Note where the hind prints fall in relation to the front prints. (Hind prints usually are narrower than front prints.) An overlay indicates tracking up. Anything shy of that is failure to track up, while anything ahead is overtracking.

A horse that fails to track up is not using his hindquarters well. Ask him to walk with more energy by giving light alternating squeezes with your calves (i.e., left leg as his right shoulder moves forward; right leg as his left shoulder moves forward) in rhythm with his steps. Your goal is to produce longer and freer strides, not quicker and hastier ones. Make sure that your hands and arms are allowing the increased forward movement and are not inadvertently holding him back. Riding frequent walk-halt-walk transitions will also improve the quality of the walk by helping him to develop better balance and encouraging him to push off from behind.

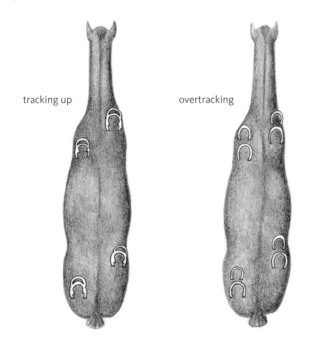

tracking up   overtracking

TRACKING UP *(left).* The horse steps far enough forward with his hind feet to meet the hoofprints of his front feet.

OVERTRACKING *(right).* In the medium and the extended walk, stepping with the hind feet ahead of the prints of the front feet shows good energy and quality in the gait.

THE JIGGING HORSE. Some horses have trouble relaxing into a regular, rhythmic walk stride and instead act like racehorses in a post parade. It takes patience and quiet riding to settle a jigger.

Jigging

Nervous and excitable horses can have difficulty settling down enough to produce a steady, flat-footed, four-beat walk. They jig, prance, and fuss. Although jigging is comfortable to sit, it can be exasperating to the rider who wishes his horse would just walk. Pulling back with the reins tends not to eliminate the jigging and may even exacerbate the problem.

Relaxing a jigging horse requires stoicism. No matter what he's doing, remain calm and relaxed so your body language models the desired behavior. You may need to do a self-inventory to identify any areas of your body that harbor tension and stiffness. It's difficult to let go in front when you want him to slow down, but you need to break the jig-and-pull cycle.

Engage the minds of easily distracted horses to keep their thoughts off potential spooking opportunities and other things to gawk at. Ride frequent transitions and changes of direction to keep their minds and bodies occupied.

Jigging can also be a sign of freshness. If you suspect that your horse has excess energy, try lungeing him for a few minutes before you ride. Regular turnout can do wonders, too, both mentally and physically. If you suspect that the jigging is temporary and will disappear after you take the edge off, don't continue trying to force your horse to walk. Trot and canter briskly for a little while instead. Later, he may be glad to have a walk break.

Jigging is not the same as true explosiveness, which requires professional intervention. The same goes for jigging as a form of not wanting to go forward, which also must be handled with great care lest it turn into rearing.

Adjusting the Walk

The walk, like the trot and the canter, takes various forms in dressage. In competition, the rider is required to show various *paces* within a gait. The different paces refer not to miles per hour covered, but to the degree that the horse is asked to lengthen or compress his stride and the outline of his body. The more advanced the horse, the more he is expected to be able to lengthen and compress.

When you walk, jog, or run, you're able to make similar adjustments to your stride and movement. Think of the difference, for instance, between a high-stepping band member marching in a parade and a fitness walker striding it out. The band member takes short, measured steps, marked by energy and elevation, as he lifts his knees high with each stride. This type of movement is roughly equivalent to what dressage riders call *collected* work. In contrast, picture the person walking with long strides, trying to cover as much ground as possible with each step. At the lower levels of dressage, when not as much elongation of the stride and frame is required, this is called *lengthening*. At the upper levels, where maximum stretch and reach are needed, it's called *extension*. Between lengthening and extension is the appropriately but unimaginatively named *medium* pace, which requires more length of stride than a lengthening, but with a degree of collection and "lift" over the ground.

Now let's look at how these concepts apply to the walk. We'll examine each pace separately.

Medium Walk

The medium walk is the all-purpose version of the same gait at the lower levels of dressage. The rule book of the United States Equestrian Federation (USEF), the national governing body of equestrian sports in the United States, describes the medium walk as "a clear, regular and unconstrained walk of moderate lengthening" (*2006 United States Equestrian Federation Rule Book* [Lexington, KY: USEF, 2006], Art. DR103.4[b]). In other words, the medium walk is a tad bigger than your horse's usual amble-across-the-field pace, and it has a regular four-beat rhythm and appears easy and unhindered.

We've already discussed the importance of tracking up and overtracking. In the medium walk, overtracking is required. Failure to do so is a sign of insufficient lengthening of the strides.

In the medium walk, as in almost everything else in dressage, your horse is supposed to be on the bit, or on contact.

MEDIUM WALK. Emily Gershberg has asked Paul to lengthen his stride while maintaining his balance and energy.

On the Bit

Dressage riders' preoccupation with the position of their horses' heads and necks is literally misplaced. A horse whose nose is poking out of the end of a snaking, giraffelike neck can be a miserable ride.

It's understandable that the average rider would want to reel in the rubbery neck and get the nose in to gain some semblance of control and comfort. Unfortunately, doing so via the usual methods — seesawing the reins, pulling, or resorting to the use of "draw reins" and other head-and-neck-controlling gadgets — only exacerbates the problem because it's a form of riding front to back (see page 91), which sooner or later hinders your horse's gaits, willingness to go forward, and ability to advance in dressage. Put simply, it's a quick fix in a sport in which there are no quick fixes.

What goes on in front of the saddle is a direct result of what goes on behind the saddle. Most of the sins of head and neck position that horses can commit are symptoms of "engine" problems and also of straightness and bend. If you fix the problem, the symptoms will disappear.

These head-and-neck-position issues are subtle, so don't fret if you don't feel their nuances right away. Regular feedback in the form of an instructor, a mirror, or a videotape will help you develop a mental connection between what the outline of your horse looks like and what you're feeling in your hands and beneath you.

On the bit means "on contact" (as opposed to a loose, looped rein), with the horse softening his neck, poll, and jaw and generally proceeding in a contented and forward manner. Accepting the contact requires that the horse engage his hindquarters and use his body in a gymnastic and athletic manner — to work. Weakness, pain, stiffness, lack of understanding, laziness, and a noncompliant attitude can make accepting the contact seem like less than a good thing to your horse. He will express his feelings by doing one or more of the following, often at different times during his training; all are common deviations.

● ***Above the bit.*** Poking the nose out and raising the head and neck. Often accompanied by a hollow back and a generally inverted outline. Head-tossing is a form of going above the bit, although it's ruder and may signify pain in the mouth or jaw.

● ***Behind the bit.*** This evasion feels better than a horse that's above the bit, but it's actually more difficult to correct. A horse that's behind the bit evades the contact by shrinking away from it. He refuses to maintain a steady contact because doing so engages his musculature and causes his entire body to work in a gymnastic fashion. Fear of contact caused by heavy

On the bit

hands, harsh bits, overuse of training gadgets, or being "crammed together" between the driving and restraining aids too strongly and too soon by an impatient or inexperienced rider can also cause a horse to be behind the bit.

You can tell if a horse is behind the bit because you feel as if you have nothing in your hands; the reins are strangely weightless. There may be slack in the reins if he curls up his head and neck like a snail. His nose will almost certainly be *behind the vertical* (behind the plane of an imaginary plumb line dropped from the front of his forehead). You'll feel overly light, as if there's nothing in front of you; it's a false lightness. How can you tell the difference? For a couple of strides, squeeze the reins by making a fist, as you would when wringing out a sponge. If your horse comes together beneath you and slows his stride, he's at least partially on correct contact. If nothing happens, he's behind the bit, and the action of your rein aid was like sending radio signals into space: there may be life out there, but so far there's been no response.

● ***Behind the vertical.*** This is different than behind the bit. A horse can be perfectly accepting of the

contact and yet be behind the vertical, simply because his rider has caused his head and neck to assume that position through use of the reins. When a horse is behind the vertical, his profile falls somewhere behind an imaginary vertical line. In this position, his poll (the place behind his ears where the crownpiece of the bridle rests) is not the highest point of his outline, as it should be. Instead, the highest point is partway down the neck. When this occurs, the energy produced by the horse's hindquarters cannot travel as it should: unimpeded over his topline and through his poll to the bit and the rider's hands, where it is channeled back to the haunches via the horse's abdominal muscles in a natural sequence of muscular impulses that dressage trainers call the muscle ring. (See page 276 for a definition.)

It is common for horses to occasionally come behind the vertical as they work. Perhaps the rider's hands acted too strongly, or perhaps the thrust of the horse's hindquarters flagged momentarily. If the position happens briefly and infrequently, then it's generally not a problem. Behind-the-vertical positioning becomes a red flag when it's persistent, which would

Above the bit   Behind the bit   Behind the vertical

indicate either incorrect front-to-back riding or incorrect training.

Spend some time in the dressage world and you are bound to hear about riders — particularly some well-known European champions — who regularly school their horses extremely "deep" and grossly behind the vertical. The theory goes that doing so stretches the muscles of their "hot" and tense horses and makes them more relaxed and obedient. They bring them up into a correct frame just before they enter the show ring.

This training method is hotly debated. Although a bit of "deep" stretching can be OK from time to time (my own horse likes to warm up that way when he's feeling stiff through his back), it's generally not a good idea to practice it constantly, particularly if you haven't yet developed the experience and feel to ascertain when a horse really needs the stretching and to be able to adjust his frame and outline at will.

● *Leaning on the hand.* Some horses find all this dressage business a tad too much effort and would prefer that you hold them up so they don't have to hold themselves up. They like to use your hands as a fifth leg of sorts, to support the weight of their heads and necks. No shyness about contact here; instead, they bear down on the bit and lean contently for as long as your arms hold out.

You can tell the difference between a correct seeking of contact and leaning on the bit by the way the reins feel in your hands. When my horse takes the contact correctly, there is weight in the reins, but it doesn't feel like dead weight. The reins have an elastic and energetic feeling. When he's hanging on my hands, the weight feels as if it's pulling straight down instead of stretching out. The reins feel heavy and dead.

Free Walk

The free walk is also required at the lowest levels of dressage and is one of the few times the horse does not necessarily maintain contact with the rider's hands. *On a long rein* indicates that contact should be maintained as the reins are made longer; *on a loose rein* indicates

A BALANCED AND FORWARD FREE WALK. Paul's frame is stretched and relaxed, with free and forward strides on a loose rein. Emily has loosened the reins to give him complete freedom of his head and neck.

COMMON FAULT IN THE FREE WALK. Paul is on his forehand, too low in the neck, and curled behind the vertical in this free walk. As a result, his strides are inhibited.

that there should be no contact and that you should be able to see a distinct loop in the reins.

The objective of the free walk is to get your horse to relax and stretch outward and down with his head and neck. The walk should remain active and rhythmic, as in the medium walk, but there should be a distinct elongation of the horse's entire outline.

Most horses go into a free walk pretty happily. The biggest mistake that some riders make is to pump too hard with their seats in an effort to encourage bigger and freer strides. Too much of this and the horse may break into a trot. How much can you push your horse before he breaks into a trot? Experimentation is the only way to find out.

Collected Walk

Once you advance beyond the lowest levels of dressage, the tests call for a collected walk rather than a medium walk. *Marching* is the keyword for this pace: it is active, measured, and stately, as the word suggests. Because some of the horse's energy is being expressed upward and not just outward, the strides of the collected walk are shorter than those of the medium walk.

The collected walk is probably the most risky gait to ride in terms of corruptibility. Excessive shortening of the reins and attempts to fiddle with the horse's basic walk rhythm and tempo can spell disaster in the form of a lateral (pacing) walk, which can be difficult to correct. Less is usually more when it comes to riding the collected walk, so resist the temptation to override.

Extended Walk

At the medium and higher levels of dressage, the free walk is replaced by the extended walk. (The exception is the postscript to the dressage test, following the final halt and salute, in which horses at all levels leave the arena at a free walk on either a loose or a long rein.)

In the extended walk, the horse shows his maximum length of stride and stretches out his head and neck while remaining on contact. He is expected to show considerable overtracking with his hind feet. The tricky part for the rider is achieving the elongated strides without quickening the walk tempo. If your horse has been taught to stretch his head and neck outward and down to seek the contact when you give the reins (an exercise that we will discuss in detail in chapter 9), and if you stay balanced and encourage him to lengthen his stride by tactfully using your seat and legs in rhythm with his stride, developing the extended walk should be a natural progression of your training.

COLLECTED WALK. The difference between the medium walk and the collected walk is subtle. Here Paul's neck is slightly more elevated and his outline is slightly more compressed than in the medium walk. The energy is maintained, with a somewhat shorter stride and more lift.

CHAPTER 9

THE TROT

$\mathcal{Y}$ou'll spend much of your training time in the trot. It's versatile, lending itself to both dramatic extensions and some of dressage's most collected movements. The trot is a clear-cut, straightforward gait that's relatively easy to ride, although sitting its natural bounciness can be challenging. In this chapter, you'll learn to sit the trot and regulate its paces.

The Trot Defined

The trot is a two-beat gait in which the horse's legs move in diagonal pairs: left hind, right front; right hind, left front. Between the movement of each diagonal pair of legs is a moment of suspension, in which all four limbs are off the ground.

The regular one-two, one-two rhythm of the trot is the simplest and easiest of the three gaits to follow, even if you're rhythmically challenged. Ideally, you should be able to set a metronome to it. This clarity, and the fact that irregularity is fairly easy to see and hear, is why the trot is used when evaluating a horse for soundness. As a sound horse trots, his body stays relatively still because of the even diagonal leg motion — we don't see the head nodding typical of the walk or the

characteristic rocking-horse up-and-down of the canter. When a lame horse trots, he nods his head as he attempts to shift his weight to protect the sore leg. This head nodding is not part of the normal trotting gait, so it sticks out like a sore thumb.

What English riders call a *trot*, Western riders call a *jog*. Biomechanically, it's the same gait; however, in practice, the two can be quite different. Western pleasure horses, in particular, are notorious for exhibiting a sort of head-dragging, listless shuffle at a speed that's barely above a walk. In dressage, activity is key. Judges love to see a free, even, forward-going trot, with energetic, regular steps, clearly powered by a strong push with each hind leg. This type of trot generates quite a bit of motion under the saddle, which can be challenging for the rider to absorb gracefully. The Western jog is

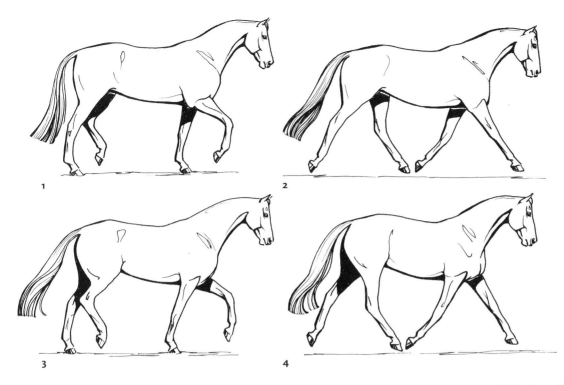

PHASES OF THE TROT STRIDE. The trot is a two-beat gait in which the horse's legs move in diagonal pairs, with a moment of suspension in between (2) during which all four limbs are off the ground.

easier to sit, but the dressage trot is more lofty and impressive to watch and to sit. Never let it be said that dressage uses ease of riding as its standard. In fact, it's quite the contrary: a horse's gymnastic ability rules the day.

The Rising Trot

Many English riders never, or hardly ever, sit the trot. Instead, they stave off jarring and fatigue by posting, or rising: coming out of the saddle slightly with one beat, then sitting down in the saddle with the second beat. This action produces the characteristic up-down, up-down motion of the rider's upper body.

In dressage, the *rising trot,* as it's commonly known, is practiced only at the lowest levels. Once you and your horse are past that stage, it's sitting trot only, although riders at all levels use a rising trot when warming up to let their horse's backs stretch and loosen to the point that they can comfortably handle the sitting trot. The rising trot may be easier, but recall that your seat is the primary way you influence your horse. It's impossible to use the seat aid when you're out of the saddle.

When you rise to the trot in dressage, as in all riding, less is more. In one beat of the trot, the horse's motion throws you gently forward and up out of the saddle; in the other beat, you sink back down into the saddle. Your hip, knee, and ankle joints open and close, absorbing shock and the excess motion, as you rise and sit. Done correctly, rising doesn't take much effort, strength, or gripping, but balance is key. Sitting the trot is where the work comes in!

RISING TROT: UP. Emily Gershberg in the "up" moment of the rising trot.

RISING TROT: DOWN. The "down" moment.

The Sitting Trot

Sitting the trot correctly is one of dressage's greatest challenges. It is also one of its greatest rewards because it teaches you body awareness and control, and sensitizes you to your strengths, weaknesses, coordination and balance issues, and asymmetries, not to mention fitness and endurance levels.

Those naysayers who dismiss riding as a lesser athletic pursuit ("The horse does all the work, doesn't he?") clearly have never tried to sit the trot. Absorbing and going with the horse's movement requires core strength, a supple lower back, decent overall strength, and a healthy dollop of aerobic fitness. If you lack sufficient core strength, your lower back will take up the slack — and feel it later. If you lack lower-back suppleness, you'll bounce in the saddle; unabsorbed movement has to go somewhere, and it'll show up in wobbling ankles, lost stirrups, flapping elbows, unsteady hands, and a bobbing head. If you lack sufficient overall strength, you'll tire easily and have trouble keeping everything together. If you lack sufficient aerobic fitness, you'll huff and puff like an overtaxed runner.

The bigger your horse's movement (and, to an extent, the bigger your horse), the more effort it takes to sit the trot. Big, airy movement typical of the warmblood, with a marked moment of suspension, is a lot to ride. A smaller, shorter-strided horse, whose back may not round and get in on the action quite as much, can be less of a challenge to sit.

That's one reason it can be an advantage to learn dressage on a horse other than a warmblood, despite the breed's continuing dominance in competition. I could not have learned to sit the trot aboard my current mount, a Swedish Warmblood. Instead, I acquired my basic dressage skills riding a motley crew of school horses and others. The warmbloods, when they rolled around, served as an ongoing finishing school, challenging me to take my strength, fitness, and seat to ever higher levels.

If you've already undertaken seat lessons on the lunge, you're probably way ahead of me. But just in case you haven't, and with full awareness of how difficult it is to impart useful how-to instruction pertaining to feel and balance, I'll share some pointers that have helped me over the years.

Level the Playing Field

If the seat of your saddle slopes forward or backward, it doesn't fit your horse correctly (see chapter 4), and you'll find it nearly impossible to sit in it correctly because you'll always be sliding in one direction or the other. Give yourself and your horse a break by starting out in a saddle that fits him properly. Otherwise, you'll be fighting gravity, and you'll lose.

Get Comfortable

Just because a saddle fits your horse doesn't mean it will be comfortable for you. Always test-ride a saddle. You'll know within a very short time whether it's terrible, tolerable, or terrific. A comfortable saddle is like a good pair of athletic shoes: it offers needed support but doesn't call attention to itself and lets you concentrate on what you're doing. If a saddle bothers you, it's not the right one.

Finding the right saddle can and frequently does take time and effort. Your search may be punctuated by moments of impatience, frustration, and sticker shock, but don't let that deter you. A qualified saddler can help you determine whether a saddle fits your horse. Your instructor or another knowledgeable person on the ground can tell you whether the saddle appears to help you sit correctly and in a balanced way, but only you can make the final decision. Will you be able to tolerate having this slab of wood, fiberglass, metal, and leather between you and your horse for the next umpteen hours and probably years? Don't despair: you can and will find a saddle that fits you and your horse.

Dress the Part

Wear breeches or riding tights and boots (or jodhpurs and boots). Trust me, you don't want to learn to sit the trot while wearing jeans. Chaps, on the other hand, are too "sticky." Wear full-seat breeches if you feel you need extra grip.

Consider padded underwear for comfort. Proper position should help keep you comfortable, but if you lack natural padding, these undergarments can help.

Sitting the trot is a high-impact activity. A good sports bra can provide needed support for women. (For more on proper attire, see chapter 3.)

Strengthen Your Core

Many people lack strength in their abdominal muscles and inner thighs. In all my years of riding, I have found only two things that help build strength in these areas: dressage and Pilates. I assume that you will take care of the riding part; see chapter 17 for a discussion of Pilates and other helpful adjuncts that promote rider fitness.

Find Your Seat Bones

Lots of dressage books show illustrations of the rider's pelvis and how it should be positioned in the saddle. Unfortunately, these never helped me figure out where my seat bones are or what I should be doing with my seat as I rode.

STRENGTH TEST. The muscles in the hips and thighs must be strong and flexible for the rider to have a secure upper leg that does not need to clamp on to stay on. Here Emily lifts one leg up and away from the saddle — a tough exercise, but a great one for improving strength and flexibility. (To find your seat bones, try it simultaneously with both legs.)

My instructor, Todd Flettrich, gave me the easiest exercise in the world for locating my seat bone: While seated on your horse at the halt, lift your upper legs out to the sides so that both thighs come completely off the saddle. (You'll feel this in your hip muscles right away.) You should immediately feel two bony protuberances pressing down into the saddle, one on either side of your spinal column; these are your seat bones. Repeat this exercise whenever you need a quick seat-bone check.

Then ride with your legs in their usual position and concentrate on feeling your seat bones. Are they roughly perpendicular to the horse, as they should be? Are they evenly weighted? Experiment with weighting your inside seat bone more heavily than your outside seat bone by simultaneously stretching tall with your upper body, and forward and down with your inner hip and thigh.

Do the Hula

Well, not really, but to sit the trot and follow your horse's motion, you need to develop a supple lower back, which requires pelvic movement. Dancing is a great way to loosen up your lower back and get a feel for following your horse's motion, so crank up your favorite tunes and get started. As you dance, notice how your lower back and hips feel. Then imagine being on your horse and moving with maybe one-fourth as much motion — motion initiated not by you, but by your horse. The idea is to be just loose enough in the lower back and pelvis to follow his movement, rather than so rigid that you inhibit it.

While you're following his movement, make a conscious effort to engage your abdominal muscles to support your lower back. If you don't, you'll feel it in your back.

Drop Your Stirrups

Stirrups are a great invention, but sometimes they can hinder you from improving your riding position. For example, the tendency to lose one or both stirrup irons as you ride is a symptom of position problems. Some riders tend to draw up their legs in an attempt to grip and balance. Others have floppy ankles because they don't absorb the horse's movement effectively with their seats or allow the shock to distribute itself evenly down their legs to their ankles. Still others brace against the irons, ankles locked, and assume a water-skiing stance atop the horse.

If you drop your stirrups, then you have nothing to lose or brace against. Riding without stirrups forces you to use your muscles to balance. Riding without stirrups and reins, as in a lunge lesson, forces you to use your muscles to balance *and* to learn not to rely on the reins as a handhold. Both are tiring, even to seasoned riders, so don't expect to be able to trot around without stirrups for your usual 45-minute training session. Take breaks as needed. Push yourself a little more each time, but pick up your stirrups when genuine fatigue sets in. Proper form is essential in riding, so you should always strive to maintain it. Practicing with poor form is marginally useful, and risky because you're likely to injure yourself.

RIDING WITHOUT STIRRUPS is one of the best ways to develop strength, balance, and endurance. Lunge lessons allow you to focus on your position without having to steer the horse at the same time.

Oddly, there may be times in your riding when you find it easier to maintain good position without stirrups. This may be because you're unwittingly resuming bad habits when you retrieve your irons, or it may be because the placement or length of your stirrup leathers is incorrect. If the design of your saddle is such that it doesn't naturally place you in proper shoulder-hip-heel alignment, you may find yourself forever struggling with your stirrups. Only a saddle with stirrup bars positioned correctly for your conformation and for that of your horse will remedy this problem.

Many dressage riders adjust their stirrup leathers too long in a misguided attempt to achieve an elegant long leg. If you constantly feel yourself reaching for your stirrups or cannot ride with your toes up and heels down without losing your irons, then try shortening your leathers by at least one hole. A too-long leg cannot wrap correctly around a horse's sides because it is too straight, and the angles of the joints are too open and locked to serve as effective shock absorbers. Experiment — ideally, with instructor input — realizing that even a slight change in the length of the stirrup leather may feel wildly different at first. Stick with it for at least one full session, and see how you look and feel at the end of the ride.

Be a Weeble

I'm dating myself here, but as a dressage rider I can relate to Weebles, the toy popularized in the 1970s and 1980s with the slogan "Weebles wobble, but they don't fall down." These little egglike figures are bottom heavy; they tip, but they always bounce back upright. Not that I'm trying to convince you to take that "bottom heavy" part literally, but you'll go a long way toward developing a balanced and secure seat if you can learn to anchor the lower half of your body firmly in the saddle.

The well-known British instructor and author Mary Wanless calls this concept "plugging in," as into a socket. When your seat is deeply rooted in the saddle, your center of gravity remains low. As a result, you're not easily dislodged or shifted out of place. You can go with your horse's motion better because you're sitting "in" him, not on him. You're also better prepared to stay seated in the event of a spook, a stumble, or another sudden movement.

Picture a tall, strong tree. Reaching deeply into the ground, the roots anchor the tree into the earth. Solid and firm, the trunk stands fast, bearing the weight of the branches and easily withstanding the whims of Mother Nature. The pliable branches grow up and out toward the sunlight. Wind may bend or break the branches, but their movement does not affect the trunk.

When you ride, your seat acts as would the roots and trunk of a tree. The muscles of your hips and thighs pull you down into the saddle, while your abdominals and the muscles of your torso lift upward. In a sense, you use the muscles of the upper and lower halves of your body in opposition, with your seat anchoring everything. Because the muscles in the lower body are the biggest and strongest, they create a Weeble effect. Engaging these muscles makes you bottom heavy in the saddle, which means you can't be easily dislodged.

Zip Up those Abs

When first learning to sit the trot (and to ride the canter), many riders complain that they bump to the back of the saddle and then have to try to catch up to the horse's motion. Engaging your abdominal muscles can prevent this by helping to pull you forward as you ride, with your pelvis in a neutral or slightly tucked position, as if you are trying to lift your pelvic floor. Some fitness professionals call this action "zipping up the abdominals" because it has an up-and-in feeling. Others, particularly Pilates instructors, call it "navel to spine."

What it *isn't* is merely sucking in your gut; that simply hollows your gut and forces you to hold your breath. Learn to engage your abdominals while breathing normally. It takes work and practice, but your horse and your lower back will thank you.

Follow Your Own Training Scale

Did you think all that stuff about suppleness, straightness, and relaxation was just for your horse? Well, it is, technically, but you would do well to assess these qualities in yourself as you learn to sit the trot. Crooked posture will prevent you from maintaining a balanced and even posture over both seat bones, for example. Tightness on one side of the body (often on the dominant side) can make you draw that leg up and back instead of stretching it down. Many riders collapse a hip; that is, they sink to one side through their midsection. A collapsed hip actually happens when one side of the torso is strong (tight) and the other is weak (slack). To correct it, the rider has to stretch the strong side and strengthen the weak side.

No human being is perfectly symmetrical and evenly strong and supple on both sides, just as no horse is perfectly symmetrical and evenly strong and supple on both sides. If you're lucky, your strong areas will correspond to your horse's weak ones and vice versa, and you'll help balance each other out. More than likely, however, he'll have some areas of tightness where you are naturally weak. Your challenge is to improve your overall strength and balance so you can influence your horse with your position, not the other way around.

Adjusting the Trot

Much more so than in the walk, in the trot you'll be able to really feel yourself influencing the tempo and length of your horse's strides. You can take advantage of the forward momentum and suspension, and use that energy to adjust the gait in various ways.

Let's take a look at the trot paces you'll encounter at the lower levels.

Stay the Course

Some of the world's best dressage riders are slight women, weighing barely over a hundred pounds. Yet they can transform a clunky-looking, fifteen hundred–pound warmblood into a graceful dancer, using little more than their strength and balance. How do they do it?

Although most top riders are fit, trim, and strong, they're generally not possessed of body-builder-like strength. However, they have learned to maintain their correct position and effective aids even when the horse's body makes it difficult to do so. For example, horses can become quite uncomfortable to sit when they're getting tired. They feel as if they're sprawling in all directions and "falling apart" beneath you. The trot feels as if it's in two counties, and the canter becomes a four-beat gait with an unpleasant downhill feeling, like a car hurtling down a mountain road. When traveling on a circle or curved line, stiffness through the horse's back and midsection can literally bounce you off your inside seat bone so that, before you know it, you're sitting to the wrong side (the outside) of the saddle. (Note that I'm talking about general fatigue and crookedness here, not outright unsoundness, which is a matter for your veterinarian.)

It's really difficult to maintain correct position and body alignment when your horse feels awful. A good eye on the ground will help guide you in the right direction. Beyond that, it's lots of discipline, feel, and body control.

Working Trot

The working trot is the basic pace at the lowest levels of dressage. These are its hallmarks: The horse remains on the bit while moving with regular and elastic steps with good hock action (signifying good thrust from behind). He is in balance and moves freely but is not collected, with an elevated head and neck. The frame is round but not especially compressed; it's more "together" and energetic than that of the comparatively strung-out hunter hack or that of the Western pleasure horse.

For most horses, the working trot most closely resembles their natural trot, the one you see when they're moving at liberty. The gait is in the horse's natural tempo, and he appears balanced and gymnastically supple yet not overly "put together."

If your horse is sound, you can achieve a passable working trot simply by practicing the basic exercises and movements provided in chapter 11. In the show ring, the working trot is ridden either rising or sitting, depending on the level.

Lengthened Trot

After you and your horse move beyond the most basic levels of dressage, the tests call for a lengthening of stride, first in the rising trot and later in the sitting trot. How to get a horse to lengthen his stride and not just trot faster (hasten his tempo) puzzles many riders. The trick is to use your seat and legs in the same rhythm and tempo as your horse's regular working trot, while simultaneously creating more forward energy. By doing so, you're telling your horse, "More trot!" and "Trot in this same rhythm." Give with your hands a little, and keep your upper body back to drive him forward and help him maintain his balance. With a little practice (and luck), he should catch on and begin to take a longer stride without quickening the pace.

Although, generally, the paces and movements in dressage are behaviors that horses exhibit naturally (watch frisky horses playing in a field: they'll lengthen and collect their strides, do flying changes of lead at the canter, and even passage), you're now trying to teach your horse to exhibit these things on your command

BALANCED, ACTIVE WORKING TROT. Chris Hickey and Brenna Kucinski's Regent, a Dutch Warmblood gelding by Flemmingh, in a balanced and active working trot. Regent uses his hind legs well, and he reaches for the bit with his head and neck.

ENERGETIC LENGTHENED TROT. Regent in an energetic lengthened trot. The gelding has increased the size of his stride yet maintains his balance.

and from specific sets of aids. It's not surprising, then, that he doesn't instantly understand everything you're asking him to do. You're bound to issue some unclear instructions, and he's bound to misinterpret you from time to time.

Lower-level dressage tests help the rider by asking for the lengthened strides in the rising trot. You don't rise to the canter, so rising is a clear signal to your horse that the trot is the desired gait. When you're starting out, this extra cue helps to keep both of you in trot mode. And it's easier to rise to a trot lengthening than to sit a trot lengthening because of the additional impulsion and suspension; there's more movement under the saddle. You only get a break at the lowest levels, though. When you advance beyond that, you ride everything sitting.

Positive Reinforcement

The masters of horsemanship remind us to reward even small steps in the right direction, to be patient and consistent in our training, and to be content with slow and measured progress. There's an expression used in animal training that I really love: "Catch him doing something right." Too often we focus on what's wrong and overlook what's going well.

We should be prepared to reward a good effort, even if it comes when we don't expect it. Say, for example, that you're trotting along in a nice working trot. You ask your horse to canter, but instead he lengthens his stride, catching you a bit off guard (and off balance) as you feel him push off beneath you in ground-covering strides. You don't necessarily want to reward him for not obeying your canter aids, but a wise rider will consider the possibility that the fault was hers — that her preparation and aiding were to blame.

Instead of immediately pulling him back down into a more modest trot, take advantage of what your horse has offered by feeling the sensation of the lengthened strides for a moment; then calmly regrouping and asking again for the canter. Try to discern what you did differently in your body to get the lengthening versus the canter. You've gained a new level of awareness and feel, merely by taking advantage of the situation when it presented itself.

Collected Trot

The collected trot is the natural evolution of the working gait. Collection is not, as so many people mistakenly assume, a frame that is imposed on a horse through the use of heavy hands or, worse, inexperienced and indiscriminate use of auxiliary reins and other so-called training gadgets. Neither is it (or any collected gait) a slow version of the working gait. Although the tempo of the horse's strides may slow somewhat as his degree of collection increases, the amplitude of those strides increases greatly. Each limb has more lift and "air time" as a result of increased impulsion from the hindquarters and bending of the joints. A horse moving in collection gives an impression of great energy, power, grace, and elasticity.

It is said that collected work teaches the horse to coil his body and energy like a spring. This gathering — which should not to be confused with tension — causes the horse's entire frame to compress and elevate. He lifts and rounds his back, and you can actually feel this under the saddle. As he shifts more of his weight back to his hindquarters, his shoulders appear to lift and his neck and head rise up out of his lifted and free-moving shoulders, his neck arching gracefully. The elevation of his neck and head, combined with the lifting and rounding of his back, cause his entire outline to shorten. He moves in a heightened state of athletic balance. He gives the impression that he could move his body with ease in any direction — forward, sideways, left, right.

COLLECTED TROT. Chris and Regent in a collected trot. The horse's outline is shorter than in the lower-level working trot. The steps are airier, with lift as well as forward reach.

Collection evolves from consistent, correct basic gymnastic work; it cannot be imposed on a horse. Transitions between gaits and between paces within a gait (such as from a working trot to a lengthening trot and then back again) teach your horse to balance himself and to push off energetically using his hindquarters. Working on turns and circles helps to make him supple and to strengthen his inside hind leg, which carries more weight on curved lines than on straight lines. Lateral movements, such as shoulder-in, further strengthen and engage the inside hind leg, and they develop balance and freedom through the shoulders. (See chapter 11 for a discussion of these and other movements.)

There are two cardinal rules of collection:

1. Collection is never achieved by a mere shortening of the reins to force your horse's head and neck into a constricted bowed shape.

2. There should be more energy and oomph to his strides in collection, not less.

These principles may sound simple, and they are, but they're not simple to put into practice. Collection cannot be forced or rushed. It happens gradually over time as the result of patient, diligent, and correct training. This may be welcome news to some and a source of frustration to others. Those who stick with it typically find its subtle challenges oddly addictive and ultimately greatly rewarding.

Avoid Gadgets

Although you're bound to see auxiliary reins and other gadgets in tack shops and tack catalogs and you may see other riders using them, dressage training is best done in a simple snaffle bridle. Improper use of gadgets can undermine a horse's confidence, can hinder or ruin his training, and can put the rider at risk. Leave gadgets to seasoned experts who understand when special circumstances warrant their careful and judicious use.

Medium Trot

Medium doesn't sound like much, but a medium gait is actually quite dynamic. Introduced at the point in your horse's training in which he is developing collection, the medium trot combines the elevation and suspension of the collected trot with the reach and ground-covering stride of lengthening. The result is an impressive extension of the stride that maintains some of the roundness and elevation of collection. The horse's nose reaches slightly in front of the vertical, and his head and neck lower. However, his overall frame is not as flat as in the more elementary trot lengthening, and his strides are less earthbound.

If your horse has been schooled correctly, you don't have to do a lot of hocus-pocus to achieve a medium trot. Say you're in a collected trot down the long side of the arena, and you want to prepare for a medium trot down the next long side. You coil your horse's springs by riding a few half-halts (see box on page 125) as he trots through the corners and the short side of the arena. As you reach the beginning of the next long side, he feels revved and ready to go. Maintaining his rhythm and tempo with your seat and legs, you "let him out the front door" by giving a little bit with your hands without throwing him away. He should reach for the contact as he's been taught.

Some of the energy goes into maintaining a degree of collection and push with the hindquarters. Simultaneously, some goes forward into an elongated stride and a slight forward and downward reaching of the head and neck.

You may be wondering how to teach your horse to reach for the contact. It's simple: just practice the exercise known in dressage tests as the "stretching circle."

MEDIUM TROT. Chris and Regent in an eye-catching medium trot. Note that this trot shows more collection than the lengthened trot on page 119. Regent's hind legs are as active as his front legs, as shown by the fact that the cannon bones of his left hind leg and right foreleg are parallel.

How Not to Trot

The photographs below depict four common "way of going" faults that crop up in the trot as well as in the other gaits.

HOLLOW. Regent remains active in the medium trot, but he has momentarily hollowed and tensed his back and raised his head and neck. The result is that he has lost some engagement of his hindquarters; he is slightly "out behind."

"STRUNG OUT." Having lost the collection and the energy, Regent now looks like a nice hunter hack. Note how earthbound his stride looks, as compared with the photo on page 122.

BEHIND THE VERTICAL. Here's what "behind the vertical" looks like. Note that Regent's poll is no longer the highest point, a telltale sign. A momentary dip behind the vertical is not cause for alarm, but some riders mistakenly keep their horses in this frame. The horse may feel nice and soft to sit on, but he's unable to come through with his hind legs or to lift his shoulders.

ABOVE THE BIT. Regent has come above the bit in an effort to evade the connection between Chris's seat, leg, and rein aids. Chris hasn't panicked; he keeps his hands low and continues to ride forward. With tactful riding, Regent will relax and drop his head.

THE STRETCHING CIRCLE

The pyramid of dressage training is built in part on the premise that the horse follows the rein — that is, he willingly goes forward into steady and elastic rein contact. Because he is accustomed to being ridden from the rider's seat and legs into a comfortable contact (in what I suppose is the equine equivalent of a reassuring handhold), and because the rein does not restrict his movement or frighten him, he becomes conditioned to reach out and down with his neck and head as his balance and the length of the reins permit.

Asking your horse to stretch out and down with his head and neck and then gathering him back up again, all while maintaining an even tempo and degree of collection, is an excellent test of his relaxation, suppleness, and balance. It's such a good test, in fact, that it's been incorporated into some of the lower-level dressage tests in a movement that's been dubbed the *stretching circle* or the *stretchy-chewy circle*. The rider trots on a large circle and commences rising, gradually allowing the reins to lengthen. If all goes well, the horse "chews the reins out of the hands," his soft mouthing of the bit evidence of his relaxation and acceptance of the contact. His neck reaches forward and down but still retains a degree of roundness. After the horse has reached down, the rider gradually shortens the reins and resumes sitting the trot. With the tempo undisturbed, the horse's outline returns to where it was before the stretching circle began.

Taking the reins forward and down is an excellent check of your horse's basics and can be done anywhere in the arena, on straight or curved lines, and in the trot or the canter. The accordion-like exercise is itself a transition and is a great gymnastic and stretching exercise for horses at all levels of training.

Even if you never plan to show and so have no need to master the stretching circle for a judge's keen eyes, make the exercise a part of your daily training routine. Problems riding this movement will point out areas of weakness in your training. Common faults are failure to follow the rein forward and down, or literally taking the rein by snatching it out of the rider's hands. Both have similar origins: usually tension in the horse's neck and back muscles, often accompanied by the use of too much hand and not enough seat and leg as forward driving aids.

The stretching circle, like all dressage movements, is not an end unto itself. Rather, it is a means of

STRETCHING CIRCLE. Emily rides Paul in the stretching circle at the trot, in which the horse "chews the reins out of the hands" and stretches down as the rider gradually gives the reins. Judges want to see the horse maintain his balance and tempo and stretch forward as well as down, as Paul is doing here.

developing your horse gymnastically and also a way of evaluating his progress against the principles of the training scale. Problems in the exercises reveal weaknesses in his basics. Then it's back to the drawing board as you work to shore up those basics. And lest you think that only beginners have to revisit the basics, know that even Olympic-level horses and riders go back to the drawing board in one form or another every single day.

FAULT: BEHIND THE BIT. Paul is no longer stretching out toward the contact (as evidenced by the slack rein) and has ducked far behind the bit, an evasion.

FAULT: ON THE FOREHAND. Paul has momentarily lost his balance and fallen on his forehand. When a horse is on the forehand, he feels earthbound and heavy in the rider's hands.

What Is a Half-Halt?

Half-halt is one of the most misunderstood terms in dressage. Equestrian writers have spilled pages of ink trying to describe this elusive concept. Actually, it's pretty simple.

A half-halt is a split-second rebalancing. You use it to contain your horse's energy somewhat as preparation for an upcoming movement (such as a transition), or when he's truckin' along at a good clip but gradually losing his balance and falling on his forehand. (How will you know he's falling on his forehand? Because the weight in your hands will increase, and he'll start to feel sprawling, ungraceful, and downhill underneath you.)

A half-halt cannot happen if your horse is not moving energetically forward with good activity. In her seminal book *Centered Riding,* the legendary Sally Swift presents a marvelous image of a rider trotting along, her arms like curved garden hoses with water rushing through. You should feel that whooshing sense of forward energy as you ride. If you're not whooshing along, you can't half-halt.

Now back to the mechanics of the half-halt. As you're trotting or cantering (the walk doesn't have enough forward energy to warrant half-halting), your horse is obedient to your driving aids (seat and legs) and has attained a good rhythm. He feels lively and reaches into the elastic contact you're maintaining at the other end of the reins. (These qualities are half-halt prerequisites. If you don't have them, then you need to fix the problem first.)

You begin to feel him tip forward a bit and start to get strung out. What do you do? You sit up even taller for a moment (lift the sternum, navel to spine,

LOSS OF BALANCE. Regent has momentarily fallen on the forehand. Time for a half-halt!

shoulders back and down) and close your fists on the reins as if you are squeezing water from a sponge. Doing so increases the pressure on your horse's mouth. The magical effect of the circle of the aids (the muscle ring) causes his forward energy to boomerang back to his hindquarters. In no more than a stride or two, he has rebalanced himself. He's more collected, moving in better balance, and is athletically positioned for whatever you have planned next.

All of this happens in an eyeblink. A half-halt lasts no longer than a stride or two. When you become comfortable with the concept and hone your timing and coordination, you'll find that some half-halts last only a fraction of a stride. In fact, after a while, you won't even be aware that you're riding half-halts: they'll become automatic, the same way changing gears while driving a car or riding a bicycle become automatic. This is a good thing for three reasons. First, it frees up your mind to concentrate on other things, like how to get that left-lead canter to look like less of a crab walk. Second, timing is everything in riding; the moment that you think, "Oh! I should half-halt now," it's too late to initiate the action. (Timing is, in my experience, one of the most crucial feel issues in riding, and one of the most difficult to learn. Watching yourself in a mirror helps, as does

watching videos and watching other people ride. But a lot of it comes down to experience and a healthy dose of experimentation.) Third, there will be times in your training when your horse needs a half-halt. If its administration requires mental gymnastics, you'll get really tired really quickly.

A half-halt is a subtle action. When you have an opportunity, watch a videotape of Olympic dressage competition or some other prestigious international show; or go watch the Grand Prix–level classes if you're lucky to have a big dressage show in your area. Usually, the highest-placing rides are fairly seamless, mistake-free performances that appear to flow effortlessly from one movement to the next. Now, while you're watching those top horses and riders, think to yourself, "They're giving half-halts all the time." Yes, they are, even if you can't see them, and that's the point. If you watch carefully, you may see the horses appear to "come underneath themselves" from time to time or to assume a certain air of readiness. Those moments are half-halts at work — no big efforts on the riders' part, no interruption of the horses' rhythm. Half-halts are important in dressage, but they are literally no big thing.

REBALANCING ACT. Regent is shifting his weight back onto his hindquarters as Chris half-halts and downshifts from medium trot to collected trot. The horse has raised his head and neck, and his nose is a slightly farther in front of the vertical than is ideal, but he is rebalancing himself effectively.

Extended Trot

Jewelry, logos, bumper stickers — whatever the item — if it has a dressage theme, chances are it's an image of the impressive and photogenic extended trot.

In the extended trot, the horse gives it all he's got: maximum stride length and ground covering, powered by great impulsion from his hindquarters. As in trot lengthening and the medium trot, he's allowed to extend his head and neck somewhat forward, and his nose is expected to come slightly in front of the vertical. His entire frame should be lengthened, as well. As in the medium trot, he should retain some of the feeling of collection, however.

True extension of stride is an all-out effort for the dressage horse, and for this reason trainers and riders ask for it sparingly. It's the same reason that jumper riders don't school their Grand Prix horses over big courses every day, and that racehorse trainers don't ask for top speed day in and day out. These maximum efforts are breathtaking to watch but also take a toll on the equine athlete's body. Most top dressage riders save the blow-your-doors-off extensions for the show ring. At home, they'll ask for maybe 75 or 80 percent if they school an extension at all, always keeping something in reserve. They know the movement; the horse knows the movement. Why tax the horse's body needlessly? Impressing family, friends, and spectators is not a good reason to ride a full extension.

If you thought sitting the working trot was difficult, the extended trot will require an even higher level of athletic effort. If your horse has a big trot, the movement beneath your seat can be tremendous. It takes solid core strength, a healthy fitness level, and good balance to sit a big extended trot well. Some riders are caught by surprise and wind up almost clutching the saddle in an attempt to stay with the movement. They're probably in no danger of falling off, but the bumping in the saddle and feeling of being left behind the motion is disconcerting.

To ride an extended trot, you leave nothing in reserve. Like the medium trot, it comes from a basis of collection. Within that collection, you ready your horse with half-halts and then give him the gas: driving seat and leg aids (shoulders back and down, core strongly engaged while you scoop your seat bones slightly forward in a small movement similar to a pelvic tuck, knees and thighs firmly on the saddle without gripping, calves making even contact yet "breathing" with each stride), while allowing forward movement with giving hands. The give of the hands comes partly from the hands themselves (which are holding the reins softly and firmly — not so softly that the reins slip through your fingers, and not so firmly as in the half-halt) and partly from your elbow joints, which open and close softly to allow your horse to reach forward with his head and neck.

EXTENDED TROT. Grand Prix dressage horse Harmony's Weiss-muller and Susan Jaccoma show the tremendous power, thrust (impulsion), and lengthening of frame needed for the extended trot. Extensions require so much strength and balance that they are not ridden until later in the horse's training.

To bring your horse back into a collected trot from the extension, you make the allowing movements of your entire body smaller. You quiet your elbows by your sides, close your fingers on the reins, deepen your seat, and hug him with your upper legs (knees and thighs) to tell him to bring himself back underneath you and gather himself back together, all the while maintaining a regular and even trot tempo. After he's downshifted and his weight has been redistributed back over his hindquarters, relax and proceed forward in regular collected trot. You again allow him to move forward freely but no longer ask for maximum ground-covering output.

ALTHOUGH MAINTAINING TEMPO AND BALANCE on curved lines can be challenging to horses, some actually lose their balance more easily traveling on straight lines.

Terrible Trots: Flaws and How to Fix Them

The two-beat rhythm of the trot is the most distinct of the horse's three gaits; therefore, irregularities tend to be glaring. Lameness aside, there are several instances in which trot tempo or rhythm can be disrupted.

Slow: Curves Ahead

The most common disruption of tempo or rhythm is caused by the horse's tendency to slow the tempo in turns, corners, and circles. This is because it can take more energy and engagement for a horse to maintain his tempo and balance on a curved line than it does on a straight line.

There are two ways to avoid this problem. First, get in the habit of riding all curved lines (later on, this holds true for lateral movements, as well) in a driving seat, with your shoulders well back and down and your seat and legs working to keep your horse using his hind legs actively to push off with energy and metronome-like regularity. Even a relatively shallow turn, such as on a 20-meter circle or through the short side of the arena, presents your horse with some measure of physical challenge. Encourage him to meet the challenge, and you'll strengthen and supple him, thus making the challenge less difficult over time. Ensuring that you ride curved lines in a driving seat also keeps your center of gravity well back, which encourages your horse to keep his weight back over his hindquarters and to maintain his balance.

Second, use these measures proactively. If you do not assume the driving position until you're partway through the short side of the arena and your horse's tempo has started to flag, you're too late. If you were preparing for a movement that was supposed to begin immediately after you came out of the second corner of the short side — such as a medium trot across the

DRIVING SEAT. Chris uses a driving seat as he rides Regent in a medium trot. His shoulders are well back, his hands are low, his seat is driving Regent forward and maintaining the tempo of the gait, and his legs are on at the girth.

diagonal — chances are you won't be able to build up a new head of steam, rebalance your horse, and prepare sufficiently for a strong and crisp transition into the medium trot. The entire effort would look lackluster and muddy, which tends to draw comments such as "no visible difference between collected and medium trots" from dressage judges. Prepare for the start of the turn or curved line by assuming the driving position and aids a couple of strides in advance, and your horse will find it much easier to maintain his nice active trot all the way through.

Irregular, Uneven Rhythm

The other major trot flaw happens when the rhythm becomes irregular or *uneven,* which can be synonymous with *lame,* but sometimes is created by the rider

and is not a symptom of a physical problem. Let me give you two common examples.

● *A horse whose hind legs are not equally strong and do not push evenly, or whose joints cannot bend to the same degree, or both.* This inequality can be the result of his innate "sidedness" (like our right- or left-handedness) and can be addressed through a gymnastic program of strengthening the weaker hind leg or teaching the horse to bend the joints of both hind legs more evenly. The inequality can also result from pain or stiffness caused by arthritis in one or both hips, stifles, or hocks. (See chapter 19 for more on common health problems of the dressage horse.)

Irregularities caused by physical limitations may be helped through gymnastic training and through various therapeutic modalities, but you may not be able to eliminate them completely. Judges must eliminate horses that appear obviously irregular or lame, so if you have a gallant old campaigner that just can't keep the beat anymore, you may not be able to show him in recognized dressage competition. (Almost no drugs or medications are allowed in recognized equestrian competition, so don't count on those to get the old guy through.)

● *Rein lameness.* Particularly in certain lateral movements, a horse may come down more heavily on one front or hind leg, looking as if he's lame. Here the problem is not physical pain but improper riding: unyielding or overbearing hands, insufficient use of the driving aids, and incorrect degree of bending are common causes. The rider interrupts the horse's energy and connection and causes him to move with stilted steps. A period of correct riding is usually all that's needed to eliminate irregularity caused by rein lameness.

CHAPTER 10

THE CANTER

A good canter bounds with power and energy. This gait becomes increasingly important as you and your horse move up the levels. Its quality can be improved through correct training, but a naturally poor canter may ultimately hold you back. Fortunately, the canter of the average horse, assuming he's sound, is perfectly serviceable for the lower levels.

The Canter Defined

People like to say that the canter is a three-beat gait, which it is. More correctly, however, the canter is a three-beat gait with a moment of suspension: a split second during which all four feet are off the ground.

The canter is decidedly directional, unlike the walk and the trot, in which the pattern of footfalls is the same to the left and to the right. It is considerably easier and more comfortable for a horse to canter on what is known as the correct lead, the lead being indicated by the foreleg that produces the gait's third beat. On the *left lead,* then, the footfalls are as follows: right hind; left hind/right front (together); left front; moment of suspension. On the *right lead,* the footfalls are opposite: left hind; right hind/left front (together); right front;

moment of suspension. The left hind leg strikes off in the first beat of the canter. In the second beat, the right hind and left fore (the diagonal pair) touch down simultaneously. The third and final beat is produced by the right (leading) foreleg. Then, for just a moment, all four legs are gathered underneath the horse's body. The single hind leg touches down, and the sequence begins again.

The action of the canter produces a rolling, rocking-horse feeling. The rolling movement begins with the outside hind leg and ends with the inside (leading) foreleg. The side-to-side motion of the canter is a greater challenge to the horse's balance than are the walk and the trot. When a horse canters, he naturally "rolls over" his foreleg during the gait's third beat, and that hoof planted on the ground acts as a mini pivot

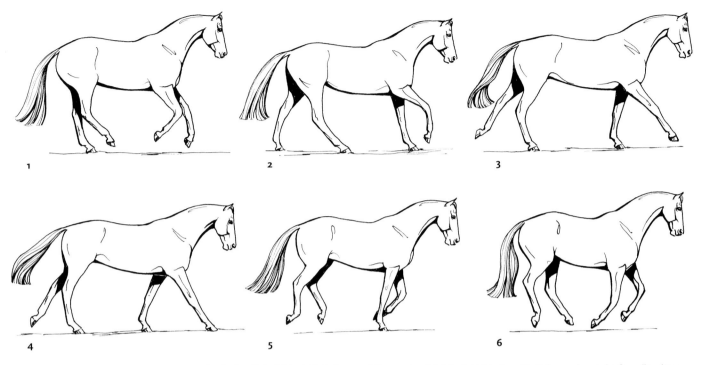

PHASES OF THE CANTER STRIDE (right lead): left hind (1); left hind, right hind, and left fore together (2); right hind and left fore (diagonal pair) (3); right hind and left fore, plus right fore (leading leg) (4); right fore only (5); moment of suspension (6).

point of sorts. For this reason, horses naturally prefer to canter with the leading foreleg to the inside because they can balance over it while in turns. Watch a horse canter loose in a pasture; he'll almost always choose the right lead when traveling clockwise and the left lead when traveling counterclockwise. We do the same when we ride. Unless told to do otherwise, we ride on the right lead to the right and on the left lead to the left.

Please Stay Seated

In riding the trot, you can choose to sit or to rise. Because the canter does not produce any up-down motion, it does not lend itself to rising (posting), so riders always sit the canter.

Sitting the canter is much less bouncy than sitting the trot, and therefore it is less challenging for your back, abdominal muscles, and trunk to absorb the motion. If you're tight in your hip joints and lower back, however, you may find yourself being rocked out of the saddle after the third beat of the canter and coming back down with the first beat of the next stride. Learn

Which Lead Is It?

It's easy to tell which lead a horse is on. If you're watching and not riding, simply follow the action of the horse's forelegs. One or the other will touch down by itself in the third beat of the canter. If it's the right leg, then he's on the right lead. If it's the left leg, then he's on the left lead.

RIDING THE WAVE. Absorbing the bounding, rocking motion of the canter requires supple back and hip joints.

to follow the motion of the gait with your seat (some have likened it to swinging on a swing), but don't get carried away, pumping hard with your seat at each stride; that will cause your buttocks to sweep the seat of the saddle from back to front. Your seat bones should stay rooted in the deepest point of the saddle, which should also be the most balanced place in the saddle. Follow the motion mainly with your hip joints, your abdominal muscles and lower back working in concert with them to undulate rhythmically.

The Canter Aids

How to get a horse to strike off on the desired canter lead can be puzzling to novice dressage riders. Riders and trainers each favor slightly different combinations of "buttons," which means that even an experienced rider may have difficulty getting a strange horse to canter off promptly and on the desired lead. Unlike the walk and the trot, which have straightforward aids (you can't go wrong with an even squeeze with both legs), riding the canter requires that you indicate a lead preference to the horse. This is accomplished partly by weighting your inside seat bone (the one on the side corresponding to the desired lead) and partly by positioning your legs in a slight scissors fashion (and I mean slight; we're talking a difference of a few inches) so that your inside leg is at the girth and your outside leg is slightly behind the girth.

To complicate matters further, dressage riders and trainers have differing opinions as to which leg should give the main cue for the horse to strike off in canter. I began riding hunter seat, and the conventional wisdom in that discipline was that you squeezed with your outside leg to ask for the canter. So if you wanted a right-lead canter, you drew your left leg back slightly behind the girth and gave a squeeze. Your inside (right) leg remained fairly passive at the girth. Some dressage riders use this same method. Others believe, however — and I tend to agree with them — that using the outside leg aid is somewhat counterproductive because it tends to push the horse's haunches to the inside. This is problematic because horses already naturally want to canter haunches-in, and the objective of dressage is to straighten the horse. It's best not to use a method that encourages precisely what you are trying to eliminate.

A better way to ask for the canter is to give the aid with your inside seat bone and leg, which remains on the girth. Your outside leg is positioned slightly behind the girth to help indicate the desired lead to your horse and to "guard" his haunches from swinging to the outside. The outside leg is not entirely passive, but it doesn't do the heavy lifting.

Olympian Carol Lavell rides Much Ado through flying lead changes that show her canter aids. Landing on the right lead, her weight is over her inside (right) seat bone and her inside leg is close to the girth.

To prepare for the change to the left lead, as in a regular canter depart, Carol brings her new outside (right) leg back and shifts her weight onto her new inside (left) seat bone.

Much Ado changes to the left lead. Note that, although Carol's body language is telling him "left lead," the horse remains straight through his body.

CLOSE-UP
The Weight Aids

In chapter 6, you learned how to find your seat bones and how they, and the muscles of your core, anchor you in the saddle as you ride. We also discussed how to use those muscles and the joints of your hips, knees, ankles, and elbows to follow your horse's motion as he walks, trots, and canters.

Sometimes you want to follow the motion passively; other times, you want to dictate the motion, whether it be tempo, rhythm, or gait. Your seat is your primary aid, whether you want to speed up, slow down, maintain the status quo, or change gait. I say *primary* because the seat is used first — before the leg and definitely before the rein. The aids may be only split seconds apart and may feel nearly simultaneous, but the seat is always first.

WEIGHTING A SEAT BONE
So how do you weight a seat bone? By engaging the muscles in opposition. Try this exercise. Sit erect in a chair, feet flat on the floor. Push your right hip bone forward. Can you feel which muscles are working? When I do this, I feel the muscles at the front of my right hip engage. I also feel my lower back begin to arch, so I engage my core muscles as well. When my core muscles are engaged, I can pull my right hip forward and down while stretching my upper body up and even back a little bit. Lower body stretching down, upper body stretching up — my muscles are working in opposition, pulling in opposite directions on either side of my hip joint. Picture a tall tree, with roots reaching down into the ground, holding fast, and limbs

stretching up and out, reaching for the sky. On your horse, your body mimics a tree. Your seat and legs "grow" downward, while your upper body stretches upward. You look and feel tall in the saddle.

This movement is subtle. You won't see much if you look in a mirror, but the feel is unmistakable. Engaging opposing muscle groups is how you avoid rounding and collapsing forward as you weight your inside seat bone. It's how you maintain an elegant, erect posture in the saddle while giving invisible aids to your horse. It's also how you spare your lower back.

Practice this exercise unmounted until you get the feel of it; then try it on your horse. Your goal is to maintain the feeling of stretching down with your hips and upper legs while simultaneously "zipping up" your abdominal muscles and stretching up with your upper body and sternum. You'll maintain the engagement of your muscles in opposition while pulling your inside hip forward and down to weight an inside seat bone in preparation for a canter depart, while riding through turns and corners and on circles, and (later) in all lateral movements and while riding flying lead changes at the canter.

THE DRIVING SEAT

You can also weight both seat bones in the driving seat. The driving seat does just what its name suggests: it drives the horse forward. Because your upper body stays well back, the driving seat helps the horse remain balanced over his hindquarters. (In circles, turns, and lateral movements, the inside seat bone is weighted slightly more than the outside seat bone, however.)

The classic example of the use of the driving seat is in riding a lengthening, medium, or extension of a gait. By using both seat bones as strong weight aids, the rider says to the horse, "Turn up the volume! Amplify your stride!" Because the weight aids increase in strength but not in tempo, the rider says: "Take a bigger, stronger stride, not a faster one." The regularity of the weight aids also tells the horse to remain in the current gait; that's how he knows you're asking him to extend his trot stride, for example, instead of asking him to pick up a canter.

Some books explain the use of the driving aids by describing the motion as "scooping" your seat bones forward. At first, I thought that meant I should engage in some sort of pumping action, complete with lower-back undulation. The result was a collapsed midsection, insufficient refinement of the aid, and a sore back — for me and for my horse. I finally realized that scooping the seat bones is less of a shove and more of a pelvic tuck or tilt. As with all things pertaining to riding, to do this movement correctly and without producing the action with your lower back, you must strongly engage your lower abdominal muscles throughout. The abdominals not only prevent your lower back from overarching, but they also create the pelvic tilt.

THE PELVIC TUCK/TILT

Unfamiliar with the correct way to perform a pelvic tuck or tilt? Try this easy unmounted exercise. Lie on your back on a firm, comfortable surface; a carpeted floor or exercise mat is perfect. Bend your knees and rest your feet flat on the floor, arms at your sides. Relax and breathe normally. When your back and abdominal muscles relax, your lower back naturally has a slight arch. You can feel this arch by sliding one hand underneath your lower back as you lie on the floor. (There's probably enough room to slide your hand under with little difficulty.)

Now, thinking "navel to spine," engage your abdominal muscles. Sink your navel toward your spine and flatten your lower back until it touches the floor. That's a pelvic tuck! Now relax and allow the arch to return to your lower back. Practice alternating between the starting position (neutral spine) and a tucked position. When you think you've mastered the action, try it while sitting in a chair, and then on your horse. Now file it away in your riding repertoire for use as the major element of the driving seat.

Because this slight pelvic tuck is accompanied by a firming and flattening of the lower-back muscles, in their texts some equestrian masters referred to the motion as "bracing the back." This implies a tightening or clenching action, which produces only an exaggerated swayback and an immediate, unpleasant tightness in the lower back, not the desired effect at all. If the pelvic tilt is done rather firmly and held for just a stride

NEUTRAL SPINE. Meghan Jackson demonstrates neutral spine, the starting position of the pelvic-tuck exercise. She's raised her arms overhead to give you a better view of her torso and lower back, but you can rest your arms at your sides. Her lower back is relaxed and shows a slight lumbar curve.

PELVIC TILT. Meghan engages her core muscles (navel to spine), thereby flattening her lower back against the floor and tucking her pelvis slightly. The sinking of her belly is evident when compared to the previous photo.

or two, however, it can actually help to slow or stop your horse, because it momentarily stops your seat bones from following his motion. The pelvic tilt is an integral part of the body language that asks your horse for a half-halt and, if held a tad longer, to downshift into a slower gait or even to come to a full halt.

TIMING OF THE AIDS

The differences between the driving seat, the weighting of the inside seat bone, and the down-transition or halt aids are slight in terms of physical action, but over time, they'll become more and more distinct and clear to you and your horse. Timing of the aids, which also includes timing of their cessation, plays a crucial role in this differentiation. And, unfortunately, timing is difficult to teach and difficult to learn from a book.

Read, analyze, take lessons and clinics, and watch other riders — all of these steps will help. Ultimately, however, timing is something you have to figure out and feel for yourself. Experiment (carefully) with different timing and amplitude of aids to see how your horse reacts. Pay attention to the ways your body influences his body. Watch yourself in a mirror. Ask a friend to videotape you. Most important, enjoy the journey of self-discovery. It will be peppered with moments or even days of frustration when you feel you just aren't getting it, but then all of a sudden you'll try something and your horse will react immediately. That feeling of connection is exhilarating.

Inside Leg/Outside Rein

When you ride the canter, it's important that you maintain a connection that is a dressage mantra: "Inside leg to outside rein." This phrase, which you will hear during countless lessons and clinics, means that you should ride your horse forward from your inside leg (your inside seat bone, too) and then contain him gently with a steady outside rein. Although you use both legs and both reins as you ride, the inside-leg/outside-rein maxim serves as a reminder that these are the two primary and most dynamic aspects of your aiding system. Your inside leg and outside rein are the stars of the show, while your outside leg and inside rein play supporting roles.

Although neither rein should be held rigidly, the outside rein maintains a firmer connection than the inside rein because it contains your horse's shoulders, neck, and head the way a garden hose contains the water inside. This is contrary to most riders' instincts, because it seems natural to pull or flex the inside rein to turn the horse in the desired direction. In fact, the inside rein serves mostly to position your horse's head and neck laterally to the inside. (Riding through a turn or on a circle, you should see only his inside eye, no more.) The turning aids are the weight aids of your inside seat bone and the position of your upper body, with your inside shoulder slightly back so your shoulders are parallel to his shoulders. Your inside leg maintains your horse's activity and gives him a support around which to bend.

The outside-rein connection should feel firm but not heavy or dead. You should get the feeling that your horse is "filling up" your outside rein, not hanging on it. When the connection is right, the rein feels firm and steady yet alive and elastic. The inside rein is similarly steady, although the connection feels less firm. There's more solidity in the outside rein than in the inside rein, which should almost always feel lighter in your hand.

The outside rein helps to keep your horse straight, but what does it do when you want to circle, turn, or begin a lateral movement? Its role remains the same — to keep your horse aligned — but keep in mind that he will appear to form an arc with his body as he turns and bends (see page 164). The outside rein must allow this change by becoming slightly more elastic while giving his outside shoulder steady support. This allowance is slight; no big movements with your hand or arm are necessary. Simply relax your elbow joint a bit; don't open your hand or allow the rein to slip through your fingers.

Adjusting the Canter

The canter, like the trot, has a complement of paces and degrees of extension and collection, depending on your horse's level of training and physical development. All should retain the gait's characteristic three-beat rhythm. The gallop, which is actually a four-beat gait, is not recognized in dressage training and competition.

Working Canter

The working canter is the regular, garden-variety canter practiced at the lower levels of dressage; it is also the standard warm-up pace of many upper-level dressage horses. Between the collected and medium gait is the working gait. It is the not-ready-for-collection pace shown by the young and the lower-level horse.

A good working canter shows balance, even strides in a regular three-beat rhythm, and is on the bit, of course. The gait has a feeling of lightness and energy, with plenty of impulsion as evidenced by what the USEF calls "good hock action" (*2006 United States Equestrian Federation Rule Book* [Lexington, KY: USEF, 2006], Art. DR105.4[b]). "Good hock action" does not mean that your horse's hind legs should move like the needle of a sewing machine or like those of a high-stepping Hackney pony. Instead, it underscores the importance of the horse's initiating the canter stride with his hindquarters, bending the joints of his hind legs and placing them well underneath his body for lots of vitality and forward thrust.

Judges and trainers do not expect to see as much hind-leg bending, reaching, and "carrying" in the working canter as they do in the more advanced collected canter. The working canter should be nice and forward, with your horse's hind legs remaining active and not appearing to drag out behind the point of his croup. A canter with insufficient hindquarter impulsion looks sprawling and strung out, and may even become four-beat because the inside hind leg and the outside fore-leg fail to touch down at the same time, as they should. (For help correcting a four-beat canter, see Canter Catastrophes on page 144.)

Most horses canter in a similar range of tempos. You'll know when your horse is cantering in his own natural tempo because he'll be able to maintain balance and impulsion. As my instructor, Todd Flettrich, puts it, your horse will feel as if he's cantering on his own, and

you won't have to push and beg with every stride. If the canter is too hurried, it begins to turn into an on-the-forehand scramble. If it's too lethargic, it'll become four-beat because there isn't enough jump, as dressage trainers call it, to keep the hindquarters sufficiently engaged and the gait pure.

Some riders think of the canter as a fast gait, perhaps because they perceive it as a jumping-off point to a gallop. In truth, a good dressage canter, particularly a collected one, doesn't feel much faster than a lively and energetic trot. The canter is no less controllable than the trot, although it can be much easier to sit. A big extended canter will get you from point A to point B in a twinkling because each stride covers a lot of ground, not because the horse is running fast.

Lengthened Canter

Some of the lower-level dressage tests ask the rider to lengthen stride in the canter. As with the corresponding lower-level trot lengthening, this requirement introduces horse and rider to the concept of taking a longer stride without changing anything else.

WORKING CANTER. Chris Hickey has Regent in a pleasant working canter. The more collected the horse's gait, the more he bends the joints of his hind legs and reaches underneath himself with each stride, as Regent is doing with his inside (right) hind leg.

LENGTHENED CANTER. From the working canter shown at left, Chris has asked Regent to lengthen his stride. Regent's stride is covering more ground, and he has lengthened his neck and frame, yet he remains in longitudinal balance.

Imagine that you're walking down a sidewalk. Being somewhat superstitious, you don't want to step on any cracks, and because you live and breathe dressage, you refuse to alter the rhythm and tempo of your strides. Speeding up and slowing down aren't options, so you have to change the length of your stride to avoid stepping on cracks.

To take an extra-long stride without altering your walk rhythm and tempo, you push off hard with one leg to generate the energy needed for the stride, then you reach and stretch the other leg forward to complete it. Try this for several strides. It requires some effort to coordinate pushing with reaching, and that's exactly what you want to teach your horse to do in the lengthened canter. Like you, he'll find lengthening his strides challenging athletically, so start slow, build gradually, and ask for only a few strides at a time. Don't bomb around the perimeter of the arena or across the diagonal like a freight train. Your horse can't sustain that kind of effort, especially when he's first learning.

Use your seat to ask your horse to lengthen his canter stride. Yes, once again, your seat is the primary means by which you communicate the desired gait and tempo to your horse. Here's how it works in the canter.

Let's say you've established your horse's comfortable working-canter pace. He's motoring along steadily like a car in cruise control. You can feel the regular da-da-DUM, da-da-DUM rhythm under your seat, and the muscles of your lower back and hips are relaxed enough for your seat to follow the motion, more or less passively. If he speeds up, you ask him to come back to the desired tempo by leading instead of following the motion for a moment — keep your seat moving in your tempo, not his, even if it means a few strides of disconnect until he falls back in synch with you. If he slows, refresh his energy by assuming the driving-seat position (eyes up, shoulders well back, seat bones scooping forward as you zip up your abdominals) and closing your legs for a moment. Don't panic if he responds a little too eagerly and quickens his tempo. When he goes more forward and you feel a nice surge of energy from behind, relax your driving aids and return to following his motion; this will allow him to settle into his regular working tempo.

You will need to make adjustments continually as you ride. Don't expect your horse to maintain a perfectly steady tempo on his own. The top dressage horses may appear to have effortlessly flawless gaits, but their riders make minute adjustments nearly all the

Do You Feel Your Horse's Pain?

My empathy for my horse soared when I stopped just riding and got involved in other athletic pursuits.

Run, jog, lift weights, do yoga or Pilates, do heavy yard work — these activities and many others are great for improving your strength, flexibility, aerobic capacity, and overall fitness. (See chapter 17 for more on rider fitness.) And with physical exertion comes a certain amount of unavoidable soreness and fatigue, like the way you feel the morning after a challenging workout or like the huffing and puffing that comes with aerobic exercise. Assuming you're

healthy and not overdoing it, the discomfort is relatively minor and short-lived. Still, there's no denying that some days you feel better than others.

Let your own aches and pains sensitize you to how your horse might be feeling. Some days, I feel like a super-woman; others, I'm drained, stiff, and sore. By keeping these fluctuations in mind when I'm with my horse, I'm less apt to become impatient when he's having an off day and more inclined to understand his travails as a fellow athlete.

time. You may not be able to see the adjustments happening because some riders' timing and feel are so good and they're so attuned to their mounts that they can correct problems at their first inkling. They don't wait for the canter to slow noticeably before they refresh the energy and "jump," for example. The problems are slight, so the corrections are slight. Done well, the result is a seamless performance.

Don't be discouraged if for a while your horse travels like a car with an unreliable gas pedal. Split-second timing takes time to develop, and you may over-rev and under-rev the engine for a while. Doing so is part of the learning process. What's more, if you don't overcorrect and undercorrect once in a while, how do you know how much or how little you really need? Never forget that riding requires some experimentation.

Collected Canter

As your horse's gymnastic development progresses and he gains the ability to make his hindquarters more active while making his shoulders lighter and more mobile, his working canter will naturally evolve into the collected pace that's required in the more advanced dressage tests.

The strides of the collected canter are shorter than those of the working canter (because the horse's entire body has lifted and compressed), but they are more active due to the increased bend-and-thrust action of the hindquarter joints, which bear more weight and are "spring loaded." The entire horse looks and feels lighter and easier to maneuver. He remains on the bit while his head and neck are raised higher than in the working canter, and his neck has a pronounced arch.

Once again, collection is not a destination but an evolutionary process. You raise the bar for your horse as he becomes more advanced in his training.

The lower levels of dressage call for the more introductory paces, while the medium and upper levels call for more advanced and physically demanding paces. It's not uncommon for a rider to show a horse in the highest test of a lower level and in the lowest test of the next-highest level, however. (See chapter 13 for an explanation of the differences among levels and tests.) In making the jump up to a new level, a rider may have to show a working canter in the first test and a collected canter in the second — on the same horse.

Ideally, our intrepid rider will go into the ring and show a distinct difference between the working canter and the collected canter. In reality, the canters shown may be pretty much the same.

So which is working and which is collected? Is one sufficient (judge-speak for demonstrating the required qualities and level of difficulty) and the other insufficient? The spectator might be hard-pressed to tell and, for that matter, so might the judge.

I like to think of the various paces within the gaits as natural partners in the horse's overall gymnastic development. In other words, I don't go in the ring and decide to "do" collected canter for a while. Instead, I try to keep the training scale (see page 89) in mind as a

COLLECTED CANTER. Here is Regent again, now demonstrating the collected canter. Chris has asked him to shorten his outline while maintaining his activity. As a result, Regent comes off the ground more with each stride, like a bouncing ball.

road map guiding me toward dressage progress. I know that I must cross-train myself to develop overall fitness: strength, flexibility, aerobic capacity. Likewise, I know that I must find similar ways to cross-train, or "gym-nasticize," my horse: ride forward and back; do transitions between gaits; do transitions within gaits; supple him both laterally and longitudinally; and develop his strength, flexibility, and endurance.

So, for example, when I ride a transition from walk to canter and in that first moment of push-off feel my horse's haunches sink and surge underneath me as his forehand lightens, I realize that it is a glimpse of the feeling of collection. I continue riding those and other transitions, as well as the lateral movements and exercises that I'll discuss in the next chapter, as a means to an end as well as ends unto themselves. Gradually, I find that I'm able to maintain that feeling of collection (what my instructor refers to as the "speedboat" feeling: stern [haunches] lowered, bow [forehand] elevating as you throttle forward) for longer periods by keeping my horse's hind legs active and well underneath him through the well-timed use of my seat and legs. His collected canter, and indeed all of his work, evolves in a natural progression. Collection is not a frame that I impose on him.

Medium Canter

Take a collected canter, boost it up a notch by asking for a vigorous increase in length in stride, and what do you get? If all goes well, a medium canter.

Falling between the working canter and the extended canter, in terms of stride length and elongation of frame, the good medium canter is marked by moderately extended strides that are free, balanced, and with distinct impulsion from the hindquarters, according to the USEF. Although there is not as much stretch in the frame in the medium canter as in the extended canter, the horse is allowed to stretch his

head and neck slightly lower and more in front of the vertical than in the working and collected paces.

To shift gears from collected canter to medium canter, I think of turning up the volume. When you hear a great song on the radio and crank it up, all you're doing is amplifying the music. The tempo, rhythm, and melody remain the same. Similarly, you make your horse's strides and movement "louder" by preparing with a balancing half-halt, then asking for more volume with each stride: you give more seat and legs, keep your shoulders well back and eyes up, and maintain an elastic contact that "opens the door" and lets the energy you've created travel through his slightly lowered and extended neck and head.

To come back to collected canter, turn down your aids. Still your seat by quieting the undulations of your lower back and hips: abdominal muscles engaged and zipping up, navel to spine, upper legs firm against the saddle. With your shoulders back, maintain an elastic rein contact, but keep your hands low over the withers, elbows against your sides, gently containing your horse in front without pulling back on the reins or riding him from front to back.

MEDIUM CANTER. Chris has Regent in an energetic medium canter. Regent clearly stretches his frame, as he takes big bounding strides over the ground.

Extended Canter

If you enjoy speed, you'll love riding the extended canter. In the extended canter, the horse lengthens his stride to the utmost to cover the most ground possible. A correct extended canter retains lightness, relaxation, and control. *Gallop* can connote being run away with or racing at top speed. An extended canter, in contrast, is completely under the rider's control — a powerful unleashing of maximum impulsion while the horse remains obedient and mentally calm.

Contrary to what you might think, horses generally aren't fazed when doing the extended canter, the same way that they aren't fazed when doing extended trot. Remember the stepping-over-the-sidewalk-cracks exercise (see page 138)? Did it make you feel anxious or panicky? Of course not — it was too much effort! Most horses seem to enjoy a brisk extended canter (it "puts air in their tires," my instructor says); to them it's all in a day's work.

A horse in extended canter should elongate his frame to the maximum. His head and neck should lower and stretch even more than in the medium canter, and his nose should come even farther in front of the vertical.

When I ask my horse for a medium canter, I think of asking for about 85 percent of his maximum stride length. When I ride the extended canter, I'm going for 100 percent — 110 percent if I'm in the show ring. I don't hold anything back. When I'm competing, I know the judge wants to see the biggest difference possible between my collected canter and my extended canter. The worst thing I can do is let him wonder when, along this long side or that diagonal, I might finally open my horse up and show something.

Let's return to our sidewalk exercise again for a moment. If you tried it, you know that taking long strides requires a fair amount of effort. Now think about what extensions demand of your horse. They're not beyond his ability but they are at the outer limit, so do them sparingly. I may ride an all-out extension once or twice a week, usually during a lesson. The rest of the time, I keep those exercises in the medium range, asking for no more than about 85 percent of my horse's maximum effort. What I will do frequently during schooling sessions, however, is test my horse's adjustability by sending him forward for a few strides and then bringing him back.

Wrong Lead on Purpose?

When learning to ride, many of us are drilled so often on being on the "correct" canter lead and on the "correct" posting diagonal that the *counter-canter* — a useful dressage training exercise that's even a test requirement — may seem counterintuitive. Why would anyone deliberately canter on the "wrong" lead?

Horses naturally prefer to canter on curved lines on the correct lead, with the inside foreleg completing the stride. Doing so allows the horse to be at his most balanced and thus requires the least effort. It is easier for a horse to bend in the direction of the leading leg than away from it, therefore the horse's body appears to conform to the arc of the turn or circle when he canters with his inside leg leading. (Although the equine spine has little or no ability to flex laterally, horses can bend; that is, they can arrange themselves in such a way that they appear to conform to an arc.)

The canter lead is of little consequence if you only travel in straight lines. In circles and turns, however, cantering on the wrong lead poses a considerable challenge to your horse's balance — he is unable to bend to the inside of the circle or turn, and the hind leg that initiates the canter stride suddenly has to bear more weight. Remember the footfall pattern in the canter? Outside hind leg; inside hind leg, outside foreleg (together); inside foreleg. Now let's think about the footfall pattern in the counter-canter.

Say you're cantering on the right rein (clockwise), on the right lead. To transform a right-lead true canter, as it's called, into a right-lead counter-canter, you have to keep the right lead but change direction so your horse travels on the left rein (counterclockwise). In the right-lead canter, the left hind leg is the first beat of the stride, followed by right hind and left front, and finally the right front. If you canter in a circle to the left but stay on the right lead, the left hind leg still initiates the stride, but now it's on the inside of the circle instead of on the outside and bears more weight.

Because it challenges your horse's balance and strengthens his outside hind leg, the counter-canter is an excellent gymnastic exercise for improving balance and collection. It's all about strengthening those hind legs. (For a refresher on inside and outside, see page 94.) To ride the counter-canter, canter as you normally would but in the opposite direction. OK, that may be an oversimplification, but don't make the counter-canter more complicated than it is. Many riders exaggerate the position of their legs, crank their horses' heads and necks around to the inside, and run their mounts off their feet in a superfast tempo, all in an effort to ensure that their horses (1) remain on the desired counter lead and (2) continue cantering. As a result, the horses are more off balance than they'd otherwise be.

Before you attempt a counter-canter, be certain that your horse's true canter is of decent quality and that he has achieved at least a moderate level of suppleness, strength, and balance. If an ordinary canter challenges him, then a counter-canter may be beyond his abilities at the moment. (If you can't tell whether Dobbin is ready for the counter-canter, ask a qualified instructor.)

When introducing the counter-canter, keep all turns and circles big and shallow. Cut the corners if you're riding in an arena. Make all circles at least 20 meters (the width of a standard dressage arena) in diameter. The smaller the circle or the tighter the turn, the more challenging the counter-canter will be for your horse. (It is not appropriate to ask for smaller circles until much later in his training.)

Because the counter-canter challenges your horse's balance, be sure he has good footing. Never ride the counter-canter on muddy, icy, or otherwise questionable footing. Plain old grass, especially when it's soaked with dew or atop sun-baked, rock-hard ground (or worse, both), can be surprisingly slick. The ideal surface for dressage training is level, free of rocks and other debris, firm enough to provide good traction, cushioned enough to provide shock absorption, and minimally dusty. It's a tall order. If you have no access to groomed and manicured riding arenas, do your best to select naturally level, forgiving surfaces and be willing to scale back your training plans on days when Mother Nature compromises the footing. (See chapter 19 for more on footing.)

Here's a low-key way to begin working on the counter-canter. Pick up whichever canter lead feels strongest and most balanced, and go on a 20-meter circle in true canter at one end of the arena. (Not in an arena? Pick an area where you're not hemmed in next to trees or other obstacles and can maneuver out of the circle easily.) Canter around the circle a few times until you and your horse feel relaxed and confident.

The next time you come out of the corner, canter across a short diagonal so you're heading for the midpoint of the long side of the arena (see illustration). As you reach the wall or rail, let it guide your horse straight down the long side for a few strides; he'll now be in counter-canter on a straight line. Before you reach the next corner, quietly bring him down to a trot and then a walk.

Practice this exercise until you get a feel for cantering on the counter (outside) lead on a straight line. You shouldn't have had to make any drastic adjustments to your position. Just keep riding the canter lead you're on: inside leg at the girth, outside leg slightly behind the girth in a slight scissors position; slight inside lateral flexion; weight on the inside seat bone. Focus on the canter and on keeping its balance, rhythm, and tempo the same, whether you're cantering on the circle, across the diagonal, or down the long side on the counter lead.

When you and your horse are comfortable with the circle-diagonal-straight line exercise, try maintaining the counter-canter through the next corner, after the

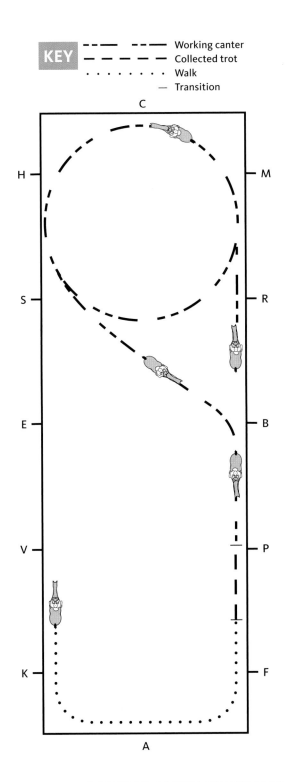

INTRODUCING COUNTER-CANTER ON LEFT LEAD

long side. Remember to cut the corners and to make the turn as wide and shallow as you can. You'll want to do something as you enter the corner in counter-canter, but try to resist the temptation. Instead, focus on keeping your shoulders well back and down and your eyes up (it will help your horse balance) and on maintaining your position and the quality of the canter. Say "da-da-DUM, da-da-DUM" or hum a tune aloud as a reminder of the canter rhythm.

Canter Catastrophes

The problems that may arise as you school counter-canter are similar to those that happen in true canter. Don't worry — all are just speed bumps on the road to better dressage and can be corrected.

Breaking into a Trot

If your horse breaks back into a trot instead of maintaining the counter-canter, you may have lost the impulsion needed to keep the canter going. Regroup by going back to the 20-meter circle in true canter and refreshing the energy. Step by step, work back up to counter-cantering through the next corner. Make sure that your seat and leg position continue to say "canter" throughout and that you don't inadvertently stop the action by blocking him with a fixed hand.

Speeding Up or Losing Balance

If your horse speeds up or yaws to one side in the counter-canter, he's trying to compensate for a loss of balance. This is your cue to go back and to break the counter-canter exercise into teensy baby steps. When you work back up to counter-cantering through the corner (or even just part of the corner), cut the corner even more so the curved line is as gradual a turn as possible.

Try this exercise: Establish a regular, rhythmic working canter on a 20-meter circle on your horse's "good" lead. Turn down the center line of the arena (or ride on any long, straight line in an open area in true canter), and then make a very shallow serpentine line, maintaining the canter lead (see illustration). If you're on the right lead, for example, the loop to the right will be in true canter and the loop back to the left will be in counter-canter. Ride just a few strides in either direction so the serpentines are mere undulations. This exercise will teach your horse to remain on the desired lead and will improve his balance. (It's so good, in fact, that it's in some dressage tests.)

The Unasked-for Flying Change

Some clever and athletic horses, when confronted with the challenge of counter-canter, will volunteer a flying change of lead (a change of lead executed in midair, during the moment of suspension in the canter). Horses do flying changes naturally, and flying changes are an important part of upper-level dressage work. So if you're the owner of such a horse, don't punish him for executing a movement that you're going to want later on. But how do you correct this?

You'll need patience and finesse. Many riders encounter this problem a little further on in their training, when they're teaching their horses flying changes but showing at a level that asks for counter-canter but no changes. The horse gets mixed messages, and the rider must curtail work on flying changes before the show, or else ride with incredible precision, lest any minor weight shift or leg movement be misinterpreted as the aid for a change.

If your horse does a flying change, don't pull back on the reins or do anything else that he might interpret as a reprimand. Allow him to canter on the new lead for a few strides, then quietly return to the trot or the walk and pick up the counter lead again, making sure that your legs are scissored correctly and that your weight remains steady over your inside seat bone. You don't

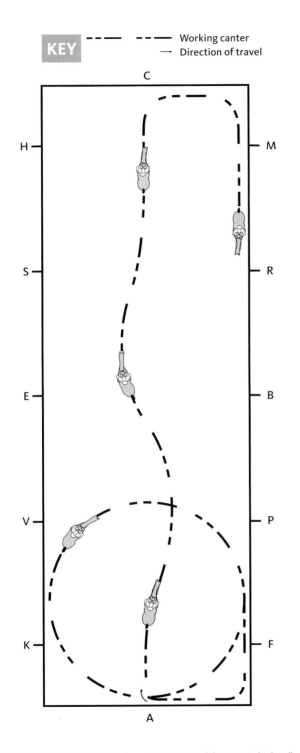

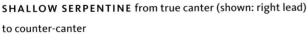

------ Working canter
→ Direction of travel

SHALLOW SERPENTINE from true canter (shown: right lead) to counter-canter

have to pose like a statue, but know that shifts of weight and changes of leg position are the primary flying-change aids. In time, your horse will learn that steady and unchanging weight and leg aids and positioning mean "Keep cantering just as you are." This is important for him to know because, eventually, you'll want to be able to ask for counter-canter and flying changes in the same schooling session or dressage test, and the aids must be clearly differentiated.

Cross-Cantering

In between the horse that breaks into a trot and the one that offers an unasked-for flying change is the individual that lapses into a cross-canter, also known as a *disunited canter*. A cross-cantering horse feels awful — completely discombobulated. He may be cantering in front and trotting behind, or cantering on one lead in front and on the other behind.

Simply asking a horse to counter-canter probably won't cause him to cross-canter. Cross-cantering tends to happen during a botched transition — say, from trot to canter, or as a result of a flying change that isn't clean (with all four legs changing simultaneously). The resulting tangle is not a gait but an unbalanced mess, and there's no way out of it other than to quietly downshift to a lower gait, regroup, and try again.

Refusal to Pick up a Lead

Just as you are either right- or left-handed, your horse has an innate preference for one canter lead over the other (and one direction of travel in general). The lead he prefers is generally the one on his stronger side. Strong muscles tend to be less flexible, and so a horse's strong side is often referred to as his *stiff side*. The weaker side is known as his *hollow side*. Horses tend to be stiff on the right and hollow on the left, although this is not always the case.

Striking off in the canter requires the outside hind leg to push off. If that leg or hoof is sore, then your horse may be understandably reluctant to pick up that lead.

If you notice that your horse picks up one lead without hesitation but refuses to pick up the other, or obviously objects by doing something like kicking out or bucking, the first call you make should be to your veterinarian. Chances are good that your horse is hurting somewhere, and your veterinarian can help figure out where and what to do about it. There are myriad possible causes — everything from arthritic hocks to a sore back caused by an ill-fitting saddle — and it may take a process of elimination to pinpoint the culprit.

Physical problems seem to manifest themselves in odd, unwanted behavior during canter departs. Years ago, out of the blue, my horse began tossing his head violently every time I asked him to pick up a left-lead canter — never the right lead; only the left. Turns out the problem was an insufficiently floated (rasped) tooth that, for some mysterious reason, bothered him only in one direction. After his teeth were corrected, the head-tossing disappeared and never returned.

A flat-out refusal to pick up a canter lead or a strong objection is reason to suspect a physical problem. Garden-variety differences between the quality of one lead versus the other are usually normal reflections of your horse's natural "sidedness" and are indications of areas in which his body needs to be strengthened or made more supple. (As you can see, we're always going back and comparing our horses' progress to the levels of the training scale.)

Your horse may canter more crookedly in one direction, for instance, or have more trouble with collection. Interestingly, as your training progresses, you may see his "good side" and "difficult side" switch from time to time; this is a result of trying to fix one problem through zealous work that inadvertently renders one area stronger than the other. If you've ever done any strength or flexibility training yourself, you know the differences between one side and the other can be startling. It is nearly impossible to achieve perfect symmetry in humans or horses, so your goal should be to balance your physical development with that of your horse.

CHAPTER 11

BASIC DRESSAGE MOVEMENTS

ou didn't think dressage was just walk, trot, and canter, did you? The sport is much more complex and fun than that! This chapter covers important fundamentals that will help you and your horse improve your skills and realize new levels of proficiency. As you undertake these deceptively simple exercises, enjoy each discovery you make and each nuance you master.

In addition to the three basic gaits, it's necessary to stop and steer, which I'm sure you already know how to do. However, in dressage, razor-sharp precision is key, so you may need to refine your techniques or learn totally new approaches.

In chapters 8 through 10, you learned how to make transitions within the three gaits (from collected trot to medium trot and back again, for example), but you also need to know how to make clean, smooth transitions between gaits: from walk to trot to walk, and from trot to canter to trot, for instance; I'll cover them here. I'll also delve into some dressage-training classics — the figures that are the basis of much dressage schooling: circles, half-circles, and serpentines. These basic shapes

are essential training building blocks: simple, timeless, and always useful.

Last, I'll review basic lateral exercises that are all-around great moves for your horse. Lateral movements enhance strength and flexibility and so are invaluable tools in developing and improving all aspects of the training scale, from suppleness to collection.

Most of the movements and exercises in this chapter are required elements in one or more levels of dressage competition, so if your aspirations include showing, plan to master them. Transitions, figures, and movements are fun, challenging, gymnasticizing exercises that all dressage riders — even those who don't compete — can and should use in their daily training.

Believe it or not, the more advanced dressage movements, such as half-passes, flying changes, and pirouettes (which are not covered here), are simply extensions of the basic exercises. Serious advanced riders and horses do not skip over such basics as walk-canter transitions in order to get to the fun stuff. Show me a rider who spends most of her time schooling what some derisively refer to as the "tricks," and I'll show you a rider who will eventually ruin her horse.

The movements in this chapter are presented in the order in which they're introduced in the dressage tests. Achieve a solid foundation in one before you move on to the next. If you're unsure whether your horse is ready to progress to the next step, consult a knowledgeable instructor.

The Halt: Be There and Be Square

In dressage, there's more to *whoa* than just getting the job done. Ideally, the execution of the halt should reflect the same positive qualities as the gait it's performed from: specifically, balance, straightness, activity, and evenness.

The ideal halt is *square;* that is, the horse stands with his weight distributed evenly over all four legs, with his legs forming a perfect rectangle underneath his forehand and his hindquarters. Viewed from the side, a horse that is halted this way appears to have only one front leg and only one hind leg; the opposite-side legs are placed so precisely that they are hidden from view.

A good halt is a state of motionlessness. The horse is expected to remain on the bit, looking straight ahead. Looking around, fussing, head tossing, pawing, and other displays of inattention and restlessness are not permitted, nor is dozing. The horse should have an air of alert readiness as he stands at attention, focused on his rider and awaiting her next instruction.

A square halt is not symmetrical just for the sake of appearance. In this balanced position, your horse is optimally poised for whatever comes next. He doesn't have to redistribute his weight or rearrange his legs before he can move off, and therefore can respond smoothly and promptly.

You know that uncomfortable, nose-diving feeling you get when a car stops short and you're suddenly thrown forward? Well, a good halt feels nothing like that. In order to halt in a balanced fashion, your horse must keep his hindquarters active even as he's downshifting. That way, he halts with his hind legs neatly beneath him and avoids sprawling downhill. A good halt is light in your hands; you don't feel like you're trying to stop a freight train. The transition to halt is prompt yet not abrupt. Even from a trot or a canter, the horse gives the feeling of settling to earth ("like a snowflake," as one of my instructors used to say) instead of crash-landing.

So how do you achieve such perfection? It's all in the setup and timing.

GOOD HALT. Emily Gershberg's horse Pancratius ("Paul") in a good halt. He is standing square and balanced over all four legs, and he remains on the bit.

Preparation

A balanced, square halt is impossible unless your horse is balanced and active. If you want to practice halting, don't ask for the halt transition unless he feels reasonably together and is moving in a good rhythm and with sufficient forward energy. If he feels like a giraffe or an eighteen-wheeler on a mountain descent, in the halt transition you'll just get more of the same. (Having said that, here's an exception: Occasionally when you ride, it might feel like things are falling apart. If you or your horse is discombobulated, or the two of you are out of synch, it's a good idea to halt quietly, perhaps walk and regroup, then try again. Here halting is not the objective; what you want is the chance to start over.)

Start by establishing a nice, free-strided, rhythmic medium walk. Can you feel your horse's back swing underneath your seat and his head nod in time with the walk rhythm? Good. Now let's try a halt. When you walk to halt, look out between his ears and think of closing your body gently around him while you engage your core muscles. Close your legs to remind your horse to continue stepping actively forward; engage your abdominal muscles to momentarily still your seat, rather than following his movement; and close your fists on the reins as if you are wringing out two sponges. Notice that I didn't tell you to pull back on the reins. If you had a nice, steady elastic contact to begin with (you did, didn't you?), you already had sufficient communication between your hands and his mouth. Closing your fists on the reins firms the bit pressure in his mouth and "closes the door" in front of him.

Timing

The tricky part about halting is not getting the horse to stop, but learning to relax the halt aids (especially the rein aids) just before the horse's final forward step, as he steps into a square halt. That final split second of relaxation gives the last bit of necessary momentum and impulsion somewhere to go. If you "hold the door closed" with your hands until the halt is completed, the halt may tip onto the forehand, be abrupt, not be square, or some combination of the three.

Try not to overthink the halt, and don't do too much with your body. After you and your horse get a feel for the halt aids from the walk, try thinking "Halt" and see what happens. Your mind-body connection is so strong that just thinking the command causes the muscles involved to contract slightly. You may even find that your horse halts when you do this.

Walk-Halt-Repeat

After your horse has halted, look up, give with your hands a little more, firm your upper legs against his sides, and give a gentle squeeze with both inner calves to ask him to walk on. If he doesn't respond, use firmer leg aids until he moves off. Walk a few strides and then halt and repeat the exercise. Remember, your constant goal is to use the lightest aids possible. Don't let your horse cajole you into using ever-stronger aids. If he doesn't respond, use a stronger aid, then repeat the drill, beginning again with the light aid. Eventually, he'll learn that it's easier and more pleasant to do it right the first time.

Repeat the walk-halt-walk exercise until you get the feel for the timing and the amplitude of the aids. Later, after you feel comfortable performing trot-walk-trot and canter-trot-canter transitions (see Shifting Gears: Transitions between Gaits on page 152), will be time for you to try halting from the trot and then from the canter. When you do, the principles and the aids are the same as for the walk-halt transition. The main difference is the amplitude of the aids: stilling your seat, using driving leg aids, and applying unyielding rein aids that "close the door." The trot and canter have more momentum and energy than the walk, so the halt aids from those gaits must have correspondingly more oomph.

Common Faults and How to Fix Them

Even the most experienced riders don't get perfect halts 100 percent of the time. Following is a list of the most common imperfections, their causes, and how to fix them.

NOT SQUARE

One front leg or hind leg (or both) may be positioned slightly ahead of its mate when your horse halts. If this happens, he may have been a bit off balance coming into the halt, or one leg may have simply gotten lazy.

To correct this problem, insist that your horse squares up for every halt. When he halts, look to see if he's square. If the shoulders are even, the front legs are square. To check the hind legs, you may have to crane your neck and lean over. If the left hind leg is out behind, ask your horse to square up by giving him a gentle nudge slightly behind the girth with your left leg. If you want him to bring his left front leg forward, give a little nudge at or slightly in front of the girth on that side. Don't snatch the reins or punish him if he takes more than one step forward or if he moves off — his correct response is more important. Walk forward, quietly halt, and begin again.

Two leg corrections in the halt are about the limit. Don't fiddle endlessly, step after step, trying to get your horse to square up. Make your adjustments; then move on. If you don't, your horse might begin to resent the halt and become bored, fidgety, or worse. (Competitors have to pick their battles in the show ring, as well. More than one competitor has ruined her chances for a decent halt score by fussing to correct a not-quite-square-halt when she should have just continued.)

If you ride into the halt in good balance and always ensure that your horse is square, eventually he'll learn that that is the way he should halt. Square or nearly square halts should be the rule, not the exception.

NOT STRAIGHT

If a horse is not straight in the halt, his forehand and hindquarters are not on the same axis. My horse halts a wee bit crooked by stepping slightly to the side with his right hind leg. This puts him in a "wide behind" stance (hind legs spread wider than his front legs), with his haunches cocked slightly off to the right. This stance is habitual for him and reveals his natural "sidedness" — something I'm always working to overcome.

POOR HALT. Regent is not square in this halt; he is not standing balanced over all four legs. He has also hollowed his back and come above the bit.

> ### TIP | Think Forward
>
> Always correct a halt that isn't square by asking your horse to bring the lagging leg or legs forward. *Never* try to get him to square up by backing up. Stepping backward in the halt is interpreted by dressage judges as an *evasion*, a sign that the horse is attempting to avoid contact with the bit. If established, it can be a difficult habit to break. Always think and correct forward.

My horse's tendency toward crookedness in the halt is not uncommon, and it's one that I must remain diligent to counteract. The goal, of course, is to evenly strengthen and supple both sides of the horse's body so the sidedness disappears. It may never go away completely, however, so I must always guard against it.

The other common cause of a crooked halt is uneven rein or leg pressure from the rider. If you inadvertently push harder with one leg, for example, your horse obeys by shifting his haunches to one side, away from the stronger leg pressure. Likewise, if you're hanging on one rein, you may pull his forehand in that direction. If you're pulling and overbending his neck laterally, you may displace weight onto his opposite shoulder and cause him to step in that direction — away from the side to which he's overbent — to regain his balance.

THE "FRONT TO BACK" HALT. This is a common mistake. By relying on the reins to halt, Emily has caused Paul to shorten through the neck and to overflex longitudinally, tipping his nose behind the vertical. The crest of his neck, instead of his poll (the highest point of the neck, right behind the ears), is the highest point. If Emily rides forward in this frame, Paul will be unbalanced and on his forehand, with tension in his neck and with shortened strides.

As a rider, it can be truly astonishing to discover how deeply ingrained a tendency to overuse one rein or leg can be. In my own riding, there have been times when I was convinced that I wasn't hanging on one rein, only to discover later that I actually was. In my case, the culprit has always been some previously undiscovered area of crookedness and weakness in my body that somehow made me feel as if my rein contact was even when it wasn't. If your horse continually halts crooked and you can't figure out why, seek the help of a reputable instructor. She can help you discover the reason for the crookedness and can devise exercises to address the problem.

ON THE FOREHAND

Halting on the forehand is my horse's favorite way of halting. I ask for a halt and he thinks, "Goody! I get to stop moving." He parks his hind legs where they are while momentum carries his front legs a couple of extra steps forward, Slinky style, until he grinds to a halt, shoulders down, neck down, and with what feels like 90 percent of his weight slumped on his forehand.

A good halt requires good activity. If your horse likes to halt the way my horse does, the only solution is to insist that his hind legs keep moving up until the last second — no quitting early.

Overthinking your halt preparations can be a problem, too. If, through your body language, you give your horse lots of advance notice that a halt is coming up, he may start downshifting on his own, before you want him to. Your horse is perfectly capable of stopping on a dime: just watch him romp in the pasture sometime. Not that you want your dressage halts to have that slam-on-the-brakes look, but he can get his ducks in a row and halt nicely with surprisingly little notice. So instead of thinking, "Trot . . . trot . . . get . . . ready . . . to . . . halt . . . and . . . halt," try thinking, "Trot . . . trot . . . and . . . halt."

It's also important to ask for the halt transition (or any transition, for that matter) at the moment that your horse can best accomplish it while still remaining balanced. This is somewhat less of an issue in the walk and the trot than it is in the canter. In the third and final beat of the canter stride, your horse's weight "rolls over" his leading foreleg. By default, in this moment he's effectively on his forehand. If you ask for a halt at this point, you'll get a nosedive. Instead, ask for the halt during the moment of suspension in the canter, when all four feet are airborne and your horse's hind legs are already gathered beneath him.

Practicing series of halt transitions can help to teach your horse to engage his hindquarters and to halt and move off more neatly and compactly. For a detailed discussion of transitions, see below.

ABRUPT

If your halts leave you feeling susceptible to whiplash, then they're a little too much "Western sliding stop" and not enough "gracefully landing snowflake." You're probably aiding too strongly and failing to relax the unyielding rein aids in that split second before the halt. Ease up a little to allow the last one or two steps of the gait before the halt actually occurs.

NOT PROMPT

At this point in our discussion, you may suspect that the "Goldilocks principle" (that is, that somewhere between "too strong" and "too light" an aid is "just right"; see page 104) also applies to halt transitions, and you're right. Too strong an aid, and you'll get an abrupt halt. Too light an aid, or an incorrectly timed aid, and your horse may halt several strides later instead of at the moment you ask. Your job is to figure out how much seat, leg, and hand to use to produce a prompt halt of good quality.

If your horse ignores your aids, imagine that you're riding toward the edge of a cliff. I'll bet you could halt

in time if your life truly depended on it! Halt like you mean it, and let him know that plowing through your aids like a steamroller is not acceptable.

Practice halting promptly as well as precisely. In a dressage test, you must halt (and perform other transitions) at specific points in the arena that are marked with letters. (See chapter 13 for more about tests.) *At the letter* means at the point that your horse's shoulder is directly opposite the letter marker. Challenge yourself: can you halt so your horse's shoulder is directly opposite a letter, a tree, or some other landmark?

FUSSING OR JIGGING

If I let him, my horse will happily go to sleep when he halts. Hotter or more impatient horses can't tolerate inaction: they paw and jig if they're asked to stand still for more than a nanosecond. These eager beavers need to be taught patience and obedience. They need to learn that you decide when to go and when to stop. Teaching this lesson, of course, takes lots of patience.

Gradually increase the time spent halted until the horse learns that he must stand quietly until he's told to go forward. You won't correct a jigging horse in a day. Aim for modest improvement over a period of days to weeks. Catch your horse doing it right, and reward him for standing quietly by moving off and saying "good boy" before he starts to fuss again.

Over time, he will begin to associate the halt with something pleasant rather than with something inherently unlikable (standing still with a lot of scolding and rein snatching).

Shifting Gears: Transitions between Gaits

I've taken many dressage lessons that were organized in the following way: First, we walked. Then we trotted. Then we cantered. Then we walked to cool down.

What a mistake! Treating each gait as a stand-alone robs horse and rider of arguably the most versatile and useful gymnastic exercise there is: doing transitions from one gait to another, including into and out of the halt.

To execute a balanced "up" transition — say, from walk to trot — your horse must gather himself and push off with his hind legs. In the process, he bends the joints of his hind legs, lowers his croup, strengthens the muscles of his "engine," and raises and lightens his shoulders and forehand.

Likewise, to execute a balanced "down" transition, he must shift his weight to the rear and bring his hind legs farther beneath his body. There's a moment when he almost crouches slightly. Sounds a little like collection, doesn't it?

Practicing transitions is the single best way to improve virtually every element of the training scale. Because you're forced to pay attention to the quality of the gaits before and after the transition, transitions can improve your horse's rhythm and regularity. Because transitions naturally compress your horse between your seat and legs and the reins, they help improve his acceptance of the contact. Because they strengthen his hindquarters and encourage him to push off from behind, transitions develop impulsion. Done in both directions, transitions strengthen each side of your horse's body, aiding straightness. At their most sophisticated level, transitions develop his ability to "sit" behind by bending the joints of his hind legs, thereby developing what's known as carrying power; they also elevate his forehand, thus improving collection.

We've already discussed walking and trotting into and out of the halt. There's also walk-trot-walk and trot-canter-trot. As you and your horse progress, you'll be able to walk into and out of the canter, too — no trot steps! Still more advanced, and practiced less often, is canter-halt-canter.

Common Faults and How to Fix Them

The following transition flubs tend to crop up at all levels of dressage. Here are some of the most common problems, their causes, and their fixes.

CHANGE IN TEMPO

A common example of a change in tempo is when a rider asks her trotting horse to canter, and the horse speeds up in the trot before, or instead of, cantering.

If this happens, don't panic or snatch at the reins and give your horse a kick. Remember that the quality and purity of the gait is most important. In this example, the quality of the trot was lost. Restore it by calmly bringing your horse back to his normal working or collected trot, then again asking for the canter. Make sure that your aids are clear and distinct so your horse knows exactly what you want. Don't say "canter" with your scissored leg position while continuing to say "trot" with your seat, for instance.

Interestingly, the quality of the trot-canter transition serves as a good barometer of the degree of relaxation and suppleness of your horse's back and topline. U.S. Olympic dressage team bronze medalist Steffen Peters once told me that practicing trot-canter-trot transitions — which many upper-level riders overlook, preferring to pick up the canter from the walk — is a good way to supple the horse longitudinally, and it also serves as a check of his muscular looseness. Sure enough, I've learned that my horse's trot-canter transitions are not fluid until he's loosened and is moving freely over his back and forward into the rein contact. Repeated transitions improve the quality of both the trot and the canter.

CHANGE IN RHYTHM

If your horse anticipates the transition or if you're holding him too tightly in front, the resulting tension in his body may manifest itself as an alteration of the rhythm

Here's a frame-by-frame look at how the horse shifts his weight and rebalances his body as he executes transitions from trot to walk and from walk to canter. Note how the rider uses his weight and the position of his upper body to help his horse remain in balance.

"DOWN": TROT TO WALK. Chris Hickey and Regent execute a good transition from trot to walk. With his seat and legs, Chris asks the gelding to keep stepping actively with his hind legs, even as he slows to the walk. Doing so ensures a balanced transition and no falling on the forehand.

"UP": WALK TO CANTER. Chris and Regent demonstrate a smooth and balanced transition from walk to canter. Note the absence of trot steps in between.

of the gait. A walk may become lateral (pacing); a canter may become four-beat. The horse may hollow his back and raise his neck, further adding to the tension and the erosion of the gait quality.

Lots of practice hones your timing and gives the transitions a smooth, no-big-deal quality that relaxes the horse. Vary where in the arena you ask for transitions. Some riders habitually ask for a canter in the corner or ask for some other transition at a particular letter, for example. No wonder the horse anticipates! Do the transitions in unexpected places, between letters, away from the wall of the arena, or even outside the arena to keep him alert and attentive.

If the prospect of a transition has your horse so tightly wound that he feels as if he's going to explode, leave that work for a while and go on to something else. Incorporating lots of transitions into your schooling work is great, but too much drilling will challenge the patience of even the most willing horse. Take a walk break, practice something else, get out of the ring and go for a hack, or just ride energetically forward to clear the cobwebs out of his brain. Like us, horses have different levels of tolerance for "classroom" work. My current horse loves it because the repetition makes him feel secure; my event horse would get bored, however, and would mentally tune out. I'd have to get him out of the ring for a hack or a jumping session to recharge his batteries.

UNWANTED WALK STEPS

A transition into and out of, say, trot-halt should be just that, with no walk steps in between, but that's easier said than done. Unwanted walk steps (or trot steps, in a walk-canter transition) happen for a variety of reasons. You may not have timed your aids properly for the transition, thus forcing your horse to take at least one walk step to rearrange his legs. Your aids may not have been assertive enough. Your horse may not have been properly on the aids, balanced and ready to respond. Or perhaps he's just being lazy.

Crisp, clean transitions, like square halts, require vigilance on your part. Once you've halted and you ask your horse to trot off, pay attention. Does he sneak in a walk step or two? If he's allowed to do it even some of the time, he'll naturally assume that it's OK with you and will continue doing it. If you decide to enter a dressage show, he won't suddenly change the way he's been doing the transition, so teach him the right way now.

What's the big deal about a silly walk step or two, anyway? Do they really matter? In the grand scheme of things, no. But if your goal is to create a better and more enjoyable equine athlete through the time-honored tradition of classical equitation, then, yes, they do. In dressage, details matter. Those few innocuous walk steps suggest that your horse isn't 100 percent on your aids and obedient, or that your riding isn't quite as precise and well timed as it could be, or a combination of the two. The goal, elusive though it may be, is perfection. In the show ring, you'll lose points for unasked-for walk steps. So whether you're motivated by a competitive nature or a quest for equestrian art, always hold yourself and your horse to a higher standard of performance. There's always more to learn and achieve.

Sharpen your timing and your horse's response to your light aids by practicing a series of fairly rapid transitions. From a regular, energetic working trot or collected trot, walk for a step and then trot off again. This is a great exercise, and it's harder than it sounds! Many horses think "break time" every time they're asked to walk. Getting them to trot off again promptly can take quick aiding (strong if needed to make the point, then back off) and quick thinking. This exercise is also an excellent way to develop impulsion and collection, because it requires the horse to stay forward-thinking and to push off strongly from behind as he goes back into the trot.

THE REIN BACK. Here is Paul in a good rein back. He is active and balanced. His legs are moving in clear diagonal pairs.

Put 'er in Reverse: The Rein Back

The rein back (stepping backward) requires good forward energy. Why does backward movement require forward energy? Simple. Because it is achieved by pushing the horse forward into an unyielding hand, not by pulling the horse backward with the reins. The forward energy you've created can't go forward as usual, so instead it's channeled in reverse, between your "guarding" legs, which keep him straight and prevent him from swinging his hindquarters to either side.

Biomechanically, the rein back is interesting because although it's done at the speed of a walk, the footfalls are not walk footfalls in reverse. In a correct rein back, the horse lifts and lowers diagonal pairs of legs, much like a trot in reverse but done at the speed of a walk.

Rein-Back Prerequisites

Before you attempt to teach your horse to rein back, he must be comfortable doing transitions into and out of the walk and the halt. He must connect the aids with forward movement, with no inclination to evade the forward driving aids by backing up or rearing. A horse that "thinks backward" can be difficult to retrain and even dangerous. Seek help from a professional trainer if you have trouble getting your horse to go forward.

Assuming that all is well going forward, introduce the rein back with the help of someone on the ground. Start by quietly halting your horse; halting next to a solid wall or other barrier is ideal because it will help keep him straight. When he's square (or nearly so) and on the bit, have your assistant give your horse a nudge in the chest while gently shaking the reins and saying "Baaack, baaack," just as you would on the ground if you wanted him to back up. As the rider, maintain steady contact with your seat, legs, and hands during this process.

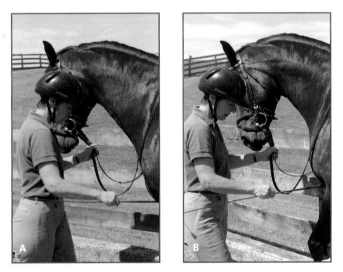

A. Introducing the rein back. Bonnie Olie demonstrates the initial rein-back training. She's introducing Sultan to the concept of stepping backward by tapping his chest with the butt end of a dressage whip while stepping toward him and saying "back." Note that she's positioned him against the rail to help keep him straight. **B.** The desired response. Sultan obligingly yields in his poll and jaw, and takes a step backward.

As soon as your horse takes a step or two backward, halt and praise him. Do this exercise a few more times until he gets the hang of it. Next, use the voice command as a bridging aid to help your horse make the connection between your assistant's directions and your aids. From the halt, slide your lower legs back a couple of inches, lighten your seat in the saddle slightly (but don't lean forward or stand up in your stirrups), keep your hands low by his withers, and think of asking him to step forward while at the same time squeezing your fists on the reins and saying "Baaack." If he stands rooted to the spot, have your assistant give him a nudge on the chest. Be patient. Eventually, he'll take a step backward, at which time you'll praise him profusely and end the lesson.

Segue to reining back without your helper's assistance, but keep her on call so she can step in and give your horse a refresher if he gets confused or stops responding. Gradually work up to reining back from your seat, leg, and rein aids alone, with no voice command. (Use of the voice is not allowed in the show ring, so don't become dependent on it.)

Common Faults and How to Fix Them

If backing up has its share of bobbles, here's some advice to help simplify the process. These are the most common faults seen in the rein back.

LURCHING INTO REVERSE

Occasionally, you'll see a horse resist going into reverse. He'll tense his topline and raise his head and neck, then step backward awkwardly without the desired even rhythm. His legs may lack the required diagonal pairing, as well.

He looks uncomfortable because he is uncomfortable. He's tense and hollow to start, which makes any movement feel stilted to him and his rider. Compounding the problem is the fact that backing up is unnatural

RESISTANCE IN THE REIN BACK. Paul has tensed and raised his head and neck as he steps backward. Clearly, he is resisting the exercise at this moment.

and a leap of faith for the horse. As a prey animal, he doesn't want to step anywhere that he can't see. Horses' willingness to rein back is proof of their trust in us.

Any horse may resist the rein back if he's not relaxed, round, and on the bit in the halt beforehand. But if most of your attempts to rein back are met with protest, have your helper reassure your horse and rebuild his confidence from the ground. If the problem persists, consult your veterinarian. Hock, stifle, and hindquarter pain can manifest as an unwillingness to step backward.

> **TIP** | **Consult a Vet**
>
> Persistent or exaggerated foot-dragging in the rein back can be a symptom of a neurological or other health-related problem. If your horse doesn't show marked improvement after judicious use of the *schaukel* exercise described on the opposite page, consult your veterinarian.

UNBALANCED REIN BACK. The rein back requires that the horse take more weight over his hindquarters. Some horses try to avoid the difficulty by curling their necks behind the vertical and becoming too low in front, which shifts the weight to the forehand.

DRAGGING THE TOES

Some horses rein back by dragging their feet backward, raising them as little as possible instead of lifting and placing them. Make sure that you're not asking your horse to start the movement when he is on his forehand and very low in his head and neck. If he's "buried" in front, he may be too off balance to shift his weight to the rear and step lightly and deliberately. To lighten his forehand, try an exercise that at the upper levels is known by the German word *schaukel* (swing); as the name suggests, the back-and-forth motion of this exercise is swinglike (see illustration). Halt, rein back several steps, immediately walk forward several steps, halt, rein back several steps, and repeat. This excellent gymnastic exercise sharpens your horse's responses, helps you learn quickness and timing of the aids, and improves balance, impulsion, and collection.

RUSHING BACKWARD

The proper rein-back tempo is measured steps taken at about walk speed. Some horses, however, have the tendency to double-time in the rein back. Often low in

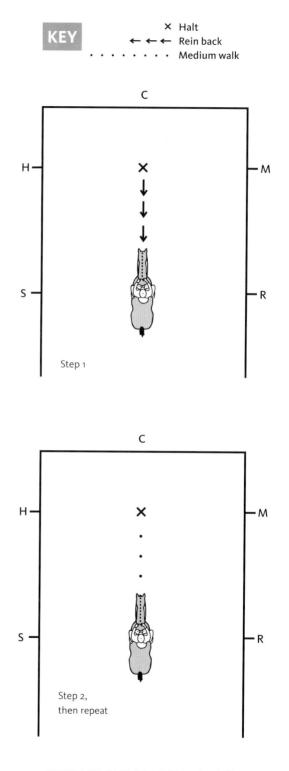

FORWARD AND BACK (the schaukel)

Arena Dimensions

If you have access to a standard, or regulation-size, dressage arena, consider yourself lucky. Many riders make do in rings of various sizes that are littered with jumps and nondescript flat and uneven areas; still others use no ring at all, just an open field or vacant pasture or paddock.

The standard dressage arena is 20 meters wide and 60 meters long. The *center line,* an imaginary line running lengthwise down the center of the arena, is 10 meters from either side. Two *quarter lines,* each 5 meters from the long side (wall or rail) of the arena, run parallel to the center line.

Because the standard arena is three times as long as it is wide, the space can conveniently be divided into thirds for the purpose of executing various figures, such as 20-meter circles, which are as wide as the arena itself.

Most dressage figures and movements are sized and spaced so they fit neatly between, or commence on, the perimeter of the arena, the center line, or one of the quarter lines.

The *small arena,* a 20-meter-wide and 40-meter-long arena used only for some low-level dressage tests, is smaller than the standard dressage arena. You can practice all of the basic movements and figures in a small arena, but as you advance you'll need the added length of the standard arena.

If you have a suitably large riding space to work in, you can measure out an area equivalent to a dressage arena by marking the corners, center line, and quarter lines with cones. If you ride in a field, a fence line could do double duty as one long side, or a tree could serve as a corner marker. Be resourceful when laying out your arena space.

If you don't have access to a metric tape measure, convert meters to feet. Ten meters equal 32.81 feet, so:

> **20 meters = 65.62 feet**
> **40 meters = 131.24 feet**
> **60 meters = 196.86 feet**

If you want to replicate the 90-degree corners and other geometric aspects of a regulation dressage arena, consult the *USDF Directory,* an annual publication of the U.S. Dressage Federation, which provides step-by-step instructions on arena setup. For the figures and movements in this chapter, all you need to do to get started is mark the basic arena dimensions and the center and quarter lines. (We'll save our discussion of dressage letters, that alphabet soup of markers placed at specific points around the dressage arena, for chapter 13. See chapter 19 for a discussion of arena footing.)

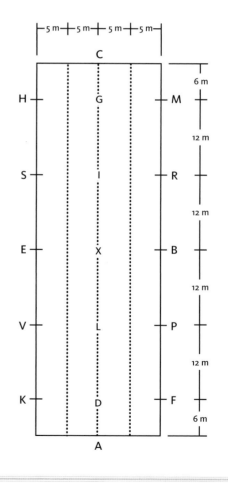

front, with their necks bowed, they rush backward. They may manage to maintain the diagonal footfalls, but the steps look absurdly hurried.

If this happens, first make sure that you are not inadvertently pulling your horse backward through overuse of the reins and insufficient support from your seat and legs. When you rein back, limit the movement to just a few steps and then go forward again. Careful use of the *schaukel* exercise (see page 159) can help teach your horse that he must think forward, even in the rein back.

If your horse is a bit of a backward thinker, don't overschool the rein back; reining back will allow him to do what he'd like to do anyway, at the expense of forward movement and energy. Backing up is in many horses' bag of tricks: they resort to it when they're stressed, scared, or feeling naughty. I don't practice the formal rein back much with my horse because the reverse button is already firmly in place.

Circles and Half-Circles

The circle ranks right up there with the transition as the most basic, universal, and well-rounded element of dressage schooling. It develops and tests every element of the training scale, even straightness. (Recall that in dressage *straight* means "aligned," so straightness on a circle means that your horse's body, from nose to tail, appears to conform to the arc of the figure.)

If the circle is the basic dressage figure, then the 20-meter circle is the meat and potatoes. The 20-meter circle is the largest circle that can be made in the standard dressage arena, and so is the least challenging to execute. Bend and balance become more critical for the horse as the diameter of the circle is reduced.

When riding a circle, precision is key. The circle must be perfectly symmetrical, without any suspicious bulges. A 20-meter circle is exactly 20 meters in diameter, not 19 or 21 meters in diameter.

Geometry Basics

It's generally easier to control the size of a circle than it is to control its shape. To make a circle accurately, practice in a dressage arena or a correctly marked space. Many a rider has gotten an unpleasant surprise on entering a regulation arena for the first time, when she discovers that the circles she's practiced so diligently were larger or smaller than the standard arena width.

Visualize how the circle will look in the arena before you go out to practice. Let's say you want to ride a 20-meter circle at one end of the arena. The circle will touch the arena at four critical points: the midpoint of the short side of the arena, two points on the long sides, and a point on the center line opposite the short side. Your horse's body will meet the rail and cross the center line at these four points, then immediately leave them to follow the arc of the circle. If you find yourself riding along the rail for several strides, the shape of the circle is off. Similarly, if you don't ride all the way out to the rail, the circle will be smaller than you intended.

The center line and quarter lines are convenient reference points that will help you make accurate smaller circles as your horse progresses in his training. If you start at one side of the arena, a 15-meter circle will touch the far quarter line, and a 10-meter circle will touch the center line. You can even use these imaginary lines to help you ride figures of in-between dimensions. An 18-meter circle, for instance, extends to approximately halfway between the quarter line and the rail.

A half-circle is an elegant way to change direction. Put two half-circles together, and you have half of a figure eight or a two-loop serpentine (see page 165 for more on these figures).

With time and practice, you'll get a good feel for the arena dimensions and for the geometry of the various figures. I don't use metric measurements outside of the arena, but if my instructor says, "Bring in the circle a meter," I know just how much smaller to make it.

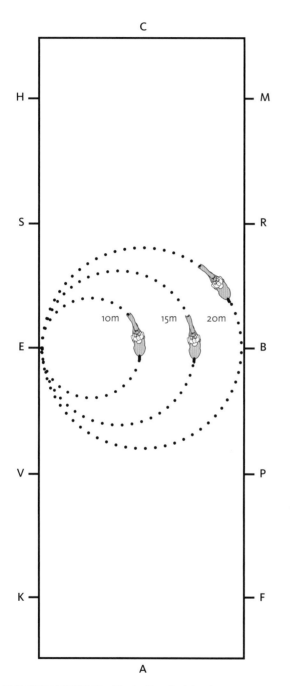

CIRCLE GEOMETRY. The illustration depicts a horse on a 10-, 15-, and 20-meter circle. The smaller the circle, the greater the balance challenge and the more the horse has to engage his inside hind leg.

Which Came First, the Circle or the Egg?

Because achieving perfect alignment on a circle is challenging for most horses, many riders' circles resemble eggs and other odd shapes. Even if you have a careful eye, your horse's natural crookedness and "sidedness" may make it difficult for you to keep him from falling in or bulging out on the circle arc. Most horses tend to fall in in one direction and to fall out in the other, depending on which side is stiff and which is hollow.

And what do falling in and bulging out feel like? They both give the rider the sense that the horse is not evenly between the legs and the reins. Your horse may feel heavier on one rein, or his shoulder may feel like it's bulging through one rein like a bubble in a tire. His

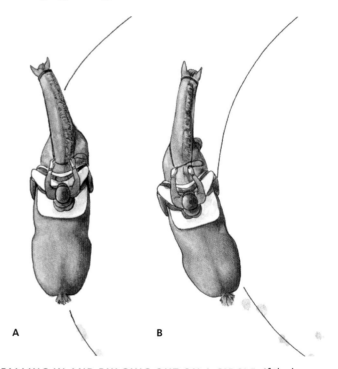

FALLING IN AND BULGING OUT ON A CIRCLE. If the horse "falls in," he runs through the rider's inside aids with his inside shoulder (A). More common is the horse that bulges out or "pops" his outside shoulder as he runs through the outside aids (B). Both faults indicate lack of straightness (perhaps caused by poor aiding on the rider's part) and balance issues.

rib cage may feel as if it's pushing against one leg, while your other leg feels as if it has nothing to wrap around. You may also find that when moving in one direction your circles tend to become smaller, while in the other direction they tend to drift outward.

Circles can be ridden in all three gaits, with the walk generally being the least challenging to your horse's bend and balance, and the canter being the most challenging. You may find that he can comfortably trot a circle of a size that he can't yet manage at the canter, and that's normal for a young or green horse. Always keep the size of the circle manageable for your horse. If he's careening around or feels alarmingly off balance, increase the size of the circle and decrease it again gradually only when he feels comfortable and confident on the larger figures.

Use circle work as a gymnastic exercise and for the valuable training insights it can give you. If you notice that your horse is having trouble remaining properly aligned on circles, try to pinpoint the problem, using the training scale as your guide. (For more on the training scale, see chapter 7.) Here are some examples of questions you might ask yourself:

- In which direction is the problem happening?
- Does the same problem occur when I reverse direction? Or do I encounter the opposite problem?
- Which part of the horse is failing to conform to the arc of the circle — the forehand or the hindquarters?
- Is the body part in question falling in or falling out? (Falling in usually means that the horse needs to bend better around the rider's inside leg [see page 164] and step better underneath his body with his inside hind leg. Falling out can signify weakness in the outside hind leg or that the rider isn't using her outside leg properly to contain the horse's body through the turn.)
- Am I sitting in the middle of the saddle, weight distributed evenly over my seat bones, with elastic contact in both reins? (A crooked rider or one who's

hanging on one rein is a surefire cause of crookedness in a horse.)

If you think your position might be to blame for your horse's difficulty on the circle, realign yourself in the saddle (ask an instructor to help you if you're not sure how) and try the circle again. If that doesn't help, try riding in the opposite direction for a while, or leave the circle entirely and refresh your horse's energy by riding freely forward on straight lines. Be sure to give him walk breaks during all this work. His muscles fatigue the same way yours do, and he can and will reach a point at which he's physically unable to do what you want.

Some horses weave if they're not moving with sufficient impulsion. Circles, turns (even through the corner of the arena), and lateral movements present different challenges to the horse than proceeding in a straight line. The extra effort required by these movements causes the horse to slow down somewhat to compensate. His rhythm and tempo should remain steady whether he's trotting down the long side or making a circle. If you can't tell whether he's easing up on the circle, count the footfalls. Unless you can set a metronome to the beat, you need to rev up things a bit as you enter the circle. Sit a little deeper in the saddle, with your shoulders well back, and use a bit more leg to continue to drive him energetically forward. When he is moving on the circle with good energy, he'll be better able to develop his balance and strengthen his inside hind leg, thereby laying the foundation for the more advanced work ahead.

If you continue to struggle with some crookedness on the circle (don't worry if you do; doing circles isn't enough to make most horses straight), you may need to incorporate more gymnastic exercises in your repertoire. There's an exercise for helping to strengthen whatever part of your horse needs strengthening. Following are some of my favorites.

What Is *Bend?*

Experts in equine biomechanics point out that when applied to horses, the term *bend* (the apparent lateral curvature of the horse's neck and body as they conform to the arc of a circle or curved line, and in most lateral movements) is something of a misnomer. The horse's spine cannot bend or flex laterally as we might expect; instead, only the horse's musculature contracts and stretches. When a horse bends, the muscles along the inside of his body contract and those on the outside stretch, so his outline appears to conform to the shape of an arc. In the photo below from the 2000 Sydney Olympics, U.S. team bronze medalist Guenter Seidel rides Foltaire in a trot half-pass left. Foltaire is bent left and flexed left laterally, toward the direction of travel. The stretch along the outside (right side) of his body is obvious from this angle.

Guenter Seidel aboard Foltaire in a trot half-pass left at the 2000 Sydney Olympics.

Even though the horse's spine cannot bend or flex laterally, it sure feels like bending when you're riding. The basic principle of bend is that the rider's weighted inside seat bone and leg, acting at the girth, cause the horse to engage the muscles of his midsection on that side and to elongate the muscles of his midsection on the opposite side. Weighted somewhat more than the outside seat bone, the inside seat bone tells the horse, in effect, "Balance under here." The horse naturally positions himself under the weighted seat bone to achieve optimal balance.

The rider's active inside leg acts as a support around which the horse yields his rib cage. The rider's "guarding" outside leg, placed slightly behind the girth, is less active and serves mainly to ensure that the hindquarters continue to travel straight and do not drift to the outside.

The inside rein does not pull the horse in the desired direction; rather, it lightly flexes the horse's poll laterally in the direction of the bend, so that his head and neck are aligned with the rest of his body. The outside rein "guards" the horse's outside shoulder and helps to contain the energy generated by the rider's inside leg.

The smaller the circle or the steeper the lateral movement, the greater the degree of bend required. Low-level movements like 20-meter circles hardly require any bend; a little lateral flexion and inside positioning are all the horse needs to follow the circle's shallow arc.

Figure Eights and Serpentines

Figure eights and serpentines build on the basic circle by incorporating changes of direction.

In dressage, a figure eight is two circles that touch at the midpoint (see illustration). The challenge to the rider, then, is to make two circles of equal size on opposite reins, and to execute a seamless change of bend at the figure's midpoint. The diameter of the circles determines the figure's level of difficulty; smaller circles are more challenging.

To get a smooth change of bend, you must produce a single straight stride just as the horse crosses the midpoint of the figure. This moment of straightness is the bridge between the bend of the old direction and the bend of the new direction. If you try to ride the figure eight without this moment of straightness, you'll probably get an unsteady change of bend, with your horse's neck flexing suddenly from one side to the other.

When you're starting out in dressage, you'll likely ride figure eights only in the trot. Later, you'll ride them in the canter, with a few walk steps at the midpoint,

A PROPERLY RIDDEN FIGURE EIGHT or serpentine shows a clear moment of straightness at the midpoint between circles or loops, as shown.

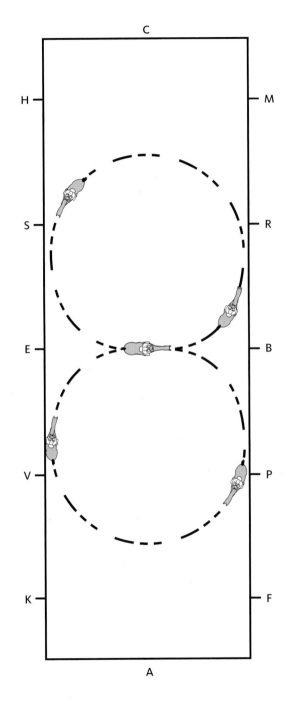

FIGURE EIGHT

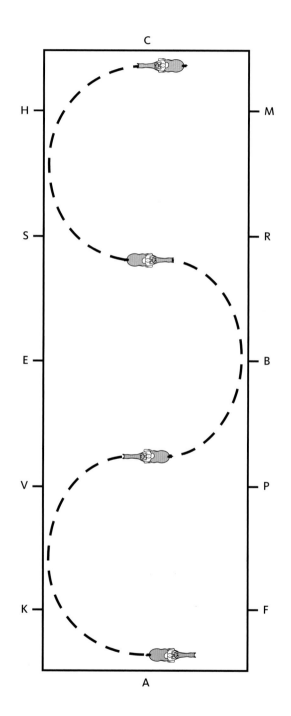

THREE-LOOP SERPENTINE

from which your horse will pick up the new canter lead (*simple change of lead*). It's difficult to ride an accurate figure eight in the canter with a trot transition because your horse will tend to travel too far along the midline before turning in the new direction.

Serpentines are S-shaped figures. They range from shallow undulations to loops the width of the arena. The more loops and the steeper the turns, the greater the challenge.

In the previous chapter, I mentioned that shallow serpentines are an excellent way to school the counter-canter, because very little turning and balancing is required (see page 144). Another type of serpentine is the classic three-loop serpentine shown in the illustration. It spans the length and width of the arena.

Begin a three-loop serpentine at one end of the arena, just as you cross the center line. Because each loop is a circle, you must cut the corner slightly to start the circle movement.

As you and your horse become comfortable with serpentine figures, challenge yourselves by decreasing the width of the loops, increasing the number of loops, or both. A somewhat more advanced horse can comfortably trot a five- or six-loop serpentine. Later in their training, horses can canter three-, four-, or five-loop serpentines, going from true canter to counter-canter.

The greater the number of loops, the tighter the turns and the more rapid the changes of direction and bend, thus making it more challenging for the rider to control and maintain the size of the loops. Controlling loop size is easier if you have access to an arena marked with the traditional dressage letters. For example, "The middle loop of my three-loop serpentine should touch the rail at B." (See chapter 13 for more on the dressage letters.)

Serpentines are challenging because they require the horse to change direction and bend, and they are an excellent suppling and balance exercise.

Lateral Movements

Circles, corners, and curved lines, such as those in figure eights and serpentines, are bending and balancing exercises but not true lateral movements. In dressage, a *lateral movement* is one in which the horse simultaneously moves forward and sideways. Because you can walk, trot, and canter, your horse has obviously learned that the leg aid means "go forward." At this stage of his training, he also must learn to yield laterally to your leg and to distinguish different meanings in the position and use of your leg and weight aids.

When your horse moves laterally, all four legs step sideways and forward. But the inside hind leg does most of the work. As the inside hind steps forward and sideways, the horse places it underneath his body mass. Some of the weight once borne by his forehand is shifted to the rear as his inside hind leg reaches farther forward and under, supporting him.

As your horse steps underneath himself with his inside hind leg, he narrows the distance between his hind legs. Horses are narrower in front and wider behind; that and the greater weight of the forehand explains why they carry 60 percent of their weight on the forehand. When a horse learns to place his hind legs closer to his body mass through lateral work and other gymnastic exercises, the joints of those legs bend to a greater degree and his hindquarters accept more weight. In this way, he develops straightness, impulsion (pushing power), and collection (lowering of the haunches and elevation of the forehand), making lateral work the cornerstone of more advanced dressage training.

AN EXTREME EXAMPLE of the degree to which some horses can bend the joints of their hindquarters: a Lipizzan stallion of the Spanish Riding School in the levade, a *haute école* movement that is not performed in dressage competition.

TROT HALF-PASS RIGHT. Horses can step forward and sideways. Here are U.S. competitors Flim Flam and Susan Blinks at the 2000 Sydney Olympics in a trot half-pass right. Flim Flam is stepping forward and to the right with his left front and right hind legs in this moment of the movement.

Lateral Positioning: It's All Relative

Before we discuss specific lateral movements, you need to wrap your mind around a concept that some of us non-spatially-oriented people have trouble grasping: the horse is positioned *exactly the same way* in most lateral and bending work; only his position in space (that is, his relationship to the line of travel) changes.

Many riders don't fully understand this concept and subsequently encounter difficulties with the various lateral movements as they attempt to push, pull, and maneuver equine body parts, when in fact they should be doing *exactly the same thing*.

Now that you're completely befuddled, let me explain. Look at the illustrations. All are aerial views of horses positioned correctly for circles, turns, and most lateral movements. Notice that each horse's outline is identical; the only thing that is different is the position of the arena wall. Move the horse in space and you get the relative positioning for almost every lateral movement.

So why should you bother with the various exercises if most are essentially the same? Because horses respond differently depending on where the wall is. And because different forms of lateral positioning are helpful in overcoming different issues, such as straightness, depending on the direction of travel and on the horse's stiff and hollow sides.

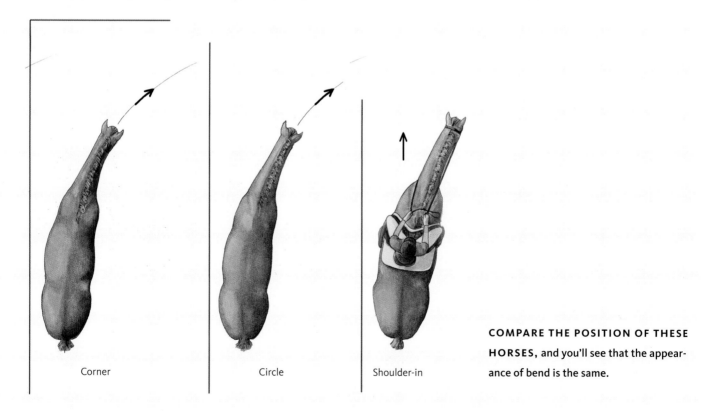

Corner

Circle

Shoulder-in

COMPARE THE POSITION OF THESE HORSES, and you'll see that the appearance of bend is the same.

TURN ON THE FOREHAND. Emily asks Paul to yield to her left leg as he executes a turn on the forehand. Although it is not a true lateral movement because there is no forward motion, this exercise can be helpful in introducing the horse to the concept of stepping sideways, away from the leg.

Turn on the Forehand

In the turn on the forehand, the horse's forehand remains in one place while his hind legs step around, yielding away from the rider's inside leg. It is not a recognized lateral movement, and no dressage test requires it. There are a few reasons for this. First, there's no forward movement, a prerequisite in dressage. (That's why a Western-style sidepass isn't executed in dressage.) Second, in dressage, lateral movement is always achieved by positioning the horse's shoulders ahead of his haunches. In the turn on the forehand, the shoulders remain relatively still and the haunches do most of the moving.

Still, the turn on the forehand is a simple, time-tested way to introduce a young or green horse to the concept of yielding sideways away from one leg. Some trainers like to introduce the movement from the ground. Stand on your horse's left side, opposite the saddle. With the reins over his neck in riding position, grasp both reins below the bit with your left hand.

A COMMON FAULT. An unfortunate moment in the turn on the forehand. Emily is leaning to the right as she attempts to move Paul over from her right leg. The horse is clearly resisting and has stiffened through his midsection.

Then, using the butt of a dressage whip, nudge him in the ribs where your leg would be. If he begins to walk off, calmly halt him and give another nudge with the whip. Take gentle hold of the reins to give him the idea that he shouldn't walk off, and he'll eventually take a step sideways, possibly with just one leg. When he does, praise him lavishly. Repeat the exercise in the opposite direction. Gradually work up to a full turn; then try the exercise mounted. If your horse has trouble associating the unmounted work with the mounted work, have a helper hold the reins and nudge him sideways until the horse makes the connection between the whip and your leg. Again, repeat the entire sequence in the opposite direction.

The goal of the turn on the forehand is even, measured steps; your horse shouldn't spin like a whirling dervish. He also should lift and lower his front legs, not plant and pivot. His front legs should remain in a relatively small area, so don't be concerned if they don't stay exactly "on the spot."

You can segue to the leg-yield (the first real lateral movement) by doing the following exercise: From a walk, halt and turn on the forehand for two or three steps. Walk forward, then halt again and turn on the forehand. Repeat the sequence several times, then try it from the opposite leg. The combination of walking forward and turning on the forehand helps to give your horse the idea of going forward and sideways.

INTRODUCING THE TURN ON THE FOREHAND. To give Sultan the idea of stepping sideways away from her leg, Bonnie starts by nudging him gently with the butt end of her dressage whip in the area where her leg lies. She's holding the reins near Sultan's chin so that she can stop him if he starts to walk forward.

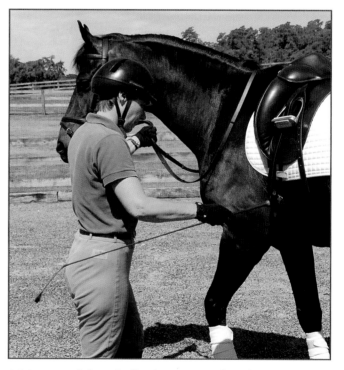

GOOD BOY! Sultan obediently steps away from the pressure. His calm expression, pricked ears, and relaxed demeanor show that he's paying attention but not worried.

Leg-Yield

The *leg-yield* is the most elementary lateral movement called for in U.S. national-level dressage tests. It is usually practiced at the walk and trot, and occasionally at the canter. No dressage test calls for a canter leg-yield, so that exercise would be done only for schooling, never competition.

In the leg-yield, the horse steps forward and sideways, away from the rider's inside leg, and he flexes slightly away from the direction of movement. This movement is unlike all other lateral dressage movements, in which the horse flexes toward the direction of movement. For example, *leg-yield right* means that the horse is moving to the right, away from the rider's left leg, and is flexed slightly to the left, away from the direction of movement.

Some dressage trainers believe that the leg-yield is neither a classical nor a useful exercise because the body of the horse remains almost straight and therefore is not suppled. Despite this, the movement is commonly used to loosen the horse's body and to develop his responsiveness to the sideways-pushing seat and leg aids. At any rate, the leg-yield remains a fixture in the official dressage-test repertoire; therefore, it seems that most believe its usefulness outweighs any possible drawbacks.

If your horse has mastered the concept of the turn on the forehand, introducing the leg-yield should be simple. The easiest way to begin is by establishing a regular medium walk along the wall or rail of the arena. (The wall will serve as a guide, so you won't have to think as much about using your reins to steer.) Start off on the right rein (clockwise). Step into your left stirrup to weight your left seat bone slightly (you'll be leg-yielding away from your left leg in this direction, so your left leg becomes your "inside" leg, even though you are traveling on the right rein). With your right leg doing guard duty to keep your horse

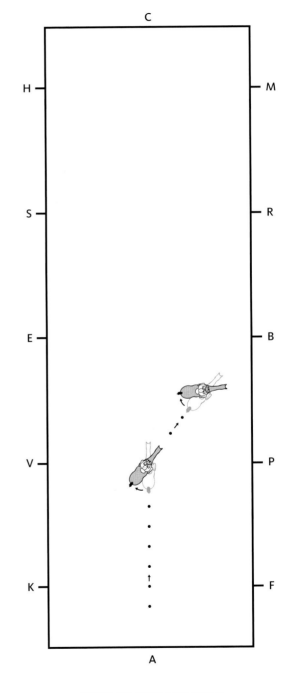

INTRODUCING LEG-YIELD

Trot Leg-Yield

FRONT VIEW OF LEG-YIELD. A correctly positioned trot leg-yield (here, to the left, away from Emily's right leg). Paul is flexed slightly laterally, away from the direction of travel. His head, neck, and shoulders are aligned. His shoulders are correctly leading his haunches, and he is moving forward as well as sideways. Note that his body remains quite straight.

LEG-YIELD ALONG THE WALL. Emily rides Paul in a trot leg-yield along the wall, away from her left leg. Paul's body remains straight, and he is flexed laterally slightly to the left, away from the direction of travel. The angle of the movement is fairly shallow; any steeper and balance and forward energy would be lost. In all lateral work, good forward energy is the prerequisite to sideways movement.

COMMON LEG-YIELD FAULT. Emily is using her inside (right) rein too strongly in her attempt to leg-yield Paul to the left. She has overbent the horse's neck, and he is no longer aligned. In trying to get him to move sideways, she has drawn her inside leg too far back; it should remain at the girth. She's also dangerously close to crossing her right hand over his withers, another common fault that breaks the correct alignment and causes the horse to lose balance over his outside shoulder.

walking forward and to prevent him from moving his haunches too far to the right, use your left leg actively in a forward and sideways manner. Push with your left leg as your horse's right shoulder moves forward; that way, you'll influence his hind legs at the correct moment and your aids will coincide with their cycle of movement.

As your horse begins to step sideways away from your left leg, his hindquarters will come slightly away from the rail. The operative word here is *slightly*. The angle of the leg-yield is only about 30 degrees. If the angle is any greater than that, the movement becomes more like a Western sidepass, with the horse's inside hind leg stepping mostly sideways and not forward, which defeats the purpose of the exercise.

Unlike other lateral movements, in the leg-yield there is no bend. Some riders mistakenly try to create bend, which causes the horse's shoulders or haunches to fall out of alignment. The horse's body should remain almost straight, with his forehand leading his haunches ever so slightly.

Likewise, his neck should remain almost straight. The lateral flexion created by light use of the inner rein brings the horse's head just inside the straight line that the rest of his body is on; there should be no obvious bow in his neck.

After your horse has taken a few steps forward and sideways along the wall, praise him and straighten him by relaxing your left-leg and left-rein aids while making your right leg more active so it resumes its role as the inside leg. Repeat the sequence a few times in this direction; then reverse and try the leg-yield along the wall from your right leg, with your horse traveling on the left rein (counterclockwise).

When you and your horse are comfortable with the leg-yield along the wall, try leg-yielding a few steps away from the wall, this time remaining parallel to it (see illustration on page 171). As always, repeat the

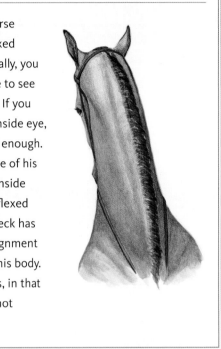

TIP **Lateral Flexion**

When your horse is properly flexed (or bent) laterally, you should be able to see his inside eye. If you can't see his inside eye, he isn't flexed enough. If you see more of his face than his inside eye, he's overflexed laterally; his neck has broken the alignment of the rest of his body. In other words, in that position he's not straight.

exercise in the opposite direction so that you don't end up with a one-sided horse. Later, challenge yourselves by leg-yielding away from the wall for a few steps, walking straight ahead for a few steps, then changing the lateral flexion to the opposite direction and leg-yielding back to the track (the rail; see illustration on page 174). This zigzag pattern is an excellent loosening exercise and test of your horse's understanding and acceptance of the forward and sideways driving aids. If there are any inequities, they will be immediately obvious during this exercise.

When you feel confident leg-yielding in the walk, try it in the trot, beginning as before, with your horse's head to the wall. Build up systematically, just as you did in the walk. If at any time either of you become confused or uncertain, go back to the walk until you feel confident again and he's leg-yielding smoothly.

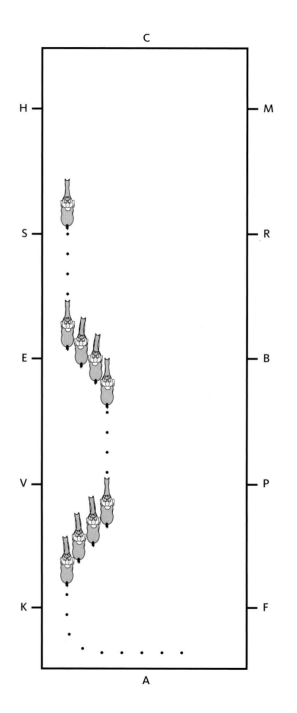

LEG-YIELD EXERCISE

COMMON FAULTS AND HOW TO FIX THEM

As you practice the leg-yield, keep in mind that the most important part of the exercise is the quality of the gait. The leg-yield is a mildly gymnastic exercise but is not an enormous test of your horse's abilities. Unless he's hampered by a physical problem, he's perfectly capable of performing this movement while maintaining a decent walk and trot. If the gaits become compromised, rider error is probably to blame. Following are the most common leg-yield faults and their fixes.

RIDER'S INSIDE LEG TOO FAR BACK, HAUNCHES PUSHED OUTSIDE These two problems have a cause-and-effect relationship. If their horses don't respond to the forward-and-sideways driving aids the way they'd like, many riders pull back their lower legs in the mistaken belief that doing so will make the aid more effective; in fact, it creates two problems. First, drawing back the leg too far pushes the hindquarters sideways (which usually makes the horse crooked; the haunches should never lead the forehand) and fails to maintain forward activity or to engage the inside hind leg. Second, it teaches the horse that ignoring the driving aid at the girth is OK.

If you suspect that your horse has ignored your leg aid, first ask yourself whether he understands what you want him to do. Does he know that you want him to step

TIP Both Ways, Always

Your horse must master any new exercise from both directions. Just because he learned something when traveling on the right rein doesn't necessarily mean that he'll be able to replicate the exercise when you go left. Plus, his body must be made equally strong and supple in both directions.

forward and sideways? If you're not sure, revisit the turn on the forehand, then try the leg-yield again.

If you're convinced that your horse understands what you want, then perhaps the way you asked was the problem. Were your aids completely clear, and was your body positioned correctly? Perhaps you were sitting to the outside and therefore blocking him from stepping forward and sideways? Maybe you were hanging on one or both reins? Even something as simple as looking down (always a no-no) can throw your horse off balance. Before you correct him, make sure that you are not the culprit.

If you're positive that your horse knows exactly what you want, that your position and aiding are impeccable, and that he is simply being lazy, now is the time to sharpen his response to your aids. No matter what gait or movement you're practicing, your horse should always respond to the lightest aids possible. When the correctly placed aid doesn't work in the leg-yield, don't

TIP ## Self-Scrutiny

Always evaluate your riding first before you blame your horse for a problem.

get suckered into squeezing or kicking harder and harder or drawing your leg back. If he doesn't respond to a light squeeze, give a little kick with the flat of your calf; don't turn your toes out or draw your heel up. If that gets a response, fine. Next time, ask again with a light leg aid. If he doesn't respond, kick and then try again with a light leg aid. Eventually, he'll understand that you won't tolerate laziness or be content riding with stronger aids.

If a kick doesn't get his attention, tap him with a dressage whip. (At some point in your training, you'll need or want to learn how to use a whip correctly. Safety should be your first priority.)

TOO MUCH SIDEWAYS, NOT ENOUGH FORWARD *(left).* Emily is trying too strongly to leg-yield Paul away from her right leg without paying attention to the horse's straightness and continued forward movement. His neck is flexed too much laterally to the right, and he is "falling" through his left shoulder while his right hind leg trails behind.

HAUNCHES LEADING IN LEG-YIELD *(right).* The horse's body should remain parallel to the wall in the leg-yield, but here Emily has used her right leg so strongly in this leg-yield left that Paul's haunches are actually ahead of his forehand. He is stepping too wide with his hind legs and has lost his balance as a result.

Using the Dressage Whip

Have you ever carried a whip or crop with your horse before? If so, is he whip-shy or otherwise overly reactive to the whip?

If your horse has no experience with a whip or is whip-shy, then a reputable professional can help with the all-important familiarization lessons. The goal is for the horse to learn to respect the whip — by going forward and not bucking or kicking out at it — but not fear it.

If you and your horse are OK with a whip, then you'll want to use it to help address the dilemma of the lazy leg-yield. The whip is an amplification of, not a substitution for (except in certain special circumstances, such as a rider's physical disability), the leg aid. The dressage whip is longer than the crop commonly seen in the hunter/jumper ranks so the rider can apply it without removing the whip hand from the reins. The rules of recognized dressage competition permit a rider to carry one whip of no longer than 43.3 inches (110 centimeters), including the lash, unless otherwise indicated in the class rules. Longer whips are available, and some riders like to use them for schooling, but they are

THE AMBIDEXTROUS RIDER. Learn to carry and use the whip safely and comfortably in either hand and to switch the whip from hand to hand. Here, Bonnie is ready to switch her whip from her right hand to her left.

THE SWITCH. Bonnie turns her right hand over so that the whip is pointed skyward, then grasps the shaft with her left hand.

VOILÀ! Bonnie is now holding the whip in her left hand. Practice this move in both directions until you can switch the whip from hand to hand smoothly at will.

not allowed in competition. You'll want to carry a regulation-length whip, especially if you decide to enter a dressage show in the future.

Generally, because of the footfall patterns of the gaits, you'll hold the whip in your inside hand for the walk and the trot, and in the outside hand for the canter. The hand that needs the whip will depend on the exercise you're working on and on the side of your horse that tends to be less quick in responding. You'll want to become adept at using the whip with both hands. This can be challenging, because the less dominant hand can be more difficult to control. Keep practicing and it will get easier.

Learn to switch the whip quickly and easily from hand to hand without accidentally smacking your horse or scaring him. The classic way is to turn your whip hand so that the shaft is angled toward your free hand; turn your free hand thumb down to grasp the handle, and carefully bring the shaft down on the new side.

Hold the whip firmly with the rein, thumb up, so the shaft rests on your thigh. When you need to use it, give your horse a tap behind your leg by flicking your wrist outward. Smacking a sensitive horse can provoke a cow-kick or a buck, so be careful. Strive to make a tap with the whip short and crisp. Timing is important: If your horse fails to respond to your leg and then to a light kick, the tap should follow immediately. As with the kick, always go back and try the light leg aid again. The whip augments the leg aid, but it shouldn't replace it.

TOO MUCH SIDEWAYS, NOT ENOUGH FORWARD

In their zeal to execute the movement, riders frequently forget that a leg-yield should be more forward than sideways. They push too hard with the inside leg, and the movement loses its free-flowing nature.

To correct this problem, go back to the "stair-step" exercise: go forward, leg-yield a few steps, go forward, leg-yield a few steps. Focus on keeping the rhythm and tempo of the gait consistent throughout.

DON'T WORK THIS HARD! Emily has collapsed her right hip (as evidenced by the fact that her shoulders are not level) and is leaning to the right as she attempts to push Paul into a leg-yield left. Your upper body should remain erect and centered in the saddle.

RIDER SITTING TO OUTSIDE In most lateral movements, you're supposed to sit a little heavier on the seat bone on the side around which you want your horse to bend. But in the leg-yield, because there is no bend, your weight remains over your inside seat bone. For instance, in a leg-yield left, away from your right leg, your right seat bone remains weighted. Some riders tend to push so hard with their legs that they literally pull themselves across the saddle until they're sitting to the outside. Others sit to the outside because that's the direction they want their horses to go. If you find yourself doing this, focus on sitting in the center of the saddle, with your weight distributed evenly over both seat bones. Remember, your horse's body is supposed to remain nearly straight in the leg-yield. Your seat and upper body therefore also must be straight and aligned.

Shoulder-In

Along with transitions and circles, the shoulder-in completes the triumvirate of classic dressage gymnasticizing exercises. Invented by the French master François Robichon de la Guérinière, the shoulder-in is the best all-around exercise for strengthening the horse's inside hind leg and developing straightness and the carrying power needed in the hindquarter for collected work. Like almost everything else in dressage, the shoulder-in is deceptively simple but can be extremely challenging to do correctly.

In the shoulder-in, the horse's shoulders are brought to the inside of the hindquarters' line of travel. The proper angle is such that his feet move on three "tracks," or lines of travel: inside foreleg on the inner track, outside foreleg and inside hind leg on the middle track, and outside hind leg on the outer track. The horse is bent around the rider's inner leg, but continues to move straight ahead; he is bent away from the direction of travel.

FRONT VIEW OF SHOULDER-IN. Emily and Paul in shoulder-in right. Paul is bent around Emily's inside (right) leg, and he is flexed laterally slightly to the right. From this angle you can see that he is moving on four tracks, with each leg on a separate line of travel. This degree of angle is useful for schooling, but the definition of shoulder-in in the *USEF Rule Book* is "three track," with the outside fore and inside hind on the same track — a slightly shallower angle than in this example.

Shoulder-in positioning is challenging for the horse because to maintain it correctly, he must step actively up and under with his inside hind leg; as a result, that leg has to bend more and bear more weight. He also must engage the muscles of his midsection on the inside and elongate the muscles of his midsection on the outside in order to create the bend. Shoulder-in is, therefore, both a strengthening and a suppling exercise. It is challenging to the rider because horses like to glue their shoulders to the arena wall and leave them there.

Shoulder-in is generally performed at the collected trot. (If your horse is doing working trot but not collected trot, he may not be ready for shoulder-in. Introduce it carefully to help develop the collected trot.) To introduce shoulder-in, first establish an even, balanced circle in a collected trot along the long side of the arena, not far from the first corner. Then simply ride the first step of the circle that leaves the wall and maintain that position as you travel straight down the long side (see illustration).

COMMON FAULTS AND HOW TO FIX THEM

Doesn't the shoulder-in sound easy? In theory, it is, but in practice it can be quite difficult. Horses come up with creative evasions to skirt the difficulty of the exercise, and riders aren't always quick to catch and correct them. Following are the major problems and what to do about them.

NECK-IN Too much inside rein pulls the horse's head and neck to the inside while his shoulders remain on the track. In neck-in, the horse does not bend around the rider's inside leg, and his inside hind leg is not working. With these results, the shoulder-in exercise has no benefit, and the horse is crooked to boot.

Correct this common problem by using your horse's inside eye as your guide, and be careful not to overflex your horse laterally. If you do, you'll find him happily traveling straight ahead instead of bringing his shoulders off the track. Help unglue those shoulders by moving from the rail to the second track (a horse's width from the rail) and interspersing some small (10- to 12-meter) circles with strides of shoulder-in to encourage him to bring his shoulders around.

Shoulder-in, like any gymnastic exercise, is fatiguing to your horse. Don't overschool any movement or exercise. Five or six strides of shoulder-in at a time is plenty. Ride straight ahead and refresh his energy

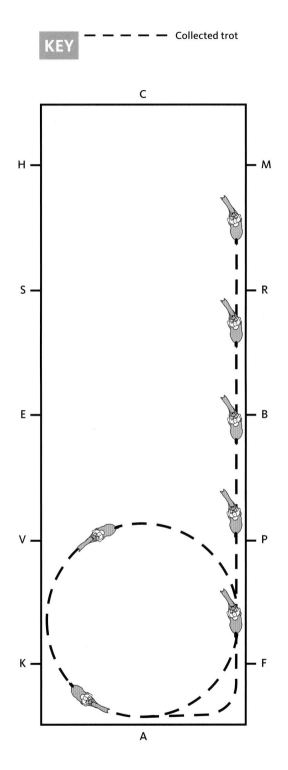

KEY — — — Collected trot

INTRODUCING SHOULDER-IN

NECK-IN. Many riders attempting to ride shoulder-in instead achieve what's termed *neck-in*. Here, only Paul's neck is flexed laterally to the inside. There is no appearance of bend in his body, and his forehand has not moved to the inside, off the rail, as it should.

TOO MUCH ANGLE IN SHOULDER-IN. The opposite of neck-in is too much angle, as Emily demonstrates here. At such an exaggerated angle, the shoulder-in becomes a leg-yield with the haunches to the wall. The engagement and bend are lost, and the movement is far less challenging for the horse.

before returning to the movement. Change direction frequently. Become attuned to his body language. You should know him well enough to be able to tell when he's running out of gas, and whether he needs a short walk break or should quit for the day. That's good horsemanship.

ANGLE TOO STEEP For the purposes of schooling (and occasionally for competition), riders sometimes use a *four-track shoulder-in,* in which the horse's shoulders are brought a shade more to the inside, so he travels on four tracks instead of the classic three. The four-track shoulder-in (and even the three-and-a-half-track) challenges the horse's inside hind leg to a greater degree, and it also shows the angle of the hind leg a little more clearly.

Inexperienced riders sometimes think that if a little more angle is good, then a lot more angle must be better. They ask for nearly a 45-degree-angle shoulder-in, which the horse can't do biomechanically. What's produced instead is a leg-yield with the horse's head facing the inside of the arena; there is no bend, no inside hind leg engagement, no suppling effect, and therefore no benefit.

Aside from having an instructor or knowledgeable helper standing in the ring to tell you whether the angle of your shoulder-in is correct, the best way to check the angle is to ride shoulder-in toward a mirror mounted at one end of the arena. If a mirror isn't available, ask someone to stand at one end of the ring and videotape your horse doing shoulder-in toward (or away from) the camera. Eventually, you'll develop a sense of what the correct angle feels like, but in the beginning you may need visual reinforcement.

IMPULSION AND TEMPO SUFFER The shoulder-in is prone to the same problem as the leg-yield: as the movement grinds on, the horse slows down. In the case of the shoulder-in, the rider focuses on the angle and the bend, not on forward movement and impulsion.

Fix this problem by disciplining yourself to ride with a metronome in your head. Count or sing aloud if it helps.

ANGLE NOT CONSISTENT IN BOTH DIRECTIONS Horses have one stiff side and one hollow side, so shoulder-in is usually easier for the horse to perform in one direction than in the other. Your goal is to supple the stiff side and to strengthen the hollow side. The shoulder-in is one of the best exercises for doing just that. (See box for more on this topic.)

It will take time for your horse to learn to perform this movement symmetrically in both directions. If you've ever done yoga or Pilates or undertaken anything else that heightens your body awareness, you know how tough it is to overcome inherent imbalances, weaknesses, and other quirks. The same is true for your horse. Be patient and practice.

TIP	**Keep the Beat**

Lacking rhythm? Get an inexpensive digital metronome, and clip it to your belt loop or pocket. Set it to coincide with the tempo of your horse's "good" trot, and then strive to maintain the tempo as you ride transitions into and out of shoulder-in.

Shoulder-Fore

Shoulder-fore is a mini version of shoulder-in and is a great exercise to use in straightening your horse. Shoulder-fore is shoulder-in at about half strength. There's a suggestion of bend and a corresponding amount of inside lateral flexion, but the angle is not nearly as steep as in shoulder-in; the horse's shoulders are slightly displaced from the rail.

You can ride shoulder-fore in any gait, including the canter. Shoulder-fore in the canter is closer to straight than many horses' preferred way of going (that is, hindquarters to the inside and shoulders glued to the wall). Use shoulder-fore liberally in your training. Do frequent transitions between shoulder-fore and straight, including on circles and curved lines as well as

SHOULDER-FORE. Shoulder-fore is a mini-shoulder-in, with the horse's forehand positioned slightly to the inside and a slight inside lateral flexion. Paul's neck is flexed laterally more than we'd like to see, and there's slightly too much angle as well, a common mistake.

Haunches-In (Travers)

In haunches-in (travers), the horse brings his hindquarters to the inside of the track, appearing to bend around the rider's inside leg while remaining fairly straight in his head and neck. This is another useful exercise for developing balance and engagement of the inside hind leg.

FRONT VIEW OF HAUNCHES-IN (travers) right. Paul's head and neck are straight, and his haunches are positioned to the inside, bent around Emily's right leg. He is bent in the direction of travel.

REAR VIEW. Haunches-in left as viewed from the rear. Paul's head and neck remain parallel to the track.

EMILY DEMONSTRATES COMMON MISTAKES in riding haunches-in. There is too much angle in the movement. The rider is crooked and leaning to the outside as she uses too much outside (right) leg in an attempt to push the haunches to the inside.

Leg-yield, shoulder-in, and the other dressage movements are gymnastic exercises designed to make horses better athletes and more pleasant mounts. They are not neat-looking tests of what a horse can do, and you shouldn't execute them solely to get good scores in competition.

Instead of thinking, "OK, today I'm going to work on shoulder-in," and riding that movement for the better part of an hour with varying degrees of success, use the training scale to assess the movement's strengths and weaknesses; then think of other exercises that might improve the weaknesses (see page 88 for an overview of the training scale). Sometimes the exercise itself is the best exercise. Don't be frustrated because your shoulder-in isn't perfect. Ride shoulder-in knowing that if you ride it correctly, it will improve over time, as will all other dressage movements you perform.

on straight lines. All of the aids and caveats for shoulder-in apply to shoulder-fore, although loss of impulsion is usually less of a problem because less bend is required. Above all, make sure that you're bringing the shoulders, not just the neck and head, off the rail.

Haunches-In (Travers)

Haunches-in, or *travers* (tra-VAIR), is essentially the opposite of shoulder-in. In haunches-in, the horse brings his haunches to the inside of the wall while his shoulders remain on the track; the horse is bent in the direction of travel. In haunches-in right, for example, you're on the right rein, and your horse's body is bent right.

Many horses seem to relish haunches-in because it's how they'd travel if they had their druthers. The challenge to the rider becomes maintaining sufficient forward energy and keeping the horse nearly straight from shoulder to poll through use of the outside rein.

Haunches-in, like shoulder-in, is generally ridden only at the trot. The canter is susceptible to becoming haunches-in, so don't exacerbate the problem.

Start by establishing a balanced, energetic collected trot around the perimeter of the arena. As you ride into the first corner of a short side, concentrate on maintaining rhythm and energy with your driving aids (see illustration on page 184). As your horse rounds the second corner, keep sitting on your inside seat bone and using your inside leg to maintain the forward movement and the bend, but use your outside leg in a "guarding" fashion to prevent his hindquarters from coming back to the rail. Ride haunches-in for a few strides, then straighten him by relaxing your outside leg as your inside leg becomes more active to maintain the activity of his inside hind leg. Repeat in the opposite direction.

It happens naturally, but as you begin riding these lateral movements you may notice that your upper body changes position as your horse does. Generally, your shoulders should be parallel to his shoulders. That is, when you ride a bending line or a movement like shoulder-in, your inside shoulder should come back and your torso should twist slightly to the inside. Your entire torso should align with your horse's shoulders (your oblique abdominal muscles at work); it's not just a matter of yanking back one shoulder blade.

COMMON FAULTS AND HOW TO FIX THEM

The main fault encountered in riding haunches-in is overflexing the neck laterally to the inside, which "pops" the horse's outside shoulder, compromises his alignment, and inhibits his inside hind leg from engaging. When done correctly, you should feel a fairly strong, steady connection between your inside leg and your outside hand, and your horse's neck should be roughly parallel to the wall.

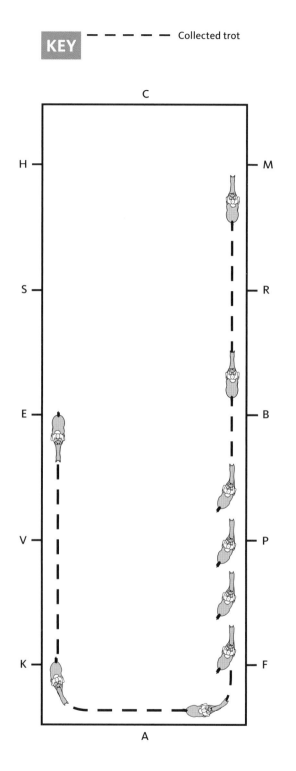

— — — — — Collected trot

C

H — — M

S — — R

E — — B

V — — P

K — — F

A

INTRODUCING HAUNCHES-IN

Turn on the Haunches

In the turn on the haunches — a bona fide dressage movement and a required element in dressage tests, unlike the turn on the forehand — the horse describes with his forehand a small circle, or portion thereof, around his hindquarters. All four legs lift and lower in a regular walk rhythm, but his hind legs — especially the inside hind — remain fairly "on the spot." This is a challenging collecting exercise, and it's a real test of your ability to bring your horse's shoulders around his hindquarters.

It's best to ride a turn on the haunches away from the arena wall to avoid the shoulders-glued-to-the-wall phenomenon. Turn across the width of the arena and ask for the turn as your horse approaches the wall; the barrier will help turn him (see illustration on page 185).

Let's say you're walking on the right rein. Turn right across the arena and proceed straight toward the opposite wall in a medium walk with your horse positioned in shoulder-fore right. A few steps before he reaches the wall, step more firmly into your inside stirrup, look in the direction of the turn, and guide him into the turn by gently opening your inside (right) rein a few inches away from his withers. Your inside leg at the girth provides forward-driving oomph, while your outside leg, slightly behind the girth, "guards" his hindquarters and

> **TIP** **Shoulders Lead**
>
> Always create a lateral movement, or fix a problem, by bringing the shoulders ahead of the haunches. Don't try to maneuver the hindquarters and not the shoulders. And yes, this advice even holds true for haunches-in because the horse's position stays essentially the same in most lateral movements; only his relationship to the wall changes.

helps maintain bend and impulsion. Your inside rein maintains slight lateral flexion inside, while your steady outside rein helps bring his shoulders around yet is elastic enough to allow him to move in the direction of the turn.

It's OK if initially your horse makes a larger circle with his hind legs. The turn on the haunches is demanding, and green horses may not yet have sufficient strength in the inside hind leg to perform this movement. Your goal is to achieve the feeling that he is coming around smoothly with his entire body. Later, you can ask him to stay more "on the spot" by using your outside leg and rein a little more firmly as your inside forward driving aids ask for continued activity.

Be happy with just a few steps at first; then walk straight out of the movement. The turn on the haunches is fairly intense work, and horses can begin to feel cramped when asked to exert so much effort in such a small space. Practice the movement in both directions (pay attention to which side is easier, and think about the reasons this is so), but don't drill it for long stretches or even every day. Gradually work up to completing a half-turn (180 degrees).

COMMON FAULTS AND HOW TO FIX THEM

You will probably encounter one or more glitches as you school turns on the haunches. Following are the most common problems and what to do about them.

TOO MUCH INSIDE REIN You can open the rein gently to guide your horse into the turn, but don't pull him around. If you hang on the inside rein, you'll stop the activity of his haunches and will throw his shoulders to the outside. After the movement has commenced, you need surprisingly little inside rein. The outside rein and leg aids bring the horse around. The inside rein plays a supporting role, ensuring that necessary bit of inside lateral flexion.

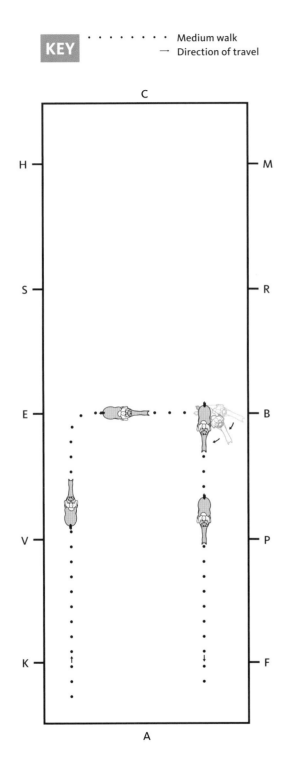

KEY   · · · · · · · · Medium walk
      — Direction of travel

INTRODUCING TURN ON THE HAUNCHES

Turn on the Haunches: Two Views

TO THE RIGHT. Paul in a good turn on the haunches to the right. He is showing good crossing of his front legs and proper lateral flexion to the right. His legs remain active, stepping in the regular four-beat walk rhythm.

TO THE LEFT. Paul in a turn on the haunches to the left, as viewed from the front. Emily is supporting him strongly with her inside (left) leg. Note that in both photo sequences, Emily holds the whip in her outside hand so, if necessary, she can encourage Paul to keep stepping actively with his hind legs.

PLANTING THE HIND LEGS, ESPECIALLY THE INSIDE HIND The hind legs should remain active, stepping up and down in the walk rhythm. Some horses like to walk around the turn with their front legs and simply pivot behind. Make sure that you're not asking for a turn smaller than your horse can handle at this point in his training. Back off a notch and ask for a "working" turn on the haunches, in which the entire turn is bigger than the textbook version. Use your inside leg strongly at the girth to keep that inside hind leg active; if he's being really lazy, carefully give taps with your whip behind your inside leg. Time the taps so the whip touches his side just before or as his inside hind leg is supposed to leave the ground. Experiment with the timing; different timing pushes horses' buttons in different ways and produces different reactions or amplifications thereof.

SPINNING AROUND The opposite of a horse that plants his hind legs is a horse that does an imitation of a Western reining spin. He whips around the turn, taking a few giant strides with his front legs instead of stepping around in a measured fashion. This is another creative attempt to evade the difficulty of the exercise.

Slow the go-getter by doing a few steps of turn on the haunches, then halting for a split second (more of a pause than a full halt). Turn, halt, turn, halt. You can also try alternating between turning and taking a couple of walk steps straight ahead. The idea is to interrupt the turn so the horse can't work up a head of steam. Alternatively, use your outside rein to give a series of half-halts throughout the turn, being sure not to block his movement.

HALTING OR STEPPING BACKWARD Your horse's inside hind leg can step up and down in place, or it can move forward slightly with each step. If your horse stops the turn altogether or if he steps backward, it is a warning sign that he is no longer going readily forward from the leg and into the hand ("in front of your aids") and that you may be blocking his movement by overusing the reins.

The horse must always think forward, even in a movement like this, which covers little actual ground. If you get a halt or a backward step in a turn on the haunches, immediately stop trying to ride the movement and go forward and straight ahead, perhaps even trotting in a big circle to refresh the energy. Reinforce your horse's obedience to your inside forward driving aids by riding leg-yield to reestablish the feeling that he is moving from your inside leg into your supporting, elastic outside rein. Your outside rein should feel solid. If there's nothing there, then you don't have the necessary outside connection to ask your horse to bring his shoulders around in a turn on the haunches.

After you've established order, try the turn again. Ride steps of a turn punctuated by a few walk steps straight ahead so that you and your horse keep thinking forward and he doesn't get claustrophobic. (Don't laugh; horses can become claustrophobic in collecting movements in tight quarters.) Ride a working turn. Ride a few steps forward, then a few steps of leg-yield. When he's nicely into your outside rein, step into your inside stirrup, turn your shoulders in the direction you want to go, open your inside rein a little, and bring him around for a few steps.

Renvers (Haunches-Out)

Renvers (rahn-VAIR) (haunches-out) is the mirror image of haunches-in. The horse moves in the direction of the bend, but this time his hindquarters, not his forehand, are next to the wall.

Renvers is developed using the same principles as in the shoulder-in, but the inside and outside are reversed. Let's say you're trotting on the right rein. Your inside leg is your right leg. When riding renvers, your inside leg becomes your left leg because your horse is bent left. To develop renvers from a collected trot tracking right, sit on your inside (left) seat bone, engage your inside (left) leg at the girth to ask for the bend, and support the movement with your outside (right) rein and leg. Since the left leg is asking for the bend, the horse's shoulders come away from the wall. To straighten, simply revert to the usual right-rein pattern of aiding.

Renvers, yet another excellent suppling and collecting exercise, teaches the horse to move his shoulders while at the same time strengthening the hind leg that's closest to the wall. It also can be used to develop straightness. Renvers to a short diagonal in a medium or extended trot helps to develop impulsion and straightness in the extension.

As in riding haunches-in, when riding renvers make sure that you don't overflex your horse's neck laterally.

FRONT VIEW OF RENVERS (haunches-out) left. Paul's haunches are on the track, and Emily has brought his forehand to the inside. Renvers is the mirror image of haunches-in.

REAR VIEW OF RENVERS RIGHT. Paul appears bent laterally to the outside, with his shoulders to the inside of the track.

CHAPTER 12

TRAINING AND CROSS-TRAINING

*A*s you'll doubtless recite countless times to puzzled friends and family members, dressage is like ballet or gymnastics on horseback. Dancers and gymnasts are superb athletes, and your horse needs to be in good shape, too. Careful training and sufficient variety will keep him interested and challenged mentally and physically.

Particularly as a horse moves up through the levels, dressage demands endurance, strength, and suppleness. To sustain the highest degree of collection for the five to seven minutes of an FEI-level dressage test, for example, an exceptional level of fitness is required.

Dressage training will help get your horse fit, but incorporating other activities will increase his level of conditioning and will refresh his attitude and minimize the boredom that sometimes comes with too much ring work. In this chapter, you'll learn about some common cross-training methods, as well as strategies for coping with conditions (such as cold weather) that can challenge your ability to keep him fit and are tough on the equine athlete's body.

The Training-Session Setup

Properly structuring your dressage-schooling sessions will go a long way toward keeping your horse healthy and will help build his fitness in an appropriately gradual, methodical way.

A schooling session should consist of three phases: warm-up, work, and cooldown. Even if you're under time pressure, resist the temptation to hop on, walk a couple of circles, and then pick up a trot and go to work.

The horseman's adage about walking the first and the last mile of every session applies to dressage, as well. Give your horse a chance to loosen his muscles — especially if he's been standing in a stall — by walking on a loose or long rein for at least five minutes. Continue to warm up by proceeding to a relaxed and forward working trot, rising (his back isn't yet sufficiently warmed up for you to sit), and making circles and changes of direction to loosen the muscles on both sides of his body as well as his neck and topline. Some riders like to warm up their horses in a long and low frame, with the neck stretched out and down, similar to the stretching-circle movement in which the horse "chews the reins out of the hands." This frame helps to loosen the topline, but be certain that your horse is stretching out as well as down; otherwise, he's just schlepping around on his forehand.

Begin to incorporate transitions from trot to canter and back again, also with circles and changes of direction. According to U.S. Olympic dressage team bronze medalist Steffen Peters, the smoothness and balance with which a horse makes (or doesn't make) a transition from trot to canter is a good gauge of his degree of looseness, forward movement, and acceptance of the aids. These transitions also help to warm up the horse's back muscles because he changes the way he uses his body as he segues from the diagonal trot movement to the three-beat canter movement.

After your horse feels sufficiently warmed up (usually about fifteen minutes into the ride — you'll know because he'll feel loose and forward moving, with a "swing" beneath the saddle as his back muscles undulate), it's time to go to work. Make the next fifteen minutes count by methodically choosing gymnastic exercises and transitions within and between gaits to develop your horse's strength, aerobic fitness, and suppleness. (If you need help designing a program, ask a qualified dressage trainer.) Give your horse occasional walk breaks, during which you loosen the reins and leave him alone. Don't continue to nag at him with your legs.

Start the cooldown process by riding your warm-up in reverse. Rise to the trot and allow your horse to stretch out and down through a few 20-meter circles; this will stretch out a topline that's been working hard, particularly if you've been doing any collected work. Then let him walk and relax for a few minutes until his respiration slows and he's cooled down. If he's worked very hard or it's hot, you might want to hop off, loosen the girth, and hand-walk him for a few minutes before you return to the barn. If there's a chill in the air, get off, toss a cooler over him, and walk until he's cool and dry.

Cross-Training for Physical and Mental Fitness

Human athletes know that if they repeat the same form of exercise day after day, they may plateau and even suffer injury. Their fitness and achievement levels will stabilize at a certain point, and they'll have a hard time improving. To get past a plateau, one must usually challenge the body by *cross-training*, or doing different forms of exercise. A competitive swimmer, for example, might incorporate weight training and jogging into his routine.

WARMING UP "LONG AND LOW." Bonnie Olie warms up Sultan's body by riding rising trot in a long-and-low frame. Sultan is stretching over his back and topline into a pleasingly light and elastic rein contact.

Cross-training can help your horse in the same way. As an added benefit, variety eases the boredom and "ring sourness" that some horses develop after too much drilling, a phenomenon shared by many humans who are easily bored with exercise. Although some horses don't mind the routine of ring work — my horse, who's timid and hates to go on a hack, thrives on the predictability — many others relish a change of scenery and activity.

Following are some excellent ways to incorporate cross-training into your dressage schooling routine.

Ground Poles and Cavalletti

Using ground poles and cavalletti is an easy way to spice up your training without leaving the ring. Walking or trotting over poles laid on the ground or raised slightly encourages your horse to move in cadence and rhythm and to use his hind end to thrust himself into the air with each stride, especially at the trot. On the lunge, trotting over ground poles can be a great warm-up exercise.

Ground poles must be heavy enough not to roll easily when struck with a hoof. Jump poles are usually used and are good choices. Start by walking and trotting over a single rail, and work up to four or five rails in succession, spaced appropriately for your horse's size and the length of his walk and trot strides. If you don't know how to space them, ask an experienced trainer for help.

After you and your horse are comfortable walking through a series of poles, try trotting over a single pole, and gradually work up to a series, readjusting the spacing accordingly. Rise to the trot at first, and give your horse a little extra freedom with the reins to lower his head and neck as he trots over. You'll feel his back spring up beneath you at each stride as the poles encourage him to step higher and to push off the ground with extra energy. Resist the temptation to look down at the poles, because doing so will throw him off balance. Gaze straight ahead, and pick a point to focus on if you need to.

A more advanced horse's back is strong enough that the rider can sit the trot during ground-pole work, but

TROTTING GROUND POLES. USDF-certified instructor Susan Hoffman Peacock trots Sandstone's Corvette over ground poles. To clear the poles, he has to take a loftier, springier stride.

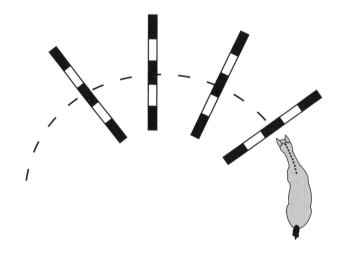

LUNGEING OVER GROUND POLES arranged on a circle is a useful gymnastic exercise. Ask an experienced trainer how to set the poles to suit your horse's trot stride.

continue rising unless you're sure that your horse is fit enough to tolerate your sitting.

Ride over the ground poles in both directions. A knowledgeable trainer can show you how to arrange the poles in a fan shape so that you can negotiate them on a circle for an added challenge.

Cavalletti work can be done under saddle or on the lunge line. It is more advanced than ground-pole work because the poles are raised a foot or so off the ground, thereby requiring the horse to step higher and push off more forcefully with his hindquarters. Cavalletti should be introduced carefully, preferably under the supervision of a knowledgeable trainer, because an inexperienced horse, particularly one that's never jumped, may catch a leg and trip or fall if caught unaware.

Keep ground-pole and cavalletti work brief; it demands extra effort. Done properly and judiciously, it can be a valuable addition to your training routine. (For more on using ground poles and cavalletti, see appendix C.)

TROTTING OVER CAVALLETTI. Using specially made PVC blocks, Susan has raised one end of the ground pole to add an extra challenge to the cavalletti work. Her horse must spring off the ground with more power to clear the higher poles.

Hacks and Trail Rides

Many dressage instructors urge their students to get out of the ring from time to time. If you're lucky enough to have access to horse trails or open space on which riders are allowed, make time for a relaxing hack now and then. It can be a fun and refreshing change of scenery for you and your horse.

Keep hacks and trail rides short (thirty minutes or less) if you're unsure of your horse's behavior or fitness

Trail Safety

Observe these safety rules when you hit the trail.

- Ride with a buddy if possible.
- Tell someone where you're headed and when you expect to return.
- Wear an approved, ASTM/SEI-certified safety helmet.
- Carry a hoof pick and a fully charged cell phone.
- In warm weather, give your horse a generous application of fly spray before you leave.
- Apply sunscreen and if bugs are a problem, insect repellent.
- Use caution if footing is questionable. Deep mud can suck off shoes or cause soft-tissue injuries. Rock-hard ground jars hooves and legs at gaits faster than a walk. Ice and snow can be dangerously slippery. If you're not sure that the footing is safe, stay home rather than risking injury to yourself or your horse.
- Avoid riding on paved roads or at dusk or nighttime. If you must ride at night, wear reflective gear.
- Use common sense if you're riding with others. Stay out of kicking range. Decide the pace as a group; don't canter off unexpectedly, which may cause the other horses to panic and bolt. If a horse acts up, everyone should walk or halt. If a rider is timid and fearful, don't try to coerce him into doing anything.

level, especially if temperatures are high. Don't subject a horse whose usual work routine is to trot in circles for twenty minutes to a two-hour trail ride over hilly terrain. Build up ride times gradually.

As you and your horse become accustomed to hacking, you can add some additional variety by introducing a little extracurricular training. Leg-yield from one side of the trail to the other and back, for instance. Some horses go more forward when they're out of the ring, so you might be able to get a nice trot lengthening on good, even, level ground.

Hill Work

If you've ever walked or jogged up or down a hill, you know that it's considerably more challenging physically than negotiating flat ground. Done in moderation, hill work is an excellent way to condition your horse. It can be a good way to help strengthen weak stifles, but get your veterinarian's approval before you begin.

Footing is paramount when doing hill work because of the risk of slipping or falling on wet, grass-slick, muddy, icy, or uneven ground. Choose your hills and your schooling days wisely.

Forgo mountain climbing. Gentle slopes are best for hill work. Start by riding up and down the hill at a walk. Make a series of loops instead of going straight up and straight down.

As you ride uphill, put a little extra weight in your stirrups to lighten your seat, and incline your upper body slightly forward. Give your horse extra freedom in his head and neck, as he'll reach out and down to help himself balance as he climbs.

Loop your way back down the hill, again at a walk. Keep your horse together underneath you by supporting him with your legs and with an elastic rein contact. Sit with your upper body erect or slightly behind the vertical, and keep your legs at the girth for balance.

Introduce hill work carefully, and gradually increase the number of trips up and down. Your goal is to improve your horse's fitness, not to exhaust him.

GOING UP. Bonnie walks Sultan up a hill. She's lightened her seat and is leaning forward in order to remain in balance and to give her horse ample freedom to use his back and hindquarters.

GOING DOWN. Descending the hill, Bonnie is keeping her weight and upper body well back to help Sultan, who has clearly shifted his weight rearward, to maintain his balance.

After you and your horse are comfortable and confident walking up and down the hill, try trotting up the hill. Rise to the trot to give him freedom to use his back, and strive to maintain a steady and even pace. Don't let him rush up the hill. If he breaks into a canter, quietly bring him back.

Gallops

Some riders like to do interval training by occasionally letting their horses go for a brisk *hand-gallop,* a controlled version of the gait instead of a flat-out race. Although this may not be an exercise appropriate for a horse that tends to bolt, it can be a great way to energize the lazy or dull horse and is also a good conditioning exercise.

Wear a helmet, of course. Your horse could probably benefit from leg protection, as well.

An ideal place for a galloping stretch is a training track. In Europe, where pastureland is scarce in many areas, some outdoor rings are encircled with tracks approximately a quarter-mile long and wide enough to accommodate two or three horses. Such tracks are rarer in the United States, but some facilities have them. Another option is an even stretch of flat land, *only* if you're positive there are no holes. Failing access to those, you can always send your horse strongly forward down the long side of the arena, smoothly bringing him back to a canter before he enters the turn through the short side.

Assume a half-seat position (weight in your stirrups, seat slightly out of the saddle, upper body inclined

HALF-SEAT. The half-seat (or two-point) position, as demonstrated by legendary U.S. jumper rider Joe Fargis on course at the Devon Horse Show in 2005.

slightly forward) when you hand-gallop. The purpose of the exercise is to have fun and perhaps reawaken in your steed the joy of going forward, not to ride uncontrollably fast. Often a brief gallop is all that's needed to put color in everyone's cheeks.

Jumping

In much of Western Europe, horses are schooled over jumps at the same time they receive their basic dressage training. American sport horses tend to have more specialized careers, and many U.S. dressage horses never clear anything higher than a ground pole.

BASIC JUMPING TRAINING can be a fun change of pace for the dressage horse and rider. Play it safe and jump only under an instructor's supervision, as this rider is doing.

If your horse is sound and healthy and you're so inclined, basic training over fences can be a fun way to add variety to your work. Jumping also teaches a horse many skills that are transferable to dressage, specifically the bending of the joints of the hind legs, pushing off, and rounding and using his back.

If you think you and your horse might enjoy jumping, take some lessons from a knowledgeable instructor. Someone who teaches event riders would be ideal because dressage is already part of that regimen. Your local USDF group-member organization should be able to help you find eventing instructors in your area.

Jump Safely

Don't try to learn to jump on your own, and never jump without supervision. Always wear a helmet. Your instructor will tell you whether you need to buy or borrow any special equipment, such as a forward-seat saddle.

Strategies for Suppleness

Fitness and conditioning are just part of what it takes to train a winning dressage horse. Like the ballet dancer and gymnast, your horse must develop comparable suppleness on both sides of his body as well as a general looseness and freedom of movement.

The dressage exercises and movements contribute to this process, as do the proper warm-up and cool-down procedures. But there are other things you can do to keep your horse's muscles comfortably loose. Some can be particularly useful in times of bad weather or when your normal routine is disrupted, such as when you're away at a show.

Stretching Work

The occasional long-and-low session, in which you ride your horse while he stretches out and down, as in the stretching-circle dressage-test movement, can be a nice break from the usual schooling routine, particularly if

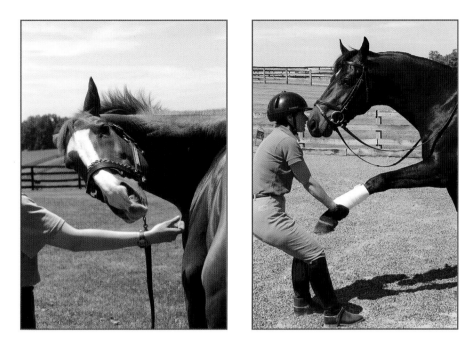

THE CARROT STRETCH *(left)*. Entertainer, a Swedish Warmblood gelding, is only too happy to demonstrate the carrot stretch.

MANUAL STRETCHING *(right)*. Before she mounts up, Bonnie stretches Sultan's forelegs. The exercise provides a little shoulder-limbering and has the added benefit of smoothing any folds of skin that may be beneath the girth.

your horse is doing a lot of collected work. The day after an intense clinic or lesson, or on the first day back to work after a show, a short stretching session may feel good to tired muscles.

Know your horse. Does he feel especially tired today? Perhaps this would be a good day to do a little long-and-low and leave it at that.

This kind of low-intensity work, complete with large circles and changes of gait and direction, is a good idea on extremely cold days, when getting your horse's muscles warm enough to work is a challenge. Most horses are frisky and happy at temperatures below freezing (although their riders may not be), but temperatures in the single digits or teens may require that the schooling routine be adjusted. Again, know your horse and how he usually warms up. If he's feeling a little stiffer than usual, choose stretching movements and transitions over extremes of collection and extension.

Some stretches are done unmounted. "Carrot stretches," in which the handler slowly brings a carrot or other treat around to the horse's side to encourage

him to stretch the muscles of his neck and midsection on the opposite side, are fun for both horse and handler. Be sure to repeat on both sides.

Before I mount up, I lift each of my horse's front legs one at a time, holding it at the fetlock, and gently pull it forward. This exercise stretches his shoulder muscles and also smoothes any skin that's folded beneath the girth.

Hand-Walking and Hand-Grazing

Lacking access to pasture (and also because of fears that they'll hurt themselves if turned out), many top European dressage horses get most of their nonworking out-of-the-stall time on the end of a lead. Grooms hand-walk and hand-graze the equine superstars once or twice a day to give them a chance to stretch their legs and nibble some grass.

At a show, hand-walking and hand-grazing are your only options for similar out-of-stall rest and relaxation, because there's no turnout. Horses are grazing animals designed to eat small amounts frequently and to keep

Hand-walking is a common prescription in equine rehabilitation and is beneficial for lameness and other physical problems. It's also a light-exercise option for those days when you feel too tired or too stressed to ride. Walk out for a good thirty minutes or so. It can sometimes get tedious, but both of you will feel better!

Most horse owners enjoy hand-grazing their animals. Standing quietly with your horse, breathing in his scent and listening to his rhythmic chewing sounds, is relaxing. With our busy lifestyles, many of us rarely have time to do more than dash to the barn, groom, ride, put away, and dash home or to work. When we hand-graze, we spend time just being with our horses, and that's time well spent.

Turnout

Many top veterinarians believe that turnout is the single best thing you can do for your horse's health and well-being. Time spent outdoors just being a horse can do wonders to improve or ward off a host of problems, from vices to health and performance issues. Particularly on days when you can't get to the barn to ride, it's nice to know that your horse won't be cooped up in a stall for twenty-four hours or more.

Critics of turnout cite fears that their valuable animals will injure themselves, especially if they're not accustomed to being turned out. It's true that a horse new to turnout, or one that's been on stall rest for an extended period following lameness or another health problem, could potentially run himself into a frenzy, literally drunk with freedom. If your horse is such a case, talk to your veterinarian before you turn out for the first time. Mild tranquilizers can take the edge off until the novelty of being turned out wears off.

You can't protect your horse from every dumb thing he could potentially do to himself while in the pasture or paddock, but you can take some precautions. First, make sure that the fencing and gate are safe, solid, and

HAND-WALKING is good gentle exercise for you and your horse when you can't or don't want to do a full schooling session. It's also a prescribed element in the rehabilitation of some equine injuries.

moving. Standing in a small box is inherently unnatural and has been shown to have deleterious effects on a horse's physical and mental health and well-being. Muscles stiffen if a horse can't move around (think about the way you feel when you first get up after sitting too long), and bored horses frequently resort to such undesirable habits as chewing and weaving.

secure; horses have a way of getting into altercations with substandard fencing, and the horse rarely emerges the winner. Second, make the footing as safe as you can. There should be no holes, potentially sole-bruising rocks, or sharp objects. Some farm owners seem to regard their pastures as extra storage space and see no problem with parking machinery or depositing unused jumps. All of these things, of course, are potential hazards, which is why it's not a good idea to turn horses out in arenas with jumps. Finally, safeguard the part of your horse most vulnerable to injury — his legs and feet, particularly in front — by turning him out in bell and leg boots. Boots must be clean, well fitted, and properly adjusted or they can cause more damage than they prevent.

Even if there are no Olympics in your horse's future, he works hard and needs the fitness and consideration that any athlete deserves. Keep him fit enough to do the job and he'll be happier and able to work up to his potential, whatever that may be. Incorporate variety and cross-training into his fitness regimen and you'll challenge him in new ways. You may even discover that the new activities deepen your partnership and create a new sense of connection between you and your horse.

R&R. After a productive schooling session, Sultan enjoys being turned out in a nice big paddock to enjoy the lush grass. He's outfitted with bell boots in front and leg boots all around for protection.

PART III

SHOWTIME!

Even if you aren't interested in competing in dressage, understanding the logic behind the levels and the tests will give you fresh insights into the training process and the application of the training scale. A noncompetitive rider should consider showing from time to time because getting a judge's objective opinion is an excellent way to assess your progress. If you're itching to get out there to see how you measure up, then by all means do so, but not before you learn the ins and outs of dressage competition. Read on to learn more.

◄ **WILL AND GRACE:** Kingston, ridden by U.S. competitor Leslie Morse, is a picture of power and beauty in a canter pirouette left at the 2005 FEI Offield Farms Dressage World Cup Final.

CHAPTER 13

LETTERS AND LEVELS

t some point in your dressage studies, you might get bitten by the competitive bug and yearn to test your skills at a show. You also might recognize that competition is an excellent way to get an expert's impartial assessment of where you are in your training, as well as a road map for your continuing education. Even if you have no desire to compete, you might attend a dressage show and discover the unique learning opportunities that come from being a spectator.

Whatever the case, before going to a show, it's helpful to understand how dressage shows are run and what the riders are doing. In this chapter, you'll learn more about the dressage arena, and I'll explain the different levels of competition and what each requires.

Dressage Letters from A to X

In chapter 11, I introduced you to the dimensions and basic proportions of the small (20-meter by 40-meter) and standard (20-meter by 60-meter) dressage arenas. I neglected to discuss the letter markers on the arena perimeter because the letters aren't needed when riding the basic gaits and movements. You may not have access to a regulation-size arena space with letter markers, but if you want to show or simply watch dressage competition, take time to familiarize yourself with the letters and their locations. I will limit this discussion to the standard dressage arena, because it is used at the vast majority of dressage shows.

The letters around the perimeter of the arena are displayed on markers of various styles, customarily black type against a white background. In an outdoor arena, the markers may be attached to metal stakes that are driven into the ground, or they might be freestanding white pylons. Upscale shows tend to use fancier markers, such as tall box planters, with letters painted on the side and attractive flower arrangements on top. In indoor arenas, flat letter markers are usually nailed to the walls at the appropriate locations.

The letters along the center line — D, L, X, I, and G — are not posted in the arena itself because that's where you're riding. However, the letters for the center line are frequently listed on the letter markers for the perimeter. The perimeter letter is large, and the center-line letter is smaller and set beneath, as shown in the photograph below.

There's only one way in and out of a dressage arena at a show, and that's the opening at A. At large shows, volunteers stand a discreet distance away from A and place a section of arena rail across the opening to close it off after the horse enters the arena; they remove it to let the horse exit after the test is completed. At smaller shows, the opening remains throughout.

As you can see from the arena diagram, placement of the letters is precise. Memorize the arena dimensions and the distances between the letters so you can ride accurate figures and tests.

THE LARGE LETTER on this marker indicates the position on the rail; the small letter beneath it indicates the position on the center line.

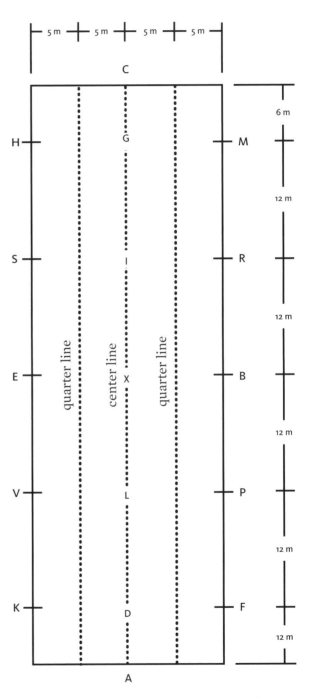

The standard (20-meter by 60-meter) dressage arena, showing placement of letter markers.

Most dressage shows have only one judge per class. A single judge always sits at C (technically, the judge sits behind C, allowing room for a horse to pass between the rail and herself) because this position affords the best view and perspective of the entire arena. At some larger shows and in certain higher-level classes, more than one judge views each class; the head judge always sits at C. In a three-judge panel, the judges are seated at H, C, and B, or at E, C, and M. The largest classes, such as at the Olympic Games and other international competitions, require panels of five judges; the judges sit at C, H, M, E, and B.

A Fat Black Mare Can Hardly Ever Kick

This silly saying is a mnemonic device for remembering the major dressage letters at the endpoints, corners, and midpoints of the arena. Beginning at A and working your way counterclockwise (on the left rein) around the arena, you'll pass F, B, M, C, H, E, and K. There are other mnemonics, but "Fat Black Mare" was the first one I learned, and it stuck. Feel free to substitute another one or to make up your own.

It's easy to remember where X is because it's the center point of the arena. Every test or competition dressage ride begins and ends with a halt and a salute to the judge or ground jury (panel of judges). X is where most such halts and salutes are designated to occur.

The in-between letters (P, R, S, and V around the perimeter of the arena and D, L, I, and G on the center line) aren't associated with any mnemonic devices that I'm aware of, so when the time comes you'll just have

PROPER SALUTE for a female rider. She takes both reins (and the whip if she is carrying one) in her left hand, drops her right arm to her side, and bows her head.

to pound those letters into memory. They are seldom used in the lowest-level tests, so you may not need to learn them for a while.

If you're riding in a small arena, only the perimeter letters A, F, B, M, C, H, E, K and the center-line letters D, X, and G are used, as shown in the diagram below. Note that the letters are spaced differently than in the standard dressage arena.

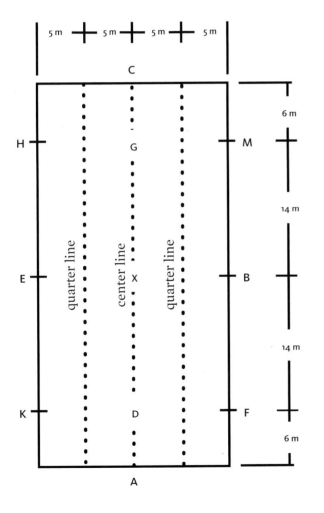

THE SMALL ARENA, measuring 20 meters by 40 meters, is sometimes used at the lowest levels of dressage.

But I Have No Dressage Arena!

In chapter 11, I discussed ways to mark out a standard 20-meter by 60-meter arena space if your ring has the wrong dimensions or if you don't ride in a ring (see page 160). Once you've measured out your space, the hard work is done. All that's left is indicating the letters. If you or your barn can't or won't spring for a set of official letter markers (available from dressage specialty companies and tack catalogs), get creative. Paint the letters on the arena fence. Paint them on traffic cones, buckets weighted with sand, or some other marker that won't tip over or blow away in a stiff breeze and won't hurt your horse if he kicks it or steps on it.

Use the measurements shown in the illustration of the dressage arena on page 203 to position the letters

Alphabet Soup

Every beginning dressage rider asks about the origin of the arena letters. Despite the fact that the origins of classical equitation can be traced back for centuries, the rationale behind the letter assignments and positioning remains unknown. The letters and their positions are universal, however, and are used in dressage competition and training worldwide.

Unfortunately, when said aloud, some of the letters are difficult to distinguish, particularly E, B, V, and P. This can cause confusion in lessons and clinics if the instructor fails to enunciate his directions well or if wind and background noise make it difficult for the rider to hear clearly. At shows, dressage tests (patterns) may be read aloud unless the class rules specify otherwise. More than a few competitors have been penalized for going off course because of a misheard direction, good reason to memorize your test.

correctly. Don't just estimate the letter placements; be precise. Even though you don't count strides in dressage the way you do between jumps, you and your horse will become accustomed to a certain amount of preparation time between movements if you practice dressage tests regularly at home. With the adrenaline and excitement of a show atmosphere, elements in the tests often seem to happen faster than real time; the last thing you need is to get in the ring and discover that your measurements at home were wrong. Imagine how it would feel to realize that the distance between C and the corner letter H is less than you thought and that you don't have enough time to get organized in the corner for the movement that's supposed to begin at H. Being precise now will help you later.

The Levels

Simply put, the *levels* are the dressage-training progression delineated for the purposes of competition. They are a tangible expression of the dressage training scale, or pyramid of training (see page 89). To test the

horses' and riders' mastery of the training progression, gaits, paces, and movements that are considered skill-appropriate for various progressive stages in training are identified and pieced together in pre-choreographed patterns called *dressage tests* or *tests*. Each level is designated by a name. The tests at the various levels are written by the organizations that govern those particular competition levels.

Every country that sanctions organized dressage competition has a national federation that writes and governs its national-level dressage tests and rules. In the United States, the U.S. Equestrian Federation (USEF) is our national federation, and it's responsible for Training through Fourth Level. The USEF Dressage Committee writes these tests and amends and updates them every four years.

Other countries refer to their dressage tests by different names, and the tests have different patterns, but the level divisions and levels of difficulty are usually fairly consistent from country to country.

The USDF, which is primarily an educational organization, not a dressage governing body, saw a need for

Levels in U.S. Dressage

LEVEL	INTENDED FOR	GOVERNED BY/TESTS WRITTEN BY
Introductory	Young and green horses; horses and riders new to dressage	U.S. Dressage Federation
U.S. national (Training Level, First Level, Second Level, Third Level, Fourth Level)	Horses and riders of an intermediate skill level	U.S. Equestrian Federation
International (Prix St. Georges, Intermediate I, Intermediate II, Grand Prix*, plus some special levels for specific horse and rider sizes or age groups: FEI Pony, FEI Young Horse, FEI Junior, FEI Young Rider)	Advanced horses and riders (Prix St. Georges through Grand Prix); ponies; five- and six-year-old horses; children and young adults competing in tests of advanced skill appropriate to their ages and stages of training	International Equestrian Federation (Fédération Equestre Internationale, or FEI)

*Olympic dressage is at the Grand Prix level, the highest level of international dressage competition.

tests that were less difficult than the Training Level, the most elementary USEF level. So the USDF developed Introductory Level as an inviting educational alternative so that novice dressage horses and riders could get their feet wet and familiarize themselves with dressage-show protocol.

If you're thinking even vaguely about showing, first you need to determine which level is most appropriate for you and your horse. Start by reading through the lists of required gaits, paces, and movements for each level in the pages that follow. I'll take you up through Second Level, which corresponds to the most advanced paces and movements discussed in chapters 8 through 11. (Third Level and above are beyond the scope of this book and therefore are not included.) If one of the required elements is not a strong part of your repertoire, it would be best to become proficient in the element before showing or to drop down a level.

Picking the Right Level

In Germany and some other countries, dressage riders are required to start competing at the lowest level and must earn the right to move up; that's not the case in the United States. With the exception of certain championship classes and other classes with age and membership requirements, we are free to enter any class we please. Whether this policy is the American way or the road to mediocrity is a subject of lively debate among dressage enthusiasts.

Because you can put your horse in the ring at any level, whether he's up to the task or not, it's your responsibility to ensure that you're not challenging him past his strength and ability. Asking a horse for too much too soon risks injury and an erosion of confidence, neither of which qualifies as humane training. Therefore, thoroughly understand the requirements of each level, and select the one that both of you can handle most competently and comfortably.

As you read through the descriptions of the levels in this chapter, you might think, "Aha! We practice trot lengthenings, serpentines, and changes of lead through the trot all the time at home. Those elements are required at First Level, so that's what I should show, right?" Actually, wrong.

Riding in a competition environment is not business as usual. In addition to the riding, you'll have to contend with show nerves (yours and perhaps your horse's), unfamiliar surroundings, strange horses, spectators, loudspeakers, odd ride times, and unpredictable weather, among other things. Coping with a show atmosphere can be challenging, which is why virtually all experienced dressage riders and trainers follow the step-down rule: *always* show one level *below* the level you're riding at home. If you're happily schooling First Level movements, therefore, do yourself and your horse a favor by entering Training Level classes. Do you find Training Level work boring? Perhaps. A piece of cake? I hope so. But won't it be nice to have that level of comfort and confidence when you need it most?

Another valuable rule of thumb when selecting a level is the "ten times test." As a self-check before you enter a class, ask yourself this question, "Out of ten attempts to execute a given movement, how many times do I nail it?" Let's say the test you're thinking of entering calls for a canter depart at the letter — that is, when your horse's shoulder is exactly opposite the letter marker. In ten attempts to execute a good canter depart precisely at the letter, how many times do you get it right? If it's eight, nine, or ten, you're probably ready to show that movement. But if it's only five or six, then stay home and continue practicing or drop down to a level at which the canter departs are less challenging.

Unless you know exactly where you and your horse belong, get an expert instructor's opinion. Doing so will boost your confidence, and when show day comes you'll be ready.

The Levels Explained

The lists that follow summarize the key gaits, paces, and movements of the levels covered in this book. Each level consists of two or more tests (patterns), which increase in difficulty somewhat as the test numbers increase. The required elements are listed in the order in which they're introduced in the tests; the later movements present new challenges.

The requirements will keep you busy. The test-writing committees for the various organizations work hard to ensure that the tests and levels reflect the correct training progression, and to encourage riders and trainers to use the training scale in developing their horses.

Introductory Level

The USDF Introductory Level tests aren't offered at all USEF/USDF-recognized (sanctioned) dressage competitions, but they're a staple at dressage schooling shows, which are low-pressure affairs designed to give horses and riders valuable competition and educational experience.

If you or a child you know has ever been involved in the U.S. Pony Clubs (USPC), you may already be familiar with the Introductory Level tests, as they do double-duty as the USPC D-1 and D-2 dressage tests. The Introductory Level tests are referred to as Tests A and B, with Test B being slightly more challenging than Test A.

Introductory Level is walk-trot only; there's no cantering. As such, Introductory Level is often ridden in the small arena because the extra room of the standard arena really isn't needed.

KEY ELEMENTS
- Medium walk
- Free walk
- Working trot, rising
- 20-meter trot circles
- Halt through medium walk

Training Level

Almost every dressage show, whether recognized or unrecognized, offers Training Level classes, which are the lowest of the USEF national levels. The biggest difference between Introductory and Training Level is that all Training Level classes include canter work.

Training Level classes may be held in either the standard or the small arena. The show's *prize list* (booklet of competitor information and entry forms) should mention the size of arena to be used.

KEY ELEMENTS
- Medium walk
- Free walk
- Working trot (either sitting or rising is acceptable, unless otherwise stated)
- 20-meter circles in trot and canter
- Trot-canter and canter-trot transitions between two letters or at the letter
- Halts through the walk are OK
- 20-meter stretching circle at the trot (rider allows the horse to stretch forward and downward, then takes up the reins at the conclusion of the circle)
- One-loop serpentine in trot

First Level

First Level introduces the lengthening of the stride and some basic lateral work in the form of the leg-yield. Serpentines test the horse's balance, bend, and suppleness.

KEY ELEMENTS

- Medium walk
- Free walk
- Working trot
- Trot lengthenings
- Trot work is done sitting unless the test states otherwise
- Halts from the trot (halts executed through the walk are no longer permitted)
- 10-meter half-circles and full circles in trot
- Three-loop serpentine in trot
- 15-meter canter circles
- Trot leg-yield
- Canter lengthenings
- 5-second halt in the middle of the test
- Change of canter lead through the trot (two or three trot strides before picking up the new canter lead)
- One-loop canter serpentine, maintaining the same lead (shallow counter-canter in middle of loop)

Note: If you need a refresher on the terms and movements listed, see the descriptions in chapters 8 through 11 or the glossary. For more details on the tests, see chapter 14.

Second Level

Second Level is a significant step up from First Level because collection is introduced and with it some more-advanced lateral movements. At this level, all trot work is done sitting.

KEY ELEMENTS

- Medium walk
- Free walk
- Collected trot
- Medium trot
- Collected canter
- Medium canter
- Two- and three-loop serpentines in collected trot and canter (canter loops with no change of lead)
- Shoulder-in in trot
- Rein back of three to four steps
- Simple changes of lead (change of canter lead through the walk, with just a couple of walk steps [no trotting!] between canter leads)
- 10-meter circles in canter
- Travers (haunches-in) in trot
- Counter-canter
- Stretching circle in canter (horse is expected to stretch forward while remaining round and balanced)
- Renvers (haunches-out) in trot
- Half-turns on the haunches in the walk
- Three-loop serpentine in collected canter with a simple change of lead at every crossing of the center line

CHAPTER 14

KNOW BEFORE YOU SHOW

This is the red-tape and protocol section — the fine print about showing, if you will. If you want your competitive experience to be smooth and productive, never underestimate the importance of details. Everybody agrees that riding is more fun than scrutinizing rule books and filling out membership forms and entry blanks, but be aware that incorrect

paperwork and failure to comply with rules and eligibility requirement are two of the biggest headaches for competitors. Each year, some hapless rider finds out too late that a membership or paperwork-filing glitch kept her from qualifying for a big championship show — a heartbreak if ever there was one. Don't let it happen to you. A little planning and effort before the show may save you a boatload of hassle and disappointment later.

In this chapter, you will become familiar with the various classifications of dressage competitions and learn the basic format and protocol of each. Then we'll review such important steps as finding shows in your area, the entry process, and helpful strategies for memorizing dressage tests.

Schooling Shows

Schooling shows are not sanctioned or governed by any official national equestrian authority and therefore are unrecognized. Many riders use them to school their horses, gain exposure to a competitive environment, and receive expert feedback on their riding in a low-key atmosphere. Some riders enjoy the low-pressure, casual environment of schooling shows so much that they choose not to participate in other kinds of competition.

Schooling-Show Specifics

Most dressage schooling shows are sponsored by dressage stables and clubs. ABC Farm might host a series of shows on its grounds, for instance. Or the Letter Perfect Dressage Association might organize one or more schooling shows each season to be held at a single facility or at different facilities throughout its entire membership area.

Schooling shows tend to be small, often with just one ring and one judge. Spectators don't flock to these competitions, so the experience can give a nervous rider confidence, without the pressure of a gaggle of railbirds watching.

Some schooling shows lack the formal dress codes of recognized shows. If formal show attire is not required, neat lesson attire is — specifically, collared shirt tucked into conservative breeches, belt, polished boots, gloves, helmet, and clean tack. Some riders treat these competitions as dress rehearsals, however, and no matter what the requirements are turned out in full show regalia. Helmets are almost always required because of insurance regulations. Horses' manes need not be braided, but you are free to do so if you want the practice.

Because many riders use schooling shows as practice sessions for recognized shows, most are run according to the U.S. Equestrian Federation (USEF) Dressage Division rules. The tests used, the way the classes are run, and the judging all adhere to these USEF rules.

To officiate at recognized shows, dressage judges must be licensed by the USEF; to officiate at international competitions, judges must be licensed by the FEI (Fédération Equestre Internationale; International Equestrian Federation). Schooling shows have no such requirements. Instead, most schooling shows employ judges who are "L" (learner judge) graduates — knowledgeable dressage folks who have successfully completed the USDF "L" Education Program for Judge Training. The "L" Education Program is a mandatory prerequisite of the USEF judge-licensing program. "L" graduates demonstrate broad, comprehensive knowledge of equine biomechanics, gaits, lower-level movements and tests, the scoring system, USEF dressage rules, and the training scale.

AT MANY SCHOOLING SHOWS, "neat lesson attire" and an unbraided but clean and tidy horse are the proper turnout. This is Eliza Sydnor riding Graffini Grace in a USDF National Dressage Symposium.

The class offerings at schooling shows tend to be at the lower end of the scale: USDF Introductory Level; USEF Training, First, and Second Levels; and occasionally higher-level classes, sometimes lumped together in one class and offered as "test of choice." Musical freestyle, pas de deux (a choreographed ride with two horses), quadrille (four horses and riders), costume, and other types of classes may be offered in addition to the standard dressage tests.

The relaxed atmosphere of schooling shows makes them fun and unintimidating. Many USDF group-member organizations (GMOs; the approximately 130 dressage and eventing clubs that underpin the USDF structure) sponsor schooling shows and offer year-end awards for points accumulated during their show series. Occasionally, farms that sponsor schooling shows offer similar types of awards. Many competitors take these awards seriously, so don't think schooling shows are all fun and games. Most GMOs host annual banquets and awards presentations. If you don't think such awards are as important as those given by the USDF and other national organizations, you've obviously never spoken with someone who's won one!

Finding Schooling Shows

The easiest and best way to locate dressage schooling shows in your area is to become a member of your local USDF GMO. The USDF Web site maintains listings, contact information, and links to GMOs in its nine regions. Once on the mailing list, you'll receive a newsletter and a calendar of events. (Many GMOs also have their own Web sites featuring this information.)

If you see a listing for a show that sounds interesting, call or e-mail the contact person and ask for a prize list and entry information. This booklet contains everything you need to know to enter: class offerings, entry and other fees, judge's name and credentials, location and directions, entry form, name and mailing address of the

ALL 4 YOUTH: Olympian Lendon Gray (left, pictured with 2005 Umego award winner Katherine Norkus) hosts her own annual competition, Lendon's Youth Dressage Festival. (See page 322.)

TIP Mind the Farrier

Don't plan to show when your horse is almost due for a trim or immediately after a visit from the farrier. If you do the former, your horse may throw a shoe at the show and he may not move quite as well. If you do the latter and your horse has sensitive feet, he may be uncomfortable — even the best farrier can quick (inadvertently drive a nail into the sensitive hoof laminae) a horse.

show secretary (the person who processes the entries, organizes the class rosters, and assigns ride times), size and footing of competition and warm-up arenas, availability of overnight stabling and food concessions, required certificates (virtually all shows require that horses have current negative Coggins tests, which prove that the animals are free from the deadly disease equine infectious anemia; some also require veterinary health certificates), rules about bringing dogs onto the grounds, helmet rules, legal release forms, and anything else you need to know about the competition and the facility.

More and more shows are being posted on the Web; entry forms and prize lists might be just a click away. If you can't find the information online, ask the show manager or secretary whether the necessary forms and information can be e-mailed to you. You'll need to submit your entry form by the date stipulated.

When you receive the prize list and entry information, look for the show's opening date and closing date. The *opening date* is the first day that the secretary will accept entries, and the *closing date* is the entry deadline. Entries received before and after these dates may not be honored. To avoid disappointment, make sure the form reaches the secretary well before the deadline. Some shows are popular and fill up early.

OK, so you've filled out your entry form, double-checked it, and mailed it in with a check to cover the required fees. Now what? Sit back and wait. If you didn't get in, you'll receive a postcard or e-mail from the secretary informing you that you've been wait-listed and that your entry will be accepted if one or more riders scratch. If you don't hear anything, you're probably in. Anywhere from a week before the show to a couple of nights before, you should be able to find out your ride times. That's right — dressage shows schedule each ride to the minute. This is possible because show secretaries know how much time to allot for each test at each level. In the old days, show secretaries mailed

postcards listing riders' times; today, you might receive an e-mail message noting the times or instructing you to visit a Web site for the entire show schedule. Some smaller shows require that riders phone the show secretary to learn their times.

In dressage competition, even at schooling shows, ride times are critical. If you're not there when you're supposed to be, you're eliminated. Ride times are non-negotiable; your times are your times. You may reach the show and discover that you can move up because of scratches or no-shows, but don't plan on it. Generally, the only legitimate reason for a change of ride time, which must be approved by show management, is a conflict — you're scheduled to show two horses in two different rings at the same time, for example.

USEF/USDF-Recognized Shows*

For a show to be sanctioned by the USEF and USDF, competitors, show organizers, judges, and other officials agree to adhere to a strict set of rules and standards set forth by the USEF. As with most sports, the dressage rules have become more complex and detailed over the years, keeping pace with new types of competition, new kinds of tack and equipment, and loopholes of various kinds, such as bit designs that aren't specifically allowed or prohibited in the rules. USEF also tries to keep its rules consistent with those of "big brother" FEI, so rules tend to change when the FEI issues changes.

The rules are meant to ensure a fair and equitable competition environment and to safeguard the horses' welfare. Some rules, such as the rider dress code, are rooted in tradition, but most exist to safeguard the horses and to keep the playing field level.

*Note: This discussion is limited to USEF/USDF-recognized shows because high-level competitions partially or wholly sanctioned and governed by the FEI are beyond the scope of this book.

Memberships and Fees

To enter a USEF/USDF-recognized dressage show, you need to secure several required memberships or pay a series of nonmember fees. These required memberships and fees apply not only to you, but also to your horse, the horse's owner (if someone other than yourself), and the trainer (the person responsible for your horse's care and handling at the show, if someone other than yourself).

The red tape and expense of required memberships and membership numbers make some would-be competitors throw their hands up and stay in the schooling-show ranks, where there's less bureaucracy. But if your aspirations include any sort of nationally administered year-end awards (there are more than you might think; see Awards on page 316) or qualifying for regional or national dressage championships, eventually you will need to deal with these organizations and the associated paperwork.

Some competitors believe that the required memberships are expensive and unnecessary, and for the rank beginner, that may be true. But when you reach a certain point in your dressage education, you will find that certain educational and competitive opportunities are closed to nonmembers and that the nonmember

Rider Requirements for Entering USEF/USDF-Recognized Shows

REQUIREMENTS	OPTION 1	OPTION 2	OPTION 3
Citizenship	U.S.	U.S.	Non-U.S. citizen
USEF membership (riders 18+ years old)	Senior active dressage or eventing discipline membership, *or* platinum membership (all disciplines), *or* life membership	Nonmember fee plus nominal discipline fee per show, *or* base membership fee plus nominal breed/discipline fee per show	USEF membership, *or* payment of USEF nonmember fee, *or* proof* (in English) of membership in good standing with national federation
USEF membership (riders less than 18 years old on December 1)	Junior active membership *or* life membership	Nonmember fee	USEF membership, *or* payment of USEF nonmember fee, *or* proof * (in English) of membership in good standing with national federation
USDF membership (riders less than 21 years old on December 1)	Group membership (membership in a designated USDF GMO [group member organization]) *or* intercollegiate/interscholastic membership (membership in a designated USDF IMO)	Youth participating membership, *or* 5-year participating membership, *or* life membership	USDF nonmember identification number (free)
USDF membership (riders 21+ years old on December 1)	Group membership (membership in a designated USDF GMO; fees vary) *or* intercollegiate/interscholastic membership (membership in a designated USDF IMO)	Participating membership, *or* 5-year participating membership, *or* life membership	USDF nonmember identification number (free)

*A written document from the national federation; IMO = intercollegiate/interscholastic member organization.

Contact USEF and USDF for current membership pricing. Membership requirements for owner, trainer, and coach, as defined by the USEF, are the same as for the rider. (USDF requires membership of owner and rider only, not of trainer and coach.) If a horse has more than one owner, only one must adhere to the USEF membership requirements. If the rider is a minor child, then a parent must also sign the entry form. If a minor-child rider has no trainer, then a parent must sign the entry form as trainer. In either case, the parent is exempt from paying the USEF nonmember fee.

fees you're paying to enter shows and register for educational events cost more than membership does. Fortunately, you don't have to join right away; you can pay nonmember fees as you go and decide later which option makes the most sense for you.

The charts on page 214 and below indicate the memberships (or required nonmember fees, if that option exists) and other prerequisites for entering a national-level (Training through Fourth Level) or FEI-level class at a USEF/USDF-recognized dressage competition. I'm assuming that the classes being entered are not championships, qualifiers, or other special categories and that you do not want your scores to be applied toward any national year-end awards.

Declaration of Rider Status

Ordinary dressage classes at USEF/USDF-recognized shows are categorized as *open* (anyone may enter), *junior/young rider* (open to riders until the end of the calendar year in which they turn age twenty-one), and *adult amateur* (open to adults from the beginning of the calendar year in which they turn age twenty-two and who have declared their amateur status). The USEF definition of *amateur* is lengthy, but briefly put, an

Horse Requirements for Entering USEF/USDF-Recognized Shows *(continued)*

REQUIREMENTS	OPTION 1	OPTION 2	OPTION 3
USEF membership	USEF horse ID number (free); most of the same USDF class exemptions apply (see below)	USEF annual horse recording (registration)	USEF lifetime horse recording (price varies, depending on age at application)
USDF membership	USDF horse ID number (one-time fee; applicable to USDF lifetime registration); not needed for USDF Introductory Level classes, breed-restricted classes, pas de deux, quadrille, and certain other classes	USDF lifetime horse registration; not needed for USDF Introductory Level classes, breed-restricted classes, pas de deux, quadrille, and certain other classes	—
Negative Coggins certificate (proof of negative equine infectious anemia test)	Mandatory for all competitions, either within past 12 months or within calendar year (check prize list for specifics)	—	—
Veterinary health certificate (usually issued within prior 30 days)	Required for some shows (check prize list for specifics)	—	—

amateur is someone who does not receive payment for riding, training, selling, or showing horses, or for teaching lessons. If you're reading this book, you probably don't belong to the professional category (professionals who are adults may enter open classes only), but to be absolutely certain, read the USEF definition carefully. USEF members may request printed copies of the current *USEF Rule Book*. The rule book is also available online at the USEF Web site, where it is updated when necessary.

Required Officials and Personnel

Recognized shows are bigger productions than schooling shows, partly because more officials are required. Following is a list of the folks — some paid, some volunteer — who are integral to the success of any USEF/USDF-recognized dressage competition, and a brief description of their responsibilities.

FEI veterinarian Dr. Fred McCashin *(left)* and professional show manager Klaus Fraessdorf *(right)* confer at a Florida dressage show.

- **Organizer/manager:** Responsible for the entire event; may be a volunteer or a paid professional.
- **Secretary:** Receives and processes entry fees and paperwork, schedules rings and assigns ride times, resolves ride-time conflicts and addresses incomplete or incorrect entries, and submits official results to national associations and publications.
- **Stable manager:** Oversees preparation of permanent stalls, temporary stalls, or both; assigns horse stalls and tack/equipment stalls to competitors; fills competitor preorders for feed and bedding for delivery to show grounds; handles complaints (such as a stallion stabled near strange mares); may arrange for barn security or night-watch services.
- **Announcer:** Informs competitors and spectators of official show time to help ensure competition runs on time; announces current competitor in ring and class results; makes public-address announcements and communicates other important information to competitors and spectators.
- **Technical delegate:** Trained USEF rules expert who ensures that all aspects of the competition adhere to the rules; fields and investigates complaints of violations, and issues rulings and reports as needed; supervises eligibility of competitors and checks entry paperwork.
- **Judge(s):** Evaluates each designated element of each ride according to a 0-to-10 scale of marks; assigns "collective marks" for rider position and effectiveness, and horse's gaits, submission, and impulsion; makes general comments about the test and how it could be improved; assesses point deductions for rule infractions; has authority to excuse an obviously lame horse.
- **Scribe:** Sits next to the judge and records the judge's numeric scores and comments on the test sheet so the judge is free to observe the entire ride; this is a volunteer position.

- **Ring stewards:** Shepherd competitors to keep the show running on time. They are usually armed with clipboards and show schedules and stand in or near the warm-up ring and at each competition ring. They call out the name of who's next to ride (who's "on deck") to allow competitors time to make their way from the warm-up to the competition arena. Ring stewarts are also responsible for checking bits, saddlery, and equipment to ensure they are legal under USEF rules. These are volunteer positions.
- **Runners:** Expedite completed test sheets to the show office for scoring; this is a volunteer position.
- **Scorer:** Armed with an adding machine, the scorer is the official who tallies marks, converts numeric totals to scores (which are expressed as percentages; e.g., 65.845 percent — 100 percent is a perfect score and has not yet been achieved in dressage), and calculates official class placements. The adding-machine tape is stapled to the completed test sheet so competitors can double-check the math.
- **Ring crew:** Prepares the arena footing; assembles and disassembles the competition arenas, judges' stands, and accoutrements; drags and waters the rings to keep the surfaces level and to reduce dust.
- **Veterinarian and farrier:** Must be on the show grounds or on call. If either is needed, inquire at the show office.
- **Emergency medical personnel:** On the grounds and easily identified in case of emergencies. Inquire at the show office.

Large shows have many behind-the-scenes volunteers, including sponsorship and advertising coordinators, show-program editors, awards coordinators, hospitality and decorations people, trade-fair coordinators, concessions coordinators, and even volunteer coordinators to keep track of the volunteers.

Putting on a recognized show is a lot of work. With the exception of a few paid people, most behind-the-scenes types are volunteers who enjoy giving back to the sport. Volunteering at a show can be a tremendous learning opportunity (see chapter 21), and it will certainly help you to appreciate all the work these folks do to produce a show with good footing, decent stabling, quality judging, sensible scheduling, yummy food, and nifty ribbons and prizes.

IT TAKES A VILLAGE to run a dressage show. Here, volunteers look on as show VIPs present ribbons during an awards ceremony.

USEF rules regarding use of drugs and medications in competing horses are stricter than those in some other facets of the horse industry. When you enter a recognized show, you're required to pay a USEF fee per horse, part of which is the USEF drugs and medications fee. The fee funds mandatory random drug testing of horses at shows, as well as ongoing research to detect whatever new cocktails competitors might devise.

Carefully read USEF drug and medications rules, and ask your veterinarian to help you if there's something you don't understand. Also ask your veterinarian whether the supplements and medications you currently give your horse are legal. Some substances are permitted in small amounts, and others are banned outright. Don't assume that a substance is legal simply because it's available without a prescription or because it's top-dressed in the feed and not injected. Some over-the-counter supplements contain forbidden substances and ingredients that may cause your horse to test positive on a drug screen, for instance.

Last, don't assume that your horse won't get tested or that a positive test won't have serious consequences. The winner of the 2004 FEI Dressage World Cup Final was forced to forfeit her title after her horse tested positive for a substance forbidden by the FEI. Doping is not tolerated in dressage; don't risk it.

If you and your veterinarian are unfamiliar with the list of forbidden medications, contact the USEF to obtain a copy of its "Practical Advice Regarding the 2005 Equine Drugs and Medications Rule," which provides current lists of substances both banned and controlled, along with guidelines for competition-legal administration. The list is also available at the USEF Web site.

Rules, Rules, Rules

From the moment you drive or ride onto the grounds of a recognized show, USEF rules are in effect, and there are a lot of them. The rules cover everything from when you must enter the show ring and how long your whip can be to what you can wear and what kinds of tack and equipment are permissible. Carefully read the USEF Dressage Division rules. Also study the USEF general rules, which regulate membership, conduct, drugs and medications, protests, and violations. Both are available at the USEF Web site.

Finding Recognized Shows

There are several ways to find USEF/USDF-recognized dressage competitions in your area. The USEF publishes an annual calendar of competitions and includes notices of changes and cancellations in its monthly member magazine, *Equestrian*. The USDF publishes a monthly calendar in its member magazine, *USDF Connection;* the calendar is also available at the USDF Web site. Both listings are necessarily brief, providing little more than the show name, date, city, state, and contact information. If interested, you'll need to phone or e-mail the contact person and request a prize list.

If you're a member of a USDF GMO, information about recognized area shows may appear in the club's newsletter.

Each year, some USDF regions publish books containing detailed information about most or all recognized shows in their geographic area. Such a book, an *omnibus,* is essentially a compilation of show prize lists, with complete class lists and information for competitors. Shows featured in such a publication agree to use a standardized entry form, which is included in the book. Omnibuses usually include advertising to help offset the costs of assembling and printing the books. Some large GMOs produce their own omnibuses.

You can also check regional USDF Web sites, GMO Web sites, and farm Web sites for show information; most include listings for area shows. Regional equine publications often contain event calendars and advertising; check your local tack shop. You can also ask your instructor and barn buddies. Most people who have been involved in dressage for even a short time know where some shows are because they've gone to watch.

The Tests

So you've decided which level you'd like to show, you and your instructor have agreed on a show for you to enter, and you've obtained the appropriate omnibus or prize list. Now it's time to decide which classes to enter. (The classes are listed according to which test will be judged.) But how do you find out which test you want to ride, and how do you get a copy of the test so that you can learn it before the show? The tests are copyrighted by and available through the USDF and the USEF; they also appear (with permission from the USDF and the USEF) in some dressage publications.

The USDF publishes the Introductory Level, pas de deux, quadrille, and freestyle (First, Second, Third, and Fourth Levels) tests. (The freestyle tests are not patterns but lists of required elements, time allotments, and artistic-impression elements to be judged.) Individual test sheets can be purchased from the USDF. The USDF also publishes the *USDF Directory,* a handy annual guidebook that contains every USDF, USEF, and FEI-level test as well as contact information for officials, membership and awards guidelines and forms, show protocols, arena diagrams, a glossary of terms, and more. (The *Directory* is free to certain membership categories.)

The USEF tests are also available from the USEF. You can order a complete set of Training through Fourth Level tests, or you can get them all in a handy booklet format. In addition to the test pattern, the USEF versions include *directive ideas,* descriptions of what the judge is looking for in each element of the test. These will help you understand how the movement or transition is supposed to be ridden and why. Directive ideas are not included in the USDF versions.

If you learn best visually, the tests are also available in a more visual format that includes renderings of each movement in the pattern, letter by letter. You can find these publications at tack shops and in dressage specialty catalogs. Most contain all of the tests in one level, and the pages are laminated and durable so horse slobber and sweat wipe right off. They're more expensive than the USEF and USDF options, but they can be invaluable memorization tools.

LAST-MINUTE CRAMMING: A competitor studies her dressage test before entering the ring.

Deciphering the Directions

Let's say you want to show at Training Level, and you're eager to begin mastering a test. You start to study it and are confronted with a list of numbered elements, each followed by letters and cryptic instructions. What does it all mean?

The numbered elements indicate the number of marks the judge will award for the various movements. The current (2003) version of Training Level Test 1, for instance, has thirteen required elements. Next to each number is a letter — one of the arena letter markers. Next to the letter is a brief phrase. See below for the list of movements in the test.

2003 Training Level Test 1

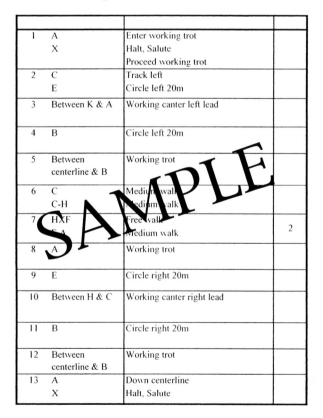

1	A	Enter working trot	
	X	Halt, Salute	
		Proceed working trot	
2	C	Track left	
	E	Circle left 20m	
3	Between K & A	Working canter left lead	
4	B	Circle left 20m	
5	Between centerline & B	Working trot	
6	C	Medium walk	
	C-H	Medium walk	
7	HXF	Free walk	
	F-A	Medium walk	2
8	A	Working trot	
9	E	Circle right 20m	
10	Between H & C	Working canter right lead	
11	B	Circle right 20m	
12	Between centerline & B	Working trot	
13	A	Down centerline	
	X	Halt, Salute	

The directions are interpreted like this:

1. **A — Enter working trot.** Ride into the arena at the letter A in a working trot.

   X — Halt. Salute. Proceed working trot. In the middle of the arena, on the center line (remember that X is one of those unmarked letters), halt your horse and, while at the halt, salute the judge. (See chapter 16 for more on saluting.) After you've finished saluting, take up your reins and proceed straight ahead in working trot toward the judge.

2. **C — Track left.** At C (the letter right by the judge), turn left.

The remainder of the test proceeds in the same fashion. Unless the test indicates that you have some leeway (e.g., "between K and A"), you're expected to execute the direction *at the letter*, that is, when your horse's shoulder is opposite the letter.

As you wend your way through the test pattern, eventually you will find your way back to the center line, facing the judge at C. Somewhere along the center line (often at X, but not always), you'll halt your horse for a final salute to the judge, after which you can sigh with relief, lengthen the reins, pat your horse for a job well done, and leave the arena in a relaxed free walk.

Choose the Best Strategy for You

When deciding which classes to enter, compare the tests within your desired level. The higher the test's number, the more challenging the test. There are four tests available in Training, First, and Second Levels, with Test 1 being the easiest and Test 4 the most difficult.

If your horse is on the verge of progressing to the next level, it might be best for you to enter Training Level Test 4 and First Level Test 1. You are not required to stay within a given level at a show. A few championship and other special classes may require that a horse not have been shown above a certain level to be eligible to compete, but generally, bridging levels is not an issue. Do what is best for your horse.

Many riders showing Second Level and below like to enter two tests per day. Those with jittery nerves or spooky horses often find that the second test goes more smoothly than the first. Having a second chance gives them an opportunity to study the judges' comments and to try to improve.

The tests are fairly short — Training Level tests take four to five minutes, for example — but with the necessary warm-up time before each ride, your horse will probably work for a good hour or more in the space of two tests. Two tests per day is considered enough for most horses. Just one test per day is fine, too, of course. (USEF rules allow for a maximum of three tests per day at Fourth Level and below.) Many upper-level horses do only one test per day because their tests are longer and more demanding.

If you're unsure of your horse's fitness level, enter one test and see how it goes. If he has energy to burn, you can always ask the show secretary whether there's a scratch (a canceled ride) in another suitable class that you might fill. Or if you don't mind losing the entry fee, you can enter two classes and scratch from the second if your horse seems too tired.

As always, your horse's welfare is most important. Don't put him through hellish footing a second time (do complain, though; there are official complaint forms for the purpose) just because you paid the entry fee. If he's wilting in the heat or fried from the excitement, scratch. It's not the Olympics, and you don't have to ride.

Test-Memorization Methods

Some riders find memorizing a test pattern challenging. If you go off course (that is, deviate from the prescribed pattern) in competition, the judge will ring a bell or blow a whistle to alert you, and will inform you of your mistake, at which point you'll have to stop and pick up the test again from the movement in which you erred. You'll be docked two points for the first error of the course. Go off course again in the same test and you'll lose another four points. The third time and you're out, as they say in baseball, although you're generally allowed to finish the test, unless the judge indicates otherwise.

There's a real incentive to ride the test pattern accurately. Here are some common test-memorization strategies. Experiment and find the one that works best for your individual learning style.

DON'T UNDERESTIMATE the degree to which an accurately ridden test can boost your score. USDF-certified instructor Laurie Moore has evidently put it all together, judging from her horse's tricolor neck sash.

RIDING THE PATTERN

Some riders learn best by doing. Riding the test, or parts of the test, at home gives you a feel for how the movements flow into one another and quickly reveals weak areas. To really polish a test, practice.

One caveat: horses learn test patterns, too. Some elements, such as a halt at X or a trot lengthening or extension across the diagonal, are included in many tests. Before long, horses begin to anticipate these movements. You'll be trotting down the center line when your horse begins to apply the brakes as he approaches X, even though you haven't asked for a halt; or you'll turn onto the diagonal and it's full speed ahead.

To prevent or cure test anticipation, practice the elements in places other than where they are called for in the tests. For instance, ride center lines without halting. Ride past X and halt at G instead. Halt on the quarter line instead of on the center line. Practice pieces of the test, but be cautious about the number of times you do a complete run-through. Your horse must learn to wait for your aids. Keep him guessing.

VISUALIZATION

If you ride the test in your mind, you can ride it as many times as you like, with no fear that your horse will master the pattern.

Visualization is used by sport psychologists and athletes to improve performance. The athlete repeatedly visualizes himself executing the event in the desired manner. Our mind-body connection is such that what our minds learn, our bodies learn, as well. Clear and detailed visualization helps produce confidence and muscle memory that kicks in during the actual performance.

You can visualize yourself riding a test in two ways: you can imagine that you are watching a videotape of you and your horse performing the test, or you can visualize the arena from the saddle, as if you are riding your horse. It can take some practice to master these techniques of mental rehearsal. When visualizing, fill in as much detail as possible — the sights in and around the arena, the smell of the horses and the dust, the sounds of the PA system and your horse's hooves, the change in vantage points as you turn this way and that as you negotiate the test.

Make your mental rehearsal even more valuable by incorporating realistic scenarios and seeing yourself ride through them. If you know your horse tends to try to halt prematurely, for example, feel him start to slow down beneath you and then feel yourself use a firm seat and leg to ride forward into an accurate halt at X. If he tends to pick up the wrong canter lead, visualize yourself preparing carefully for the depart, flexing him slightly to the inside and positioning your legs clearly as you insist that he pick up the desired lead. If a bobble wanders into your mental videotape ("Oh, no, he broke into a canter from the trot lengthening!"), don't "stop the tape," but instead visualize yourself quickly and tactfully bringing him back down to a trot and continuing the test.

UNMOUNTED REHEARSAL

"Riding" the test on foot can be a surprisingly effective way to learn the pattern. In an empty arena, or in an equivalent marked-out space in your yard, walk, trot, and canter the test on foot (and ignore the neighbors' curious glances). If you're the type of learner who has difficulty translating written directions to physical actions, this kinesthetic technique may prove useful. Make your practice sessions even more vivid by imagining the feel of your hands on the reins and your horse beneath you as you make your way through the test.

DIAGRAMMING THE TEST

Studying visual diagrams can also help you commit test patterns to memory. Some commercial test booklets contain movement-by-movement patterns, with dotted and dashed lines and other visual representations of the gaits and movements. Some riders who have a hard time remembering letter-by-letter sequences find it easier to memorize the patterns, many of which repeat in mirror-image sequences. They use the letters as markers for beginning and ending movements, not as cues for what comes next.

If you're budget minded, you can draw scale arena models on paper and create your own patterns, perhaps using different-colored pens to indicate the gaits and movements. Or you can buy a portable dry-erase board imprinted with the arena perimeter and letters and draw in the patterns with colored dry-erase pens.

USING A READER

If all else fails, in all USDF and USEF tests except those designated as final or championship classes, you may use a *reader* or a *caller,* a helper who stands beside the ring (usually at B or E, depending on which way the wind is blowing) and reads the test aloud.

A good reader gives the instruction in advance of the movement so you time to prepare for the movement, but not so early that you forget what to do by the time you reach the letter in question. He or she should have a strong voice and enunciate clearly so you can tell "B" and "E" from "P" and "V." Being a reader is not a task for someone unfamiliar with dressage, although an experienced spectator can do a fine job, even if he or she has never ridden.

A reader may call each movement only once. Errors or lateness in reading in no way frees the rider from her responsibility to know the test. Don't assume that you can coast through a test without ever studying the pattern.

If your competition ring is adjacent to another, as often happens at shows, be courteous and have your reader stand on the far side of your ring to minimize confusion. If your reader is a good distance from someone else's reader, you'll be able to hear her better, which can only help you.

SEE THE GUY standing by E? He's a reader, and he's reciting the test movements aloud to the rider in the ring.

CHAPTER 15

SHOW-RING ATTIRE AND TURNOUT

hen you compete, your horse's performance should be the focus of attention. Everything else about his and your appearance should be so tasteful and correct that it recedes into the background and does not distract. As the classic fashion saw advises, one should notice the woman (in this case, the horse), not the dress.

Like the other English equestrian disciplines, dressage is rooted in tradition. Subtle trends come and go, but in dressage the look tends to remain the same. There is no attempt to catch the judge's eye the way one might in a Western-pleasure class, with silver and sequins, for example. Let conservatism and tradition be your guide as you prepare yourself and your horse for show season.

The Well-Dressed Rider

Some schooling shows lack the formal dress codes required by recognized shows. If you'll be competing at a schooling show that doesn't require competition-legal show attire, keep the following points in mind:

- Formal show attire is OK but not required.
- Lesson or clinic attire prevails — specifically, collared shirt (or sweater and turtleneck if it's chilly) tucked into neutral-colored breeches with belt; polished boots; safety helmet (strongly recommended and sometimes required) or hunt cap; gloves (preferably buff or tan; black also acceptable).
- No dangling or flapping jewelry; small stud earrings are OK.
- Get long hair under control, preferably in a neat bun (with a hair net on top to control flyaways, if necessary); secure midlength hair under a hair net. Use hair spray and bobby pins liberally, as needed.
- If you wear makeup, keep it neutral and natural.

If you intend to compete in USEF/USDF-recognized dressage shows, then you must adhere to the dress code provided in the *USEF Rule Book*. See the rule book for details.

For riders competing at Training through Fourth Levels, the dress code is:

- Short riding coat of "conservative color" (e.g., black, navy).
- Stock tie, choker, or tie.
- Breeches or jodhpurs.
- Boots or jodhpur boots.
- Hunt cap, hard-shelled riding hat, derby, top hat, or equestrian safety helmet.
- Conservative-colored gloves are recommended.

The requirements aren't very specific, are they? The rules give riders quite a bit of leeway in terms of attire, but the vast majority of competitors choose to adhere to a fairly rigid standard. The good news is that if your short riding coat happens to be dark green, you don't have to run out to buy a new one just because most dressage competitors wear black. The same is true if your breeches are light gray, if your gloves are black, and if your riding shirt and choker are pale pink. As long as you are neat and clean and well turned out, with well-fitted attire that meets the above rules, the judge won't care what you look like, especially if she's thoroughly captivated by your fine ride.

If you happen to be a member of the armed forces or a police unit, you are permitted to compete in your uniform jacket. If you wear the jacket, you must wear either the accompanying military hat or protective equestrian headgear.

If you're shopping for show attire for the first time or if you're eager to replace those tired hunter-ring/ English-pleasure duds with "real" dressage show clothes, consider investing in the classic dressage-arena look. Here's what you'll need.

Coat

Two types of coats are worn in dressage competition: short coats, which fall to the top of the thigh and are worn through Fourth Level; and shadbellies (short waistcoats in front with two long tails in the rear), which are worn at the FEI levels. Black and midnight blue are the standard colors for both styles of coats. Short coats styled for dressage typically sport four

GOOD TURNOUT. Junior rider Chelsea Allen (here, showing her Morgan gelding Don't Tell Daddy) is an example of a nicely turned out lower-level rider: neatly contained hair, black velvet hunt-cap-style safety helmet with harness, black jacket, white shirt with stock tie, white gloves, white breeches, and black dress boots.

metal front buttons, a figure-hugging silhouette, and a back vent. In contrast, short coats designed for the hunter ring and other English disciplines typically have three buttons in a color that matches the coat fabric, and double-vented backs; they also may be a tad shorter, with a slightly less defined waist.

When you're in the tack shop or browsing an equestrian catalog or Web site, you'll know a coat is intended for dressage by the color of the fabric and the number and material of the buttons. Hunt coats are rarely coal-black, and they almost always have just three non-metallic front buttons.

Various manufacturers offer short dressage coats. Besides fit and size, which vary from maker to maker, the biggest differences among brands are likely to be button and collar color and styling. Collars were traditionally made of coat fabric; today, some collars feature velvet, contrasting piping, and even hints of color. All are fine for the show ring, but remember that you can never go wrong with simple, classic choices.

Most dressage coats are made of wool or wool/nylon blends, which is unfortunate for those of us who show in hot climes or summertime temperatures. They're hot, and black fabric absorbs sunlight and makes them even hotter. Sweat in yours for the better part of one sticky summer weekend, and it'll be ready for dry cleaning, which is how most coats must be cleaned.

A new short dressage coat will set you back several hundred dollars. Imported European frocks are the most costly. Actually, when it comes to dressage, almost everything that's imported from Europe — including the horses — commands top dollar.

UPPER-LEVEL ATTIRE. At the upper levels of dressage, the uniform is the shadbelly coat with attached *vest points* (two sewn-in fabric triangles in canary or another color that suggest the rider is wearing a vest), top hat, and white or light-colored breeches (modeled here by the silver-medal-winning U.S. 2002 World Equestrian Games dressage squad). A short jacket paired with a bowler or hunt cap may also be worn at the FEI levels, but is rarely seen.

TIP | **Shopping**

Catalogs and Web sites that offer riding wear usually include sizing and fit guidelines to help you select the right size and style for you. But if you're new to the sport, nothing beats trying on the merchandise at a reputable tack shop in front of a knowledgeable staffer. Sit in a saddle to see how the clothes look and feel when you're in riding position, and try on various brands to see which sizing and styling best suit you.

Shirt and Neckwear

A white shirt is the old standby, usually with a button front and mandarin collar, in long-sleeved, short-sleeved, or sleeveless styles. Choose from the standard oxford fabric, T-shirt-like jersey knit with comfy stretch, high-tech moisture-wicking materials, and others.

Most show shirts are plain white or subtle white-on-white patterns. A few feature colored or patterned bodies and sleeves with white bibs, so you can be conservative in front of the judge and stylish when you remove your jacket.

Don't worry too much if your horse slobbers on the front of your show shirt; you'll cover it up, anyway, usually with a folded and pinned stock tie. These blousy creations hark back to days in the hunting field, when the narrow length of fabric could be pressed into service as a makeshift sling or bandage in the event of a mishap. Today, they're strictly decorative. Learn to tie your own or take the easy way out and buy a pre-tied stock tie, which fastens around the neck with a hook-and-loop closure and then is attractively arranged and pinned in place with a stock pin. Any sturdy pin or brooch will do. Many riders choose decorative pins as subtle expressions of uniqueness amidst a sea of tradition. If you're loath to wear Grandma's heirloom cameo brooch in the dusty competition arena, your local tack shop will gladly show you its selection of equestrian stock pins.

As long as it's completely covered up by the stock tie, you can wear your favorite T-shirt under your coat, and the judge won't be the wiser. In hot weather, however, plan to have at least one decent white or pale-colored show shirt on hand in case show management waives the coat requirement. If that happens, wear just the shirt, which must have either long or short sleeves (sleeveless shirts are not permitted), and lose the neckwear.

Hat

Protective headgear is permitted at all levels. Time was you never saw a protective helmet in the show ring, but this is slowly changing. If you want to wear a helmet in the show ring, choose a conservative-looking black model or use a dark-colored hat cover.

If you want to wear a show hat instead, you have three options: hunt cap, derby, or top hat. The hunt cap is the most traditional for the lower levels and is the hat of choice for most riders. Some adults look quite stylish in derbies, while others prefer the top hat, which is paired with the shadbelly at the upper levels. If you choose to wear a top hat, be advised that some people may take it as a bit of a brag. If you wear a top hat, some say, you'd better be good!

Breeches

If you want the classic dressage look, you have two color choices: white and cream. The breech fabric is totally up to you, as is the styling. Breeches come in

---

TIP | **Stock Tie**

If you'd rather buck convention, women are permitted to wear a simple white choker; men may wear a white necktie. The stock tie prevails, however. Canadian Grand Prix–level competitor Tom Dvorak has secured his properly tied stock tie with a handsome gold stock pin.

knee-patch, extended-patch (elongated partway up the leg), and full-seat (covering every part of the body that touches the saddle) styles, with the patch and seat overlays made of either leather or faux leather. The bigger the patch or seat overlay, the grippier the breech. This can be helpful if you tend to bounce at the sitting trot, but you may find yourself glued to the saddle and unable to shift your seat around easily when you need to. Experiment to see which style you prefer.

Some kinds of leather tend to stiffen after being laundered and require special care. An increasingly popular leather is deerskin, which comes out of the washing machine as soft as it went in. Hang it to dry and gently stretch it while it's still damp, and you're good to go.

Faux leather (Clarino and similar materials) is the easiest to care for. Some synthetics don't wear as well as the real thing, and they tend to have less grip (an advantage for some, a disadvantage for others). High-end breeches usually use sturdy, long-lasting materials.

Leather and faux leather give a little bit, but they don't stretch nearly as much as the breech fabric itself. Some riders dislike the lack of stretch through the

crotch in a full-seat and opt for a knee-patch or extended-patch style instead. Again, try different brands and designs to see what you like best.

Old-fashioned peg-leg breeches, made in the days before stretch fabric, were flared through the hips and thighs to allow riders ease of movement. Then stretch fabric was introduced, and breeches were skintight for years. Today, all breeches are made with some stretch and are available with plain and pleated fronts. Retro-type breeches with a slight flare through the hips and thighs are also available.

Breeches are pricey. Expect to spend in the low triple digits for a basic knee-patch model. High-end imported full-seat breeches will set you back twice or three times that. If you're going to a multiday show, you'll need a pair for each day you'll be competing.

Young children traditionally wear cuffed jodhpurs and short boots instead of breeches and tall boots. A knowledgeable tack-shop staffer or dressage instructor can tell you what attire is most appropriate for a child.

Boots

The tall black, laceless dress boot is the standard for dressage. Boots sold specifically for dressage are usually made of leather that is thicker than the softer, more crushable leather that hunter/jumper riders favor. The thicker leather helps to steady the leg and is less likely to drop and wrinkle, thereby preserving the desired long, clean look.

In addition to thicker leather, dressage boots have a stiffener up the back shaft to prevent the upper from wrinkling. The stiffener ends about an inch before the heel so the boot can conform to the wearer's ankle. The combination of thick leather and stiffeners makes new dressage boots a challenge to break in. When mine were new, they were so tall that I could barely bend my leg to put my foot in the stirrup, even standing on a mounting block. Broken in, they look and fit fine, but I

TIP | **Coordinate Colors**

Consider your horse when choosing the color of your breeches. If you want to use a light-hued saddle pad, it should match your breeches and your gloves; otherwise, one will look dingy in comparison. If you think your horse would look nicer in a cream-colored saddle pad, then plan to wear cream-colored breeches and gloves; with a white saddle pad, wear white breeches and gloves.

White is always correct and is easier to find, in more styles of breeches, saddle pads, and gloves, than cream.

still can't squat in them, so I make sure my horse's legs are wrapped before I pull them on. Dressage boots also feature a *Spanish top:* the outside of the boot upper curves up over the wearer's knee. This feature gives the illusion of a longer leg and has no functional benefit.

Lacking laces, dress boots can be tricky to pull on and off. Manufacturers offer a variety of solutions to help ease the process. Gussets are inconspicuous elastic inserts set at the top inside portion of the upper. Zippers hidden under the back seams extend down the length of the upper for the quickest on and off. Some manufacturers install gussets and zippers in the factory, or you can have an aftermarket modification made at a tack shop or an equestrian boot specialist service (yes, they exist, but they aren't common). Bad boot modifications won't feel right and won't last, so get a solid referral before you pursue this option.

Gloves, Spurs, and Whips

Buy white or cream gloves to match your chosen color scheme. Don't fall for the argument that black gloves hide unsteady hands. Black gloves aren't a traditional choice in dressage, and judges aren't easily fooled.

Spurs aren't mandatory (except in most FEI tests), and neither are whips. Both, however, are permitted in regular USEF/USDF dressage classes. Whips are forbidden in certain championship and other classes, so read the fine print before you show.

If your horse needs a little motivation, you can don spurs — metal only — with a shank pointed straight out, curved downward, or swan neck. *Rowels* (circular pieces, with or without points, on the ends of the shanks) are currently permitted, but must be free to rotate. Metal spurs with round, hard plastic knobs on the shanks (e.g., the Impuls spur) are also permitted, as are dummy spurs with no shanks. Choose inconspicuous black spur straps of braided nylon or leather, and tuck in long ends so they don't flap distractingly.

If individual class rules permit, you can carry a single whip, no more than 43.3 inches (110 centimeters) in length, including the lash. Most dressage whips are black, with a black or white handle, sometimes adorned with a decorative metal cap. The end of the whip has a short lash and not a "popper" as on a *jumping bat* (a short crop used in jumping) or a riding crop.

The Well-Turned-Out Horse

For your horse to look beautiful in the show ring, he must have tiptop health and good conditioning. Good nutrition puts a shine on the coat that no shampoo or grooming potion can equal. A happy, healthy horse has a sparkle in his eye and a spring in his step. Keeping your horse in good health is your highest priority; grooming tips and turnout pointers are secondary.

Assuming that your horse is healthy and in good shape, how do you prepare him for the show ring? First, he must be squeaky clean. A stem-to-stern bath is a must before the show.

If you'll be stabling at the show, bathe the day you leave home. Don't count on finding a wash stall and warm water at the show grounds. Then groom, spotclean, and cool off with sun-warmed buckets of water during the event.

If your horse has white markings, make sure they're snowy. Nothing does the job quite like Quic Silver shampoo (Exhibitor Labs, Newbury Park, California), which contains bluing. Just don't leave it on too long, or your horse may turn a delicate shade of purple.

Wash, condition, and carefully comb out your horse's tail. To guard against tangles and stains and to add a brilliant shine, spray on or rub in a sheen product. Some spray-on products can also be used on the hair coat, but never apply them to the saddle or girth areas, as they make the hair superslick. Don't spray the mane, either; you'll need a good grip to braid it.

The Dressage Mane

Like hunters, dressage horses are traditionally shown with braided manes and forelocks. For most breeds of horses, the mane is pulled to a length of about six inches, with a *bridle path* (clipped area so the bridle crownpiece lies neatly) just slightly wider than the crownpiece. Dressage horses in the United States are typically braided on the right sides of their necks, so their manes are pulled and trained to lie on the right. In Europe, it's common to see braids on either side of the neck.

Exceptions to the mane-pulling rule are certain breeds of horses that traditionally sport long, flowing manes. Common examples in dressage include the coal-black Friesian (a draft breed) and the Andalusian, the Lusitano, and other Iberian breeds. These horses are usually shown with their manes long and French-braided at the ends, finishing in a plait that cascades down the horse's shoulder. Less frequently seen is the Continental braid — not a braid at all, but a style in which the long mane is sectioned and banded, forming a diamond pattern.

BRAIDING

To braid the traditional pulled mane, the hair is divided into sections, each section is plaited, and then the ends are turned under and secured against the horse's neck. This custom, like the wearing of stock ties, harks back to the hunt field: riders wanted to keep their mounts' manes neat, out of their faces, and burr-free as they galloped through woods. The practice has persisted because braiding shows off the line of a handsomely arched neck. Hunters are typically shown with as many tiny, tightly spaced braids as possible. In contrast, dressage horses' braids tend to be thicker, involving bigger sections of mane.

Braiding styles differ from groom to groom. Some favor the flat hunter braid secured with mane-colored yarn or rubber bands; for a finishing touch, some grooms wrap flat braids with half-inch-wide white tape to further accentuate the horse's neck. Other grooms make a hunter braid but push up the top of the braid to create a little bump, under which they tie off the yarn ends. Still others wrap the plaits around to make little knobs and then secure these *button braids* by sewing them in place with a big needle and sturdy braiding thread.

Whatever braiding style you choose, neatness counts. Practice at home until you can make tight, even braids that lie fairly flat against your horse's neck. Then practice turning them under and tying them off so the finished appearance is neat and uniform.

Arm yourself with a big hair clip to keep the unwanted mane out of the way, fly spray so your horse doesn't jerk at a critical moment, a safe and comfortable step stool, and a big bobby pin or other tool for turning up the plait and pulling the yarn or thread ends through. Many grooms wet the mane slightly to make the hairs stick together. Even better is Quic Braid (Exhibitor Labs), which sprays on like water but makes the hair slightly tacky for easier gripping.

If you don't know how to braid, get an experienced friend to show you how. And get *Grooming to Win* (Howell, 1991), the grooming bible by Susan E. Harris, which contains step-by-step instructions for braiding and all other aspects of grooming for dressage and other disciplines.

If you'll be competing at a multiday show, accept the fact that you may need to rebraid every day. Being braided makes horses itchy after a while, so many welcome being unbraided at the end of the day. There's nothing worse than arriving on the show grounds for an early-morning class to discover that your horse has rubbed out most or all of his braids and you didn't allow time for braiding before your ride.

Braids and Breeds

Braiding is painstaking, time-consuming work, but it shows off the line of a horse's neck like nothing else. For this reason, the custom is still going strong in the show ring, even though braiding for show serves no practical purpose.

REGULAR PULLED MANE. Sultan's mane is pulled to the proper length for braiding and has been trained to lie on the right side of his neck, as is customary in the United States.

HUNTER BRAIDS. The Andalusian stallion Levante D, being shown "in hand" in a sport-horse breeding class, displays a neat set of flat "hunter" braids secured with same-colored yarn.

BUTTON BRAIDS, in which the braids are sewn (yes, really) into tight knobs, are popular in dressage.

THE FRENCH BRAID. Traditionally long-maned breeds, like this Andalusian gelding, Faraon 31, are frequently shown in dressage with their manes French-braided and their forelocks wholly or partly loose.

THE CONTINENTAL BRAID, a long-maned alternative to the French braid. Maruxa, a Lusitano mare, is shown in a sport-horse breeding class with her mane sectioned and banded.

Hunter Braids

1. Section off a 1-inch width of mane and braid down, incorporating a folded piece of yarn that matches the mane. At the bottom, tie off the braid; leave yarn ends dangling.

2. Using the loop end of a braid pull-through, or a large bobby pin, pull the yarn ends through the top of the braid, turning the braid under.

3. Loop the yarn ends around opposite sides of the braid and tie them off with a square knot.

The Dressage Tail

Tails are much simpler than manes to get into show shape. A dressage horse is typically shown with his tail "banged" (trimmed straight across at the bottom) and trimmed or pulled short along the dock. The desired look is streamlined and neat along the length of the dock, then gloriously full to the bottom. Usual tail length is midway between the hocks and the ground.

Hunter ring–like braiding of the tail is permitted but is rarely seen in dressage. False tails (the equine equivalent of cosmetic hair extensions) are allowed but must not contain any metal parts.

To encourage lush, healthy growth, wash and condition your horse's tail regularly, including the dock.

The Banged Tail

A banged tail should be straight across at the bottom when the horse is in motion. He lifts his tail slightly and carries it away from his body when he moves, but you're giving him a trim while he's standing still. What to do? Carefully lift his tail and slide a whip or crop beneath the dock. When you let go, the whip will stay in place and will hold the tail in a similar attitude to the way the horse naturally holds it when he's moving. This enables you to trim more accurately. When you're done trimming, carefully remove the whip or crop. Use caution to avoid startling your horse and getting kicked, and don't try this if he's afraid of the whip.

Dirt and flaky skin can cause itching and tail rubbing. Detangle the tail carefully to avoid breaking hairs. Use silicone-based spray-on products infrequently, as they can dry out the hair and lead to breakage.

Dressage people aren't the tail fanatics that some breed enthusiasts are, with their endless braiding and bagging; although some people wrap tails to protect against rubbing and hair loss, particularly during shipping. But a lush, thick tail does enhance a horse's show-ring turnout, so treat your horse's tail with TLC.

Trimming

In the United States, dressage horses are usually shown with their whiskers trimmed. (The Europeans tend to leave the horse's face au naturel.) Clip a short bridle path while you have the trimmers out, and neaten any protruding fluffy ear hair. Some people clip the insides of the ears completely, but doing so leaves the horse's tender skin defenseless against biting insects. To help protect his eyes, leave the long "guard hairs" around the eyes untrimmed.

Some horses grow tufts of hair at the backs of their fetlocks. Unless you're showing a Friesian or other draft breed, trim them for a clean look. You can "boot up" the entire lower leg by running the clipper up the back of the leg to remove coarse hair growth. These steps may be unnecessary on fine-coated horses.

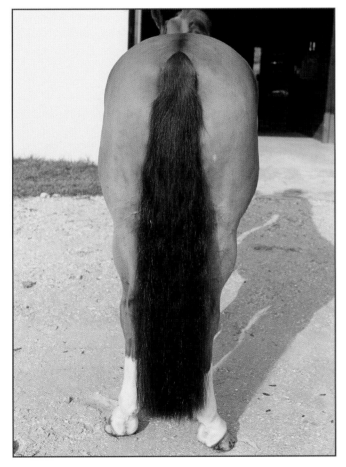

GOOD DRESSAGE TAIL. Emily Gershberg's horse Paul, whose natural tail is exceptionally full and lush, sports the traditional dressage-tail coiffure: clipped or pulled short at the top, then full to the bottom, where it is "banged."

BRIDLE PATH. Here's Levante D again. From this angle, you can clearly see his *bridle path* (the clipped area that allows the bridle crownpiece to lie neatly).

Hooves

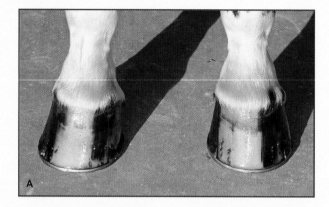

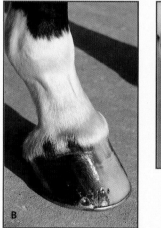

GOOD CARE AND SHOEING are important in all disciplines, but especially in dressage, where free and even movement are goals. These views of a dressage horse's front legs show good trimming and shoeing. His feet are trimmed evenly (A) and match the conformation and angles of his pasterns, which are not quite symmetrical (as is typical of most horses). His toe and heel angles match. (B) His shoe is fitted to the shape of his hoof, and the toe is slightly squared to help him "break over" for freer movement. The heels are "fitted full" (C) to give his heels and frog room for the necessary contraction and expansion — his shock-absorbing mechanism — that occurs with each stride.

Hooves

A healthy, well-trimmed, well-shod hoof is your horse's best accessory. Dressage riders usually don't bother with purely cosmetic hoof products, such as hoof polish, although its use is not forbidden. Most competitors seem to believe that the look of an artificially colored, glossed hoof is not in keeping with the classic, understated appearance expected in dressage.

Tack and Equipment

The USEF rules are quite specific about the types of tack and equipment that may and may not be used in dressage competition. Carefully read the current dressage rules in the *USEF Rule Book*, and get clarification before the show on any points you don't understand. If a question should arise during a competition, ask the technical delegate, the show's on-site rules guru.

Especially prone to changing — even between the annual rules review and changes — is the list of permitted and illegal bits. Illustrations of the permitted bit types are included in the print and online versions of the *USEF Rule Book*. Any updates can be found online. With those caveats out of the way, following is an overview of the major guidelines for tack and equipment use at USEF/USDF-recognized dressage competitions through Second Level. Rules for Third Level and above may differ, particularly regarding bit and bridle styles.

Special Provisions

Riders with physical disabilities may petition the USEF for a dispensation certificate allowing them to compete using special equipment, such as adapted reins and special stirrups. Other rules and exceptions may also apply to riders with disabilities; contact the USEF for more information.

Overview of major guidelines for tack and equipment use at USEF/USDF-recognized dressage competitions through Second Level*

MANDATORY IN THE COMPETITION RING

- English-type saddle with stirrups
- Plain snaffle bridle with regular cavesson, dropped noseband, crossed (figure-eight) noseband, flash noseband, or crescent noseband. Nosebands (except for the metal parts of the crescent and a disk of sheepskin used to cushion the figure eight) must be made of leather or leatherlike material.
- Permitted snaffles:
  - Single- or double-jointed; mullen-mouth (unjointed)
  - D-ring, loose-ring, eggbutt, full-cheek (with or without keepers), hanging or drop cheeks (Baucher), half-cheek (upper or lower)
  - Dr. Bristol
  - Fulmer
  - French-link
  - Snaffle with rotating mouthpiece
- Bits must be smooth and have a solid surface. Mouthpieces may be covered with rubber or leather or made of flexible rubber or synthetic material, as long as it gives the appearance of a permitted mouthpiece.
- Competition number (usually affixed to bridle or pinned to saddle pad)

PERMITTED, BUT NOT REQUIRED, IN WARM-UP AND COMPETITION

- White saddle pad or saddle pad of "conservative color"
- Saddle-pad logos (breed, sponsor, national flag): one on either side, area not to exceed 200 sq cm
- Breastplates
- Cruppers

LEGAL IN DESIGNATED WARM-UP AREAS ONLY

- Leg boots and bandages (without magnets)
- Running martingales
- Earmuffs
- Lunge line and standard lunge whip
- Side reins (OK for use only when lungeing with single line only; horse may be unmounted or mounted)

FORBIDDEN IN THE SHOW RING

- Leg boots (including Easy-Boots) or bandages (leg or tail) (exception: polo-wrap leg bandages are permitted in pas de deux and quadrille classes and also are acceptable in awards ceremonies)

FORBIDDEN AT ALL TIMES
WHILE ON THE SHOW GROUNDS

- Standing martingales, tie-downs
- Bit guards, tongue ties
- Auxiliary reins (side reins, draw reins, sliding side reins, etc.) used while riding. Single direct side reins are permitted only while lungeing.
- Blinkers, hoods, nose covers, seat covers
- Ear covers (unless judge gives special permission to entire class)
- "Extravagant" decorations (e.g., flowers, ribbons, etc.)
- Twisted bits, wire bits, and roller bits
- Bits with extremely thin mouthpieces
- Bridle or bit of a type not specifically permitted (e.g., kimberwickes, pelhams, curbs, Western shank bits, elevator bits, gags, bits with dangling "keys")

Rules-related information is subject to change. Make sure you're up to date by consulting the current USEF Rule Book.

Common Show-Ring Faux Pas

In addition to rule infractions, there are plenty of appearance issues that, despite being legal, can give competitors a subpar turnout. Following are some common problems.

- **Sloppy grooming job.** The horse is not sparkling clean and shiny. The tail is ratty looking or unkempt.
- **Bad braid job.** Braids are loose, sticking up, of unequal size, or fuzzy where the horse has rubbed them.
- **No braid job.** Technically, braiding isn't required, but it's one of those unwritten rules.
- **Dirty tack.** Leather is dull and dingy. Bit rings are encrusted with gunk. Metal items are not polished (see cleaning tip).
- **Poorly fitted or adjusted tack.** Your saddle and girth should fit your horse well. The bit should be the correct size for his mouth, and it and all bridle pieces should be properly adjusted. If you're not sure how everything should fit, ask a reputable trainer.
- **Poorly fitted saddle pad.** The saddle pad should be long and deep enough that a few inches extend in front of the pommel and behind the cantle of the saddle, but no more. If the saddle pad is too short, it looks like a tutu. If it's too long and deep, it looks like a blanket.
- **Unflattering saddle-pad color.** Black can look striking on gray horses but dull on others. If in doubt, choose white. And, by all means, no Black Watch plaid or other patterns, loud colors, or decorations; all can be cause for elimination. Subtle contrasting piping is acceptable.
- **Poor-fitting rider attire.** A baggy coat, too-short boots or coat sleeves, or a sloppy stock tie is distracting to the eye and detracts from the performance.
- **Unpolished boots.** Get a good paste or cream polish and get to work!
- **Sagging spurs.** Spurs too large for your heels usually point down, which reduces their effectiveness and creates the illusion that your heels are up (which they may be, as you vainly attempt to use the spurs).
- **Bad hair day.** Untidy wisps of unsecured hair and free-range ponytails are unacceptable. Don a hair net so you'll look neat wearing your hat or helmet.
- **Rakish hat angle.** The brim should be level. If your hat moves around on your head as you ride, it's too large or doesn't suit your head shape and could come off on a windy day — a potential safety hazard. *Quick fix:* Stuff the inside of the brim with tissue or newspaper. *Permanent fix:* Get a better-fitting hat!
- **Flapping leather.** Bridle-piece ends are not secured in keepers. The end of the flash noseband is too long and is unsecured. The end of a too-long stirrup leather is dangling below the edge of the saddle pad.

Parting Shots

The old saw about getting what you pay for is true when it comes to tack and riding apparel. Sure, sometimes you're paying for a brand name (especially a European one), but more often than not the really inexpensive stuff looks cheap and doesn't fit well.

TIP | **Cleaning**

Effortlessly clean bits and stirrup irons by running them through the dishwasher on the top rack. Use a good all-purpose metal polish to shine up all metal parts: buckles, spurs, saddle nameplates, stirrup irons, saddle rivets and D-rings, bit rings. Never apply metal polish to the bit mouthpiece, as the horse could ingest the chemicals; polish the rings only.

Go to tack shops and compare brands. Study the differences in the look and feel of the leather tack. Check the quality of the stitching, and the fit and finish of all parts. When shopping for apparel, look at the fabric, seams, and workmanship. There are differences.

Fortunately for those of us on a budget, tack shops and catalogs periodically have sales (you also can sometimes find deals at trade shows held in conjunction with competitions), and midpriced lines of tack and apparel are available that look nice and are a good value.

Fit and spit and polish have a lot to do with the overall picture you present. Go to shows and look critically at the horses and riders. Which ones look great? Which ones look sloppy and not well put together? What's different?

Looking terrific won't win you the class, but looking sloppy makes your first impression less than stellar and shows disrespect to the judge. It's a horse show, so rise to the occasion and show how great you and your horse can look!

IN UNIFORM. Servicemembers may compete in uniform. German police officer Klaus Balkenhol canters to team gold aboard Goldstern at the 1996 Olympic Games in Atlanta.

CHAPTER 16

SHOW-DAY POINTERS

*I*n this chapter, I'll walk you through the immediate pre-show routine as well as the dressage-competition experience, so you'll know the protocol and what to expect. If you'll be stabling at a show, you'll want to ship your horse to the show grounds the day before your first class is scheduled. Possible exceptions that might warrant trailering over on show day include a

show close to home, a class later in the day, or both. However, experienced competitors generally trailer over a day in advance, regardless of show location, even though doing so costs them a night's stabling fee. That way, they are able to settle in without pressure and can familiarize their horses with the grounds.

Many competitors like to school lightly the day before a show gets under way, in order to stretch their horses' legs, to show them the sights, and to get a feel for the footing. They know that some horses become anxious when they find themselves in a strange place and need time to get accustomed to the grounds and the stabling.

If the show is a one-day affair that lacks stabling, you'll have no choice but to trailer in and out the day you compete. Fortunately, for participating in such a

show to be feasible, it has to be relatively close to home. And the fact that it's not a multiday event generally means that it's small and low-key.

This chapter outlines the typical routine of a competitor stabling at the show grounds. The routine for a one-day show is pretty much the same once you're at the grounds, minus the extra baggage required when preparing a horse for a sleepover trip. You'll learn pointers on getting ready for your class, warming up, riding your test, and what to do once your test is over.

Show Preparation Schedule

Planning ahead will make your show experience better and less stressful. The following timeline should help keep you focused and organized.

A Week Before

By this point, you've entered the show and probably have your ride times. You have been faithfully practicing your tests and working diligently to prepare your horse to be the best he can be in the show ring. Now it's time to make preliminary preparations for your departure.

● *Get your paperwork in order.* Assemble all necessary forms before you leave: a copy of the entry form, the prize list or omnibus, copies of rider/horse/owner membership and registration certificates, a copy of a current negative Coggins test, directions to the show, a map, contact information for emergency road service if you subscribe to one, hotel reservation and contact information if you'll be lodging away from home, test sheets or booklet, and your checkbook.

● *Inspect the trailer.* Inspect tires and check tire pressure. Check that all lights and signals function properly. If this is the first show of the season and you haven't had your trailer's annual maintenance done in the last twelve months, have it done now.

● *Inspect the truck.* Check tire pressure, oil level, and all signals and lights. Have any needed maintenance done now; believe me, you don't want to break down on the road. Be sure the truck is in perfect working order before you leave.

● *Veterinary check.* If the show requires a current health certificate, get one from your veterinarian.

● *Clothing check.* If you have any doubts about fitting into last year's show boots, breeches, or coat, try them on now so you can go shopping if you need to. While you're at it, do a quick inventory of everything you'll be wearing — from gloves to stock pin — to make sure you have all the required items and will be able to find them when it's time to pack.

Three Days Before

The show is just around the corner. Create a workable preparation schedule for yourself and stick to it, so you don't have to do anything at the last minute.

● *Start packing your truck and trailer.* Load everything you won't need until you arrive: portable racks and hooks, hay (one bale per horse per day), grain and supplements (I premeasure grain into containers and put daily doses of supplements in plastic baggies; if you use the supplement-mixing service SmartPak Equine [Plymouth, MA], simply grab the appropriate number of sealed containers), show tack trunk, show horse clothing, step stool, mounting block, buckets and hardware, muck bucket and pitchfork, screw eyes, stall guard, hammer, screwdriver, braiding kit and yarn or thread, scissors, standing bandages and wraps, bagged shavings (unless you've arranged for them to be delivered to your stall at the show; either way, plan on five or six bags for the initial bedding and an additional bag for every day thereafter), spare halter and lead rope, show saddle pads, and any other gear that you won't need before you get to the show.

● *Tidy up.* Trim your horse's bridle path and whiskers. Trim any excess ear hair so it is even with the edges of his ears. Tidy up any minifeathers on his fetlocks. Pull his mane so that it's an even length and thickness for braiding. Pull or trim the hair along his dock so it lies neatly, and bang his tail.

● *Give tack the once-over.* Make sure all stitching and stress points are secure and safe.

One Day Before

Getting nervous? Keep butterflies at bay by staying busy — there's plenty to do. The day before you leave for the show:

- Pack your own suitcase. Use a checklist to make sure you pack all needed show attire and accessories.
- Polish your boots, clean your tack, and shine metal pieces (not bit mouthpieces) using metal polish.
- Load tack and as much additional equipment as you can.
- Set out shipping boots and wraps.
- Gas up truck.
- Hitch up trailer.
- Get a good night's sleep.

Departure Day

The day you travel to the show is always a busy one. A typical routine might include the following:

- Bathe your horse thoroughly, leaving time for him to dry before you leave.
- Groom and spray your horse with fly repellent as needed. Load grooming supplies onto trailer.
- Load water buckets and any other stall items not already on the trailer.
- Wrap your horse's legs using shipping boots or thickly padded wraps. If you're using shipping boots or wraps that lack protection in the vulnerable coronet-band area, add bell boots in front in case your horse grabs himself with a hind hoof. Put on his shipping halter, head bumper, and any other needed shipping gear.
- Load your horse on the trailer with enough hay to keep him occupied for the duration of the trip.
- Leave your dogs at home. Dogs are banned from many show facilities and can be a nuisance to other competitors.
- Make arrangements for a babysitter. If small children accompany you to a show, be sure to arrange for someone to supervise them while you are riding.
- Hit the road. On trips of four hours or more, stop at least every four hours to offer your horse water and to check his overall condition, his hay supply, and the condition of his shipping boots or leg wraps.

SPICK AND SPAN. Weather permitting, a thorough bath is a pre-show must.

When You Arrive

Because you organized your paperwork in advance, checking in at the show should be a snap. When you pull onto the show grounds, find the secretary's office and tell the clerk that you want to pick up your competitor's packet. The clerk will find your file and check to see that all required signatures, forms, and fees are accounted for. At that point, you'll get your packet, which contains your horse's bridle number or saddle-pad number, the class lists, the show schedule (often in a show program), your official ride times (often printed on a label affixed to your competitor's packet), and possibly a map of the grounds and other information. Your stabling assignment may be in your packet, or you may need to see the stable manager to get your assignment.

After you locate your stall, park your truck and trailer as close to it as possible without blocking the way for others. Before you unload your horse, inspect the stall carefully for foreign objects on the floor and walls that could injure him. If you paid in advance for bedding, make sure that the proper number of bags of shavings has been delivered to the stall; speak with the stable manager if there are any problems with the bedding or the stall condition. If the stall is acceptable, bed it deeply, hang and fill water buckets, and toss a flake of hay in a quiet corner.

Unload your horse, unwrap his legs, and put him in the stall to relax, sip water, nibble hay, and relieve himself while you unload the rest of your gear. If you've paid for an extra stall to use as a tack stall, arrange your gear and feed neatly so you'll be able to find what you need quickly and easily, even during those moments of pre-show pressure. If you have no tack stall, arrange your equipment neatly and unobtrusively so fellow competitors won't trip over it and so it won't get wet if it rains. You may want to keep money and other valuables, such as your saddle when not in use, locked in your truck if you don't have a tack stall and a sturdy padlock. Unfortunately, theft can and does happen.

TIP   **Stall Etiquette**

Never use a stall other than the one assigned to you without permission from the stable manager. Stall assignments reflect a painstaking assembly of requests and the need to separate stallions and mares.

SHOW YOUR ID. While on the grounds of a recognized dressage show, horses must wear their competitor numbers at all times while being exercised or ridden.

Although you may be tired by this point, your day isn't over yet. Most competitors want to get on and school, mostly to show their horses the surroundings. So get changed, put your number on your horse's bridle or saddle pad (it's mandatory), brush off your horse, and get tacked up. Walk him around the grounds, paying particular attention to the warm-up area and the competition rings. School lightly (ride in the competition rings if you can; it's not always allowed) to check out the feel of the footing and the decorations. Resist the temptation to drill; it's too late for that, so just concentrate on loosening up your horse's muscles and making him feel relaxed and confident.

After your ride, cool off your horse. He might welcome a little hand-grazing if you have the opportunity. Clean him up and put him in his stall; then clean your tack and get everything ready for tomorrow's first ride. Be sure to post your contact information (cell and hotel phone numbers) on your stall door so that you can be reached in the event of an emergency.

If you have an early ride (e.g., at 9 a.m. or earlier) or if you're not an early bird, you may want to braid the day before. (If your horse is a notorious braid rubber, however, do it the day of the show.) Braid his mane, wrap his legs if you want, fill his water buckets, give him dinner; then take care of yourself — go check into your hotel and have some dinner.

After dinner, it's back to the show grounds for a night check. Top water buckets if needed, toss in another flake of hay or two, and make sure your horse appears happy and healthy. If the temperatures will dip overnight, put a sheet on your horse. (If in doubt, opt for a cool horse. Don't risk the possibility of a too-warm, sweaty horse stuck in hot, clammy clothing.)

And now, finally, you can go to bed. Before you do, make sure your show clothes are ready to go, double-check the time of your first ride, and set the alarm accordingly.

Show Day

Get to the show grounds and allow plenty of time for your horse to eat his breakfast and for you to braid (or repair braids), groom, get changed, tack up, and warmed up before your first class. Timing is critical if your first class is early in the day. If your ride's not until later, you still need to arrive early to feed your horse, but then you'll have plenty of time to muck his stall, hand-graze him, dawdle, chat, and be a spectator before you have to start getting ready.

Warm-up Strategies

Warm-up time is the biggest variable to consider when planning your show schedule. The optimal amount of time and the warm-up routine varies with each horse. You already know how long you have to ride at home before you're in the zone. Use that as a guideline, but realize that horses can and do act differently in a show environment. Some get wound up and need time on the lunge to settle down before working. Others get

THE WARM-UP RING at most dressage shows is a busy and crowded place, with lots of "railbirds" and coaches. The attire of these riders suggests that one is getting ready to compete while the others are schooling.

increasingly rattled the longer they're in the warm-up. Still others tire easily from the extra stress. And almost all horses go differently in unexpected heat or cold.

When you plan a time frame for your warm-up, allow some extra time before and after the warm-up session. Before the warm-up, you have to get from the stabling area to the warm-up area, and at some shows that can be a lengthy hike, even on horseback. After the warm-up, you have to make your way to the competition ring, which may be some distance away. You also may need a few extra minutes to put your coat on, wipe your boots, and remove any leg wraps or bandages that you applied for the warm-up.

Shortly before it's time for you to start getting dressed and tacked up, find out from the steward for your competition ring whether the ring is running on schedule. Usually it is, but occasionally a ring will slip a little behind schedule; adjust your time frame accordingly. Occasionally, because of scratches (riders who have withdrawn in advance), the ring may be ahead of schedule. Understand, however, that you are not obligated to ride before your assigned time. If the ring is running ahead of schedule, many riders like to go early, particularly when it's their last class of the show and they're eager to leave for home.

With the ring schedule in mind, venture over to the warm-up arena at the time you've decided. Check in with the steward so she knows you're there and won't have to look for you when it's almost your turn to show. Then go about your business.

> ### TIP Lungeing Legalities
>
> Lungeing is permitted in designated areas only; ask at the show office, and also find out whether there are any time restrictions.

WARM-UP RING ETIQUETTE

Warm-up arenas are busy and can be chaotic; the hubbub can be unsettling to the novice competitor. Know these points of basic warm-up ring etiquette, and you'll be better able to focus on your horse.

● Keep right when riding past oncoming horses (pass left shoulder to left shoulder).

● Faster gaits have the right of way. If you're walking, stay off the rail.

● If you want to proceed across the diagonal to do a trot lengthening, for example, wait until the coast is relatively clear and call "Diagonal!" to warn other riders. (Do this sparingly as a courtesy.)

● Be hypervigilant about other horses and riders around you. People get nervous and don't always do what you might expect.

● Don't get too close to other horses. If your horse is a kicker, attach a red ribbon — the universal symbol of a kicker — to his tail. Remember to remove the ribbon before you enter the show ring.

● If you must stop to adjust your girth or for some

> ### Keeping Whites White
>
> The bane of every dressage competitor is trying to keep white shirts and breeches clean between the time you get dressed and the time you compete. This can be especially challenging if you're showing solo and have no helper to tack up and hold your salivating horse for you. The solution? Wear a protective garment that covers the critical neck-to-knees area. Some riders sport long bib-style denim or twill aprons. Others step into coveralls. I have a cover-up that in another environment might be considered a lightweight knee-length bathrobe. Whatever you choose, put it on the moment you slip into those pristine whites, and don't take it off until it's time to get on.

other reason, do so away from the in-gate and the rail. Don't halt along the rail to chat with friends or have a discussion with your coach.

- If another horse becomes unruly, give him room.
- If your horse becomes fractious and you can't get him under control safely and quickly, dismount and leave the ring. It's better to scratch a ride and lose the entry fee than to possibly endanger other competitors and their horses. If you decide to scratch, tell the ring steward on your way out.
- Every competitor has the right to warm up. Don't feel you have to yield to another rider just because he's showing at the upper levels. Some riders seem to use the warm-up as a place to play "chicken" or to try to psych out the other competitors. Follow the rules of ring etiquette and you'll be fine.
- Don't yell across the ring. The warm-up is noisy enough with horses neighing and instructors trying to coach students over the din.
- Wear a sturdy, water-resistant watch that is set in sync with the official show time, and check in again with the steward about five minutes before your scheduled ride time. She'll tell you which horse you follow and when it's appropriate for you to head to the competition ring.

On Deck

On deck means that you're the next to ride. So you've warmed up, donned your jacket, wiped the dust off your boots, removed any leg boots or wraps your horse is wearing, and you're ready to roll. You walk over to the competition ring, and the rider ahead of you is in the ring, partway through her test. You walk quietly near the competition area, or you let your horse stand and catch his breath for a moment (but don't let him zone out on you).

After the rider in the ring has made her final halt and salute, you may proceed around the perimeter of the competition ring. If there isn't enough room to do so outside the ring, competitors may be allowed to circle inside the ring before the start of their tests. Usually, there is sufficient space to allow you to circle the entire ring, passing between the rail and the judge's booth. If you can, ride your horse in front of the judge's booth in both directions, as the booth is generally the most spook-provoking object in or near the ring. The judge and her scribe will be busy wrapping up the comments on the previous test, so don't be surprised if they don't acknowledge you. If the judge makes eye contact, simply state your competition number and say "Good morning" or "Good afternoon."

For Whom the Bell Tolls

You won't know how many minutes you'll have before the judge finishes the previous test and calls for you to begin, so use your time wisely. Don't show off for the judge; instead, ride a few selected movements that will put your horse in the best shape possible to enter the ring. A lazy horse, for example, might benefit from a lively medium trot and a few crisp transitions. A tense horse might relax with a few circles and a little lateral suppling work.

When it's time for you to begin, the judge will ring a bell or blow a whistle — the signal for you to enter the arena. The clock starts the moment the bell rings. You have 45 seconds to enter the arena at A or face elimination. But don't panic: 45 seconds is ample time to trot to A from wherever you are, make a circle, and enter the ring.

As you make the turn to enter at A, ride in front of the letter marker. If you don't, the turn will be so wide that you'll have trouble making a straight entry.

With your head up, gaze straight ahead and trot purposefully toward the judge. Use your peripheral vision to assess your proximity to X, and aim to make a neat, smooth, straight halt with your horse's shoulders

SIGNS AND SIGNALS. Multiple arenas at shows are numbered. If rings are close together, judges will use different signals for clarity and to avoid confusion. The sign on this ring instructs riders to listen for a whistle.

directly at X. While your horse is halted, take the reins (and the whip, if you're carrying one) in one hand. A woman salutes the judge by dropping her free arm to her side, inclining her head in a slight bow, and then taking up the reins in both hands before proceeding forward. A man either doffs his hat and drops his arm to the side or simply drops his arm to the side, in the fashion of the female rider, inclines his head, and then returns the hat to his head before gathering up the reins. Only military riders competing in uniform may execute a military-style salute.

Make Every Point Count

Riding a dressage test in competition is more difficult than schooling at home, not just because of the excitement and activity, but also because you get no second chances or extra time to prepare for any given element. A test is a precise pattern of gaits, transitions, and movements. Quality is obviously important, but so is accuracy. A surprising number of points can be lost due

SALUTING. A gentleman rider (here, Denmark native Lars Petersen aboard Dansko's Success) salutes by removing his hat and dropping his right arm to his side, then replacing his hat and taking up the reins before moving off.

to incorrect geometry (e.g., circles too large or not round, center lines or quarter lines not ridden accurately), transitions not executed at the letter, and failure to prepare for upcoming movements. That's why successful dressage competitors are so fastidious about making circles perfectly round, perfecting the timing of their transitions, and riding deeply into corners to prepare for what comes next. Given two competitors of equal quality, the more accurate test will win.

One of the most difficult things to learn is to let go of a less-than-perfect movement or transition and continue on. It's easy to let a mistake rattle you. You lose focus and confidence, and it's all downhill from there. Experienced competitors understand that a blown movement means one poor mark, but that they have an opportunity to make up for that one low score (3 or 4) by bankrolling a string of better ones (6s and 7s).

Savvy competitors also make the most of *coefficient movements,* test elements that are considered especially important and therefore count for double the judge's mark. You'll know which are coefficient movements because the number 2 appears in the coefficient box on the test sheet. A score of 7 on a trot lengthening, for instance, translates to 14 points if that lengthening is a coefficient movement. Getting a good mark on a coefficient movement is a great boost to your total score, but the reverse is true if your mark on a coefficient movement is less than stellar.

With these strategies in mind, ride the best test you can, and leave a good impression by making a good final halt. Salute the judge the same way you did at the beginning of the test, loosen the reins, walk forward a few steps, and then turn and head for A. Give your horse a pat for a job well done.

After the Test

If you have another test later the same day, the time interval dictates your plan of attack. You may find yourself with only 20 minutes between tests, in which case you'll stay mounted, walk your horse back to the warm-up, relax for a minute, and then gather him up in preparation for the next test. If you have a couple of hours or more between tests, you're better off going back to the stabling area, untacking, cooling down your horse, and

DEBRIEFING WITH AN INSTRUCTOR after a test is an important part of the learning process. Here, German Olympic gold medalist and current U.S. dressage team coach Klaus Balkenhol *(left)* is evidently pleased with the performance of U.S. rider George Williams.

letting him relax in his stall or hand-grazing him before you begin the entire getting-ready process again.

Of course, you'll be anxious to know how you fared in the class. After you've seen to your horse, make your way to the show secretary's office. Somewhere in the vicinity will be large boards on which are posted the class lists, with spaces for scores and class placements. Periodically, someone will emerge from the secretary's office, pen in hand, and write in a batch of scores for classes currently under way. After the last score is in, the class will be placed, and competitors may then pick up their scored test sheets (and ribbons and prizes, if they're lucky).

DECIPHERING THE TEST SHEET

Especially if you have another ride coming up, get your test sheet as soon as possible, and carefully review the marks and the judge's comments. Comments such as "needs more bend" or "circle not round" indicate areas in which you can strive to improve, and possibly get better scores next time.

The judge awards a mark for each numbered item on the test sheet, plus collective marks, which are awarded after the test as overall scores for gaits, impulsion, submission, the rider's position and seat, and effectiveness and use of the aids. The scale of marks ranges from 0 to 10, with 0 being "not performed" and 10 being "excellent." In the past, marks tended to cluster in the midrange: scores of 5 and 6 were most common, with an occasional sprinkling of 4s and 7s. Today, judges feel free to use the entire range of marks to reward excellence and to penalize poor performance. Doing so helps competitors better understand which aspects of their tests were exceptional and which were substandard.

A majority of marks of 6 ("satisfactory") or 7 ("fairly good") indicate that you and your horse are solidly on the right track with your training and are competing at an appropriate level. The still fairly uncommon marks of 8 ("good") and 9 ("very good") are cause for celebration. A 10 ("excellent") — not quite unattainable but nearly — is a rare gem indeed. Each dressage test has a maximum number of possible attainable points, the total that would be earned if every movement and collective mark received a 10. The official scorer divides your total number of points into this number to calculate your overall score, which is expressed as a percentage. So a test that earns mostly 6s and 7s will convert to a percentage in the mid-60s.

HOW DID WE DO? Competitors, coaches, spectators, and supporters are usually crowded around the board where score sheets and final placings are posted.

After you've scrutinized the numbers, pay particular attention to the general comments at the bottom of the test sheet. Many judges strive to give competitors encouragement and practical advice that can prove useful in their training back home.

Keep in mind, however, that a judge can only assess what he sees in the ring, and that he is comparing you and your horse against a standard of perfection for that test and that level. He doesn't know that normally your trot-canter transitions are flawless, or that the spook at E was a freak occurrence, or that your horse just wasn't his usual forward self today. Show your test sheet to your instructor and get her take on the comments and marks.

Ultimately (although this can be hard to remember in the heat of competition), what's most important is that you felt you and your horse gave your best effort and that you have made progress. If you know that today's test was better than yesterday's, or the last show's, and especially if your instructor feels the same way, then you have something to be proud of. Some improvements are modest, and that's OK. My own horse finds a certain movement very difficult, and compared to other, more talented horses, he doesn't execute it particularly well. When I started getting 5s and 6s instead of 4s and 5s, I was pleased, even though 5s and 6s are modest marks. The consistency with which I was receiving the higher marks told me that judges were seeing definite improvement and reinforced my belief that I was on the right track with my training.

Who's Judging This Thing, Anyway?

Schooling shows are usually judged by graduates of USDF's "L" Education Program for Judge Training, which is a mandatory prerequisite for participation in the USEF judge-licensing program; "L" stands for learner.

Only USEF- and FEI-licensed judges, and certain foreign judges, may officiate at recognized competitions.

THREE U.S. DRESSAGE VIPS. From left, international-level judges Jessica Ransehousen (also an Olympic veteran and a longtime U.S. dressage team *chef d'équipe* [a team leader of sorts, who helps to keep things running smoothly for the competitors and has various official duties]), Janet Brown Foy, and Natalie Lamping.

In ascending order of seniority, USEF judges are classified as "r" (recorded), "R" (registered), and "S" (senior). "Little r" judges may judge only Introductory, Training, First, and Second Level tests. "Big R" judges may officiate through Fourth Level. "S" judges may officiate at all USDF, USEF, and FEI levels.

Some judges go on to earn FEI licensing, which entitles them to officiate at FEI-recognized competitions.

Licensed judges receive extensive training in many categories, from the scale of marks and the rules to the proper execution of movements and equine biomechanics. Most are experienced competitors and trainers, with a thorough understanding of the training scale and a deep love for horses. In other words, they've been in your shoes.

As a competitor, it's important to remember that the judge is there to critique your performance, not to give you a riding lesson. Although ideally the judge's comments will be constructive and instructive, they're merely snapshots of what the judge saw in the five minutes that you were in the ring. Show under different judges, and you'll get different sorts of marks and comments. Even though judges are trained to evaluate your ride against a standard of perfection, it's impossible to be completely objective and some measure of opinion is inevitably part of the process. Therefore, the clearest sign that an area is good or needs work occurs when several judges award similar marks or make similar comments. If three judges say "needs to go more forward," then it's a safe bet that this aspect of your training needs attention.

Most judges are not out to get you. Although their job is to be critical, most welcome an opportunity to award a high mark for a well-executed movement. They enjoy watching a pleasing performance as much as the rest of us. An accurate, well-ridden test by a nicely matched and turned-out horse and rider — regardless of the horse's breed and the rider's age — is usually generously rewarded. Judges know that they influence dressage-training trends by virtue of what they reward and penalize, and most take this responsibility seriously. Most feel that they play an important role in keeping the sport of dressage moving forward and on the correct path.

Ten Show-Ring Don'ts

Commit any of these violations and the officiating judge has the authority to eliminate you from competition.

1. Late entry into the arena
2. Three errors of the course (riding off course)
3. Unauthorized assistance (any help other than the reading of the test by a caller)
4. Failure to wear your competitor number
5. All four feet of the horse leaving the arena
6. Cruelty to the horse
7. Marked lameness
8. Resistance (e.g., refusal to go forward) that lasts longer than 20 seconds
9. Use of illegal equipment
10. Horse's tongue is tied down to prevent it from protruding from the mouth, often a sign of resistance

PART IV

PHYSICAL EDUCATION

Time in the saddle isn't the only way to enhance your understanding of dressage and to improve your dressage skills. You and your horse are athletes. Boosting your strength, endurance, and flexibility can have big payoffs in improved riding. In chapter 17, I'll explain how to improve your all-around fitness. As your interest in dressage deepens, you may want to learn more about the sport horse: his history, conformation, movement, and breeding. I'll cover the basics in chapter 18. Last, no matter what kind of horse you have, you want to keep him sound, happy, and comfortable in his work. In chapter 19, I'll review common challenges and how to resolve them.

◀ New Jersey–based trainer and competitor Heather Mason rides Nimbus in an FEI-level test.

CHAPTER 17

THE FIT DRESSAGE RIDER

The surest way to upset a rider is to say, "But doesn't the horse do all the work while you just sit there?" The paradox of dressage is that the better the rider, the less she appears to be doing. And the best performances do give the impression that the horse is doing all the work, when in fact it's an ongoing partnership between horse and rider.

Dressage riders do a lot. They must have the strength, endurance, and flexibility needed to engage certain muscles, relax others, and bend and straighten their joints in order to absorb and influence the horse's movement. A horse is a huge animal, weighing half a ton or more. His gaits and movements — walk, trot, canter, flying change, pirouette, piaffe, passage — are dynamic, and he performs them with a rider on his back. As he moves, his motion travels through the rider's body the way waves travel over the ocean. A good rider appears quiet because she is matching her movements to those of the horse. If she were truly sitting still and doing no work, she would flop and bounce around like a rag doll: exactly what beginner riders resemble.

How Fit Do You Need to Be?

To ride dressage well, you may need to be fitter than you are now. The good news is that you don't need to be as fit as a professional athlete to get started. (Thank goodness, right?)

Riders have a bad habit of not practicing what we preach. We whine about how we're given short shrift in the coverage of the Olympic Games and how we receive even less coverage in the general sports media. At the same time, we wear attire that elicits snickers from sports journalists, and some top dressage riders are photographed smoking, which makes us look less than serious about our claims of athleticism. Even some elite riders may not be as fit as athletes in some other sports. Still, dressage is more demanding than it looks.

To ride at the lower levels of competition, decent baseline fitness — specifically, functional strength and flexibility, and sufficient aerobic fitness to ride for thirty to forty-five minutes without stopping — is all that's required. To excel or to ride successfully at the upper levels, you'll have to attain greater overall fitness. The fitter you are and the better toned certain muscle groups are, the more effective you can be in the saddle. When you achieve this level of fitness, you can actually get more from your horse while expending less effort. Riding ceases to feel like a test of brute strength. You're free to hone the little things that make a big difference: timing, balance, and coordination of aids.

A strong back and strong abdominal muscles are assets in dressage. The sitting trot takes a toll: lower-back pain is a common complaint among dressage riders. Many riders' abdominal muscles are not strong enough, which forces the muscles of the back to compensate, doing most of the work and thus fatiguing easily and becoming prone to injury. Improved core strength reduces fatigue and lower-back pain during and after riding, and it can help you sit the trot better, too.

Keys to Rider Fitness

A fit rider possesses strength, endurance, and flexibility. Let's look at how each of these qualities relates specifically to dressage riding.

Strength

Your *seat* — collectively, the muscles from your midsection to your knees — does most of the heavy lifting when you ride dressage. These muscles absorb the horse's movement, give aids, slow his tempo, increase his tempo, help him to rebalance himself (half-halt), and help to straighten and bend his body. Your abdom-inal muscles stabilize your torso and support your lower back as it undulates with the horse's movement. Of particular importance are the transversus abdominis and the oblique internus abdominis, the deep abdominal muscles that lie beneath the rectus abdominis, the outer abdominal muscle. A toned rectus abdominis and a low percentage of body fat produce that coveted "six-pack" look, but this muscle contributes less to stability and core strength than the other two. Also important is the obliquus externus abdominis, which wraps up and around from either side of the navel to the side of the waist and allows you to twist your torso, such as when you ride shoulder-in.

Your legs, particularly from hip to knee, must be evenly toned, because they work in concert to keep your legs down and around your horse as he moves. The quadriceps (the muscle at the front of the thigh) and the hamstrings (the muscle at the back of the thigh) work together to keep your legs in the proper position against the saddle flap. The adductor (the muscle of the inner thigh) holds your thigh against the saddle, while the abductor (the muscle of the outer thigh) allows you to lift your leg up and away from your horse.

The muscles I've named are commonly mentioned in articles about rider fitness, but riding dressage requires that you use practically every muscle in your body. The muscles of your neck, shoulders, and back, for instance, help keep your upper body stretched elegantly tall, with your shoulder blades pulled back and down. The muscles of your shoulder girdle and back work to keep your elbows and upper arms quiet against your sides. And the muscles in your lower legs help to keep them draped quietly around your horse's sides, your toes pointed forward and up slightly in accordance with your conformation and that of of your horse. That's just the beginning.

All this talk about the need for strength makes more sense when you realize that the correct riding position

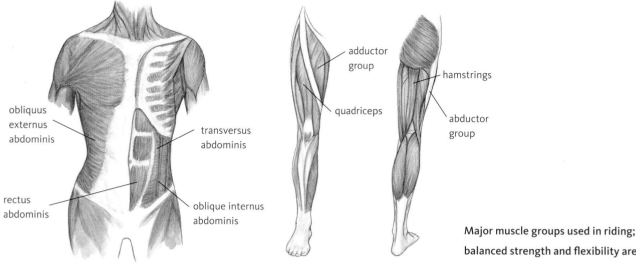

obliquus externus abdominis

transversus abdominis

rectus abdominis

oblique internus abdominis

adductor group

quadriceps

hamstrings

abductor group

Major muscle groups used in riding; balanced strength and flexibility are key.

is not really sitting, although we refer to it that way. A good dressage rider balances over her feet in a dynamic way, similar to the way that a skier stands balanced over his skis, leg joints somewhat flexed. When you ride, some weight is in your seat, of course, but a good amount is also distributed over your lower legs. You squat more than you sit. If your horse were to disappear from beneath you, you would land on your feet.

Endurance

Magazine articles that list calorie expenditures for various activities typically rank horseback riding with such modest efforts as vacuuming the house and taking a relaxing stroll. We dressage riders know better. Calorie-usage tables seem to assume that all riders are moseying down a trail, but our sport is far more challenging than that.

Riding dressage may not be as challenging aerobically as running or swimming, but walking, trotting, and cantering for a forty-five-minute lesson or training session requires a respectable level of aerobic fitness and general endurance. And riding without stirrups really gets the heart rate into the aerobic training zone.

Flexibility

Wrapping your legs around a horse takes strength, yes, but it also takes flexibility. Riders whose hip and leg muscles are tight have a hard time lengthening their legs down and around their horses' sides, and shortened calf muscles may prevent them from sinking their weight into their heels and can make them prone to losing stirrups. Tightness through the shoulders and the front of the chest — common in deskbound workers — leads to slumped posture in the saddle. And lack of suppleness in the back muscles will make sitting the trot a punishment.

To perform well, all athletes need a balance of strength and flexibility. Because of their ability to develop large muscles, men are more likely to develop strength at the expense of flexibility (think of the beefy guys who are so muscle-bound they can't even relax their arms at their sides). Hormones prevent women from bulking up like the men, so we tend to be more flexible but are not as strong, particularly in the upper body. Anyone who's suffered an injury or undergone surgery may forever have diminished flexibility and range of motion in the affected area.

Dressage riders do not need the extreme flexibility of ballet dancers and Olympic gymnasts, but riding quickly brings any areas of tightness — and we all have them — to our attention. With tightness come postural imbalances and other types of misalignment, which are killers when it comes to the desired equine qualities of straightness and bend. In time, most dressage riders learn that to develop their horses' suppleness and alignment, they must first develop their own.

Part of what makes the study of dressage so fascinating are the countless interrelationships between the mind and body of rider and horse. It is said that your horse is your mirror. If your body is weak and tense, then your horse's body will become weak and tense. If you are emotionally stressed, then your horse will reflect your state of mind in his attitude and his way of going. Similarly, the more control and mastery you gain over your own body, the better you will be able to influence your horse and ride effectively. Improving your flexibility (and strength and endurance) will make you feel more comfortable and confident in your own skin. This sense of well-being will percolate through your attitude and emotions — the mind-body connection — and will influence your horse positively, both physically and psychologically.

Dressage has a karmic sense about it: what goes around, comes around, and it all starts with you.

Strength Training

If you're interested in joining a gym, go for it. Learning to use the various weight machines, free weights, and resistance machines can be fun, as is the variety. A qualified trainer can show you how to use the equipment properly and can even design a workout that helps you meet your goals, targets problem areas, and makes allowances for any special health concerns, such as an old injury.

But you don't need a gym to improve your overall fitness and core strength. Even if you're crunched for time or money, or live in the middle of nowhere, you can still get in better shape for riding. It doesn't take hours of sweating to produce results that you'll feel in the saddle, and the difference in your riding will make the modest time investment well worth it.

Pilates

I've tried a lot of exercise and strength-training regimens, but nothing has impacted my riding the way Pilates has.

An overall strength-training and flexibility program with a decided emphasis on core strength, Pilates is named for its creator, Joseph Pilates, who devised a system of exercises in the early 1900s to strengthen his own body and, later, to help with patient rehabilitation. He dubbed his method *Contrology* because of its emphasis on total body control, stressing form over numerous repetitions.

Exercise Safely

- Consult your doctor before beginning any exercise program.
- If you are pregnant or think you might be pregnant, get your doctor's OK before attempting any new form of exercise.
- Drink plenty of water before, during, and after exercising.
- If at any time during a workout you feel dizzy, light-headed, weak, or unwell, stop exercising and consult your doctor.
- Know your own body. Know the difference between "good pain" and "bad pain." Know what's normal for you and what isn't. Trust your instincts.

Ballet dancers later discovered the exercises of Pilates, and the regimen became popular because it developed flexibility and strength without shortening or bulking muscles. Recently, Pilates has become a fitness regimen of fashion models and actors and has found its way into the mainstream fitness scene. People with back pain have found relief in the Pilates method, and fitness enthusiasts who got bored (or sore) with high-impact aerobics welcomed the regimen's gentler nature and kindness to joints. Eventually, equestrians, the most high profile of whom may be U.S. FEI-level trainer and competitor Betsy Steiner, discovered that Pilates can develop a strong, supple seat.

Pilates emphasizes core strength, flexibility, and stability. It's a dynamic and challenging workout, but it doesn't leave you an exhausted, sweaty mess. The exercises will also quickly reveal where your weak and tight areas are. Most of us are naturally stronger (and therefore tighter) on one side than the other.

Pilates is a great complement to dressage. In fact, Betsy Steiner once remarked that Pilates is like doing dressage without the horse and that dressage is like doing Pilates on horseback. As you develop a more evenly balanced physique, you will sit more evenly on your horse and will be able to influence him more effectively with your seat and legs.

Some Pilates exercises are done on special apparatus usually found only in Pilates studios. Fortunately, however, the basic exercises are done on a mat and require no equipment.

As Pilates becomes increasingly popular, studios and classes are becoming more widely available. Because form is everything, an introductory course taught by a certified Pilates instructor is strongly recommended. If you're interested in working on the apparatus, which offers variety and additional challenges beyond the traditional mat workout, access to a studio is a must. For more information, see the resources on page 332.

THE ROLL-UP

If you want to get a feel for Pilates, try the roll-up, which is part of every mat routine and also is used as a transitional movement.

Wearing comfortable, loose-fitting clothing, lie on your back on a rug, an exercise mat, or another firm, comfortable surface. With legs together and feet flexed with toes pointing up, breathe in through your nose and out through your mouth. Each time you exhale, visualize drawing your navel toward your spine by "zipping up" your abdominals and drawing your ribs closer together. Even when you inhale, try to keep your navel engaged toward your spine. As you do this, you should feel your lower back flattening toward the floor; when done correctly, there will still be a small space between your lower back and the floor. Practice the breathing until you can maintain a navel-to-spine connection.

Next, keeping your shoulders down (don't let them hike up toward your ears), reach straight arms overhead and back until they're almost touching the floor. Don't force them to the floor; reach back only as far as you can while keeping your shoulder blades down and your collarbones broad and open.

Begin the roll-up by inhaling through your nose as you bring your arms up toward the ceiling. As your arms pass over your head and begin to reach toward your feet, start exhaling through your mouth and smoothly lift your upper body off the mat: chin to chest, followed by shoulder blades, followed by torso, one vertebra at a time. Curl forward as you continue to exhale, and engage your core muscles until you're in a C shape (back rounded), with your ears between your arms, arms reaching forward, parallel to your legs. Maintain the space between your chest and your legs and keep your abdominal muscles engaged by imagining that you're reaching over a beach ball. At the apex of the stretch, you should feel muscles working in opposition: your arms and the muscles of your upper back reaching

The Roll-Up

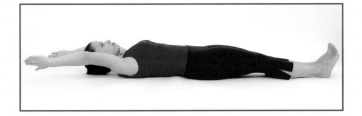

STARTING POSITION FOR THE ROLL-UP. Certified Pilates instructor Meghan Jackson demonstrates the starting position for the roll-up: belly "scooped," legs together with feet flexed, and arms overhead, as far back as possible, without lower back arching or ribs losing contact with the floor.

INHALE THROUGH YOUR NOSE while bringing your arms up and forward, past your ears, and your chin toward your chest, leaving a small space between chin and chest. Using your abdominal muscles, begin rolling your upper body up and away from the floor.

EXHALE THROUGH YOUR MOUTH as you continue rolling up, keeping your upper body rounded and your chin tucked as if you are under a low ceiling. This is the tough part of the exercise for most people. Exhaling helps, so don't hold your breath.

THE FULL ROLL-UP POSITION. Meghan's body has formed a C shape. Her head is dropped so that her arms are on either side of her ears, and her belly is pulling back toward her spine so strongly that she's feeling a nice stretch through her rounded lower back. To roll back down, she'll again inhale as she tucks her pelvis to initiate the rolling movement at her hips. She will then exhale as her arms come back overhead and she smoothly rolls her spine down, one vertebra at a time, until she reaches the starting position.

forward, while your belly pulls back. If you do it right, you'll feel a nice stretch through your lower back.

Inhale as you smoothly bring your arms back over your head, tuck your chin to your chest, and tuck your pelvis. The entire way, both up and down, imagine that you're underneath a low ceiling. This will help you to keep your back rounded and your chin tucked. As your arms pass back over your head, exhale and roll, one vertebra at a time, down to the starting position. As your shoulder blades touch down, bring your head back to touch the floor and bring your arms overhead to their starting position.

Repeat the roll-up three to five times. Challenge yourself to keep your legs together throughout the entire exercise by engaging the muscles of your inner

FEI-LEVEL TRAINER AND COMPETITOR Betsy Steiner (aboard Diamore) is dressage's best-known Pilates devotee.

thighs, and keep your feet together and flexed. Don't let your legs lift off the floor as you roll up. If it's too difficult for you to roll up with straight legs, bend your knees slightly and rest your feet on the floor, keeping your legs together.

The most difficult part of the roll-up is the point at which you have to roll your lower back up and off the floor. Make sure you're exhaling strongly as you come through what in many people is a tight area; exhalation will help your effort. Don't hold your breath!

The roll-up is a good introduction to Pilates because it gives you the feel of the breathing pattern, the navel-to-spine connection, the use of muscles in opposition, and the attention to detail and form. In virtually every Pilates exercise, some muscles are being strengthened while others are being stretched — all while the core abdominal muscles are engaged to stabilize the body and power the movement. In fact, Joseph Pilates referred to the core muscles as the powerhouse. Your core muscles are your powerhouse, just as your horse's hindquarters are his powerhouse.

Simple At-Home Strength Moves

Dressage riders need leg strength, upper-body strength, stability, and endurance. There are innumerable exercises with weights that train specific muscles or muscle groups, but there are also a few great total-body moves that train the whole body. As one who's done her fair share of circuit training on universal weight machines and other conventional strength-training regimens, I can tell you that whole-body moves, like the two that follow, produce the best results in the shortest amount of time. They work most, if not all, of the major muscle groups in concert. They also require core strength and stability, so all of those "seat" muscles get a great workout. Finally, as in riding, these exercises require coordination of multiple body parts — good practice for the coordination and motor control you need in the saddle.

THE LUNGE

Lunges strengthen the muscles from buttocks to knees like nothing else, save maybe hoisting large barbells. Lunges are stressful to knee joints and can aggravate knee problems, however, so if a move hurts, don't do it.

Wear comfortable, loose-fitting or stretchy clothing and sneakers so your feet don't slip. Stand on a firm, flat surface, feet parallel and hip distance apart and arms relaxed at your sides. Inhale and step forward with your right leg, bending both knees. Gaze straight ahead and keep your back straight. Don't lunge past vertical with the forward leg; keep your knee over your foot. Exhale and push back to your starting position. You'll feel your glutes and the muscles in your left leg working as you do so.

Repeat the exercise by lunging forward with your left leg. Do three to five repetitions with each leg. Gradually work up to eight to ten repetitions per leg.

Lunges are challenging; my thighs feel like jelly when I'm through! If you want even more challenge, try holding a dumbbell in each hand as you lunge. Start with light weights (five pounds or less), and gradually increase the weight if you are so inclined. Even an additional pound or two per hand makes a big difference in the level of difficulty of the exercise. If you feel any knee pain while doing lunges, stop immediately.

You can vary the type and direction of your lunges to challenge slightly different muscle groups and to add interest to your workout. You'll also test your stability in different ways. Try lunges as a series of steps forward. Lunge backward instead of forward, or step diagonally. As always, pay attention to the way the movement feels. Your muscles should feel challenged, but there shouldn't be any joint pain. (My knees protest a bit if I make my lunges too deep.) When you're through, you should feel pleasantly fatigued — perhaps with a little of that "jelly legs" feel — but not weak, exhausted, or dizzy.

The Lunge

STARTING POSITION. Meghan stands erect, feet shoulder-width apart. She is holding light dumbbells to provide her lower body with a little extra challenge during the exercise.

KEEPING HER EYES AND HEAD UP and her upper body erect, Meghan lunges forward with her right leg, protecting her knee by making sure that her right knee doesn't advance past her right foot. Then she'll push up and back with her right leg and gluteus maximus muscle to return to the starting position. Repeat with the left leg.

The Hover

STARTING POSITION. Meghan prepares by assuming the classic straight-leg push-up (plank) position, with her arms directly underneath her shoulders, her neck aligned with her body, and her abdominal muscles strongly engaged to keep her back from arching and her belly from sagging toward the floor.

TO TRANSITION TO THE HOVER, Meghan carefully lowers down onto her elbows, turning her thumbs up to keep her forearms aligned. Then she holds her body in a plank position, which she maintains for up to 1 minute. Breathe and keep your abdominal muscles tight to protect your lower back. Start with 15 seconds and gradually increase the duration.

CHILD'S POSE. After the intense effort of the hover, you'll appreciate this relaxing position, which provides a good lower-back stretch. Extend your arms out in front of you, or circle them by your sides, whichever feels better.

THE HOVER

The hover (also known as the *bridge*) works practically every muscle in the body, with emphasis on the abdominals, shoulders, back, and triceps.

Begin in traditional push-up position, with your hands and the balls of your feet on a firm surface, hands shoulder width apart and feet together. (A mat or carpet will provide your wrists and elbows with some cushioning.) Make sure that your back is flat and your abdominal muscles are strongly engaged so you are not in a swayback position. Gaze down at the floor but slightly in front of you to keep your neck aligned with your torso.

To transition to the hover, lower yourself down onto your elbows so that your forearms are resting on the floor. Extend your fingertips in front of you or make your hands into fists — whichever you find more comfortable. Keeping your belly pulled in and your back flat, *breathe.*

Hold the hover position for fifteen seconds to start. Work up to 30 seconds, then 45, and eventually to an entire minute. It will be a long minute!

When you are finished, gently lower your body to the floor. Stretch out your back by taking what in yoga and Pilates is called *child's pose:* Sit back with your buttocks resting on your heels and then bend forward until your forehead touches the floor, back relaxed and rounded. Either extend your arms in front of you on the floor or rest them, palms up, by your sides — whichever feels more comfortable and relaxing.

The hover is a super exercise for developing upper-body strength, stability, and core strength. You'll understand more clearly what it's supposed to feel like when your shoulders are back and down, your elbows are at your sides, and your core is engaged, as they're supposed to be when you ride. The hover may be a still position, but it's extremely dynamic, just as your upper body has to be when you ride.

Endurance Training

If you find yourself huffing and puffing after a few minutes of sitting trot, raising your level of aerobic fitness will help you keep up with your horse.

Aerobic activity is fueled by oxygen and promotes cardiovascular health by strengthening the heart muscle. Oxygen-burning activities tend to be of longer duration, in contrast to anaerobic exercise, which is of high intensity and short duration (sprints, for example) and does not use oxygen to fuel the muscles.

The general rule of thumb is that it takes approximately twenty minutes of sustained activity to get your heart rate up into its training zone, and that you'll derive maximum aerobic and cardiovascular benefit if you continue the activity for at least ten minutes more, preferably longer.

Almost any activity is of aerobic value if you sustain it long enough: walking, jogging, bicycling, in-line skating, swimming, dancing, lawn mowing, even house cleaning. There are charts and formulas for calculating your ideal training heart rate based on your age, but the easiest way to tell whether you're in the training zone is to converse; you should be able to talk with some difficulty, without gasping for breath. If you can chatter away as though you were lolling on the couch, you're not working hard enough. If you're breathing so hard that you can barely eke out a few words, you're overdoing it.

Aerobic activity is probably the easiest to incorporate into our lives because our normal activities (walking the dog, caring for home and yard and horses) already require it. Sometimes it's simply a matter of increasing the intensity: walking Fido briskly for a half hour instead of strolling and letting him stop and sniff every ten feet, switching to a push mower instead of a riding model, taking the stairs instead of the elevator, parking far from the store entrance. The important thing is to work at least thirty minutes of aerobic activity into your life at least five times a week, and preferably more often. Choose activities that you enjoy and will continue doing. If you hate step aerobics and the accompanying dance music, don't bother signing up. If your resolve to walk daily is likely to melt away in the event of cold, hot, wet, or snowy conditions, choose an activity that you can do indoors, at least on bad-weather days. I have an exercise bike and a stair-stepper machine in my basement so that I can work out even if it's dark out or weather conditions are not to my liking. By doing so, I've effectively removed any excuses I might have for not exercising, and a 30-minute pedaling spree while taking in a favorite TV show is fun, not a chore.

All Things in Moderation

As with any form of physical activity, the best piece of advice is to listen to your body. You know the difference between your usual aches and pains and something that's really not right. Don't be a weekend warrior, and don't try to do too much too soon.

Professional athletic trainers advise increasing the intensity of any activity — whether duration of exercise or weight lifted — by only 10 percent per week. So if you've started walking and can manage to do fifteen minutes the first week, by week two you should aim for just sixteen and a half minutes. Such incremental increases may seem trivial and not worth celebrating, but if you adhere to the 10-percent rule you'll greatly reduce your chances of injury or strain. And although this has been mentioned before, it bears repeating: consult your physician before you begin any exercise regimen, especially if you have a known health condition.

Get moving and have fun!

The Cross-Leg Stretch

STARTING POSITION.
Lie on your back with knees bent and feet flat on the floor.

TO PREPARE TO STRETCH her right hip, Meghan crosses her right ankle over her left knee.

MEGHAN INITIATES THE STRETCH by grasping the underside of her left thigh with both hands and gently pulling her left knee toward her chest. Altering the position of your left leg will slightly change the area of the stretch in the right hip. Experiment to find your tight spots and the stretch position that feels best to you. Breathe normally and hold the stretch for a count of ten; then switch legs.

Flexibility Training

Supple muscles are what allow you to keep your shoulders back and stretch your legs down and around your horse when you ride. You can twist at the waist to align your torso with your horse's shoulders in lateral movements such as shoulder-in. You can absorb the shock of his movement without bouncing as he trots and canters. Flexibility increases range of motion and makes our bodies feel comfortably loose.

Some people are innately more loose-limbed than others. A person who's born without a lot of flexibility can increase her range of motion over time with stretching exercises but can't be transformed into Gumby — and that's not the goal, anyway. The goal is to preserve (or increase) your range of motion and to keep muscles from tightening and shortening as a result of activity. Stretching helps to prevent injury and can ease other complaints, from stiff necks to tight shoulders.

Pilates and yoga incorporate a lot of stretching work. So if you do either, you'll definitely be meeting your flexibility-training quota. But if these regimens aren't your bag, there are many simple stretches that you can do wherever you are — at home, at work, or at the barn.

Simple Stretching Exercises

Here are two simple stretches that help loosen up areas that are tight in many people.

THE CROSS-LEG STRETCH

This move feels great and helps to stretch the piriformis, the muscle that runs up the outer thigh and over the hip. Stretching this muscle will help you to open your hips and drape your legs comfortably around your horse's sides.

Wearing comfortable, loose-fitting or stretchy clothing, lie on your back on a firm, comfortable surface — a mat or carpet is ideal — with your knees bent and your feet flat on the floor. Cross your right ankle over your left leg, slightly above the knee. Gently press your right knee down toward the floor until you feel a stretch along the outside of your right thigh and hip. Breathe normally and hold for a slow count of ten. Switch legs to stretch the left piriformis.

To increase the stretch, clasp your hands around the underside of the thigh that's not being stretched (your left thigh while you're stretching your right leg, and vice versa) and gently pull the leg toward you, maintaining the cross-legged position.

This stretch is a favorite because it loosens a big muscle that's usually tight. The stretch feels good, and the position is comfortable and relaxing.

CHEST-AND-SHOULDER STRETCH

The pectoral muscles (in the front of the chest) and shoulders tend to tighten as a result of stress and poor posture. Deskbound workers are particularly apt to assume a slumped, round-shouldered position that frequently carries over to their posture when standing, walking, and riding. Uncorrected, this unattractive posture tends to worsen over time and can lead to headaches, stiffness and soreness in the neck and shoulders, and other complaints. In the saddle, it's difficult to sit correctly and balance a horse when you yourself are canted forward with your neck lowered and your chin jutting forward.

Help ease the stresses of the day and improve your posture with a simple stretch, which can be done alone or with a friend. To do this stretch unassisted, use a length of exercise band or the frame of a doorway for resistance. Of the two methods, an exercise band best enables you to tailor the stretch to your specific comfort zone and range of motion. (For more on exercise bands, see Bands and Tubing on page 266.)

To stretch your chest and shoulders using a band, find a band that's long enough. There should be some

Chest-and-Shoulder Stretch

STARTING POSITION. Meghan shows the starting position for the chest-and-shoulder stretch using a length of exercise band. From this angle, you can see the slack in the band, which enables her to take her arms out to the side during the stretch. She grasps the band between her thumbs and the palms of her hand so her wrists stay aligned with her forearms. Holding the band with a fist can produce unwanted tension in the arms and shoulders.

FOR THE STRETCH, Meghan takes her straight arms back while exerting enough outward pressure to tighten the band between her hands. Holding the band in this manner forces her shoulder muscles to do most of the work.

slack when holding the band between your hands with your arms straight and lifted slightly more than shoulder-width apart.

You can do this exercise standing or sitting. If you stand, position your feet shoulder-width apart. If you sit, a cross-legged position provides the most stability.

With your abdominal muscles engaged so your back is in a neutral position (not arched), and keeping your shoulders down (away from your ears), gently take your arms back and down in a range that's comfortable for you while exerting enough outward pressure to tighten the band between your hands. (The goal is not to stretch the band as much as possible, but to use its gentle resistance to help stabilize the movement and to assist in the stretch. The movement is more back than down.) You should feel a "pinch" between your shoulder blades, which indicates the muscles are contracting. Breathe normally, hold the stretch for a few seconds, then control the movement as you slowly return your arms to their starting position.

Repeat the stretch two or three times. Each time, see if your arms will reach back a little bit farther, but don't force the movement. If your shoulders are tight, this stretch is intense. Take it easy, and never force your range of motion.

If you can't locate an exercise band, a door frame is a convenient substitute. Stand in the doorway with your legs hip distance apart and your feet parallel. With straight arms, gently reach back until your palms are resting on the edges of the door frame, fingertips pointing backward, until you feel a stretch. To increase the stretch, move your hands farther up the door frame or step slightly forward out of the doorway. Do not go so far that your shoulders hike up; keep your shoulder blades back and down. Hold the stretch for a count of ten.

If stretching with a friend, she'll provide the resistance rather than the band or the doorway. Stand with your legs hip distance apart and your feet parallel.

Instruct your friend to stand behind you and gently take your straight arms back until you feel a stretch. Tell your friend which way to move your arms to increase or decrease the stretch as needed. When you find a comfortable position, ask your friend to keep your arms there for ten seconds before gently letting go.

Versatile Extras for Total-Body Training

Two inexpensive pieces of exercise equipment are outstanding additions to any home gym, and one is even a snap to take with you when you travel. Use them to expand your exercise repertoire to include numerous fun and challenging variations of basic stretching and strengthening moves.

The Exercise Ball

Visit a gym, a Pilates studio, or a physical therapist's office and you'll probably find one or more colorful exercise balls of various sizes in a corner. These inflatable vinyl balls are tools for a number of exercises that promote strength, flexibility, core stability, and even relief of back pain.

You can do push-ups and hovers with your legs on the ball to develop upper-body and core strength while challenging your stabilizing muscles. You can do cross-leg stretches with your legs propped up on the ball. You can do back extensions over the ball or simply relax and drape yourself over the ball for a back, shoulder, and neck stretch. Sitting on the ball is comfortable and can provide relief to those with sore backs.

Exercise balls come in various diameters. The correct size for you allows you to sit with your feet flat on the floor and your legs bent at a right angle at the knee. Many sporting-goods stores and catalogs sell exercise balls, as do many physical therapists' offices, Pilates studios, gyms, and "big box" retailers.

The Exercise Ball

THE SHOULDER BRIDGE. This exercise works the abdominal muscles, the hamstrings, and the glutes. Because the ball can roll, this exercise challenges your core stability. Meghan is in the starting position. The ball is the perfect size for her. When she lies on her back and rests her heels and the backs of her lower legs on the ball, her legs form a 45-degree angle. She rests her arms by her sides, slightly away from her body, and engages her triceps and shoulder muscles to stabilize her body for the next move.

BEGINNER VERSION. Keeping her legs at a 45-degree angle, Meghan inhales to prepare. She then exhales and, beginning at her hips, rolls her lower back up off the floor. She presses down strongly with her arms to stabilize her upper body, and keeps her shoulders in contact with the floor. (If your shoulders lift off the floor, you'll balance on your cervical spine and neck — ouch!) Hold the bridge position for a couple of seconds, then reverse the movement, inhaling and then exhaling as you roll back down from shoulders to hips, one vertebra at a time.

ADVANCED VERSION. This is more of a balance and stability challenge than the beginner version. Meghan prepares and executes the movement as before, except that now she extends her legs so they are straight and her body is in a plank position. Full shoulder bridge on the ball is an intense workout for the hamstrings, glutes, triceps, and core muscles.

A FINAL STRETCH. After all that exertion, this move feels like a reward. It's especially good if your back, shoulders, or neck are tight and tense. Meghan drapes her torso over the ball, relaxes every muscle, and breathes normally. She holds the position as long as she wants. (It feels so good, you'll probably want to stay there for a while.)

Tubing: A Versatile Extra

PORTABLE RESIS-TANCE. Meghan uses a length of tubing for a biceps-curl exercise. (Hers has a roll of foam padding at each end and a handy connector in the middle, but a plain length of tubing, knotted to a length of about eighteen inches, also works well.) She has looped one end of the tubing around her right foot and holds the other in her right hand. She sits up straight and has tucked her left foot under her right knee for support and stability.

THE CURL. With each exhalation, Meghan contracts her right biceps and brings her forearm closer to her chest, taking care not to let her elbow drop. Do ten to twelve repetitions, then switch sides.

SIDE LEG LIFT. Tubing can also be used to provide resistance during side leg lifts. In this exercise, Meghan flexes both feet to help engage her leg muscles and keep her legs straight and stable.

Bands and Tubing

Lengths of latex, latex-free, or rubber bands or tubing (Thera-Band is a well-known brand) offer the creative exerciser many options for strength training and stretching. The bands and tubing come in varying levels of resistance and can be cut and knotted to whatever length you desire for a custom-fit loop. Accessories, such as handles and door-attachment devices, increase the workout options.

Do hamstring stretches by holding the band or tubing in one hand and hooking the other end around your ankle. Do biceps curls. Do chest stretches. Do leg raises with resistance. Best of all, the bands and tubes are lightweight and stuff easily into a corner of your suitcase or carry-on bag when you travel — the perfect exercise equipment when you're on the road.

The Role of Good Nutrition

Strictly speaking, this is not a rider-health book. However, as you continue your quest to be your very best in the saddle, don't overlook the importance of eating right.

At dressage shows, you will undoubtedly see competitors noshing on junk food and drinking all manner of sugary, empty-calorie beverages. But many top-level riders find that where athletic performance is concerned, it's garbage in, garbage out.

Always stay adequately hydrated, especially for schooling sessions, lessons, and shows in the blistering summer heat. Nothing beats plain old water, although electrolyte-replacing sports drinks can give an extra boost in extreme heat or humidity. Caffeinated beverages are dehydrating, and sugared sodas pack lots of unwanted calories. Diet sodas are the stuff of life for some, but aspartame and other sugar substitutes can trigger headaches.

Drink water before, during, and after your ride. It's easy to get caught up in the intensity and concentration of a lesson or show warm-up and forget to take a swig from the water bottle, but try to stash it somewhere accessible from the saddle, or give it to your helper to carry at a show. Keep sipping water even if you don't feel particularly thirsty. In some people, thirstiness doesn't develop until they're already quite dehydrated.

Make wise food choices to give your body the fuel it needs to perform well, with plenty of energy. You know your body's likes and dislikes best: whether you can exercise after eating without suffering any ill effects; whether you must eat at regular intervals to avoid feeling lightheaded, sluggish, or headachy; whether certain foods upset your stomach, especially if you're nervous or stressed (as you might be in a show environment); and so on.

For before-competition meals, sports nutritionists tend to recommend simple, healthful foods that are low in fat: salad and pasta with marinara sauce, for instance, or fish and fresh vegetables, all washed down with a tall glass of water. Perhaps the best nutritional advice is to pay attention to how different foods make you feel. After you eat protein or carbohydrates, do you feel energized? Sleepy? Wired? Able to concentrate? Does your energy level last until your next meal, or do you find yourself hungry and irritable just a short time later? Strive to think of food as fuel, and choose fuels that make you feel good afterward and not just during the momentary pleasure of the meal itself.

The Dressage-Riding Mother-to-Be

Should you ride dressage during pregnancy? Doctors generally advise women not to take up new forms of exercise at this time. So if you've never ridden or you're getting back into riding after a long hiatus, wait until after the baby comes before you get back in the saddle. Even if you ride regularly, riding during pregnancy is generally discouraged because of the risks of falling or being kicked by the horse.

Every woman is different, and common sense must prevail when it comes to the decision to continue or discontinue riding during pregnancy. An obvious consideration is the way you're feeling. If you're sick as a dog, you probably don't want to be riding, anyway. If the pregnancy is considered high risk, you'll be advised to quit riding for the duration.

Some diehard riders announce their intentions to ride practically until the labor pains start, but often Mother Nature has other plans. I knew a superfit eventing and dressage trainer who was forced to give up riding early in her pregnancy because she began bleeding and was warned she might miscarry if she continued. Another rider, a champion dressage competitor, competed at Grand Prix level the first few months of her pregnancy, but then abruptly fainted after completing a test and would have fallen had helpers not been there to catch her. That was the end of her riding until after her son was born. The 2004 Olympic dressage individual gold medalist, Anky van Grunsven, competed in Athens while eighteen weeks pregnant, announcing her condition only upon her triumphant return home to the Netherlands.

Some women continue to ride happily until very late in their pregnancies, simply slowing down (the sitting trot is among the first things to go) and riding only at a walk for the last few weeks. Still others find the jouncing and jostling intolerable and quit riding, even though they may not have suffered any outwardly alarming symptoms.

Take your horse's temperament into consideration, as well. Now may not be the time to be dealing with that fractious, spooky youngster, but some gentle turns on a semiretired pensioner might be OK. Ride only a horse that you know well and trust, but realize that no horse is "bombproof," no matter how placid he may seem.

CHAPTER 18

YOUR DRESSAGE PARTNER

T he dressage horse is the gymnast or ballet dancer of the equestrian world. In dressage, form and precision are everything. The objective of dressage training and the training scale (see chapter 7) is to develop an individual horse's gaits, movement, and balance to their fullest potential — to make him the happiest and most beautiful athlete he can be.

In this chapter, I'll help educate your eye to recognize the finer points of equine movement, which will help you to develop a better understanding of the biomechanics of the three basic gaits and of what movement characteristics are considered desirable in dressage. Then I'll explain why and how conformation (the way a horse is built) can play a role in dressage performance and overall soundness. (If down the road you decide to shop for a dressage horse, this information will be particularly important.)

Finally, I'll introduce you to the world of sporthorse breeding and the many breeds of warmbloods that dominate the sport of dressage, especially in international competition.

How a Horse Moves

A horse's breeding, conformation, and training influence his "way of going," or the way he moves. Some gaited horses, for instance, naturally exhibit gaits other than or in addition to the standard walk, trot, and canter. Depending on the breed or discipline, horses are encouraged to position their bodies and to move in certain ways.

Train your eye to recognize what is considered desirable in a dressage horse's movement. Although the gaits aren't quite as critical in dressage competition as they once were, they're still considered important, especially in terms of rhythm and tempo.

The photographs that follow illustrate the way of going of four types of horses: a high-stepping park-horse-type Saddlebred; a "daisy-cutting" hunter (so called because he skims over the ground with little bend in his knees, and his hooves are so low that he appears able to clip the heads off daisies as he travels); a Western pleasure horse that jogs, not trots, with very little animation or other motion that would jostle his rider, producing a smooth, easy-to-sit ride — he gets the judge's nod by moving slowly and evenly, his topline level; and an upper-level dressage horse that trots with marked activity and whose collected movement is both up and out. (Pictured is Geldnet Lingh, who with Dutch rider Edward Gal finished second at the 2005 FEI Offield Farms Dressage World Cup Final.)

What differences do you notice in the movements of the horses in these photographs? First, you might observe that the Saddlebred has the most "action" of the group: his movement is flashy and showy. With all of that up-and-down action, he moves a lot but won't win any speed contests because he doesn't cover much ground with each stride.

Saddlebred

Western-pleasure horse

"Daisy-cutting" hunter

Upper-level dressage horse

The movements of the hunter and the Western pleasure horse are similar, although the hunter appears livelier, with a more energetic stride. In contrast to the Saddlebred, the strides of the Western pleasure horse are out and low rather than up and down.

And what about the dressage horse? His movement is somewhere between that of the Saddlebred and that of the hunter and the Western pleasure horse. He has less action than the former but more action than the latter. Like the Saddlebred, the movement of the dressage horse is dynamic and powerful, but unlike the Saddlebred, his strides reach farther forward and cover more ground. (Too much up-and-down action in a dressage horse's natural trot is scoffed at: "He moves like an egg-beater.") The entire body of the dressage horse appears "round," that is, convex along his topline. Some trainers describe the desired way of going as "coming up off the ground like a bouncing ball." Ideally, the movement of the dressage horse embodies relaxation, rhythm, athleticism, balance, and dynamic energy.

The Role of Conformation

Standing in their stalls, some star dressage horses look like cart-pulling nags. And yet the popularity of dressage sport-horse breeding classes and the number of magazine articles devoted to the evaluation of dressage-horse conformation suggest that many people believe that function follows form.

You will not learn how to buy a dressage horse from this book, and you probably want to try dressage with the horse you already have. Still, it's helpful to educate your eye. Conformation contributes to a horse's athletic ability and soundness. Understanding conformation will help you understand why he does some movements well and has difficulty doing others.

Because dressage training emphasizes the lightening of the forehand and the taking of weight by the hindquarters and hind legs, a horse with so-called *uphill balance* has an advantage. Standing still, his withers are slightly higher than the point of his croup. His neck rises in a graceful arch from his shoulders. Well-built warmbloods and some individuals of other breeds display these characteristics. The effect is the opposite of the *downhill balance* frequently seen in Quarter Horses, Paints, and some Thoroughbreds: croup higher than the withers; straight, low-set neck; heavy shoulders; and an earthbound-looking forehand.

The textbook dressage horse has a neck of medium length and a throatlatch of sufficient refinement to permit him to flex comfortably at the poll. His mouth and teeth are normal (deformities could lead to discomfort in bitting and therefore lack of acceptance of the bit and the contact). He has a sloping shoulder, a back of medium length (too long and he'll be hard to collect; too short and he'll have difficulty bending and doing lateral movements), and a well-sprung barrel. Powerful hindquarters with a croup of medium slope, a strong stifle, and sturdy hocks facilitate collected work. Hocks are of medium angle, with the point of the hock aligned beneath the point of the buttocks (a horse with hocks set "out behind" may have difficulty collecting because it's inherently difficult for him to place his hind legs underneath his body).

Feet and legs are cleanly developed and sturdy. Nice big, tough feet with sufficient heel are a boon to any horse.

The proof, as they say, is in the pudding, and for a dressage horse that's his movement. Some gorgeous specimens are mediocre movers at best, while other unprepossessing individuals have lovely gaits.

It's easy to be dazzled by a huge, ground-covering trot, but pay more attention to the walk and the canter. These two gaits are more challenging to improve than the trot, and a good canter becomes increasingly important as a horse moves up the levels of dressage.

GOOD CONFORMATION FOR DRESSAGE.
Capable dressage horses come in varying shapes and sizes, but good basic conformation generally contributes to better movement and a higher likelihood of overall soundness. This is Pancratius ("Paul"), a Dutch Warmblood gelding owned by Emily Gershberg who was seven years old and competing at Third Level when this photo was taken. Paul has good uphill conformation, with a fairly high set-on neck, a sloping shoulder, a level topline, and strong hindquarters with hocks that are not set "out behind" the rearmost point of his buttocks.

A good walk is clearly four-beat, even in rhythm and tempo, and shows good overstride (placing of the hind hooves ahead of the prints of the forefeet). A good canter is even, solidly three-beat (no tendency to change to four-beat due to lack of synchrony of the diagonal pair of legs), in excellent balance, and with a tendency toward an uphill "jump." A good trot, of course, is a swingy, even two-beat, with free shoulder movement and good thrust from the hind legs. Beware the horse that throws his front legs extravagantly while his hind legs lag behind, or the one that reveals his restricted shoulder range by the telltale "flicking" of the extended foreleg, in which the toe rises higher than the cannon bone.

Arguably, the most important asset of all for a dressage horse is a good work ethic. Scores of riders have purchased wildly talented dressage prospects, only to be disappointed because the horses lacked good temperaments and did not genuinely enjoy the training work. Horses, like humans, thrive when they enjoy their jobs, and are miserable when forced into the wrong situations.

Brilliant yet difficult horses are projects for professionals. I'll take a kind, willing, modestly talented horse over a fabulous yet erratic animal any day.

The "Right" Age for Dressage

Dressage riders are fortunate in being able to enjoy longer partnerships with our horses than equestrians in other disciplines. Although upper-level dressage is demanding, it does not inflict the kind of pounding on the horse's body that racing and jumping do. A Thoroughbred racehorse is generally most competitive at ages two and three; a show-jumper, at ages nine to eleven. Most top dressage horses competing in the 2004 Athens Olympics, in contrast, were in their teens. The late Udon won team bronze with U.S. rider Steffen Peters at the 1996 Atlanta Games at age eighteen. Even past their prime, many dressage horses downshift into second careers as schoolmasters for young riders or other students, who demand less of their mounts. Some horses enjoy these roles well into their twenties.

Building the necessary strength, endurance, and suppleness needed for dressage takes years of patient, gradual training. Warmbloods, the sport horses most commonly found in dressage competition, are a little slower to mature than Thoroughbreds and some other breeds. As a result, dressage prospects usually are not started under saddle until age three or four; before that age, their bones, muscles, and minds are too immature to handle the stresses of training.

Some top trainers lunge their youngsters, break them to saddle, and then put them back out to pasture for another six months or so to do some additional growing and maturing. They say the horses don't forget the early lessons and that their patient approach pays off. The early handling "imprints" the youngsters and helps ensure that they will be tractable and willing partners down the line. This method may be far preferable to the practice of allowing a youngster to live out in a field, practically untouched, for the first few years of his life. So treated, the horse happily fends for himself and develops a sense of independence and, in some cases, entitlement to a life of leisure. Some horses that enter the working world late in life do fine, but others become sources of frustration for their owners and riders.

Many horses find their way into dressage as a second career. There are plenty of ex-racehorses, ex-eventers, ex-hunters, ex-jumpers, and ex-Western horses in dressage arenas across the United States, especially at the lower levels. Some make the switch because their owners think they're getting a little too far along in years to deal with the continued physical demands of their previous disciplines. Numerous riders adopt ex-racehorses, and several adoptees have found their way into the dressage ring. Perhaps most often, it's the rider who is tired of (or feels too old for) her previous sport and is lured by the elegance, intellectual appeal, and perceived lesser risk of dressage and therefore introduces her horse to a new discipline.

Whatever your horse's age, one thing is for certain: dressage training can help any sound, healthy horse become a more pleasant mount to ride. Even an older horse can learn some basic dressage and do a little lateral work. Assuming your critter is in decent shape, it's never too late to start.

Breed Preferences?

Entire sections of dressage-show rule books are devoted to descriptions of the qualities that judges want to see in the gaits of horses. Many of the sport's standards and trends have emerged from and been shaped in the competition arena. Since the 1960s, dressage competition, especially at the highest levels, has been dominated by the warmblood, a type of sport horse that originated in Europe and has been developed for dressage movement as well as for excellence in jumping and driving.

Warmbloods are large, robust horses, with lengthy strides (many have huge trots that are challenging to sit, especially for the inexperienced or physically unfit rider), uphill movement that facilitates lightness of the forehand and free shoulder movement, and overall athleticism. For some time, dressage aficionados were so awed by the warmbloods' jaw-droppingly big movement that more modest movers tended to get swept aside in competition. Today, the pendulum is swinging in the direction of moderation. Judges now seek a balance between good basic gaits and correct basic training, which has helped to level the playing field.

Recognizing that most dressage riders are female amateurs, sport-horse breeders have also shifted their emphasis somewhat, from massive animals that can require above-average strength to ride, to smaller, lighter horses that have excellent temperaments and are easier to sit.

What Is a Warmblood?

Pour a cup of hot water into a cup of cold water, and what do you get? Warm water, of course. Well, that's basically what horse breeders did to create the warmblood breeds. They selectively bred generations of stocky working or draft types to Thoroughbred and other light-boned types to create sport horses with versatile athleticism and good temperaments.

The thin-skinned Arabian, an ancient desert breed, is called a *hotblood* because of his origin and sensitive temperament. His direct descendant, the Thoroughbred, is also a hotblood. The draft breeds — Clydesdales, Percherons, Shires, and others — originated in cooler climates and are known for their placid natures; they are collectively referred to as *coldbloods*.

In the broadest sense, breeds of horses that are neither hotbloods nor coldbloods are warmbloods — refined crosses between the hot-blooded and the cold-blooded breeds. However, Morgans, Quarter Horses, Appaloosas, and the like generally aren't referred to that way. The warmblood distinction is reserved for certain breeds of European origin that were developed as cavalry mounts, as carriage horses, and for other utilitarian purposes and that now form the ranks of the *sport horses* — all-around athletic mounts that excel in dressage, jumping, and driving.

Several things about the warmblood breeds can confuse the novice, and they puzzle some of us who are fairly knowledgeable, too. First, there are a great number of warmblood registries, many of which are named either for their country of origin (e.g., Dutch Warmblood, Swedish Warmblood, Danish Warmblood) or the region in which they were developed (e.g., Hanoverian, Holsteiner, Oldenburg). Strictly speaking, these "breeds" aren't breeds at all, in the sense of purebreds. In fact, some warmblood owners, particularly owners of stallions at stud, boast that their horses are approved for breeding by more than one warmblood stud book (e.g., "My stallion is approved Hanoverian and Oldenburg").

These "breeds" are more accurately described as *types* and are organized by registry — aggregates of sorts, selectively bred for size, temperament, movement, and athletic ability. Bloodlines do exist, and certain lines are identified with certain registries, but warmbloods wear the *breed* moniker rather loosely.

Structure and control come in the manner in which individuals are approved for registry and as breeding stock. Just because a colt is the offspring of two Dutch Warmbloods, for example, doesn't make him a shoo-in for future breeding-stallion status. He must first be approved by licensed authorities from the breed organization at a *keuring* (examination), a rigorous judging process during which horses are presented for approval by a breed organization. Mares also vie for approval to ensure that genetic standards remain high. At a keuring, horses of various ages are evaluated on conformation, temperament, movement, and jumping ability.

Fine sport horses, warmbloods still dominate the dressage ranks, particularly at the upper levels. But they're not suitable for every rider, and having a warmblood does not guarantee dressage success, in the show ring or otherwise. If you have a perfectly nice, sound, off-the-track Thoroughbred or a cute Appaloosa or a Heinz 57 "mutt," by all means don't rush to trade him in. You can do dressage with almost any horse. Also, dressage training can improve the gaits, fitness, and suppleness of almost any horse, and make him generally better to ride. And that's the real fun of this sport.

OLD-STYLE WARMBLOOD. Gifted, a Hanoverian gelding ridden to team bronze in the 1992 Barcelona Olympics by U.S. rider Carol Lavell, was the quintessential "old-style" warmblood: huge, with enormous movement and tremendous athleticism.

CHAPTER 19

KEEPING YOUR HORSE SOUND AND HEALTHY

orses are a paradox. They're big, strong animals, yet they're also fragile. Nearly every horse owner has complained that horses never lack new and imaginative ways to hurt themselves, even in the most benign situations.

Dressage, like all athletic pursuits, builds up the body, but also carries a risk of injury. Dressage horses aren't as likely to suffer the kinds of traumatic injuries to which racehorses are prone — few horses break legs just trotting along, thankfully — but the repetitive nature of the sport and the demands placed on the equine musculoskeletal system make other types of unsoundness more commonplace.

In this chapter, we'll review the most common soundness problems found in dressage horses and what you can do about them. We'll look at the ways that external factors, such as footing, can impact horses' soundness. We'll explore the importance of dental care, an often-overlooked source of training and riding problems. Finally, we'll also review some preventive and alternative-therapy options.

Common Soundness Problems

Every equine sport can lead to injuries. Although any horse can fall prey to any injury, some problems crop up more frequently in specific disciplines. Here's a rundown of some types of common dressage-related unsoundness.

Achy Hindquarter Joints

All the half-halting and collected work in dressage puts additional stress, and more of the horse's weight, on his hindquarters. When we ask our horses for actions like impulsion and extension, we require them to bend the joints of their hind legs and to push off strongly as they straighten them. Over time, hips, stifles, and hocks — particularly the latter two — can develop the wear-and-tear form of arthritis known as *degenerative joint disease* (DJD).

Show me a forty-five-year-old ex-football player, and I'll show you a guy who's stiff and uncomfortable from time to time. Likewise, a certain amount of DJD is virtually inevitable in an older dressage horse. Horses with poor hind-leg conformation are more prone to soundness problems because their bones and joints are not aligned optimally for maximum natural cushioning and minimal grinding and shearing forces. A horse with weak hindquarters as compared to the rest of his body would also be suspect. And although dressage horses literally tend to be more well-rounded than their eventing counterparts, some dressage riders seem to believe that a fat horse is a healthy horse when, in fact, extra

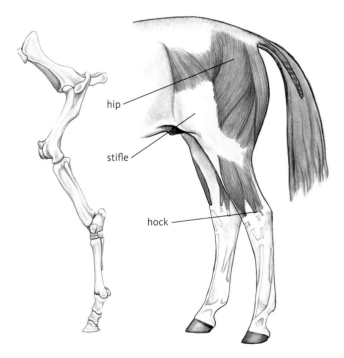

HINDQUARTER MUSCULOSKELETAL ANATOMY. The horse's hip, stifle, and hock joints do a lot of the work in dressage and are prone to unsoundness over time without careful maintenance.

blubber on the hindquarter joints is just as bad for his body as extra weight is for yours. Because of his probable warmblood pedigree and the work he does, an upper-level dressage horse is more heavily muscled and does not have the lean, "tucked up" look of the event horse (which also probably has a higher percentage of Thoroughbred blood) — but don't confuse portliness with muscle.

Achy Backs

Poor saddle fit, weak abdominal muscles, and bad riding are the three major causes of sore backs in dressage horses. The problem can be difficult to diagnose because it can manifest itself in ways that could point to any number of possible causes. A dressage horse with a sore back might flinch noticeably when he's curried and brushed in that area, hollowing his back in an attempt to escape the discomfort. He might start acting cranky and "girthy" when he's saddled and mounted. He might seem "cold backed," reacting violently if his rider lands too heavily in the saddle when she mounts. Or his performance might simply start eroding. He might become reluctant to go forward, to bend in one or both directions, to lengthen or extend his gaits, or to pick up or change canter leads. Many of these symptoms, particularly those that are performance related, could be caused by any number of things, from overtraining to DJD to dental discomfort. To help decide whether an achy back is the root of the problem, explore the three main causes.

POOR SADDLE FIT

I learned the hard way that a horse's back can change shape as he develops and progresses in dressage. I once had a gelding that I purchased as a three-year-old. I happily outfitted him and started training. A few years later, he began showing even more unwillingness to go forward than his usual lazybones self. A veterinarian discovered that the saddle, which fit perfectly for a while, now pressed on my gelding's withers. I sadly parted with my beloved saddle, found another with help from a professional saddle fitter, and the back soreness disappeared over time.

A saddle that presses on your horse's withers, spine, or both will cause pain. The cause can be a tree that is too wide or too narrow, a seat that doesn't sit level on your horse's back, or a tree that has warped or in some other way become twisted or misaligned, such as after a fall. Saddles are like shoes: different makes and models are cut differently, and not all feel comfortable.

If you're not sure whether your current saddle fits your horse properly, consult a saddle-fitting expert (your tack shop may be able to suggest someone). He or she will visit your barn and examine the saddle fit with and without you sitting in it. A good saddle fitter can tell you whether the saddle can be adjusted to fit — through reflocking (adjusting the amount and placement of stuffing in the saddle's panels) or reshaping the tree — or whether it is damaged beyond repair or fits so poorly that you're better off getting another. If saddle fit is the problem, you should notice relatively quick improvement in your horse after it is corrected.

WEAK ABDOMINAL MUSCLES

A horse's weak abdominal muscles are usually directly related to his aching back. Your horse's back muscles literally serve as a bridge between his forehand and his hindquarters. Just as your abdominal muscles support your lower back, your horse's abdominals support his back, and both have to work even harder when they're carrying you.

Your horse's abdominal muscles support his back through the action of the *muscle ring,* an interconnected sequence of impulses. When you close your legs on your horse's sides, you activate his abdominal muscles, which in turn stimulate other muscles: hindquarters, back and topline, poll, front of the neck, and chest, returning to the abdominal area. When his abdominal muscles engage, they lift upward with his back. (See page 109 for more on the muscle ring.)

In collection, a horse's back lifts and rounds considerably. A Fédération Equestre Internationale (FEI)–level horse performing a correct canter pirouette or a piaffe has a distinctly rounded shape to his topline, similar to that of a horse jumping with a good bascule (rounded back and neck position, usually signifying athleticism) over fences.

THE MUSCLE RING. The rider's aids activate the horse's musculature in a circular pattern of impulses. When the muscle ring is working correctly and the horse is "through," it really is possible to influence his hind legs with your rein aids.

Tummy Tuck

Try this experiment and watch what happens. Stand next to your horse and reach your hands beneath his belly (be careful if he's ticklish). Press upward with your fingertips. Most horses will engage their abdominal muscles in response to the pressure, and you'll see their backs lift. Although this isn't exactly the muscle ring at work, it shows the relationship between the use of the abdominals and the lifting and rounding of the back.

CANTER PIROUETTE. U.S. competitor Susan Jaccoma and the Grand Prix dressage horse Harmony's Weissmuller in a canter pirouette, in which the horse's topline, from poll to tail, is rounded.

A horse whose abdominal muscles have not been strengthened through correct, systematic training will encounter difficulty when introduced to collected work, if not before. Without sufficient support from his abdominal muscles, he may develop a sore back. Incorrect "front to back" riding or some other factor that causes him to hollow his back, such as a poor-fitting saddle, will prevent him from using his abdominal muscles as much as he should. The causes of sore backs are often interrelated.

BAD RIDING

It's easy to understand how a rider who does not sit the trot well and pounds mercilessly into her horse's back could cause him pain, but there are other, subtler ways that poor riding contributes to equine back problems.

The most notorious is the rider who inadvertently hollows her horse's back as she uses the reins in an attempt to collect him from front to back instead of riding correctly forward from her seat and legs into an elastic rein contact. When a horse's back hollows, his vertebrae are compressed and his back muscles tense. It's the equine equivalent of standing and moving with a swayback (an overarched lower back) and slack abdominal muscles, and we all know it doesn't take long for the lower back to begin complaining in that

BASCULE. Equally rounded is this hunter at the Devon Horse Show, who is showing a marked bascule over the fence.

position. Imagine how you'd feel if you had to support added weight on your tight lower back!

If you suspect that your horse has a sore back and you've ruled out saddle fit as the cause, have someone videotape a lesson or a training session. Look at the way your horse carries himself. Does his back look round and swinging, or does it appear stiff and hollow? How are you sitting? If you lean back, lower legs out in front of you instead of balanced beneath your center of gravity in that classic shoulder-hip-heel alignment, you may be "water-skiing" and using the reins for balance.

If you're not sure about what might be wrong with your position, or if you know your sitting trot has more bounce than it should, ask a qualified instructor to give you a series of seat lessons on the lunge. Learn to absorb your horse's motion with your muscles and joints instead of pounding his back. He'll thank you for it by moving more freely and willingly forward, and you'll feel more in control of and connected to his movement.

Uneven Gaits

Rhythmic, regular gaits are the cornerstone of dressage training. Therefore, it is considered a serious fault when one or more gaits lose their distinctive rhythm and become uneven.

Uneven can be interpreted in a range of ways, from an irregular pattern of movement to outright lameness. The term usually signifies a stilted rhythm, perhaps one in which a limb or pair of limbs lands more forcefully than the other. The trot half-pass, in which the horse moves forward and sideways into the direction in which he is bent, is a common trigger of unevenness. If the rider pushes the horse excessively sideways with insufficient forward impulsion, the horse may become slightly off-balance with each stride and either land more heavily on one diagonal pair of legs or take strides of unequal length. When the unevenness is caused by the rider's hanging on one rein and perhaps "blocking" the horse's outside shoulder from moving freely, the horse is said to be *rein lame*. The unevenness, which can masquerade as actual physical unsoundness, may disappear when the horse is ridden correctly forward into an even and elastic rein contact.

Another sort of unevenness is revealed in movements in which one of the horse's hind legs has more thrust (pushing power) than the other. For example, in the medium or extended trot, the horse should bend the joints of both hind legs evenly and used that stored "coiled spring" energy to push off strongly with each stride, propelling his body over the ground with a lengthened frame and long strides. If one hind leg appears to push off with less power than the other, then the strides of the diagonal pairs of legs will be uneven in their length and ground-covering ability. The result is a form of unevenness that is visible and possibly even audible.

Unevenness can be a strength or training issue, or it may be caused by unsoundness. It can be difficult for a rider to determine whether the cause of an underperforming hind leg is weakness or pain; sometimes it is both. Pain causes the horse to favor the sore limb, conserving its movement and compensating by using the opposite limb more strongly; the sore limb weakens as a result.

Have your veterinarian check out any form of unevenness that occurs suddenly and inexplicably or that persists and shows no improvement, even after a few weeks of careful gymnastic training under a qualified instructor's supervision.

Soft-Tissue Injuries

Dressage horses are less likely than racehorses to break their leg bones, but even the relatively low-impact stresses of dressage can injure the delicate soft tissues that support the lower limbs.

Horses have practically no muscle below the knee. The cannon bones lie at the front of the legs. Strung tightly behind them are the complicated tendinous and ligamentous structures that support the limbs and flex and extend the hooves and lower limbs.

Briefly, running up the back of each leg is the superficial digital flexor tendon, which attaches to the fetlock joint. Between this tendon and the cannon bone is the suspensory ligament. Under strain, which may be caused by anything from poor footing to fatigue to a bad step, these soft-tissue structures can develop small tears. The tears, called *lesions,* may or may not cause outright lameness, but the area is usually painful when palpated, and the horse's performance and movement generally deteriorate.

A bowed tendon, caused by an injury to the superficial digital flexor tendon, is easy to spot because the thickened tissue produces a distinct bowed shape along the back of the leg. An injury to the suspensory ligament can be harder to identify and may require diagnostic ultrasound to confirm the presence of lesions within the tissue. Both injuries may cause unsoundness. Soft-tissue injuries are slow to heal — as a rule, ligaments heal more slowly than tendons — and the affected area may be forever vulnerable to reinjury; however, advances in the use of stem cells may help some injury sites heal more completely and with renewed strength. Unfortunately, soft-tissue injuries are common and occur in many dressage horses at some point during their careers.

Tight Neck and Poll

A dressage horse's neck must flex laterally and longitudinally as he extends and collects and performs circles, turns, and lateral movements. In addition, he must be able to flex easily at the poll.

"Rubberneck" horses — those with long, giraffelike necks — present a unique set of challenges, but equally difficult is a horse whose neck tends to be stiff and tight. Short-necked horses seem more prone to tightness and can have trouble loosening and stretching their necks and lifting up through the withers and the base of the neck. A short-necked horse with a thick throatlatch has even more difficulty because the extra bulk makes flexing at the poll uncomfortable for him.

Although some neck issues are purely conformational, others can signify physical problems. Tension or incorrect riding and training can cause a horse to develop an "upside down" neck, in which the neck appears to curve upward the wrong way because the underside of the neck is overdeveloped and the crest is weak. It can take a long time to undo this fault and to develop the neck musculature correctly, because the horse must learn to relax the underside of his neck

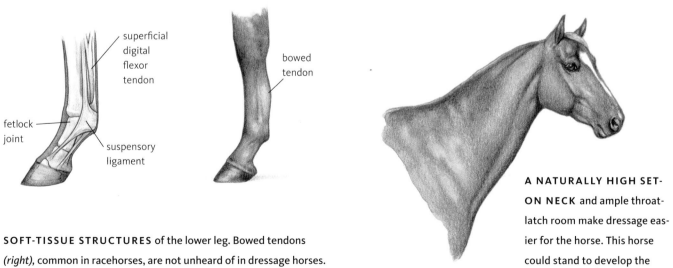

SOFT-TISSUE STRUCTURES of the lower leg. Bowed tendons *(right),* common in racehorses, are not unheard of in dressage horses. Dressage horses suffer a fair number of suspensory-ligament injuries.

superficial digital flexor tendon

bowed tendon

fetlock joint

suspensory ligament

A NATURALLY HIGH SET-ON NECK and ample throatlatch room make dressage easier for the horse. This horse could stand to develop the muscle in front of his withers.

while lifting and arching properly out of the base of the withers.

A horse that cannot flex his neck evenly in both directions may be overly tight in the muscles on one side. Equine chiropractors and many riders and horse owners believe that horses can suffer the same sorts of vertebral subluxations (misalignments) that humans can, and that a marked difference in a horse's ability to flex to the left and right may signify the need for an adjustment. Others rely on massage therapy and a riding program of exercises designed to stretch the tight side and strengthen the weak (hollow) side to improve balance.

What's Underfoot and Soundness

No foot, no horse. Healthy, correctly trimmed and shod hooves help keep dressage horses moving freely and correctly. Likewise, level footing with appropriate shock absorption and traction facilitates free, confident movement and helps keep horses sound.

Shoeing

If the average horse owner is concerned about trimming and shoeing, then the average dressage rider is positively fanatical about them. That's because correct trimming and shoeing protect the hoof and help keep its structures balanced and healthy. They also play a critical role in ensuring balanced, free, even movement — essential qualities for success in competition.

Dressage horses are shod for protection and support. Traction is not an issue the way it is for jumpers and event horses, and lightness and speed are not issues as they are for racehorses. As a result, the standard horseshoe (not lightweight, quick-to-wear-out aluminum), free of studs and caulks, is most often the footwear of choice. Many farriers use clips to help give

shoes a little extra staying power, but other than that, they're simple flat shoes.

The egg-bar shoe, whose rounded heel portion helps support the heels, particularly of the front feet, is another type seen fairly often in the dressage ring. Some large warmbloods and horses with low heels may benefit from this additional heel support.

Farriers who specialize in trimming and shoeing sport horses understand that dressage riders want their horses' feet trimmed in accordance with their unique leg conformation and also to enhance their freedom of movement. The horse should be able to use his shoulders to the full extent that his conformation allows — the "expressive" movement prized by riders and judges alike. Imbalances in trimming can lead to compromised movement, unevenness, and lameness. Most good sport-horse farriers watch new clients walk and jog on a firm surface before they trim and shoe for the first time, and repeat the process periodically thereafter or if the owner reports that the horse is not moving as well as he used to.

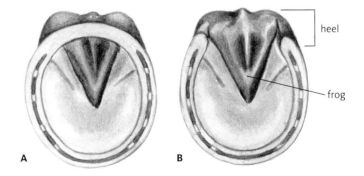

COMMON FOOTWEAR. Many dressage horses wear standard horseshoes (A). Some wear egg-bar shoes (B), which offer additional support through the heel and frog areas.

GOOD FOOTING (even, well-drained, not slippery, with enough "bounce" to lessen stress on horses' joints but not so deep that it strains tendons and ligaments) is essential. Shows without good footing have a hard time attracting repeat competitors. This is a close-up of a sand-and-rubber mix, a popular combination.

Many dressage horses are warmbloods, and many warmbloods have big feet, in keeping with their generous bone and overall size. Dinner-plate-size feet need big shoes, with generously fitted heels and toes for maximum support. The practice of trimming and rasping a horse's feet smaller for the purposes of fitting a smaller shoe is disastrous for all horses, but especially in dressage horses, where stunted feet can lead to stunted movement and chronic lameness.

Footing

More than any other group of equestrians, the dressage community has led the effort to improve the footing at boarding and private stables, fairgrounds, and show grounds. Recognizing that hard, deep, uneven, rutted, rocky, dusty, and muddy footing is unpleasant to ride in and often hinders horses' movement and performance, dressage riders demanded better footing, making their point with their pocketbooks if facilities continued to offer substandard surfaces.

Later, thanks to research efforts such as those led by equine biomechanics expert Dr. Hilary Clayton of Michigan State University, it was determined that footing is even more critical than once thought. Good footing offers traction and also absorbs much of the shock of impact, which otherwise would travel back up into the horse's feet and limbs. Repeat impact stresses can lead to career-ending injuries. And because many dressage horses enjoy fairly long careers, it is especially important to spare them as much unnecessary impact stress as possible.

With the help of sponsors, the USDF produced a booklet on the preparation and maintenance of good dressage-arena footing, and it has become a standard reference. *Under Foot* discusses how to prepare a site and build an arena, common footing materials and their advantages and disadvantages, and proper maintenance of arena surfaces. Because of these and other efforts, the larger recognized dressage shows and championship shows usually have excellent footing, and ring crews work valiantly to remedy any curveballs that Mother Nature may throw, such as torrential rain. Puddles or dust are inevitable at virtually every show, but horses shouldn't have to endure unsafe conditions.

Once you've ridden on good footing, you'll be spoiled for anything else. Many dressage arenas at top facilities feature surfaces that are blends of sand and rubber particles, expertly laid on carefully prepared bases that are designed to remain firm and flat while providing good drainage. Some types of sand (medium to coarse, irregular-surfaced industrial, or commercial varieties that have been screened and washed) offer better traction and produce less dust, and these make the best choices for footing. The rubber particles are often recycled tires and treads from athletic shoes and give the footing a pleasant springiness; plain sand feels dead in comparison. The goal is to put down enough footing to ensure a shock-absorbing surface, yet not so much that the footing becomes dangerously deep, which stresses soft tissues and can lead to tendon and ligament injuries. Dressage riders tend to prefer slightly deeper footing than jumper riders, who like the grip and speed offered by firmer surfaces.

The best footing in the world won't stay that way for long unless it is regularly maintained. Top facilities drag rings at least once a day, and show grounds drag more often. Regular watering is a must to keep dust down. In the proper proportion, water increases the footing's ability to absorb shock. Most top barns water with sprinkler systems.

Cold-weather climates make arena maintenance even more challenging. Sprinklers don't work when temperatures drop below freezing, and any moisture in the footing freezes. Judicious application of additives such as calcium chloride helps to prevent freezing and can help keep surfaces rideable until temperatures moderate and watering can resume. Calcium chloride and other salts can dry hooves and irritate horses' legs, so thorough post-ride grooming and cleaning are essential.

Complaints about footing are common at boarding facilities. If you're a boarder at a stable with substandard footing, educate the farm owner or manager about the dangers of poor footing and why improving the footing would be good for the horses. Also point out that excellent footing would be a tremendous asset and a draw for many potential boarders.

Failing that, if the footing is truly bad, you might want to consider looking elsewhere. Your horse takes a pounding on this footing day in and day out. In the interest of your horse's good health, it might be worthwhile to move to another (perhaps more expensive or less convenient) facility with better footing.

Dental and Bitting Problems

That holy grail of dressage — elastic, "alive" rein contact — is only as good as what's at the other end of the reins. Acceptance of the bit, usually indicated by soft chewing and salivating, is more critical to dressage than to any other equestrian sport because it colors every gait and movement and is one of the criteria on which the collective mark for submission is based. It is essential, therefore, that your horse's teeth and mouth be well cared for and that he feel comfortable wearing his bit.

Dental Care

Horses' teeth grow throughout their lives. Teeth wear unevenly and can develop sharp points that can cause pain when the horse eats or wears a bit and bridle. A qualified equine dental technician, working under the

AN EQUINE DENTAL TECHNICIAN uses a metal speculum to hold the horse's mouth open, as he examines the teeth and mouth and floats (files) sharp edges smooth.

supervision of your veterinarian, can "float" (rasp) the sharp edges and address other dental or mouth problems as necessary. Horses need their teeth floated at least once a year; twice a year is better.

Horses indicate pain and discomfort in their teeth and mouth in various ways, including drooling while eating. Under saddle, head tossing, tilting or yawing of the head, and reluctance to bend or turn in one direction and to pick up a canter lead may also signify problems. Some have multiple possible causes, so have your veterinarian do a comprehensive examination.

The Right Bit

Regular, quality dental care is an important step in keeping your horse happy and healthy. Another important step is finding the type and size of bit that best suits him.

As you learned in chapter 4, various types of bits (snaffles, at the lower levels) are permitted in recognized dressage competition. From the classic single-jointed snaffle to double-jointed varieties and curved mouthpieces, there are plenty of styles to choose from. Types of rings (D-, loose, full-cheek, and more) add even more variety. Each of these styles comes in various mouthpiece widths and thicknesses and types of metals.

There is no easy formula for figuring out what kind of bit your horse will go best in. Trial and error is usually the only way to find out. The one part that is simple is determining the correct mouthpiece width: the bit should be wide enough that one end isn't being pulled partway inside his mouth, but not so wide that the mouthpiece slides back and forth with room to spare.

Asking an instructor or your barn buddies to lend you bits for test rides is the easiest and least expensive means of experimentation. (Make sure all bits are clean before you put them in your horse's mouth, and wash them thoroughly before you return them.) Start with the simplest snaffles and go from there. There may not

be worlds of difference between one bit and the next. Your goal is to find the hardware in which your horse goes most quietly and happily, ideally with some soft chewing and salivation. Opening the mouth, putting the tongue out, tossing the head, refusing to take consistent contact, raising the head (going above the bit), ducking behind the bit, and excessive chomping on the bit are signs that his mouth is not comfortable, especially if the symptoms weren't present before you tried a particular bit.

The shape of your horse's palate and the thickness of his tongue can affect bit fit and comfort. Horses with low palates, for example, may be bothered by single-jointed mouthpieces, which may bump the roof of the mouth when the reins are pulled and the joint hinges. Such horses may find double-jointed mouthpieces more comfortable. Horses with thick tongues may be more comfortable in thinner mouthpieces, especially if they also have low palates. Although conventional wisdom says that thicker mouthpieces are gentler and kinder than thin ones, it's important to take your horse's mouth shape and tongue size into consideration. If you're not sure how your horse measures up, ask a qualified instructor or your veterinarian.

In the past several years, the bit-manufacturing industry has profited handsomely from the introduction

No Magic Bullet

When a horse isn't going well, some riders immediately begin fiddling with bits, as if finding the right one will make their problems disappear. It is always a good idea to check a horse's health and the fit of your tack and equipment when you encounter a training problem, but if these check out OK, try not to tinker endlessly with bits and gadgets. All too often, the source of the problem is holding the other end of the reins.

of metal alloys purported to stimulate the production of saliva and therefore to increase the desired gentle mouthing of the bit. Twenty years ago, it was almost unheard of to find a bit made of anything other than stainless steel, which wears well and needs little polishing. Stainless-steel bits are still available, but many dressage riders prefer the pricier German silver (which is not really silver at all, but combinations of metals with a high percentage of copper) or the gold-toned Aurigan (even more copper). Is the higher price worth it? It depends on your horse. Try it and see if you notice a difference. If he goes just fine in stainless, don't feel that you have to upgrade. But if he tends to have a dry mouth, one of the pricier alloys might help.

Although equine dental care is a science, bitting is largely an art. Other than complying with dressage rules and choosing an appropriate mouthpiece width, there are no prescriptions for success. Your horse's way of going and the way his mouth feels on the other end of the reins are your best guides.

Therapeutic Options

You don't have to wait until your horse sustains an injury to do something to promote soundness. A host of products and therapeutic options are available that can help keep him healthy and even give him a competitive edge. Some modalities, such as massage, are familiar in human sports medicine. Others, such as homeopathy, are gaining popularity but are still considered alternative therapies by most in the mainstream veterinary community.

Joint Health
Wear and tear on joints is a common cause of diminished dressage performance. Manufacturers of joint-health products have found in the dressage market a windfall of consumers willing to spend whatever it takes to keep their horses healthy and performing well.

Oral and injectable supplements purported to promote joint health (healthy cartilage and joint fluid) and joint function are available.

Humans, especially older folks, take joint supplements to ease the pain and stiffness of degenerative forms of arthritis. They are just now catching on to what horse owners have known for years. Supplements containing glucosamine and chondroitin sulfate, which are found naturally in cartilage, are said to promote the rebuilding of cartilage, thereby easing the stiffness and pain of achy joints. Many other substances, from yucca to vitamins, are also touted as remedies.

Walk into any tack shop or glance through any equine-supply catalog, and you'll be greeted by an overwhelming array of over-the-counter oral joint-health products (feed supplements), often with *flex* in their names. Prices, ingredients, and dosages vary. As with nutritional supplements sold for human consumption, equine supplements are unregulated and manufacturers are not required to prove efficacy. A handful of manufacturers and independent researchers have conducted studies that suggest their products help horses move more easily and freely, but the efficacy of most supplements remains questionable.

Even the most expensive oral joint supplements cost far less than the prescription-only injectable types, which are administered intramuscularly (into the muscle), intravenously (into the vein), or intra-articularly (directly into the affected joint capsule). Some experts

Buyer Beware

Before you decide to purchase a joint supplement, do some research (a Web search will turn up lots of information) and consult your veterinarian. Also, read labels carefully; some products contain lots of fillers and relatively low levels of the active ingredients.

believe that the injectable forms are more effective than the oral forms because delivery is guaranteed.

Polysulfated glycosaminoglycan (Adequan) and hyaluronate sodium (Legend) are the most widely prescribed injectable joint supplements. Adequan is available in intramuscular and intra-articular forms, and has been shown to block the enzymes that lead to cartilage degeneration and to ease pain. Legend contains hyaluronic acid, a component of joint fluid and cartilage. It is injected intravenously or intra-articularly and helps to block cartilage-destroying enzymes while promoting joint mobility.

Injectable supplements aren't for the horse owner on a budget, as they can cost several hundred dollars per application. Injections are administered intramuscularly or intravenously as needed, usually more frequently at first, and then at longer intervals on a maintenance basis; ask your veterinarian for guidance. Intra-articular injections are done less frequently because introducing a needle directly into a joint carries a risk of infection. Many dressage horses of a certain age have had their hock joints injected, and some have had other joints injected, as well. Thoroughly discuss the costs, risks, and potential benefits of supplement therapy with your veterinarian before you proceed. Some horses show dramatic improvement, but it's best not to expect miracles.

Alternative/Complementary Therapies

One person's alternative therapy is another person's mainstay. Name any method, from chiropractic to homeopathy, and some will argue passionately that it was of enormous benefit to their horses, while others will say it didn't do a thing for their animals. Part of the challenge in evaluating these therapies derives from the surprising lack of scientific study of their relative benefits. Much evidence is anecdotal and occasionally amounts to little more than a placebo effect.

Anyone who's had a horse with a frustratingly elusive soundness or performance problem understands the appeal of alternative therapies. With each new method tried comes renewed hope that perhaps this one will produce the desired result. If mainstream veterinary medicine has not helped his condition, alternative therapies are even more appealing. And some consider news of an improper diagnosis by a prominent veterinarian or veterinary hospital sufficient reason to turn away from the traditional medical establishment.

As his owner, it is your job to be your horse's primary advocate. Educate yourself and ask questions. The Internet is a tremendous resource, but always scrutinize the information you're reading and consider its source. The Web sites of some veterinary hospitals and clinics offer general information for horse owners, but sometimes it is provided with ulterior motives — promoting a practitioner's services, for example. Articles by reputable, disinterested parties, such as those featured in the magazine *The Horse: Your Guide to Equine Health Care,* tend to be more objective than those on sites promoting practitioners and products.

Following are some of the more common alternative and complementary (alternative approaches accepted and used by mainstream practitioners) therapies.

MASSAGE

Anyone who has ever enjoyed a relaxing back rub knows that massage feels good. Moreover, therapeutic massage has been shown to ease stiffness and improve equine performance while promoting relaxation and a sense of well-being.

Some muscle soreness is a fact of life for high-level equine athletes. A good equine massage therapist can ease muscle aches and pains and help horses feel and move better.

Your horse might benefit from massage therapy if he shows obviously sensitive or tight muscle areas

AN EQUINE MASSAGE THERAPIST identifies muscles that are tight or in spasm and then uses pressure and kneading to break up the knots.

while being groomed or if he has a particularly grueling training, competition, or travel schedule.

CHIROPRACTIC

Chiropractors believe that proper skeletal alignment is essential to good health and overall functioning and that subluxations (misaligned joints) can lead to stiffness, pain, pinched nerves, and even other problems.

Human chiropractors adjust (realign) a patient's spine and other joints through carefully directed movements. It remains to be seen whether a human being has the strength necessary to adjust a horse's spine or joints, however.

Your horse might benefit from chiropractic care if he shows signs of obvious stiffness, such as a marked decrease in range of motion when he turns his head in one direction.

ACUPUNCTURE

Acupuncture is a form of ancient Chinese medicine. Practitioners believe that the *chi* ("chee") of a living being — its energy or life force — normally flows freely along many *meridians,* or energy pathways in the body. Interruptions in chi, particularly at points of the body that control various impulses and functions, are thought to produce symptoms that can range from pain and stiffness to disease. Acupuncturists restore the free flow of energy by inserting thin, hollow needles into the blocked points, sometimes rotating the needles, heating them, or injecting a saline solution for added therapeutic benefit. Insertion of the needles causes little or no pain, and many horses appear markedly more relaxed at the conclusion of an acupuncture session.

Acupuncture's meridians have no corollary in Western medicine, and Western medicine cannot explain why acupuncture treatments ease the pain of some patients. This is consistent with the experience of owners of horses who have seen improvement that other conventional or complementary therapies failed to achieve.

Your horse might benefit from acupuncture if he has a persistent stiffness or lameness that has failed to respond, or has not responded completely, to conventional treatment.

HOMEOPATHY

Homeopathy is the practice of administering extremely diluted doses of substances — frequently tinctures of herbs or flowers but sometimes substances that can be toxic at full strength — that in stronger forms can cause symptoms similar to those currently exhibited by the patient. The belief is that "like cures like" — that is, the body responds by developing an immunity.

The theory behind homeopathy is a bit of a mind bender. Practitioners assert that the more dilute the substance, the more potent the remedy. Suffice it to say that adherents use homeopathy to combat everything from injuries and colic to mental stress and muscle soreness. Keep in mind, however, that homeopathic remedies are not substitutes for conventional veterinary care for injury or illness; they may speed healing but cannot take the place of getting a wound stitched, for example.

Your horse might benefit from homeopathy if you like the idea of helping his body help itself, particularly when you're waiting for a veterinarian to arrive. As always, however, it's best to consult with your veterinarian before you administer a homeopathic remedy to your horse. If the veterinarian comes to call, provide a complete list of all medications and other substances your horse is on.

OTHER THERAPIES

Some dressage riders use still other forms of noninvasive therapy in the belief that they help their horses feel and perform better. They include the following:

● ***Pulsating electromagnetic field (PEMF) therapy:*** Low-grade electrical impulses are delivered to key muscles in order to stimulate and eventually relax them. For horses, the pulses are usually administered through a special battery-powered blanket that covers the shoulders, back, and croup. In some studies, PEMF therapy has been shown to alleviate pain and to speed certain kinds of healing; other studies have indicated conflicting results.

● ***Therapeutic ultrasound:*** A gel is applied to the area to be treated to facilitate contact between the skin and a special metal wand that delivers ultrasonic waves. The treatment is believed to increase circulation and speed healing, particularly of the soft tissues of the lower legs. Therapeutic ultrasound is a fairly common modality used to speed the healing of suspensory injuries, bowed tendons, and the like.

● ***Low-level laser therapy:*** Laser beams, emitted at low levels from special machines, are used in an attempt to speed the healing of soft-tissue injuries, abscesses, wounds, and even bone injuries. Although lasers are known to affect cells to a shallow depth, the jury is out as to whether they can penetrate the skin deeply enough to have a substantial therapeutic influence in the horse. (Lack of scientific evidence does not keep horse owners from swearing by this and other therapies mentioned in this section, however. For a provocative look at the subject, read Dr. David Ramey's book, *Consumer's Guide to Alternative Therapies in the Horse* [Howell, 1999].)

● ***Magnetic therapy:*** Nonelectrified, magnet-implanted wraps, leg boots, and blankets are applied based on the theory that magnetic forces increase circulation and speed healing. There is little conclusive evidence about the efficacy of this therapy.

ELECTROMAGNETIC BLANKET.
The Andalusian stallion Otelo models a special blanket that delivers electromagnetic pulses to major muscle groups. The various hookups (red plugs) were detached from the battery pack (saddle area) for the photo.

PART V

FUN EXTRAS

We close this book with the beauty, fun, and spectacle of dressage to enhance your enjoyment of the sport.

For a sport that is so focused on the horse, dressage is also a remarkable journey of self-discovery for the rider. As you learn, you will continue to refine ever-subtler nuances in your riding and yourself. You will develop new levels of self-awareness and body awareness. You will tune in to your horse's feelings and body language, and you will let him guide you in the best way to work with him. If we learn to listen, our horses will tell us what they want and need. After all, they are our best teachers. Enjoy the journey.

◄ THE RIBBON is a dead giveaway, but the other reason we know Amy Gimbel and Travolta M are in an awards ceremony is the horse's polo wraps. Leg bandages are not permitted while showing.

CHAPTER 20

DRESSAGE WITH A TWIST

So you thought dressage was a solitary sport: just you and your horse, alone in an empty arena? Think again. You might enjoy several dressage-based activities. Some involve riding with others, which can be a fun way to combine your equestrian interests with social activity; others represent new challenges for the rider who's itching to do something different.

Dressage has many forms, each of which takes the classical equestrian art in a slightly different direction. If you get the chance to watch any of the events mentioned in this chapter, by all means go. You'll broaden your dressage horizons and be treated to some fun and exciting entertainment.

Musical Freestyle

Now a standard feature in regulation dressage competition, musical freestyle (or *kür*, as it is also called) is to dressage what the free skate is to figure skating: a unique choreographed routine set to music, incorporating various mandatory elements and conforming to

rules regarding duration, permitted and illegal movements, and so on.

A performance to music is dynamic in a way that a silent prescribed pattern of movements cannot be. The music itself is a draw, of course, as is the unique choreography. Spectators enjoy watching performers interpret their musical choices and are thrilled to see imaginative moves and combinations. Done well, a routine set to music is emotionally stirring and unforgettable.

Musical freestyle made its international dressage debut in the 1992 Dressage World Cup Final. It hit the big time when it made its Olympic debut at the Atlanta Games four years later. In fact, the spectator draw for this event was so significant, it might have saved the sport from the Olympic chopping block. Today it is a mandatory part of most FEI-level competition, including Young Riders (an upper-level division for riders sixteen to twenty-one). Grand Prix Freestyle night at the famed Dressage at Devon show in Devon, Pennsylvania, is nearly always a sellout, as are many other high-level freestyle competitions at notable shows.

Riders of all levels, from First Level up, have embraced freestyle as a way to combine the discipline of dressage with creative flair, and relish the opportunity to express their individuality in a custom routine. Particularly at the upper levels, freestyle has spawned lucrative careers for professional freestyle choreographers who develop routines, select and edit music, or both. Today's freestyle music is edited using sophisticated software and recorded to a CD for flawless transitions and outstanding sound quality. Judges award technical and artistic scores, so musical and choreographic excellence are both important.

If the idea of riding a freestyle intrigues you, start by watching as many freestyle rides as you can. Almost all recognized dressage competitions offer freestyle classes. The freestyles done at the Olympics, the Dressage World Cup Final, and other international competitions are usually available on commercially prepared videotapes and DVDs.

Then learn the rules. National-level (First through Fourth Level) freestyle score sheets and guidelines are written by the USDF, but USEF rules, including prerequisite qualifying scores, also apply. For more information, see page 317.

If you want to ride a freestyle but feel overwhelmed at the prospect of music selection, music editing, and choreography, you may wish to consult a professional freestyle designer. (Ask your instructor or one at a recognized show to get some names.) Fees depend on the level of freestyle being created (upper-level routines are more complex and thus more costly) and the amount of work being done. Designers work in different ways, so ask questions. For a hefty sum, some will compose and record original music just for your horse and your ride. Others work exclusively in certain musical genres, such as classical.

Although it's true that a lower-level freestyle may lack the visual fireworks of a Grand Prix–level routine, riders at all levels enjoy performing to music. Putting together a dynamite freestyle ride at any level takes a tremendous amount of work but is an accomplishment to be proud of. If you're looking for a challenge, the timing and music interpretation required in riding a freestyle offer tremendous opportunities to take your riding to an entirely new and different level.

SATURDAY NIGHT LIGHTS. The Grand Prix Freestyle is the biggest draw at many dressage shows. George Williams rides Marnix in front of a packed house at Dressage at Devon in Pennsylvania.

Quadrille

Quadrille is dressage times four. With a heritage dating back to the Renaissance, quadrille is the entertaining art of performing a routine choreographed for four horses and riders, often set to music. Long practiced by equestrian drill teams, quadrille is now a form of competitive dressage. It is especially popular in California.

Quadrille participants ride tests written by the USDF at Introductory, Novice, Preliminary, Intermediate, and Advanced levels. (The names and the levels are comparable to those used in eventing.) The tests patterns are executed without music, as in the standard dressage levels. *Freestyle quadrille* combines the challenges of quadrille with those of riding to music and has guidelines and rules, as does regular dressage freestyle.

Pas de Deux

If you've been to the ballet, you've probably seen a *pas de deux,* or "dance for two." In dressage, a pas de deux is a routine for two horses and riders.

Unlike quadrille, pas de deux is always a freestyle performance. There are no specified test patterns, and rides are accompanied by music. Pas de deux may be offered at any level, up to and including Grand Prix. As in freestyle, the judge awards marks for technical execution and for artistic impression. Synchronization of the two horses' movement plays an important role in the artistic score. Riders enjoy dreaming up pleasing visual imagery, including mirror-image patterns.

The annually published *USDF Directory* contains the current USDF rules for pas de deux.

THE POULIN FAMILY (Katherine Poulin-Neff, mom Sharon, dad and Olympian Michael, and daughter Kate) in a quadrille.

"DANCE FOR TWO." Floridians Johnny Robb and Lisa Payne ride a pas de deux.

Eventing and Combined Tests

Some dressage riders started out in the sport of *eventing,* formerly known as *combined training.* Likewise, some event riders started out in dressage and later yearned for a little jumping excitement.

Eventing is an equestrian version of the triathlon. Originally developed by the cavalry as a test of military mounts' obedience, stamina, and overall athleticism, eventing consists of three tests, or phases: a dressage test, a cross-country jumping test, and a show-jumping test (sometimes known as *stadium jumping*). A successful event horse must do an obedient dressage test when he is fit and raring to go; gallop and jump a series of solid, natural-looking obstacles over open and frequently uneven terrain; and have enough energy left over to put in a clean round over colorful, easy-to-knock-down jumps in an arena.

At the lowest levels, eventing is a fun sport that the modestly fit horse and rider, or pony and child, can enjoy. No great speed is required, and competitors can pop over unthreatening obstacles from a gentle canter or even a trot. Many low-level eventing competitions are run as horse trials, in which all three phases are run on a single day. At the highest levels, eventing is for the elite only, with demands that far exceed ordinary horses' levels of fitness and ordinary riders' bravery. At the higher levels, each of the phases is held on a separate day because they are so strenuous.

The *combined test* is a scaled-down version of eventing, incorporating only two of the three tests (often dressage and show-jumping). As such, it's an option for the off-season, when the ground outdoors is frozen or otherwise inhospitable; for areas that lack sufficient open space to build a cross-country course; and for those new to the sport of eventing.

AN EVENTING CHAMPIONSHIP PAIR in three memorable moments that exemplify the versatility required in this sport.
A. U.S. competitors Kim Severson and Winsome Adante, 2005 Rolex Kentucky CCI**** winners, during their (muddy) dressage test.
B. The team negotiating in style the formidable Head of the Lake water jump at the Kentucky Horse Park during cross-country.
C. The pair clearing a big oxer, with room to spare, during the final phase, show-jumping.

Because event horses do not specialize the way dressage horses do, the dressage tests in eventing are not as difficult as those in the dressage FEI levels. As an example, at the advanced level of eventing (the sport's highest level), the dressage test is approximately equivalent to Fourth Level dressage.

If eventing intrigues you, take some jumping lessons, preferably from an instructor who specializes in event horses. When she says that you and your horse are ready, seek out a starter event in your area. Many dressage and eventing associations hold "green as grass" competitions for the neophyte. For more information, see appendix C.

> ### TIP **Safety First**
>
> Safety is paramount at all times when you work with horses, but particularly when you're jumping. A qualified instructor can guide you in safe practices and the selection of appropriate safety gear.

Combined Driving

If eventing is an equestrian triathlon, then the sport of combined driving is eventing done with a harness and vehicle. Like dressage, this international sport is governed by the FEI at the highest levels. Combined driving consists of three phases comparable to those in eventing. There is an actual dressage test, performed in a dressage-type rectangle but much larger than that used in ridden dressage. There is a cross-country course, during which horses and "whips" (drivers) have to negotiate some tricky mazelike obstacles. Finally, there is the "cones" phase, held back in the dressage arena, which tests whips' skill at navigating a course of orange cones topped with tennis balls that fall when bumped.

Combined driving is every bit as exciting to watch as eventing, even though there is no jumping involved. The sport demands skill, finesse, and teamwork. The driving horses are quite skilled in basic dressage, and many whips school dressage under saddle as well as from the driver's seat.

DRIVEN DRESSAGE. Combined driving is the driving world's answer to eventing, and it commences with a dressage test in an oversized arena.

If you have a horse that you use for pleasure driving, you may enjoy training him in dressage. Making your dressage horse into a driving horse might be more of a challenge and isn't something to be attempted without expert help. For more information, see appendix C.

Reining: "Western Dressage"

Reining is one of the fastest-growing equestrian sports. Once the province of Quarter Horse and other Western-riding–dominated breed shows, it is now recognized by the FEI, with world-championship competition held at the World Equestrian Games. It has been an exhibition sport at the Olympic Games, and enthusiasts hope that reining will be added to the Olympic roster in the future.

Many refer to reining as Western dressage, and for good reason. The sport tests a horse's obedience, athleticism, speed, agility, balance, and coordination. *Reining patterns* (they're not called tests) require transitions within and between gaits (walk, jog, and lope instead of walk, trot, and canter), circles, flying lead changes, and other movements. The two most crowd-pleasing and often-photographed moves are the spin (imagine a canter pirouette on speed) and the sliding stop, in which the horse literally skids to a halt from a dead gallop, scrabbling his hind legs and practically sitting down in the dirt. There's even an equivalent to dressage freestyle: freestyle reining, in which competitors in costume execute choreographed patterns to music.

Western riding is more flamboyant than the English disciplines, so it's fitting that reining is dressage's more boisterous cousin. There's more flash and less precision. Even the audiences are different. Dressage spectators maintain a respectful hush, while reining enthusiasts clap and holler when they see something they like. Still, the two sports share common ground. Both develop the horse in a gymnastic fashion, although purists can and do argue the fine points. The end products reflect the different equestrian cultures — certainly no reining horse can be said to be "on the bit" — but many of the underlying horsemanship techniques are similar. Dressage riders and reiners have performed pas de deux that were wildly popular with audiences at shows and exhibitions. Clearly, enthusiasts from both camps appreciate the similarities and differences. For more information, see appendix C.

REINING. The grace, balance, and athleticism of this sliding stop shows why some call reining *Western dressage*.

CHAPTER 21

LEARNING OUTSIDE THE ARENA

Your home arena is your classroom, and that's where the lion's share of your learning takes place. However, many top trainers recommend taking advantage of other kinds of educational opportunities. You can gain valuable perspective and insights, including the following, when you're out of the saddle and from people other than your regular instructor:

- You can broaden your theoretical knowledge of the development of the dressage horse.
- In unmounted activities, you can focus on what is being presented, without having to try to replicate it.
- Watching other riders address challenges may lead to new insights and will reassure you that other people struggle, too.
- You'll meet other dressage enthusiasts.
- Some activities offer opportunities to meet and ask questions of well-known riders, judges, and trainers.
- Many are less expensive than regular riding lessons; some are even free.

In this chapter, I'll introduce you to several such learning opportunities. There is no shortage of educational activities to satisfy your thirst for learning. Most program standards are high. Try one; you won't be sorry!

Participating in Clinics

In dressage, a clinic is a lesson with a guest instructor. Some clinics are hosted privately by a stable, with participation limited to its clients; others are hosted by dressage clubs and are open to members and nonmembers, who trailer in their horses. Some barns invite the same clinician back yearly or several times a year; others prefer to expose riders to a variety of instructors.

AUDITING A DRESSAGE CLINIC lets you watch the action close up. This audience is at the USDF FEI-Level Trainers' Conference in Florida.

For some riders, a clinic is an opportunity to ride with a dressage notable (domestic or imported) with whom they wouldn't ordinarily train. For others, particularly those living in areas without easy access to good dressage training, clinics are a lifeline to quality, mounted instruction.

A clinic may be presented over one, two, or even more days. The most common format is the two-day weekend clinic, with forty-five-minute or one-hour lesson slots beginning at 8 a.m. and concluding in the late afternoon, with eight or so rides per day and a one-hour break for lunch.

The host facility or club sets the fee for each ride slot — usually the clinician's day rate plus travel and lodging expenses, divided by the total number of slots being offered. The average clinic ride is therefore more expensive than the average lesson because the fee helps to offset the clinician's travel expenses. Big names also command hefty daily rates. Put the two together and it's not uncommon to pay several hundred dollars for one session with a top trainer. (Lesser names, and those whose travel expenses don't include airfare and lodging, may cost much less.)

Although some riders seem to participate in clinics for bragging rights — "I've ridden with So-and-So!" — and others participate whenever an opportunity presents itself, you'll get far more bang for your clinic buck if you're selective. Different instructors have different teaching methods. They also have different personalities, different styles of interacting with students, and different ways of explaining things. Some will work for you and your horse; others won't. Find out as much as you can about a clinician before you commit to participating in a clinic. Study her credentials and achievements. Ask your instructor and other knowledgeable dressage folks whether they recommend taking her clinic. Post a question on an online dressage forum (see appendix C) and ask respondents to e-mail you privately with their opinions and experiences. If you can, audit a clinic before you register to ride (see page 299); you'll see firsthand whether you like the clinician's style and approach.

If you decide to sign up, reserve your slot(s) early. The clinic organizer can tell you what you need to do. Occasionally, such as when your own barn is hosting the clinic, a verbal commitment is sufficient, with payment made on the day of the event. In others, such as more formal events hosted by a large dressage club, you may have to send an entry form and payment by a closing date, much as you would if you were entering a show. In some special cases, in order to be considered, you may have to send a videotape of yourself riding to a selection committee.

If you like the clinician and want to get the most out of the event, sign up for both days of a two-day clinic if there are slots available and you can afford it. When you first meet the clinician, day one is spent partially on skill assessment and identification of areas that need improvement. Oftentimes, the bulk of the progress is made on day two. The second day can produce "aha" moments, breakthroughs, and dramatic improvement that make the investment worthwhile. If you ride repeatedly with the same clinician, she gets to know you and your horse, and you establish a working rapport that can carry over from session to session.

Before the clinic, spend some time thinking about what you want to accomplish. A clinic isn't a magic bullet, so don't expect the clinician to fix all of your training and riding issues. It's more realistic to go with one or two goals in mind, such as "I'd like help with my walk-canter transitions." Doing so gives the clinician a starting point and a clear understanding of your expectations. If she believes that you need to address another area first, she'll tell you.

Tips for Clinic Day

The day of the clinic, arrive at the facility in plenty of time to tack up and warm up by your starting time. You don't want to waste the first fifteen minutes of the session loosening up your horse so you can get to work.

Show respect for the clinician by turning out yourself and your horse nicely. Braiding isn't necessary, but a spotlessly clean horse and tack are. For yourself, a collared shirt or nice sweater paired with gloves, breeches, and polished boots present a tidy appearance. Protective headgear is always recommended and is mandatory at some facilities and events.

At the start of a session, most clinicians ask for a brief summary of your experience and level. Be prepared to give a short introduction: "I'm Jane Jones, and this is Dobbin. Dobbin is a twelve-year-old Thoroughbred–

Quarter Horse cross, and we're schooling Training Level. His walk and trot work are OK, but I'm having trouble keeping him balanced in the canter; he tends to get strung out and just goes faster. I'd love it if you could give me some exercises that might help."

The clinician may ask to ride your horse for a short time during your session. This can be helpful because some problems are more easily felt than seen. Keep in mind, however, that ultimately you are responsible for your horse's welfare. If you believe that the clinician is being abusive toward your horse — something I have never seen happen in a clinic — you are entirely within your rights to politely and diplomatically request that the session be concluded.

Likewise, the clinician expects you to respect her expertise and to treat your horse well during the session. I once saw a famous trainer halt a clinic session prematurely because the rider argued with the clinician's assessment that a young horse had had enough for one day.

Be prepared to try new exercises and for the possibility that you will be asked to do some things differently. You shouldn't be asked to do anything that's dangerous, but you might be pushed out of your comfort zone a bit. Again, unless you feel strongly that what you're being asked to do is jeopardizing your horse's welfare or your health or safety, try to be open to new concepts and approaches. "But this isn't the way my instructor does it" doesn't sit well with most clinicians.

Some clinicians have encouraging teaching styles, whereas others don't mince words and say exactly what they think is wrong with you and your horse. Such frankness can come as a rude shock to some, who take the comments as personal insults. A clinician may come right out and say, "That horse isn't suitable for you," and proceed to state why.

I once saw a lower-level rider reduced to tears after a clinician told her that she would be able to sit and ride better if she lost some weight. That clinician was pronounced "too harsh" by the people at the facility that invited her and was not asked back.

You'd think that every rider who takes clinics wants to learn and to find out what she can do to improve, but that's not always the case. Some people are more interested in being praised. Some cringe at the thought of being corrected in front of an audience and are afraid to make a mistake. Others really don't want to hear the clinician's unvarnished, unbiased opinion about things like horse suitability and rider fitness, or to be told that they shouldn't be schooling their five-year-old horse in piaffe and passage when the horse can't yet make a decent circle.

Maximize Your Clinic Experience

You can do several things to maximize your clinic experience. First, have a friend videotape your rides. Review the tapes as soon as possible after the session, while the ride is still fresh in your mind. Then replay the tapes at home and any time you want a refresher course.

Second, as soon as possible after your ride, make some notes. Jot down exercises, comments, insights, and any questions that come to mind. Review the questions with the clinician or your instructor. If your instructor can watch your session, so much the better.

Third, watch as many of the other sessions as you can. You'll invariably miss some when you're getting your horse ready and cooling him off, but hurry back to the ring to catch some of the other horses and riders. You'll probably hear some familiar phrases and exercises repeated, which will reinforce your own learning. It's also instructive to see how the clinician works with horses and riders of different skill levels and with different training and riding issues.

Auditing Clinics

If you're on a budget, auditing clinics is a valuable way to further your dressage knowledge. An auditor is a spectator, and watching a good clinician work with different horses and riders for a day or two can yield insights into ways to resolve various training problems and to work with different types of horses. Auditing multiday clinics is especially beneficial because it lets you see how horses improve from one day to the next; sometimes the changes can be quite dramatic.

In many cases, auditing is free. If your stable is hosting a clinic, for example, clients and friends may be permitted to watch at no charge. Other times, facilities charge a modest daily auditing fee. Still others charge higher fees but provide lunch in return.

AUDITORS, the nonriding audience at a dressage clinic, watch and listen intently, often taking notes for future reference.

If you hear or read about a clinic that you're interested in auditing, contact the clinic organizer for details. Find out whether you need to reserve a spot in the audience and what it will cost, if anything. Ask whether seating will be provided (often it's not, so be prepared to bring a lawn chair) and whether refreshments will be available (often they're not, so be prepared to bring a bag lunch). If you're not familiar with the facility, find out whether the clinic will be held indoors or outside, and dress appropriately.

Bring pen and paper, and take careful notes. Ideally, you'll review your notes when you get back from the clinic (doing so will help you remember up to 83 percent of the material, according to one source), but even if you don't, take careful notes, anyway. Doing so will force you to pay close attention to the clinician and to the riders and horses. Studies have shown that the act of note-taking improves comprehension and retention of information. To get the most out of your auditing experience, pay attention. You'll be surprised at the number of spectators who tune out the lessons to chat with their friends. You may not be riding, but auditing doesn't have to be a passive experience. Focus on what the clinician says to the riders. Watch how the horses change and improve during the course of the sessions. When the clinician tells a rider to do something, watch the horse closely to see if you can figure out why that correction or exercise was recommended at that moment; then watch to see if you notice any improvement in the horse's way of going. In other words, start thinking like a trainer: analyze the situation using the training scale (see page 88), identify areas that are good and areas that need improvement, choose exercises that will help the weak areas, and gauge their effectiveness.

Unless the clinician or the clinic organizer tells the audience otherwise, save any questions you might have for between rides, the lunch break, or the end of the day. The clinician may not be prepared to engage in a lengthy discourse with auditors, but most are happy to answer brief questions or to clarify points that may be confusing.

Auditing also gives you perspective and exposes you to different teaching and training styles. You'll realize that the way your dressage instructor does things is not the only way to train a horse and that methods, exercises, emphases, and expressions differ. Watch enough trainers in action, and you'll begin to recognize the common threads that run through reputable trainers' approaches, even when their personal styles differ. You'll also develop a sense for which trainers are solidly classical in their approaches and which are closer to the fringe. All of this is extremely helpful when deciding which clinicians you might like to ride with someday, and which you'd rather avoid.

Equine Expositions

Equine expositions are just plain fun. They're all-breed, all-discipline affairs. Most large public equine expositions and trade shows include educational sessions and demonstrations in a multitude of equestrian disciplines. For the price of admission, attendees can hear a lecture or watch a demonstration given by a well-known rider or trainer, not to mention browsing the trade-show aisles and checking out all of the tempting offerings.

If you're lucky enough to live within striking distance of an equine expo, check out the lineup of presenters and vendors. If a notable dressage expert is scheduled, you may be able to glean valuable insights for a fraction of the cost of a clinic. But be advised that when audiences are large, opportunities to ask questions and for one-on-one conversation may be limited.

In the United States, the best-known series of equine expos is Equine Affaire, which features dressage clinics with top trainers. In addition, there are regional expos hosted by colleges, universities, and other organizations. To learn of expos in your area, consult the

DRESSAGE EXHIBITIONS, whether traditional or flamboyant (like this flamenco dancer performing with Grand Prix–level rider Sabine Schut-Kery and the Andalusian stallion Capprichio), wow audiences at dressage shows and equine expositions.

events listings and advertisements in local and regional equine publications. Broaden your equestrian horizons by watching breeds and disciplines that wouldn't ordinarily cross your path. You just might gain a new appreciation for the challenge and elegance of dressage.

Dressage Shows

Dressage shows offer countless opportunities for learning, and most of them are absolutely free. Some larger shows offer organized educational programs, usually for a fee.

Learning at the Rail

Want to learn more about dressage, usually without spending a dime? Go to any dressage show, notebook and pen at the ready, and stand at the rail of the warm-up arena. The bigger and more prestigious the show, the better the horses and riders and the more well-known the coaches. A few of the biggest shows, such as

Pennsylvania's Dressage at Devon, charge admission fees, but most are just happy to have spectators. (For more on shows, see the next chapter.)

While you watch, pay attention. Listen to the coaches as they warm up their riders and horses. Watch the riders get their horses ready for the show ring. Observe their warm-up routines, their exercises, and their methods of coping with excited horses and other challenges of competition, and take notes. Too often, show spectators overlook the warm-up in favor of the actual classes. Although watching tests is educational, seeing competitors prepare their horses offers a behind-the-scenes glimpse into riders' training methods and can give you a new appreciation for what a rider has to do to get her horse into show form. Some horses mosey into the warm-up looking as if they just finished pulling a plow. Then the rider goes to work, and thirty minutes and a number of gymnastic exercises later, the plow horse becomes a graceful dancing dressage horse. The transformation can be truly amazing.

SPECTATORS. Want to learn? Be a railbird at the warm-up ring or at the show ring, and study the riders and horses.

It's great to train your eye and to learn to spot flaws, but don't succumb to rider- and horse-bashing. Some railbirds spend their time making fun of the competitors and seem to relish finding fault, often loudly. If you wonder whether something you see is incorrect, discreetly ask your instructor or a knowledgeable friend when you're out of earshot of the rider and his or her entourage. More than one spectator has made a catty comment only to be embarrassed by the discovery that the rider's mom or husband, or the horse's owner, overheard the remark.

Educational Programs at Shows

Increasing numbers of dressage shows are offering special educational programs to spectators to encourage extra revenue, additional sponsorship, increased attendance, or all three. Especially popular are sessions offering commentary by experienced judges. Participants rent headphones for designated classes, and the judge assigned to the class gives a running critique of the tests to help educate the eyes of the spectators.

Some shows host mini-forums on various dressage-related topics that are open to the public. Participants must usually register in advance and pay a fee.

If you're live near the site of a large dressage show that offers such activities, by all means participate. These types of educational programs are great ways to increase your dressage knowledge, and they're even more fun when you can combine the experience with the excitement of attending a quality competition.

Scribing

Any volunteer position at a dressage show offers a unique learning experience, but for the richest educational gold mine, nothing beats scribing.

A scribe is a volunteer who sits next to the judge during a class and records the judge's marks and comments on the test sheet or in a computer, freeing the judge to watch the test uninterrupted. Scribes have immediate access to the judge's assessment of each ride. At most shows, only the final score is made public; the marks for the individual movements are not announced or published. Even when individual marks are made available to the press or to the public, judges' comments are publicized only rarely, such as during an annual international dressage competition for young horses.

Scribing is a detail-oriented job that demands focus, concentration, knowledge of the level being judged, and a solid grasp of the basic rules. The scribe must know enough about the test being ridden to be able to follow the test sheet easily, and to be able to look at the horse and rider and know where they are in the test. As you might imagine, the higher the level, the more challenging scribing becomes. Scribes need to know how to mark errors, such as for going off course. They also need to understand the test sheet well enough to be able to tactfully remind the judge that she forgot to give a score for a shoulder-in, for example. (Yes, it happens!)

Many USDF group-member organizations (GMOs) and show committees offer training sessions for prospective scribes. If you're interested in volunteering as a scribe, taking such a course is a good idea and may even be required by the show's volunteer coordinator if you're a first-timer.

If you're new to scribing, you'll probably be assigned to a low-level class, in which the action happens relatively slowly. The challenge in scribing at more advanced tests is keeping up with the marks and movements, which follow one another rapid-fire. It can also be a challenge to write down verbose judges' comments after each movement, and that's why experienced scribes use as many abbreviations and symbols (like ☐ for "square," as in "halt not ☐" and ⊙ for "circle") as they can, while keeping the comments legible.

Just because you're a scribe, don't expect a private clinic with the judge or opportunities for extensive chitchat, although some judges will do so if the opportunity arises, such as during a scheduled break or when there's a lull in the action because of *scratches* (competitors who withdraw before the class). But even if you're not assigned to a chatty judge, you're bound to learn a lot from watching and listening. By watching horse after horse come down the center line to do the same test, you'll also begin to form your own opinions about who does the best job.

A SCRIBE records the judge's marks and comments during a dressage test, thereby freeing the judge to scrutinize the action.

National Programs and Dressage Symposia

Some of the dressage world's biggest names headline a variety of national educational programs, many of which are organized by or through the USDF (see appendix A for more on the USDF offerings). Some of these programs are essentially clinics on a grand scale; others offer participants opportunities for certification.

Adult Dressage Camps

It's many an adult dressage rider's idea of heaven: a long weekend away from job and family pressures, with nothing to do but eat, sleep, train, learn, and talk about dressage. Most dressage camps are put on by USDF GMOs and are held at facilities, such as colleges with riding programs, that offer both stabling and riding facilities and lodging for campers. One or more clinicians come in and teach lessons. Evenings consist of convivial meals and lectures and other educational activities.

USDF produces guidelines for dressage-camp organizers. Check USDF event listings for information about camps in your area.

Other Dressage Symposia

Some groups outside USDF organize their own dressage symposia. The New England Dressage Association, for instance, produces a symposium each fall, usually with a famous European trainer. The Kentucky Horse Park produces an annual spring symposium at its facility in Lexington. On a smaller scale, many dressage clubs organize lectures and various other educational activities.

To find symposia and other activities in your area, start by checking the USDF calendar, your local member newsletter or Web site, advertisements and event listings in local equine publications, and other dressage-related publications and Web sites.

CHAPTER 22

MUST-SEE SHOWS AND EVENTS

Watching top horses and riders is educational and inspiring, not to mention fun. As was mentioned in the previous chapter, studying competitors' warm-up and test-riding strategies — especially when you're accompanied by an instructor or a knowledgeable friend — gives insights into the training and handling of different types of dressage horses.

The best place to find top horses and riders, of course, is at top shows. That's not to say that good competitors can't be found at smaller competitions — big-name riders often introduce young horses to the show ring at these — but certain competitions tend to attract the crème de la crème.

What Makes a Top Show?

Prestigious shows share a number of characteristics that lure competitors. They include:

● *Location.* Certain parts of the country are bastions for dressage. The East and West Coasts have traditionally been dressage strongholds, for example. In winter, top riders and trainers from all English disciplines, including dressage, flock to Florida for warm-weather training opportunities and for a bevy of prestigious shows. Major metropolitan areas around the United States, perhaps because of their concentration of good-paying jobs, seem to spawn dressage-training facilities and dressage riders. All play host to respected dressage competitions.

● *Management.* Top shows are run efficiently by experienced show-management teams. A show at which stabling, class scheduling, and arena maintenance are first-rate is every competitor's dream.

● *Footing.* Quality footing in warm-up and competition arenas is critical for dressage riders. An otherwise great show with poor footing won't stay a great show for long.

● *Judging.* Top shows tend to hire experienced and highly respected judges, some of whom may be licensed by the Fédération Equestre Internationale (FEI), imported from abroad, or both. Because European dressage competition is considered the gold standard, aspiring international competitors relish the opportunity to have their performances evaluated by officials who judge their counterparts across the pond.

● *Championships and other designations.* A show is automatically more prestigious if it hosts championship competition. For instance, annual USEF/USDF Regional Championships are held in conjunction with an *open show* (a regular recognized dressage competition, with classes open to all eligible horses and riders) in each of the USDF's nine regions.

Some shows are designated as qualifying competitions for various national and international championships. A qualifying competition for the Dressage World Cup Final, for example, is run according to strict FEI guidelines.

● *Extras.* Sponsorship, trade fairs, competitor goodie bags, competitors' parties, prizes and prize money, educational events, and exhibitions are to be expected at the biggest dressage shows. A modest local recognized show, in contrast, may be a no-frills affair with a small concession stand.

Standout Shows

Although the list that follows is by no means comprehensive, it will provide you with an overview of some of the most prestigious annual dressage competitions in the United States. Attend as many of these shows as you can. See appendix B for contact information.

● *Dressage at Devon.* Held on the grounds of the Devon Horse Show in Devon, Pennsylvania, Dressage at Devon is the premier U.S. dressage performance and sport-horse breeding competition.

Open only to competitors at Fourth Level and above, Dressage at Devon showcases the dressage elite. Competitors must achieve minimum qualifying scores to enter, and only the top scorers gain admission.

The multiday extravaganza also features a huge sport-horse breeding show. Horses of all ages and sexes are evaluated for their conformation and movement in in-hand classes. Watching the sport-horse classes, to which top breeders from across the nation send their best stock, helps train your eye to recognize desirable and undesirable sport-horse attributes.

● *The Florida winter circuit.* The Florida winter dressage circuit is an aggregate of well-known competitions that cater to the sport's snowbirds. Many, if not most, top trainers from the Northeast and Mid-Atlantic areas, as well as some from the Midwest, relocate to Florida for the winter months along with their horses, clients' horses, and those clients who either winter in Florida themselves or travel to Florida for weekends or stints of several weeks. Most of the dressage facilities and competitions are located in the Wellington-Loxahatchee area, inland from West Palm Beach.

Because they draw so many top riders, the Florida shows have a high standard. A win here is prestigious indeed. Many of the shows are designated qualifying competitions for a variety of national and international championships. Aside from Dressage at Devon and some of the California shows, the big Florida shows are among the best opportunities to see many big names all in one place.

● *California Dressage Society Annual Championship Show.* The California Dressage Society (CDS) has the largest membership and is the mightiest of the USDF group-member organizations. Its annual championships are tough to qualify for and an honor to win.

The championships, held at varying locations in the state (frequently at the Los Angeles Equestrian Center in Burbank), feature competition at the national and international levels and are usually the designated USEF/USDF Region 7 championships, as well.

California boasts a wealth of top riders and trainers — among them, Olympians Susan Blinks, Charlotte Bredahl-Baker, Hilda Gurney, Steffen Peters, Guenter Seidel, and Christine Traurig — and its dressage standards are very high. The CDS Annual Championship Show is a standard of excellence on the West Coast.

● *Dressage in the Rockies/High Prairie Dressage.* Colorado likes to bill itself as dressage's "third coast" in the United States because of the large amount of interest and activity in the sport. The Colorado Horse Park in Parker (formerly High Prairie Farms) hosts two important multiday shows at its spacious facility, with sweeping views of the Rocky Mountains.

THE OLYMPIC GAMES are like no other athletic event. U.S. veteran Robert Dover rides Rainier, owned by Jane Forbes Clark, to team bronze in Sydney, 2000.

● *Concours Dressage Internationale* (CDI). CDI, or international dressage competition, is the designation awarded to shows recognized by the FEI. Asterisks following CDI indicate the level of competition offered. One asterisk is up to Intermediate I, two asterisks is up to Grand Prix but excluding the Special and the Freestyle, and three asterisks is all levels.

● *CDI*** Cincinnati at Paxton Farm, Batavia, Ohio.* Paxton Farm is a state-of-the-art, privately owned facility in Batavia, in southwestern Ohio.

● *CDI*** Raleigh and Capital Dressage Classic.* The Hunt Horse Complex at the North Carolina State Fairgrounds in Raleigh is the home of this well-known June competition, which includes a trade fair, equestrian exhibitions, a silent auction, and several educational forums and activities.

● *CDI*** Darien and Ox Ridge Summer Dressage Show.* Northeasterners flock to this August event at the Ox Ridge Hunt Club in tony Darien, Connecticut.

● *Fall Festival of Dressage CDI***.* Also known as the New England Dressage Association (NEDA) Fall Festival, this prestigious show is held each autumn. Like Dressage at Devon, the Fall Festival combines a breed show with a performance show. The Fall Festival's performance show offers competition at all levels, from Training through Grand Prix. A trade fair and "ride on the side" expert ringside commentary are also featured.

> **TIP** **Finding Shows**
>
> To find more shows in your area, visit the USDF Web site for its online competition calendar.

CADRE NOIR. The famed instructors and horses of the French National School of Equitation at Saumur perform in an exhibition.

Extra-Special Shows

Some dressage competitions are one of a kind. Held annually or even less frequently, they bring together the best horses and riders on the continent or even the world. See appendix C for contact information.

● **_FEI North American Young Riders' Championships (NAYRC)._** The FEI sanctions annual continental championships in dressage, show jumping, and eventing. The North American competition, which is held each summer, attracts riders ages sixteen to twenty-one from the United States, Canada, Mexico, Bermuda, and the Caribbean Islands.

The NAYRC is for advanced young riders; the official FEI Young Rider team and individual dressage tests are equivalent in difficulty to Prix St. Georges, the lowest of the international levels.

Each USDF region may send a team of four horses and riders or one or two individuals, and qualifying for Young Riders is difficult. For many, the event serves as an introduction to the bells and whistles of FEI-sanctioned competition, complete with veterinary inspection of horses. Winning a team or individual gold medal is the height of achievement for a talented youngster, and more than a few former young riders have gone on to international success in the Olympic equestrian disciplines. The NAYRC is held in different host locations across the country.

● **_FEI Dressage World Cup Final._** This Grand Prix–level annual international championship pits against one another winners of FEI-designated leagues (currently numbering five: Western Europe, Central Europe, the United States, Canada, and Pacific [Australia and New Zealand]). The Final is held in locations around the world and last visited the United States in 2005, when both the Dressage and the Show Jumping World Cup Finals were held in Las Vegas.

● **_Pan American Games._** This intercontinental, multisport, Olympic-styled championships is held the year before the summer Olympic Games, every four years. All sports on the Olympic program, plus some others, are featured. The Pan Am Games attract athletes from all over North and South America. In 2007, the Pan Am Games dressage competition will be at Grand Prix level (they were formerly Prix St. Georges/Intermediate I), making the event a true preparatory competition for the Olympics.

- **World Equestrian Games (WEG).** These world championships of equestrian sport are held every four years, midway between summer Olympic Games. Unlike the other international championship competitions, which are limited to dressage only (Dressage World Cup Final) and the three Olympic disciplines (NAYRC, Pan Am Games, Olympic Games), the WEG features competition in each of the seven FEI disciplines: dressage, jumping, eventing, driving, endurance, vaulting, and reining.

- **Olympic Games.** Nothing stirs the sports fan's imagination like the Olympics. Those who have participated say the experience is like no other competition. To win a medal here, especially if it's gold, ensures an athlete a place in the history books.

The Summer Games are held every four years. Equestrian competition has been part of the "modern" Olympic movement since 1912. A few sports, including polo, have come and gone; but dressage, show jumping, and eventing have endured.

Equestrian sports have history on their side, but Olympic organizers and the governing body of the Olympic movement, the International Olympic Committee, are keenly aware of two things: that horse sports cost a lot of money to produce, and that they're far from the biggest spectator or media draw. Dressage was said to have had a tenuous hold before musical freestyle was introduced at the 1996 Atlanta Games, injecting new life and boosting ticket sales. Meanwhile, eventing draws ire because of the expense of constructing the cross-country course

and because of negative publicity generated by spills. Whether the three equestrian disciplines will remain on the Olympic roster remains to be seen, although their place is assured through the 2012 London Games.

Even if competition is not your goal, it's fun and educational to attend these and other noteworthy dressage shows. Usually, a handful of rides stand out as truly exceptional, proving again that dressage at its best melds sport and art. Attending the Dressage World Cup Final, the Pan Am Games, the World Equestrian Games, or the Olympic Games is a once-in-a-lifetime experience not to be missed.

Other Don't-Miss Events

After all of this dressage learning, a rider has to have a little fun. Some dressage-related events aren't for educational purposes but instead are intended to showcase the elegance and grandeur of this sport-cum-art. Following is a sampling of events that even the non-dressage-obsessed can enjoy.

- **Spanish Riding School of Vienna.** The granddaddy of all dressage exhibitions, tours by the famed Lipizzans and their tricorn-hatted riders are rare treats not to be missed. The Spanish Riding School embarks on overseas tours occasionally; if a tour brings the Lipizzan stallions your way, go. You'll be glad you did. The riding, the baroque horses, the attire and tack, and the airs above the ground are all exceptionally beautiful and classical.

If your travels ever take you to Vienna, visit the school and attend a performance in the chandelier-bedecked arena. Visitors may also watch the morning exercise sessions and tour the school, including the stables. Tickets must be purchased in advance for all of these activities.

- **The Tempel Lipizzans.** The Tempel Lipizzans of Tempel Farms in Old Mill Creek, Illinois, are somewhat more accessible than those of the Spanish Riding School. The largest privately owned herd of "dancing white stallions" in the world, the Tempel Lipizzans are named for the late Tempel and Esther Smith, who in 1958 imported twenty stallions from Piber, the Austrian stud farm at which the Spanish Riding School's stock are bred. The Tempel Lipizzans have performed for presidents and other dignitaries, and the horses and riders give public performances at the Illinois farm as well as on occasional tours.

Former Spanish Riding School riders, including USDF Hall of Famer Karl Mikolka, have served as trainers and riders at Tempel. Among Tempel's former riders is the well-known Grand Prix–level dressage competitor and current USDF vice president George Williams, who studied under Mikolka and others.

- **Cavalia.** Conceived by one of the founders of the immensely popular Cirque de Soleil, Cavalia is an equine-infused extravaganza that includes live music, dance, and a variety of equestrian performances, including dressage with baroque Lusitano horses.

- **Medieval Times.** This equestrian dinner-theater chain isn't strictly dressage, but there are performances by Andalusian stallions, including airs above the ground. Successful Grand Prix–level competitor Cherri Reiber is the head horse trainer at Medieval Times in Toronto, Canada. There are a number of Medieval Times locations in the United States.

- **Exhibitions at nondressage horse shows.** Dressage is a popular exhibition sport not only at equine expositions but at other types of horse shows, as well. Most large shows incorporate at least a few exhibition rides during lunch breaks and off-hours, and dressage (musical freestyle, pas de deux, quadrille, and others) is commonly selected. Usually, the demonstration duties are handled by a well-known local upper-level rider and horse, or perhaps by an area quadrille team. It's possible you might find some dressage at a large hunter/jumper show, for example. Most big shows list planned exhibition rides under *spectators, entertainment,* or a similar heading on their Web sites.

PART VI

APPENDIXES

Appendix A. All about the USDF 313

Appendix B. Dressage-Related Associations. . . . 317

Appendix C. Resources. 319

Appendix D. Outfitters 325

◀ U.S. competitor and Olympic medalist Steffen Peters rides Floriano at the 2005 FEI
Offield Farms Dressage World Cup Final in Las Vegas.

ALL ABOUT THE USDF

The USDF is an umbrella organization that ties together approximately 130 dressage and eventing clubs around the country, including such groups as the California Dressage Society, the Eastern States Dressage and Combined Training Association, and the Virginia Dressage Association. Clubs affiliated with the USDF are known as USDF group-member organizations (GMOs).

To become a GMO, a club must have at least twenty-five members and must agree to file its bylaws with USDF and to include certain USDF information in its communications with its members, among other requirements.

A number of affiliated schools that offer dressage or equestrian programs fall into another category, interscholastic/intercollegiate-member organizations (IMOs).

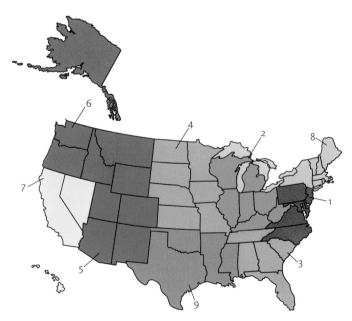

EACH OF USDF'S NINE REGIONS is represented by a regional director and holds its own Regional Dressage Championships.

Organizational Structure

The USDF divides the country into nine regions, each of which is represented by a regional director, who is a voting member of the USDF Executive Board. The executive board is headed by a president, a vice president, a secretary, and a treasurer.

Members of the executive board are elected by the members of the USDF Board of Governors, who themselves are elected representatives. As in the U.S. House of Representatives, each GMO is entitled to appoint a certain number of delegates, each with a certain number of total votes, depending on the size of the club being represented. USDF's participating members (people who join USDF directly in order to obtain additional benefits) are represented by delegates, as well; these delegates are chosen at the regional level, with the number of delegates contingent on the number of participating members in the region.

The board of governors meets once a year, at the annual convention of the USDF. There they vote for officers and regional directors; they also discuss and vote on any motions that may be brought before them by the USDF's twenty-five councils and committees.

Much like the U.S. government, the USDF accomplishes its work by committee. Its members represent every facet of the dressage world: judges, competitors, show managers, instructors, and many others. Each of these special-interest groups is represented within the USDF by a council or committee, whose chairpersons and members are volunteers and, typically, respected experts within the dressage community.

The terms *council* and *committee* may seem synonymous, but there are important differences. A council has ten members: a chairperson and nine regional coordinators, each representing a particular USDF region. The regional directors appoint representatives to each of the eleven USDF councils.

A committee's structure is looser. Each committee has a chairperson, but there can be any number of committee members, and their expertise is more important than where they are from. Committees tend to be informal groups of people with a common interest or specialized knowledge.

Each council and committee chairperson presents an annual report at the convention, summarizing the year's accomplishments, outlining the coming year's objectives, and seeking approval for new measures and programs. If the USDF annual convention is starting to sound like something you might see on C-SPAN, it is; lots of important decisions are made there. And the great thing is that *any* USDF member can attend the open council and committee working sessions at the convention, as well as the board of governors assembly, and stand up and express an opinion. (Only official delegates can vote, however.)

The USDF volunteer effort is commendable. Supporting the work of the volunteers is the paid staff, most of whom work at the USDF headquarters in Lexington, Kentucky. They process memberships, track awards status, handle competition results, and manage programs. Some are designated as council and committee liaisons. All employees report to the executive director of the USDF, a person hired by the executive board and charged with carrying out its wishes.

USDF Programs

For a nonprofit organization with a relatively small staff, the USDF runs an impressive number of programs. Most relate to at least one of its mission objectives: "education, recognition of achievement, and the promotion of the sport of dressage." Of the three, education is the

Creating a Legacy

It makes sense for nations to offer strong educational and competitive opportunities to help create a "feeder system" and develop the international champions of tomorrow. As excellence in dressage has increased in the United States, so has U.S. performance in the international medal hunt.

cornerstone. (Details on the programs that follow and other programs are available at the USDF Web site.)

Instructor Certification

In the United States, equestrian education is unregulated. Anybody who knows one end of the horse from the other can, as they say, hang out a shingle and proclaim him- or herself to be a professional trainer and instructor. The result is the expected mixed bag. The United States is blessed with many top-notch equestrian professionals — some of the finest in the world — but we're also cursed with trainers who range from so-so to sorry. They may be ineffective at best or downright inhumane at worst.

In an attempt to establish a standard of humane, classical, effective dressage teaching and training, the USDF launched its Instructor Certification Program in 1990. Led by a panel of expert trainers who serve as examiners and faculty members, the program offers educational and preparatory workshops and subsequent testing sessions. Instructor candidates strive to attain certification in various categories and at various levels. Examinations are rigorous, and to be certified the instructors must demonstrate competence in such skills as teaching riders, training and riding horses, and lungeing (working with mounted and unmounted horses on the ground, at the end of a lunge line). (See chapter 5 for how to find qualified dressage instruction.)

All USDF members can learn from the Instructor Certification Program. Even those who do not aspire to becoming certified instructors are able to attend the open workshops that certification candidates are required to complete in preparation for their certification examinations.

Judge Education

For most riders, dressage education starts with lessons in the schooling ring. But not all dressage education takes place at home. Many riders compete because they enjoy showcasing their horses' skills and training, and because the judging process is a valuable opportunity — unique in the horse world — to receive expert feedback. It stands to reason, therefore, that dressage competitors would want a well-trained, experienced, and impartial eye in the judge's booth.

In another attempt to raise standards, USDF began a program of judge education in 1989. Now formally known as the "L" Education Program for Judge Training (the *L* stands for "learner"), it indoctrinates aspiring officials through a multiphase program of workshops, mock-judging sessions, apprenticeships to licensed judges, and examinations. All USDF participating members can enroll in and benefit from the workshops, but apprenticeships and examinations are required of those who want to go on to earn their judges' licenses through the USEF.

The purpose of the "L" program is to prepare participants to earn their dressage judges' licenses, which they can do by enrolling in the USEF's "r" judges' program if they graduate from the "L" program with a

---

TIP | **Finding an Instructor**

To find a USDF-certified instructor in your area, visit www.usdf.org.

---

certain minimum score. ("Small r" judges, as they're called — the *r* stands for "recorded" — are the lowest classification of licensed dressage judges and are permitted to judge only certain lower levels.) It's a testament to the success of the USDF "L" program that it's now a mandatory prerequisite for USEF "r" candidates.

Even if you have no interest in becoming a dressage judge, attending "L" program sessions can help to expand your knowledge of equine biomechanics, the scale of training, test riding, the system of marks and how they are awarded, and how the judge critiques a ride. The sessions are taught by designated "L" program faculty members, who are themselves distinguished American judges.

Clinics, Trainers' Conferences, and Symposia

Recognizing that young people are the future of the sport, the USDF offers clinics with internationally respected trainers to promising young dressage riders in various age classifications. The USDF also sponsors a series of regional clinics for adults, and these are open to both amateur and professional riders. Two levels of invitation-only USDF Trainers' Conferences, aimed primarily at professionals, enable participants to observe internationally renowned trainers working with carefully selected demonstration riders and horses. The annual USDF National Dressage Symposium, held concurrently with the annual USDF convention and open to the public, spotlights one or more dressage notables in multiple days of clinics and lectures.

USDF ANNUAL CONVENTION

Apart from the National Dressage Symposium that is held during the same week, the USDF Annual Convention is rich in educational offerings. Convention-goers may choose from sessions on topics as diverse as veterinary issues, riding and training, and increasing volunteer turnout at GMO events. The educational lineup usually includes some big-name trainers, judges, and others. The Salute Gala, held during the convention, honors USDF Hall of Fame inductees and USDF Lifetime Achievement Award recipients.

USDF UNIVERSITY

No, you can't yet earn a college degree by majoring in dressage. Until that time, USDF University, as the educational program is called, may be the next best thing. The university program recognizes USDF members who participate in USDF's educational programs and independent educational programs accredited by USDF, based on their educational content. University participants earn certificates and "diplomas" for amassing various numbers of credits. Lists of accredited seminars and other programs are available from the USDF.

Regional Dressage Championships

Held in each of the USDF's nine regions, the USDF Regional Dressage Championships feature head-to-head competition among the region's top horses and riders, at all levels, including the popular musical freestyle. Competitors qualify their mounts for the regional championships by earning certain numbers of scores at or above a designated level, in special qualifying classes at recognized shows. The championships themselves are classified by rider designation, meaning that youngsters, adult amateurs, and "open" riders (typically professionals) compete in their own groups and don't have to go up against one another.

Awards

Broadly speaking, USDF awards are designed to recognize dressage rider achievement, horse achievement, and the achievement of a breeder in producing a fine sport-horse specimen. Following is a brief overview of the major award categories. Who knows? You might decide to go for one someday.

● *Rider medals.* You may never wear Olympic bronze, silver, or gold, but don't let that stop you from striving for a dressage medal of your own. USDF awards bronze, silver, and gold medals to recognize the achievements of riders who earn minimum scores at designated levels. Lower-level achievement earns the bronze rider medal, success at the medium levels earns silver, and the highest levels of dressage are recognized with the gold rider medal.

● *Horse of the Year awards.* Ultimately, it's the horse that's judged in standard dressage competition. Scores earned by eligible horses competing in USEF/USDF-recognized dressage shows are compiled in a USDF database. After the conclusion of the competition year, the number crunchers tally the results and identify the highest equine achievers at each level. The number-one horse is proclaimed the USDF Horse of the Year at his level. The proud owner gets to collect assorted goodies at the annual USDF awards banquet, which is held during the USDF convention.

There are Horse of the Year awards in breeding categories, too. The Dressage Sport Horse Breeding Horse of the Year awards recognize outstanding colts, geldings, fillies, stallions, and mares. The Breeder of the Year awards recognize breeders of top-placing horses.

● *All-Breeds awards.* This huge category constitutes the biggest slice of the USDF awards pie. Equine breed organizations and registries of practically every stripe seed the program by contributing monies that the USDF uses to track and recognize outstanding dressage performers at various levels within that breed. Got a registered Paint horse? A Quarter Horse? A Morgan? He may be eligible to earn one or more USDF All-Breeds awards. Whether your mount of choice is an Appaloosa or a Welsh pony, chances are there's an All-Breeds category for you, provided you and he meet the requisite membership and eligibility requirements.

DRESSAGE-RELATED ASSOCIATIONS

Club and association memberships afford a variety of privileges: opportunities to meet and socialize with like-minded individuals, access to activities and educational events, news and information, and other perks. Some memberships are prerequisites for special activities or to be eligible for awards.

Here is a rundown of the major dressage-related organizations in the United States and a list of their major benefits. Double-check dues and other information before you join, as these and other factors are subject to change.

LOCAL, STATE, AND REGIONAL DRESSAGE AND EVENTING ASSOCIATIONS

What they are: Clubs for dressage enthusiasts, eventing enthusiasts, or both.

Benefits: Group-member status in the USDF (benefits: subscription to monthly member magazine, *USDF Connection;* eligibility to compete in USDF-recognized shows, earn USDF rider awards, and earn USDF University credit; member-discount rates for USDF events). Club newsletter and calendar of events. Eligibility to ride in or attend club-sponsored clinics and schooling shows. Eligibility to earn club-sponsored year-end awards, if given. Eligibility to attend club meetings, lectures, and other events. Other benefits may vary with the individual club.

How to find a club in your area: Visit www.usdf.org.

USDF PARTICIPATING MEMBERSHIP

What it is: The USDF is the only U.S. national organization devoted solely to dressage. Its mission: education, the recognition of excellence, and the promotion of the sport of dressage. Participating members (PMs) are those who join the USDF directly (at a higher rate than group membership). PMs obtain an expanded list of benefits.

Benefits: All benefits of group membership (see above), plus: complimentary copy of annual *USDF Directory,* which contains all current dressage tests; a directory of dressage officials; guides to all USDF educational and awards programs; glossary of dressage terms; guide to arena setup; and more. Discounts on USDF merchandise. Regional newsletters. Eligibility to qualify for all USDF awards, including Horse of the Year and All-Breeds. Eligibility to qualify for USEF/USDF Regional Championships. (Additional membership and horse-recording requirements apply for Regional Championships and other USDF awards.) Eligibility to participate in the Instructor Certification Program, the "L" Education Program for Judge Training, and other educational programs.

How to join: Visit www.usdf.org or call 859-971-2277.

U.S. EVENTING ASSOCIATION

What it is: USEA's mission is to educate participants and to promote the sport of eventing. Unlike USDF, USEA has an official role in the making of rules and the sanctioning of national-level eventing competitions in the United States.

Benefits: Eventing USA, USEA's bimonthly member magazine. *USEA Omnibus,* a quarterly listing of registered competitions. Regional newsletters. Copy of the United States Equestrian Federation's Rules for Eventing. Eligibility to compete in USEA-recognized events, to qualify for regional and national adult and young-rider team competitions, and to earn USEA year-end awards.

How to join: Visit www.useventing.com or call 703-779-0440.

U.S. EQUESTRIAN FEDERATION

What it is: The USEF is the official United States Olympic Committee–designated national governing body (NGB) of equestrian sport and the U.S. national federation for equestrian sports under the FEI. As such, it sanctions national-level competitions in the U.S., establishes rules, and governs the twelve breeds and fifteen equestrian disciplines that fall under its jurisdiction, including dressage. Its governance role includes the licensing of officials, the provisions (including drug testing of horses) to ensure equine welfare and a level playing field, and the authority to discipline those who break the rules. In dressage, the USEF writes the national-level (Training through Fourth Level) tests.

Benefits: Eligibility to participate in USEF-recognized competitions and in USEF awards programs. Amateur certification for qualified members. *Equestrian,* USEF's member magazine, published ten times a year. Eligibility to become a USEF-licensed judge or steward (technical delegate, in dressage). Automatic equestrian liability insurance coverage.

How to join: Visit www.usef.org or call 859-258-2472.

BREED ASSOCIATIONS AND REGISTRIES

What they are: Organizations that establish standards, register, and promote various breeds and types of horses. Some license breeding stallions and organize inspection tours for registry approvals.

Benefits: Vary by organization, but may include publications; eligibility to stand stallions, register foals, and participate in inspection tours; and eligibility for USDF All-Breeds awards. (USDF gives dressage and dressage sport-horse breeding year-end awards to owners of horses registered with participating breeds and registries; USDF membership and horse-recording requirements apply.)

How to join: For the current list of USDF All-Breeds participating registries and breed associations and their contact information, visit www.usdf.org. Most major organizations participate.

U.S. EQUESTRIAN TEAM FOUNDATION

What it is: Formerly the United States Equestrian Team (USET), the organization was renamed the USET Foundation and transformed into the elite-competition fund-raising arm of USEF as part of the settlement of a dispute as to which organization should be designated equestrian sports' official national governing body. Member dues are used to help offset the costs of fielding teams for such international competitions as the Olympic Games and the World Equestrian Games.

Benefits: *USET Foundation News,* a quarterly newsletter. Other benefits vary with level of membership and may include auto decals, lapel pins, discounts on USET Foundation merchandise and on admission tickets to the USET Festival of Champions competition, and others.

How to join: Visit www.uset.org or call 908-234-1251.

THE DRESSAGE FOUNDATION

What it is: A nonprofit corporation that administrates various funds whose monies are used toward the advancement of dressage education in the United States.

Benefits: TDF is not a dues-supported membership organization.

How to contribute or apply for funding: Visit www.dressagefoundation.org or call 402-434-8585.

RESOURCES

Is your thirst for dressage knowledge unquenchable? Then I have great news. Publishers have long known that dressage enthusiasts are avid readers, and they happily cater to this market with a never-ending stream of new books. Add these to the plentiful supply of dressage classics, and you'll never lack for something to read. Then, of course, there is the Internet, a forum in which dressage enthusiasts of all persuasions post their questions, beliefs, and gripes.

Here are some good starting points, in print and online. Many of the books mentioned are required or recommended reading in the USDF's Instructor Certification Program and are available from the USDF, booksellers, and libraries.

CLASSICAL CLASSICS: TIME-TESTED TEXTS

Some of these are heavy reading, but they're among the granddaddies of classical horsemanship.

Albrecht, Brig. Gen. Kurt. *Principles of Dressage*. London: J. A. Allen, 1981. *A classic from the director of the Spanish Riding School of Vienna from 1974 to 1985.*

de la Guérinière, François Robichon. *École de Cavalerie (School of Horsemanship)*. Paris, 1733. *Eighteenth-century bible considered the foundation of modern horsemanship, including such movements as shoulder-in, which de la Guérinière invented.*

Klimke, Ingrid, and Dr. Reiner Klimke. *Cavalletti: The Schooling of Horse and Rider over Ground Poles*. Guilford, CT: Lyons Press, 1985. *A classic reference on using cavalletti and ground poles in training.*

Ljungquist, Col. Bengt. *Practical Dressage Manual*. Boonsboro, MD: Half Halt Press, 1976. *A staple from the Swedish-born former U.S. dressage team coach, who trained some of today's top riders and judges. Excellent illustrations and photographs.*

Mairinger, Franz. *Horses Are Made to Be Horses*. Hoboken, NJ: Howell, 1983. *Thoughtful work by a former Spanish Riding School instructor and the first-ever Australian Olympic equestrian-team trainer.*

Müseler, Wilhelm. *Riding Logic*. New York: Simon & Schuster, 1985. *Best-selling equestrian text by the late German Olympic rider and cavalry officer.*

Podhajsky, Col. Alois. *The Complete Training of Horse and Rider*. North Hollywood, CA: Wilshire, 1979. *A classic by the Spanish Riding School's most famous director.*

Seunig, Waldemar. *Essence of Horsemanship*. Canaan, NY: Sydney R. Smith Sporting Books, 1986. *Another classic from the late rider, teacher, and international judge; a native of Austria, he became an equestrian instructor in the German army.*

Steinbrecht, Gustav. *The Gymnasium of the Horse*. Cleveland Heights, OH: Xenophon Press, 1995. *A nineteenth-century classic that influenced equestrian sport in the German army and nation.*

Wätjen, Richard. *Dressage Riding*, 2d ed. London: J. A. Allen, 1979. *Born in Germany, Wätjen studied and taught at the Spanish Riding School of Vienna and went on to train and coach several Olympic teams.*

Xenophon. *The Art of Horsemanship*. Translated by Morris H. Morgan. Canaan, NY: Sydney R. Smith Sporting Books, 1999. *Oldest known work on horsemanship (4 BC), by a Greek general who advocated humane training practices.*

CONTEMPORARY DRESSAGE TEXTS

More recent additions to the dressage literature are also worthy reading.

Boldt, Harry. *The Dressage Horse.* Translated by Sabine Schmidt and Dane Rawlins. Germany: Edition Haberbeck, 1978. *Translation of one chapter of an immense book by the legendary German trainer and rider, with uniquely detailed diagrams of the aids.*

de Kunffy, Charles. *The Athletic Development of the Dressage Horse.* Hoboken, NJ: Howell, 2002.

———. *Training Strategies for Dressage Riders,* 2d ed. Hoboken, NJ: Howell, 2003. *Two popular modern texts by the well-known author and judge.*

Gahwyler, Dr. Max. *The Competitive Edge: Improving Your Dressage Scores in the Lower Levels,* rev. ed. Boonsboro, MD: Half Halt Press, 1995.

———. *The Competitive Edge II: Moving Up the Levels.* Boonsboro, MD: Half Halt Press, 1992.

———. *The Competitive Edge III: Gravity, Balance, and Kinetics of the Horse and Rider.* Boonsboro, MD: Half Halt Press, 2000. *Insights and advice from the Swiss-born trainer and judge and former president of the American Dressage Institute, a forerunner of the USDF.*

German National Equestrian Federation. *The Principles of Riding,* rev. ed. Boonsboro, MD: Half Halt Press, 1997.

———. *Advanced Techniques of Dressage.* Boonsboro, MD: Half Halt Press, 2000. *These companion volumes spell out the successful German training system on which the methods of the USDF's programs — and those of countless trainers and riders worldwide — are based.*

Knopfhart, Alfred. *Dressage: A Guidebook for the Road to Success.* Boonsboro, MD: Half Halt Press, 1996. *Progressive training manual through the medium and advanced levels.*

Kyrklund, Kyra, and Jytte Lemkow. *Dressage with Kyra.* North Pomfret, VT: Trafalgar Square, 1998. *The training methods of Kyrklund, an Olympic dressage rider from Finland.*

Lilley, Claire. *Schooling with Ground Poles: Flatwork Schooling for Every Horse, Every Sport.* North Pomfret, VT: Trafalgar Square, 2003. *Provides a good introduction to the use of ground poles and cavalletti and also includes tips on using ground poles to help improve straightness, bend, balance, and coordination.*

Lindgren, Maj. Anders. *Major Anders Lindgren's Teaching Exercises: A Manual for Instructors & Riders.* Boonsboro, MD: Half Halt Press, 1998. *Compilation of gymnastic exercises from the Swedish trainer who helped USDF instructor training get off the ground.*

O'Connor, Sally. *Common Sense Dressage.* Boonsboro, MD: Half Halt Press, 1990. *Useful, down-to-earth, and understandable introduction to the sport.*

United States Dressage Federation. *United States Dressage Federation Manual.* Lexington, KY: USDF, 1995. *Compilation of theories and excerpts from classic texts.*

———. *2006 USDF Directory.* Lexington, KY: USDF, 2006. *Handy, annually updated compilation of dressage information, from guides to USDF programs and dressage officials' contact information to the current dressage tests.*

von Dietze, Susanne. *Balance in Movement: The Seat of the Rider.* North Pomfret, VT: Trafalgar Square, 1999. *Detailed study of rider conformation, position, and biomechanics.*

Zettl, Walter. *Dressage in Harmony.* Boonsboro, MD: Half Halt Press, 1998. *Modern-day classic by the German-born master and former USDF Adult Clinic Series instructor.*

HELPFUL EXTRAS

These books will enhance your overall horsemanship, riding ability, fitness, and competitive and sport savvy.

Benedik, Linda, and Veronica Wirth. *Yoga for Equestrians.* North Pomfret, VT: Trafalgar Square, 2000. *Improve your suppleness, balance, and focus through yoga.*

Harris, Susan E. *Grooming to Win,* 2d ed. Hoboken, NJ: Howell, 1991. *The bible for producing a well-maintained, dynamite-looking horse for any show ring, including dressage.*

———. *Horse Gaits, Balance, and Movement.* Hoboken, NJ: Howell, 1993. *Lavishly illustrated introduction to equine biomechanics.*

Pavia, Audrey, with Janice Posnikoff. *Horses for Dummies*, 2d ed. Hoboken, NJ: Wiley, 2005. *Excellent introduction to horses and horse care.*

Ramey, David. *Consumer's Guide to Alternative Therapies in the Horse*. Hoboken, NJ: Howell, 1999. *With help from various scientists and researchers, the well-known equine veterinarian and author takes a cold, hard look at the efficacy of acupuncture, homeopathy, and a host of other "alternative" therapies in horses.*

Savoie, Jane. *That Winning Feeling! Program Your Mind for Peak Performance*. North Pomfret, VT: Trafalgar Square, 1997. *Useful introduction to sport psychology for riders by a former U.S. Olympic reserve rider and popular speaker and author.*

Steiner, Betsy, with Jennifer O. Bryant. *A Gymnastic Riding System Using Mind, Body, & Spirit*. North Pomfret, VT: Trafalgar Square, 2003. *Successful FEI-level trainer and competitor's three-pronged approach to horsemanship, including a Pilates exercise program for riders.*

Stewart, Daniel. *Ride Right with Daniel Stewart*. North Pomfret, VT: Trafalgar Square, 2004. *Fitness, strength, flexibility, nutrition, and sport psychology by the U.S. endurance-team and Paralympic dressage-squad coach.*

Swift, Sally. *Centered Riding*. North Pomfret, VT: Trafalgar Square, 1985. *Breakthrough imagery helps make the mind-body connection.*

United States Dressage Federation. *Under Foot: The USDF Guide to Dressage Arena Construction, Maintenance and Repair*. Lexington, KY: USDF, 1993. *Concise guide to arena specifications, materials, construction, and maintenance to ensure the best footing possible for dressage horses' safety and performance.*

United States Equestrian Federation. *2006 United States Equestrian Federation Rule Book*. Lexington, KY: USEF, 2006. *Annually published rule book of equestrian sports' national governing body.*

Wanless, Mary. *The Natural Rider: A Right-Brain Approach to Riding*. North Pomfret, VT: Trafalgar Square, 1987. *If you're not a "natural rider," this British instructor will help you to learn and apply the right muscles and movements.*

PERIODICALS

Several U.S. magazines are devoted solely or partly to dressage.

The Chronicle of the Horse
    Weekly bible of the competitive English-riding world covers most important national and international dressage competitions and runs occasional features on dressage riders. Publishes an annual dressage issue.
    www.chronofhorse.com

Dressage Today
    Monthly dressage-training and riding magazine.
    www.dressagetoday.com

Equestrian
    Monthly member magazine of the United States Equestrian Federation contains occasional dressage-focused articles.
    www.usef.org

Horse of Kings
    Focus on Friesians, Andalusians, and other baroque breeds often used in dressage.
    www.horseofkings.com

The Horse: Your Guide to Equine Health Care
    Reliable horse-health information and reports on cutting-edge equine veterinary research.
    www.thehorse.com

Hunter & Sport Horse
    Dressage, eventing, and hunter/jumper focus.
    www.hunterandsporthorsemag.com

Practical Horseman
    General-interest English-riding magazine contains occasional dressage-training articles (lower level) and profiles of successful riders and trainers.
    www.equisearch.com/practicalhorseman

USDF Connection
    Monthly member magazine of the United States Dressage Federation.
    www.usdf.org

THE CYBERWORLD OF DRESSAGE

The Internet was tailor-made for dressage because enthusiasts love to discuss their sport. Here is a guide to some of the most frequented sites. Be aware that although discussion boards may be monitored, you should take all advice offered with the proverbial grain of salt. The anonymity of the Web prevents most users from ascertaining details of posters' identities, and so credentials often cannot be verified.

www.chronofhorse.com; click on "Bulletin Board"
> Chronicle of the Horse *discussion boards. Very active dressage board as well as forums dedicated to the* Chronicle's *other coverage areas. Public; other areas of the online magazine are for subscribers only.*

http://cvm.msu.edu/dressage
> *Web site of McPhail Dressage Chair and world-renowned equine-biomechanics expert Dr. Hilary Clayton, who researches dressage-related issues at Michigan State University. Articles and links. Public.*

www.dressageclinic.com
> *Subscribers to this commercial site may view videos of top trainers teaching and riding.*

www.dressagedaily.com
> *News, photos, competition coverage, horses for sale, and commercial links, run by equine photographer Mary Phelps. Public.*

www.dressage4kids.com
> *Youth-oriented site run by Olympian Lendon Gray, with emphasis on Gray's annual Youth Dressage Festival competition. Message-board links. Public.*

www.dressageunltd.com
> *Commercial site containing news, classified ads, and members-only discussion boards.*

www.ultimatedressage.com
> *Classified ads, calendar of events, commercial links, and a heavily traveled bulletin board containing topic areas pertaining to all things dressage. Public.*

www.youngriders.net
> *Information and news pertaining to the FEI North American Young Riders' Championships. Discussion board for young riders. Public.*

RIDER FITNESS

Are you intrigued by one or more of the workouts you've read about in this book? Check out the following resources for more information, and then get moving! Your horse will thank you.

PILATES

Siler, Brooke. *The Pilates Body*. New York: Broadway Books, 2000. *Excellent, thorough introduction to the Pilates method; illustrated with top-notch photos.*

Steiner, Betsy, with Jennifer O. Bryant. *A Gymnastic Riding System Using Mind, Body, & Spirit*. North Pomfret, VT: Trafalgar Square, 2003. *Dressage-based training book for horse and rider includes a program of Pilates exercises for riders, selected by FEI-level rider/trainer/competitor and Pilates devotee Betsy Steiner.*

Ungaro, Alycea. *Pilates: Body in Motion*. New York: DK, 2002. *Another very good Pilates exercise book, also with excellent photos.*

www.equilates.com
> *Building on the introductory Pilates-for-riders program in her book, Betsy Steiner went on to develop Equilates, a complete Pilates regimen for equestrians, including workshops for instructors.*

www.pilates-studio.com
> *Web site of the New York Pilates Studio and the original Pilates method as developed by Joseph Pilates and passed down to Pilates master teachers.*

ENDURANCE/AEROBIC TRAINING

Schlosberg, Suzanne, and Liz Neporent. *Fitness for Dummies*, 2d ed. New York: For Dummies, 1999. *As you would expect from a "for Dummies" title, this is a useful all-around introduction to fitness in all of its incarnations; also contains information about flexibility and Pilates training.*

Strength Training

http://sportsmedicine.about.com/cs/strengthening/
About.com's guide to strength training. Guidelines and tips from the "info central" Web brand.

www.cdc.gov/nccdphp/dnpa/physical/index.htm
Centers for Disease Control and Prevention's Physical Activity site. Articles, information, and links on physical fitness from the U.S. government.

Neporent, Liz, and Suzanne Schlosberg. *Weight Training for Dummies,* 2d ed. New York: For Dummies, 2000. *The same author team that brought you* Fitness for Dummies *explores weight training in more detail.*

Flexibility Training

Anderson, Bob. *Stretching: 20th Anniversary.* Bolinas, CA: Shelter, 2000. *Also contains sport-specific stretches, including for equestrians.*

Accessories and Equipment

www.gymnic.com
Just one source of the popular, versatile, and affordable exercise balls and other items that help make workouts fun and challenging.

www.thera-band.com
Another supplier of bands, tubing, exercise balls, and more. Best known for its stretchy bands that can be used in countless stretching and strengthening exercises.

DRESSAGE-RELATED ACTIVITIES

Musical Freestyle

Anderson, Libby, and Leigh Ann Hazel-Groux. *Dancing with Your Horse.* Boonsboro, MD: Half Halt Press, 2003. *Good introduction to the various considerations in creating a musical freestyle.*

Quadrille

www.in-balance.com/CQA.htm
Web site of the California Quadrille Association, a USDF group-member organization and one of the most active quadrille groups in the country.

Eventing

www.eventingusa.com
Web site of the U.S. Eventing Association; information and links to everything about the sport of eventing in the United States.

Driving

www.americandrivingsociety.org
Web site of the American Driving Society, the national association for driving.

www.drivingessentials.com
Web site of Driving Essentials (Kennett Square, Pennsylvania), an everything-for-the-driver store that carries many books on driven dressage.

Reining

www.nrha.com
Web site of the National Reining Horse Association, the national association for the sport of reining.

DRESSAGE SHOWS

- California Dressage Society Annual Championship Show: www.california-dressage.org
- CDI Cincinnati: www.paxtonfarm.com
- CDI Raleigh: www.cdi-raleigh.com
- Dressage at Devon: www.dressageatdevon.org
- Dressage in the Rockies/High Prairie Dressage: www.cornerstonedressage.com; www.coloradohorsepark.com
- FEI Dressage World Cup Final: www.feiworldcup.org
- FEI North American Young Riders' Championships: www.youngriders.org

- Florida Winter Circuit: www.thebarnbook.com; www.pbderby.com; www.orlandodressage.com
- New England Dressage Association Fall Festival: www.neda.org
- Olympic Games: www.horsesport.org; www.usoc.org; www.olympic.org
- Pan American Games: www.usoc.org
- World Equestrian Games: www.horsesport.org

OTHER DON'T-MISS SHOWS/EVENTS

- Cavalia: www.cavalia.net
- Medieval Times: www.medievaltimes.com
- Spanish Riding School of Vienna: www.spanische-reitschule.com
- Tempel Lipizzans: www.tempelfarms.com

INSTRUCTOR CERTIFICATION PROGRAMS

www.cha-ahse.org

Web site of the Certified Horsemanship Association, an equestrian certification organization.

www.riding-instructor.com

Web site of the American Riding Instructors Association. ARIC certifies instructors in many equestrian disciplines, including dressage.

www.usdf.org/Programs/InstructorCertification

Complete guidelines for certification candidates and useful information for dressage students.

OUTFITTERS

In the market for a new show coat? Do you have to have the latest trend in European breech styling? Are you anxiously awaiting the newest browband fad or bit design? Then get thee to a dressage emporium!

Even if all you want is a decent pair of schooling tights or an everyday saddle pad, merchants who specialize in dressage items can help outfit you and your horse properly and comfortably. The better stores, catalogs, and Web sites employ clerks who know the sport and the merchandise and can steer you in the right direction for your needs and your pocketbook. Some are experts at such valuable skills as measuring riders for boots and horses for saddles.

Most English-oriented tack shops offer dressage apparel and equipment, and many of these carry top brands and hire knowledgeable salespeople.

Ask dressage enthusiasts in your area which tack shops they patronize and which salespeople are the most savvy about the sport. Dressage magazines and other publications may include ads for stores, catalogs, and Web sites that specialize in dressage apparel and equipment. Large and local dressage-related retailers also may have a presence at trade fairs held in conjunction with dressage shows, particularly the larger and more prestigious affairs.

GLOSSARY

The dressage terms defined in this section are also explained elsewhere in this book. Use this glossary whenever you need a quick refresher.

above the bit. A head position in which the horse projects his nose up and out (often accompanied by raising the entire neck) in an effort to avoid acceptance of the bit.

action. The degree to which a horse lifts his legs as he moves. A very high-stepping horse, especially in a discipline other than dressage, may be said to have a lot of action or knee action.

activity. Energetic, lively movement, especially of the horse's hind legs.

aids. The rider's means of communicating cues to the horse. The aids are: seat, legs, hands (rein aids), and voice. Use of the voice is not permitted in dressage competition. Advanced riders may use the *artificial aids* (whip and spurs) to amplify the basic aids.

allow. To "give" with the hands, seat, or both to enable a horse to go freely forward.

banged. Trimmed straight across, as the end of a horse's tail.

behind the bit/behind the leg. A horse's attempt to avoid acceptance of the bit and the forward driving aids by "sucking back" away from the contact.

behind the vertical. A head position in which the horse's profile is behind an imaginary vertical line. Indicates improper longitudinal flexion (along the neck vertebrae instead of at the poll, as is correct), which prevents the horse from being "connected" correctly between the aids. The position is sometimes used as part of a "deep," stretching warm-up routine or at certain other times during training, although experts debate its correctness and effectiveness. A momentary positioning behind the vertical is not a serious fault. *Behind the vertical* is not synonymous with *behind the bit* or *behind the leg*.

bend. The horse's body positioned such that it appears to be curved equilaterally from poll to tail. On a curved line, such as a circle, the horse's body should appear to be bent (aligned) evenly along the arc of the curve.

blocking. Tensing of the hands, seat, or both to inhibit a horse's free forward movement by creating rigidity in his musculature.

cadence. Expressive movement, with accentuated rhythm and tempo in accordance with the gait. Because cadence is possible only in gaits with a moment of suspension, the term is used only in reference to the trot and the canter.

cavesson. Noseband of the bridle.

chair seat. Incorrect position in which a rider sits back on the fleshy portion of the buttocks with the legs forward, as if sitting in a chair.

class. A single competitive division at a show, grouped by task and/or skill level.

classical horsemanship. The practice of a humane, gymnastic means of training horses as athletes for various purposes, using a common set of agreed-on principles.

coefficient movement. In a dressage test, a judged element that is weighted to give it more influence over the total score (the norm is a coefficient of 2, in which the points awarded are doubled). A coefficient signifies that a movement is considered particularly important at that stage in a horse's training.

cold-backed. Refers to a horse that does not like a rider to sit down hard on his back when first mounting.

collected/collection. A state in which the horse's energy is gathered in his body in the manner of a coiled spring. His outline becomes shorter from poll to tail, and he literally appears taller, with an arched neck and lifted back. His strides become more expressive at the same time that they cover less ground. His energy is directed up as well as forward.

collective marks. At the conclusion of a dressage test in competition, numeric scores awarded for overall impressions of the horse's gaits, impulsion, and submission; and for the rider's position and seat, and effectiveness and use of the aids.

contact. A connection between the horse's mouth and the rider's hands, maintained through the reins. Contact cannot be achieved or maintained on slack (looped) reins. The horse, not the rider, "takes" the contact by seeking the connection with the bit. The horse goes forward into the contact; the rider does not enforce it by pulling back on the reins. Good contact feels alive and elastic, not heavy and dead in the rider's hands. Good contact is also consistent; it isn't alternately dropped and picked up.

counter-canter. A canter on the "wrong" (outside) lead; used as a valuable gymnastic tool for developing a horse's balance, strength, and straightness.

disunited canter. A canter that has lost its normal three-beat pattern of footfalls; also known as *cross-cantering*.

double bridle. A bridle containing two bits (snaffle and curb) and two sets of reins. Not permitted below Third Level. Optional at Third and Fourth Levels. Required in most FEI-level tests.

downhill balance. "On the forehand" equine conformation in which the horse's weight is concentrated over his shoulders and forelegs; often seen in horses whose croups are higher than their withers.

driving seat. Rider position with assertive seat aids and the upper body vertical or (sometimes, momentarily) slightly behind the vertical in order to encourage the horse strongly forward.

engagement. Increased weight-bearing over the hindquarters through increased flexion of the horse's hip joint and the joints of the hind legs during the stance phase (the phase in a gait when the limb is on the ground). Engagement lowers the hindquarters relative to the forehand and "loads" the joints so that they can produce powerful thrust, necessary for impulsion and later for collection.

equestrian art. Another term for *classical horsemanship*.

extended/extension. A pace in which a horse lengthens his outline and his stride to their utmost while remaining in balance and contact. The walk, trot, and canter may all be extended.

figure. A dressage-test element with specific geometric designation (e.g., 20-meter circle).

flash noseband. A cavesson consisting of two parts: the regular cavesson, which fastens around the horse's jawbone; and a flash attachment: a lower strap, attached to the midpoint of the cavesson via a loop, that wraps around the horse's chin, in front of the bit. Fastened snugly, the flash helps to keep the horse's mouth closed. Used only with a snaffle bridle.

flatwork. Schooling that does not incorporate jumps; usually used in reference to hunters and jumpers.

flexion. Yielding of the horse's jaw and poll, usually to bit pressure. A horse may be flexed longitudinally (with his nose drawn closer to his chest), laterally (with his head turned to the left or to the right), or both. In correct lateral flexion, the rider can see the horse's inside eye and no more.

float. To file and balance a horse's teeth and grinding surfaces to ensure proper chewing and maximum comfort while bitted.

frame. Outline of a horse's body; the frame may be longer or shorter depending on the degree of extension and collection.

"front to back" riding. Common, incorrect form of dressage riding in which a rider attempts to "pull the horse together" by using the reins instead of pushing him forward from the leg into an elastic rein contact.

girthy. A horse that objects to the feel of having the girth tightened.

give. To relax the wrists and elbows, as after a half-halt, to allow a horse to go forward.

gymnasticize. To systematically develop a horse's strength and suppleness longitudinally and laterally.

hack/hacking. Riding outside the arena for pleasure.

half-halt. Momentary rebalancing of the horse, either as a correction for a loss of longitudinal balance (falling on the forehand) or in preparation for a transition or other movement.

haunches-in (travers). Lateral movement that supples the horse and engages his inside hind leg by displacing his haunches to the inside of the line of travel. The horse is bent around the rider's inside leg.

hollow. Inverted; with the horse's neck raised, his back dropped, and his haunches elevated. Opposite of *round*.

impulsion. Thrust; release of the energy from the "coiled springs" of the engaged hindquarters.

in front of the leg. Description of a forward-thinking, forward-going horse that reacts promptly to the rider's seat and leg aids and that energetically strides forward into the rein contact.

lateral. To the side. Lateral movements require that a horse be bent in one direction and therefore also require him to travel both sideways and forward, relative to the line of travel. Also, used to describe one form of a poor walk — a pacing gait (with both legs on one side stepping simultaneously) instead of the correct four-beat walk gait.

leg-yield. An introductory lateral movement in which the horse steps forward and sideways while flexed laterally away from the direction of travel. His body remains nearly straight. Commonly performed in the walk and in the trot.

lengthened/lengthening. Elongation of the horse's stride and outline in the walk, trot, or canter. The most introductory version of the elongation of the stride.

levels. Stepping-stone stages of difficulty in the dressage training as articulated through the requirements in the various dressage tests used in competition. The lowest level of dressage competition in the United States is USDF Introductory Level. Next are the national levels: in the United States, U.S. Equestrian Federation Training, First, Second, Third, and Fourth Levels. The international levels of competition, used worldwide, are: International Equestrian Federation (FEI) Prix St. Georges, Intermediate I, Intermediate II, Grand Prix, Pony, Junior, Young Rider, and Young Horse (Five- and Six-Year-Old).

medium. An elongation of the horse's stride and outline that is midway between lengthening and extension. The stride and outline show more elongation than in a lengthening but with a greater degree of balance and collection.

movement. A horse's way of going. In dressage, good movement is considered to be active, expressive, and free, particularly from the shoulders and hindquarters. Also, a lateral

exercise or other element, particularly as required in a dressage test.

on the bit. Accepting and seeking a steady contact with the bit.

on contact. See *on the bit*.

on the forehand. Moving in a "downhill" fashion such that the horse's front legs remain earthbound for longer than is desired in the stride.

out behind. Standing or moving with the hind legs remaining behind an imaginary vertical line dropped from the point of a horse's buttocks.

overtracking. In the walk, placing the hind hoof in front of the hoofprint of the front hoof on the same side. Indicative of a correctly free and swinging walk.

polo wrap. Long bandage, usually made of synthetic fleece, that is wrapped around the horse's leg from cannon to fetlock for protection and looks and is secured with hook-and-loop fasteners. White is the traditional color for polo wraps in dressage. Used extensively in schooling but, as with other leg wraps and boots, not permitted in dressage competition.

pyramid of training. Graphic representation of the scale of training.

rein. In dressage, refers to the direction of travel. To be on the right rein means to be traveling clockwise.

rhythm. Evenness of footfalls in accordance with the gait being performed. The walk has a four-beat rhythm (four even footfalls); the trot is two-beat (two sets of footfalls by diagonal pairs of legs); and the canter is three-beat (one hind leg, one diagonal pair, and one foreleg). As in a piece of music, a gait's rhythm should remain consistent at all times.

rising. Posting. In the trot, allowing one's seat to come slightly out of the saddle at every other stride. Used frequently when warming up because it is less fatiguing to the horse's back.

round. Refers to the convex topline of the horse's body.

scratch. Withdraw from competition.

scribe. Volunteer who sits next to the judge during a dressage competition and records his or her numeric scores and verbal comments.

seat. The rider's primary aid, consisting of the weight influence and actions of the area from hips to knees.

self-carriage. Balanced and independent carriage by the horse of his own body, without leaning on the rider's hands for support.

serpentine. S-shaped figure. Can be ridden at any gait, at any width, and with any number of loops. The wider the serpentine and the more loops, the more difficult it is for the horse because it challenges his bend and balance.

shoulder-fore. Lateral positioning of the horse such that his forehand is brought slightly to the inside of the line of travel, but not as much as in shoulder-in. Used as a straightening and bending exercise in the trot and especially in the canter.

shoulder-in. Lateral positioning of the horse such that his forehand is brought to the inside of the line of travel so that he travels on three tracks: with his outside hind leg on one track (line of travel), his inside hind and outside fore on the second, and his inside fore on the third. Usually performed at the trot. A test movement that is required beginning at Second Level.

sidedness. Similar to "handedness" in humans; the difference in strength and flexibility in one side of the horse's body versus the other. The horse is usually stiff (tight) on his strong side and "hollow" (weaker, albeit more flexible) on the other. Horses tend to be stiff to the right and hollow to the left.

simple change. Change of canter lead through the walk, with no trot steps. As performed in the dressage tests, there should be a few steps of walk before the horse picks up the new canter lead.

sitting. At the trot, remaining in the saddle at all times instead of rising (posting).

straight/straightness. With the horse's body aligned on the line of travel, be it a straight line or a curved line. Because a horse's hindquarters are wider than his forehand, for him to be straight he must learn to travel with his hind legs somewhat narrowed and his forehand brought slightly to the inside. In lateral movements, the shoulders must always precede the haunches relative to the line of travel.

stride. Cycle of limb movements for a particular gait, from starting position to starting position. Also, the amount of ground covered by these limb movements.

suppleness. Lateral/longitudinal flexibility.

tempo. Rate of repetition of footfalls within a gait. Although minute changes can occur, the tempo of a gait should not change noticeably as a horse adjusts his stride (e.g., collects and extends).

test. Prescribed pattern of gaits and movements used in dressage competition. Each level in dressage comprises one or more tests.

test sheet. Official document on which the numbered test movements are preprinted and on which the scribe records the judge's marks and comments. The judge may write additional remarks on the test sheet at the conclusion of the test and is required to sign the completed sheet.

throughness. English translation of the German dressage term *Durchlässigkeit* — more accurately, "throughlettingness." When a horse is through, his mind and body are accepting and "permeable," such that the rider's aids can influence all parts of his body.

tilting. Undesirable positioning of the horse's head such that his ears are no longer level. Tilting is a fault that crops up especially in lateral work and signifies an evasion of even contact with both reins.

track. A line of travel. To ride on the track means to travel along the rail or wall of the arena. The *second track* is a horse's width from the rail. Also used to describe the lines of travel of individual legs (e.g., a three-track or a four-track shoulder-in, with the horse's legs moving on three or four parallel lines, depending on the degree of angle of the movement).

tracking up. A horse is said to be tracking up when his hind feet are stepping into the prints of his forefeet.

turn on the forehand/turn on the haunches. In a turn on the forehand, a movement not called for in dressage tests, the horse moves around his forefeet. The movement can be a useful method of introducing a green horse to the concept of yielding laterally from the rider's leg. In a turn on the haunches, a walk movement that appears in lower-level tests, the horse describes a very small circle with his hind legs and a larger circle with his forelegs as he brings his forehand around his hindquarters. He is bent in the direction of travel and should continue stepping in an even walk rhythm with all four feet.

turnout. Horse and rider attire and appearance. Also, time that a horse spends loose in a pasture or paddock.

uneven. Taking steps of differing length, which disrupts the rhythm of the gait and causes a horse to land more heavily on one fore- or hind than the other. May be caused by lameness or poor rider position and uneven rein use — thus the term *rein lameness.*

uphill. Appearance that a horse's forehand is higher than his hindquarters; considered an attribute for dressage because it bespeaks a lightening of the forehand and an ability to carry weight and bend the joints of the hind legs. May be the result of conformation, training, or both.

way of going. A horse's usual manner of moving and carrying himself.

working. The basic forward-going, balanced outline called for in the trot and canter at the lower levels. The stride length is between that of collected and medium paces.

PHOTOGRAPHY CREDITS

© Arnd Bronkhorst Photography/www.arnd.nl: 13, 17, 237, 282

© Ed Camelli: 198, 203, 204 bottom, 210, 224, 238, 247, 252, 303

© captivespirit.com: 32 top left, 269 top right

© Frédéric Chéhu/Arnd Bronkhorst Photography: 7

© Mary Cornelius: 296

© Amy Katherine Dragoo: 32 all except top left, 45 top, 51 bottom, 58, 63, 69, 75, 97, 99, 102, 112, 127, 130, 135, 157 bottom, 170, 176, 191, 194, 195, 196, 197, 199, 225, 227, 231, 232, 233 right, 240, 241, 242, 245 bottom, 257, 259, 260, 262, 263, 265, 266, 269 bottom left and right, 277, 286, 287, 291, 293, 295, 301

© Sharon Fibelkorn: vii far left, 100, 128, 192, 193, 268

© Shawn Hamilton/CLIX Photography: vii all except far left

© Jane Jacobs: 269 top left

© Gary Knoll: 294

© Bob Langrish: ii, vi, x, 1, 2, 3, 14, 18, 19, 20, 28, 30, 37, 42, 43, 44, 45 middle and bottom, 49, 50, 51 top left and right, 52, 53, 65, 66, 67, 68, 70, 72, 73, 76, 77, 78, 79, 80, 81, 82, 83, 84, 85, 86, 87, 92, 96, 107, 110, 111, 114, 115, 116, 119, 121, 122, 123, 124, 125, 126, 129, 132, 137, 139, 140, 141, 148, 150, 151, 154, 155, 157 top left, 158, 159, 164, 167, 169, 172, 175, 177, 178, 180, 181, 182, 186, 187, 189, 201, 202, 204 top, 216, 217, 223, 226, 233 left, 234, 245 top, 246, 248, 251, 271, 273, 274, 281, 289, 290, 302, 304, 306, 307, 309, 311

© Terri Miller: 55, 200, 310

© Tim Morse/Lightspeed Photography: 212

© Jennifer Munson Photography: 16

© PhelpsPhotos.com: viii, ix, 6 top, 12 left, 133, 258, 292

© Carien Schippers: 219

© Sheri Scott/Sheri Scott Photography: v, 147, 221

© Susan Sexton: 211

© SusanJStickle.com: 250, 288

© Cealy Tetley: 12 right

Courtesy of USDF: 6 bottom, 8, 9, 10, 11; Phelps Photos 54, 60, 190; Rhett Savoie 88, 297, 299

INDEX

Numbers in *italics* indicate illustrations/photographs; numbers in **boldface** indicate charts.

Abdominal muscles
  horse, *276*, 276–77
  rider, 253, *254*
"above the bit," 108, *109*, 123, *123*
Active Walero, *x*
acupuncture, 286
Adequan (polysulfated glycosaminoglycan), 285
age of horse, 271–72
aids. *See also* canter; position of rider; training scale; trot; walk
  escalating aids, 100–101
  independent seat, 17, 66, 76, 117
  lateral movements, 147, 163, 167–75, 177–89
  leg aids, 74–75, *75*, 100, 102, 167
  rein aids, 100, 102
  "seat, using your," 71, 74, 100, *100*, 117
  timing of aids, 135, 149
  voice aids, 101
  weight aids, 71, 101–2, 133–35, *135*
airs above the ground, 5
alignment, rider, 67, 68, *68*, 117
"alive" rein contact, 282
alternative therapies, 280, 285–87, *286–87*
amateur status, 215–16
American Dressage Institute (ADI), 9–10
American Farrier's Association (AFA), 281

American Horse Shows Association (AHSA, USA Equestrian), 10. *See also* U.S. Equestrian Federation (USEF)
American Riding Instructors Association (ARIA), 61
American Society for Testing and Materials (ASTM), 18, 193
Arabians, 273
arena dimensions, 160, *160*
Arrianus, Lucius Flavius, 2
Ars Tactica (Arrianus), 2
Art of Horsemanship, The (Xenophon), 2
"at the letter," 152, 220
attire, rider, 18–27, 76, 115, 224–29, 236
auxiliary reins, 121

Backing, 157–59, *157–59*, 161
back soreness, horse, 275–78, *276–77*
balance, rider, 67
Balkenhol, Klaus, *237*, 246
ballotade, 4, *4*
bands and tubing (exercise), 263, *263*, 266, *266*
banged tail, 232, *232–33*, 233
bascule, 277, *277*
basic dressage movements, 147–89
basic training, 53–199
bathing a horse, 229, 240, *240*
"behind the bit," 108–9, *109*
"behind the vertical," *109*, 109–10, 123, *123*
bend, 164, *164*, 168, *168*
billeting system (straps), *33*, 33–34
bitting and dental problems, *282*, 282–84

Blackmon, Lisa, 60
Blinks, Susan, *167*, 306
Boomer, Lowell, *10*, 12
boots (riding), 19–22, *20–22*, 23, 76, *76–77*, 115, 228–29, 236
bowed tendon, 279, *279*
"box, the," 70
"bracing the back," 135
braiding mane, 230–32, *231–32*, 236
bras (sport), 26, 115
"break over," 234, *234*
Bredahl-Baker, Charlotte, 306
breeches, 19, 20, *20*, 22–25, *24*, 115, 227–28
breeds for dressage, 271, 272–73, *273*
Brentina, *v*
"bridge," the hover (exercise), 260, *260*
bridle path, 233, *233*
bridles, 34, 41–45, *41–45*
"bulging out" on a circle, *162*, 162–63

Cadre noir, 4, 307, *307*
California Dressage Society Annual Championship Show, 305–6
caller (reader), test, 223, *223*
camps, adult dressage, 303
canter, 130–46
canter pirouette, 276, 277, *277*
Cappellmann, Nadine, *6*
Capprichio, *301*
capriole, 5, *5*, 6, 309, *309*
carousels, 4
carrot stretch, 197, *197*
carrying power stage (collection), training scale, 89, *89*, 92–96, *92–96*, 276

"catching him doing something right,"
120

Cavalia, 309

cavalletti work, 193, *193*

cavalry and dressage, 4–5, *5*

Cavendish, William, 4

cavesson (noseband), 42–45, *42–45*

Centered Riding (Swift), 71, 125

center line of arena, 160, *160*, 161

certification instructor program
(USDF), 61–62, 88, 314–15

Certified Horsemanship Association
(CHA), 61

certified instructors, *60*, 60–63

chair seat, 30, *30*, 33, 73, *73*

Chamberlin, Harry D., 8

chaps, 115

chef d'équipe, 248, *248*

chest-and-shoulder stretch (exercise),
263, 263–64

"chewing the reins out of the hands," 191

chi, 286

child's pose, 260, *260*

chiropractic, 280, 286

Chronicle of the Horse, The, 12

circle, straight on, 93, *93*

circles, turns, *128*, 128–29

circles and half-circles, 161–66, *162,
164–66*

class, competitors, 7

classical horsemanship, *2–7*, 2–8

Clayton, Dr. Hilary, 281

clinics, 296–300, *297, 299*, 315

"closing the door," 149

Coggins test, 213, 215, **215**

"cold backed," 275

coldbloods, 273

collected canter, *139*, 139–40

collected trot, 120–21, *121*

collected walk, 111, *111*

collected work, 57, 107

collection, 89, *89*, 92–96, *92–96*, 276

"collective marks," 216

combined driving, *294*, 294–95

combined training, *293*, 293–94

"coming underneath themselves," 126

"coming up off the ground like a bouncing ball," 270

complementary therapies, 280, 285–87,
286–87

Concours Dressage Internationale (CDI),
7, 306

conferences (USDF), 303, 315–16

conformation, 268, 270–71, *271*

*Consumer's Guide to Alternative Thera-
pies in the Horse* (Ramey), 287

contact, 41, 89, *89*, 91

Contrology, 255

cooldown, 190, *191*

core muscles, rider, 74, 82, 114, 115, 135,
135, 253, 256, 258

counter-canter, 142–43, *143*, 144

courbette, 5

Cowles, Chandler, 9

cross-cantering, 145

cross-country jumping, 293, *293*

cross-leg stretch (exercise), *262*, 262–63

cross-training (gymnasticizing), 140,
190–99

croupade, 4, *4*

curl (exercise), 266, *266*

Dahlwitz, 10, *11*

"daisy-cutting" hunter, 269, *269*, 270

Dansko's Success, *245*

"deep" schooling, 110

degenerative joint disease (DJD), 275

diagramming test, 222–23

directions of test, 220, *220*

disabled riders, 234

Don't Tell Daddy, *225*

double bridles, 41, *41*

double-jointed snaffle, 46, 47, *47*, 48

Dover, Robert, *12*, 61, *306*

downhill balance of horse, 270

"down" transitions, 153, 154, *154–55*

draft breeds, 273

draw reins, 108

Dresden, *9*

dress, rider, 18–27, 76, 115, 224–29, 236

dressage, 3, 4. *See also* U.S. Dressage
Federation (USDF)

Dressage at Devon, 301, 305

Dressage in the Rockies/High Prairie
Dressage, 306

dressage preliminaries, 1–51

dressage saddle, 30, *30–33*, 31–34

Dressage Today, 58

Dressage World Cup Final, 7

driving seat, 70, 128, 129, *129*, 134

drugs and medications, 218

Dvorak, Tom, *227*

Ebeling, Jan, *55*

École de Cavalerie (Guérinière), 4, *4–5, 5*

École de Versailles, 4

École Nationale d'Équitation, 4

écuyer, 4

egg-bar shoe, 280, *280*

endurance training, rider, 253, 254, 261

Equestrian (USEF), 218

Equestrian Educational Center
(Sweden), 4

Equine Affaire, 300

"equitating," 67

escalating aids, 100–101

evenness, rider, 67

eventing (combined training), *293,* 293–94

exercise equipment, rider, 263, *263,* 264–66, *265–66*

expositions, equine, 300–301, *301*

"expressive" movement, 280

extended canter, 141, *141*

extended trot, *127,* 127–28

extended walk, 111

extended work, 57, 107

"**F**alling in" on a circle, 162, *162*

"falling out" on a circle, 93, *93*

familiarization and habitation stage, training scale, *89,* 89–91

Faraon 31, *231*

Farbenfroh, *6*

Fargis, Joe, *195*

farriers, 212, 217, 280, *280,* 281

"Fat Black Mare Can Hardly Ever Kick," 204–5

FBW Kennedy, *12*

Fédération Equestre Internationale (FEI), 7, 62, 206, **206,** 211, 305

"feeder system," 314

FEI Dressage World Cup Final, 307, 308

FEI North American Young Riders' Championships (NAYRC), 307

fetlock joint, 278–79, *279*

fight-or-flight response, 90

figure (of dressage test), 83

figure eights, arena exercise, 161, *165,* 165–66

"filling up" outside rein, 136

first dressage lessons, 65–87

First Level, 206, **206,** 207, 209, 219, 220

fitness of rider, 15, 16–17, 115, 252–67

fit of saddle, 28, 29, *29,* 34, 39, 40, *40,* 115, 275–76

Flettrich, Todd, 116, 137

flexibility training, rider, 253, 254–55, *262–63,* 262–64

"flicking," 271

Flim Flam, *167*

floating teeth, 282, *282,* 283

Floriano, *310*

Florida winter circuit, 305

"foamed up," 43

following the motion, *102,* 102–3

Foltaire, *164*

footing, 160, *280–81,* 280–82

forward and back *(schaukel),* arena exercise, 158, 159, 161

four-beat canter, 137, 156

four-beat gait (walk), *98,* 98–99, 271

Fourth Level, 206, **206,** 207, 219

four-track shoulder-in, *180,* 180–81

Foy, Janet Brown, *248*

Fraessdorf, Klaus, *216*

"frame," 77

free gaits, 57

freestyle tests, 219

free walk, *110,* 110–11

French Cavalry School, 4

Fritz, Capt. John ("Jack"), 12–12

"front to back riding," 108, 277

Gadgets, avoiding, 121

Gahwyler, Max, *9,* 10

gaits, 57. *See also* canter; trot; walk

Gal, Edward, *269*

gallop, 136, 141, 195

Geldnet Lingh, *269*

General System of Horsemanship, A (Cavendish), 4

German National Equestrian Federation, 4, 13, 57, 88

German Olympic Training Center, 4

German silver, 49, 284

Gershberg, Emily, *20, 107, 110–11, 114, 124–25, 148, 151, 157–59, 169, 172, 175, 177–78, 180–82, 186–87, 189*

Gifted, *12, 52, 141, 273*

Gimbel, Amy, *288*

girths, 34, 36, *36*

"girthy," 275

Gli Ordini di Cavalcare (Grisone), 3

gloves, 20, *20,* 25–26, *26,* 76, *76–77,* 77, 229

GMOs (group-member organizations), 59, 60, 212, 218–19, 302, 303, 313

Goldilocks principle, 104, 152

Goldstern, *237*

grab strap, 76, 81, *81*

Graffini Grace, *211*

Graf George, *13*

Grand Prix Level, 206, **206,** 207, 219

Gray, Lendon, 61

"green horse, green rider," 55

Grey Falcon, *8*

Grisone, Federico, 3

Grooming to Win (Harris), 230

ground poles, 192, *192,* 192–93

group-member organizations (GMOs), 59, 60, 212, 218–19, 302, 303, 313

"guarding" legs, 157, 164, 183

Gurney, Hilda, *10–11,* 306

gymnasticizing (cross-training), 140, 190–99

Hacks, cross-training, 193–94
half-halts ("rebalancing"), 74, 122, 125–26, *126*
half-pass, 3, *3*
half-seat (two-point), 195, *195*
halt, *148,* 148–52, *150–51*
hand-grazing, 197–98
Handler, Col. Hans, 9
"handshake," 91
hand-walking, 197–98, *198*
Harmony's Weissmuller, *127, 277*
Harris, Susan E., 61, 230
haunches-in (travers), 182, *182,* 183–84, *184*
haunches-out (renvers), 189, *189*
haute école, 3, 4, 167, *167*
helmets, 18–19, *19–20,* 76, *76,* 193, 195, 196, 227
Henry, Maj. Gen. Guy V., Jr., *8*
Hickey, Chris, *19, 67–68, 70, 76–81, 84–87, 96, 119, 121–23, 126, 129, 137, 139–40, 150*
hill work, *194,* 194–95
hindquarters ("engine"), 92
hindquarters, sore, 274–75, *275*
hip (collapsed), rider, 72, *72,* 118
history of dressage, 2–13
"hock action, good," 136–37
hollow back ("out behind"), 123, *123,* 270, 271, 277
hollow side of horse, 145
homeopathy, 286–87
The Horse: Your Guide to Equine Health Care, 285
horse care, basics of, 17
horse-rider match, 55, 57, 64, 74
hotbloods, 273
"hot" horse, 92

hover ("bridge") (exercise), 260, *260*
Hoyos, Ernst, 97
hyaluronate sodium (Legend), 285
hydration, rider, 266–67

Iberian horses, 3
IMOs (interscholastic/intercollegiate-member organizations), 313
"imprinting," 272
impulsion, 89, *89,* 90–95, *92–95*
independent seat, 17, 66, 76, 117. *See also* position of rider
inside, concept of, 94, *94*
inside leg/outside rein, 136
instructor certification program (USDF), 61–62, 88, 314–15
instructors, 54–64, 76–77
Intermediate II Level, 206, **206,** 207, 219
Intermediate I Level, 206, **206,** 207, 219
International Equestrian Federation (FEI), 7, 62, 206, **206,** 211, 305
International Horse Show Committee, 6, 7
International Olympic Committee (IOC), 6, 308
interscholastic/intercollegiate-member organizations (IMOs), 313
interval training, 195
Introductory Level, 206, **206,** 207, 208, 219
irregular rhythm, 129, *129*

Jaccoma, Susan, *127, 277*
Jackson, Meghan, *257, 259–60, 262–63, 265–66*
jigging, 106, *106*
jog, 112
joint health products, 284–85

judge education (USDF), 211, 249, 315
judges, 204, *204,* 216, *248,* 248–49
judging, advent of, 7–8
jumping, cross-training, 195–96, *196*
jumping saddle, 31, *31–32, 32*

Keen, *10–11*
Kentucky Horse Park, 303
keuring, 273
Kingston, *200*
Kirstein, Lincoln, 9
Krizisch, Klaus, *7*
kür (musical freestyle), 290–91, *291*

La Guérinière, François Robichon de, 4, 5, 178
lameness of horse, 129, 279
Lamping, Natalie, *248*
laser therapy, low-level, 287
lateral couplets, 98
lateral flexion, 173, *173*
lateral movements, 147, 163, 167–75, 177–89
lateral walk, *104,* 104–5
Lavell, Carol, *12, 52, 133, 141, 273*
"leaning on the hand," 110
leather vs. synthetic tack, 35
left lead (canter), 130, 131, *131,* 133, *133*
leg aids, 74–75, *75,* 100, 102, 167
Legend (hyaluronate sodium), 285
leg muscles of rider, 253–54, *254*
leg protection, horse, 50–51, *50–51,* 76, *76*
leg-yield, 170, 171–75, *171–75,* 177–78, 183
lengthened canter, *137,* 137–39
lengthened trot, *119,* 119–20
lengthening, 107
lesions and lameness, 279

lessons, first dressage, 65–87

letters and levels, 202–9

"letting him out the front door," 122

levade, 5, *5*, 6, 167, *167*

Levante D., *231, 233*

levels, tests, 88, **206,** *206–9*

Levin, *76–81, 84–87*

licensed judges, 248–49, 305

Lipizzan horses, 3, *3*

"L" (learner) judge, 211, 248, 315

Ljungquist, Col. Bengt, 9

lunge (exercise), 259, *259*

lungeing at shows, 243

lunge lessons, 76–87. *See also* position of rider

Magnetic therapy, 287

mane, braiding, 230–32, *231–32,* 236

manège riding, 3

Manual of Horsemanship (Chamberlin), 8

manual stretching, 197, *197*

marks on test, *247,* 247–48

Marnix, *291*

Maruxa, *231*

Mason, Heather, *250*

massage therapy, 280, 285–86, *286*

Master, Edith, 10, *11*

McCashin, Dr. Fred, *216*

McDonald, Debbie, *v*

McGivern, Nicola, *x*

Medieval Times, 309

medium canter, 140, *140*

medium trot, 122, *122*

medium walk, 107, *107*

medium work, 57, 107

memberships and fees for USEF/USDF, 214–15, **214–15**

memorizing tests, 221–23, *223*

mental fitness from cross-training, 191–96, *192–96*

Mikolka, Karl, 309

Military test, 5

mind-body connection, 255

Monaco, 10, *11*

Moore, Laurie, *221*

Morkis, Dorothy, 10, *11*

Morris, George, 61, 68

Morse, Leslie, *200*

mouthpieces of snaffle bits, 46, 47, *47–49,* 48–49, 283

movement (required element of test), 7

movements (basic dressage), 147–89

Much Ado, *133*

muscle ring, 276, *276,* 277

musical freestyle *(kür),* 290–91, *291*

National programs (USDF), 303

"navel to spine," 103, 117, 134–35

neck, "upside down," 279–80

neck and poll tightness, *279,* 279–80

neck-in, 179–80, *180*

neutral spine, 135, *135*

Nikolaus 7, *ii*

Nimbus, *250*

noseband (cavesson), 42–45, *42–45*

nutrition, rider, 266–67

Officials, show, 216–17, *216–17*

Olie, Bonnie, *102, 157, 170, 176, 191, 194*

Olympic competition, *6,* 6–7

Olympic Games, 306, 308

omnibus, 218–19

"on a long rein," 110

"on a loose rein," 110–11

"on deck," 244

"on the bit" (on contact), 97, *108–9,* 108–10, 295

"on the forehand," 151–52

"opening the door," 140

open shows, 305

origins of dressage, 2–13

Otelo, *287*

"out behind" (hollow back), 123, *123,* 270, 271, 277

outside, concept of, 94, *94*

overtracking, 105, *105*

Ox Ridge Hunt Club, 9

Paces within gaits, 106

pacing, 98–99, 111, 156

Page, Michael, 61

pain of horse, off days, 138

Pan American Games, 7, 307–8

Pancratius ("Paul"), *42–45, 92, 107, 110–11, 114, 124–25, 148, 151, 157–59, 169, 172, 175, 177–78, 180–82, 186–87, 189, 233, 271*

partnership with horse, 15–16, *16*

pas de deux, 212, 219, 292, *292,* 295

passage, 6, *6*

patterns (dressage tests), 6, 7, 208

Payne, Lisa, *292*

Peacock, Susan Hoffman, *192–93*

pelvic tuck/tilt, 134–35, *135*

PEMF (pulsating electromagnetic field) therapy, 287, *287*

Peters, Steffen, 191, 271, 306, *310*

Petersen, Lars, *245*

physical fitness from cross-training, 191–96, *192–96*

piaffe, 5, *5,* 6, 7, *7*

Pilates, 115, 117, 255–58, *257–58,* 260, 262

placement of letters, 202–6, *203, 205*

"plugging in," 117

polo wraps, 50, *50*, 51

polysulfated glycosaminoglycan (Adequan), 285

"popped" shoulder, 93, *93*, 162, *162*, 183

position of rider, 65–75. *See also* lunge lessons

positive reinforcement, 120

Poulin, Michael, 13, 15

Poulin family, *292*

pregnant riders, 267

Prix St. Georges Level, 206, **206**, 207, 219

pulled mane, 230, 231, *231*

pulsating electromagnetic field (PEMF) therapy, 287, *287*

pushing power stage (impulsion), training scale, 89, *89*, 90–95, *92–95*

pyramid of training. *See* training scale

Quadrille, 4, 212, 219, 292, *292*

quarter lines of arena, 160, *160*, 161

Rainier, *306*

Ramey, Dr. David, 287

Ransehousen, Jessica, *248*

reader (caller), test, 223, *223*

"rebalancing" (half-halts), 74, 122, 125–26, *126*

recognized shows, 213–19, **214–15,** *216–17,* 225

Regent, *96, 119, 121–23, 126, 129, 137, 139–40, 150*

Regional Dressage Championships (USDF), 313, *313,* 316

Reiber, Cherri, 309

rein aids, 100, 102

rein back, 157–59, *157–59,* 161

reining ("Western dressage"), 295, *295*

rein lameness, 129, 278

reins, lunge lessons, 76, *76,* 81, *81–83,* 82, 83

relaxation, training scale, 89, *89,* 90–91

renvers (haunches-out), 189, *189*

rhythm and regularity, training scale, 89, *89,* 89–90

rhythm change in transitions, 153, 156

Richter, Judy, 61

rider, traits of, 14–17, *16–17*

rider position, 65–75. *See also* lunge lessons

rider status, declaring, 215–16

riders with disabilities, 234

ride time, 213

Riding and Schooling Horses (Chamberlin), 8

"riding back to front," 91, 108

riding the pattern, test, 222

right lead (canter), 130, 131, *131,* 133, *133*

rings of snaffle bits, 46, 47, *47,* 283

"ring sourness," 192

rising trot, 113–14, *114*

"r" (recorded) judge, 249, 315

"R" (registered) judge, 249

Robb, Johnny, *292*

Rocher, *viii*

roll-up (exercise), 256–58, *257*

Royal Academy of Equestrian Art, 3, 4

Royal Andalusian School of Equestrian Art, 4

"rubberneck," 279

Saddlebreds, 269, *269, 270*

saddle pads, 38–41, *40*

saddles, 28–35, *30–33,* 67, 74, 115

safety, stirrup, 38, *38*

safety-conscious instructor, 55, 56

Safety Equipment Institute (SEI), 18, 193

safety importance, 17

salute to judge, 204, *204,* 220, 245, *245*

Sandstone's Corvette, *192–93*

scale of training. *See* training scale

schaukel (forward and back), arena exercise, 158, 159, 161

schedule for show preparation, 238–40, *240*

schooling shows, 210–13, *211–12,* 246

"school is in session," 97

School of Naples, 3

Schut-Kery, Sabine, *301*

scribing, 216, 302–3, *303*

"seat, using your," 71, 74, 100, *100,* 117

seat bone, weighting a, 133–34

seat bones, finding your, *115,* 115–16

Second Level, 206, **206**, 207, 209, 219, 220, 221

Seidel, Guenter, *ii, 13, 17, 164,* 306

self-carriage, 96

self-scrutiny, 175

serpentines, 145, *145,* 161, 166, *166*

Serrell, Margarita ("Migi"), 9

Severson, Kim, *293*

shadbelly coat, 226, *226,* 227

shallow serpentine, true canter to counter-canter, arena exercise, 145, *145*

shoeing, 234, *234,* 280, 280–81

Shoulder Bridge (exercise), 265, *265*

shoulder-fore, 181, *181,* 183

shoulder-in, *178–80,* 178–81, 183

showing, 201–49

    instructor selection and, 56

    learning at, 301–2, *302*

showing (*continued*)

  recognized shows, 213–19, **214–15,** *216–17,* 225

show-jumping (stadium jumping), 293, *293*

shows (must-see), 304–9, *306–7, 309*

"sidedness" of horse, 129, 146, 150

side leg lift (exercise), 266, *266*

side reins, 76, 78–79, *78–79*

Siglavy Mantua, *7*

simple change of lead, 166

Si Murray, *8*

single-jointed snaffle, 46, 47, *47,* 48

"sitting in," 75

"sitting" on a horse, 68

sitting the canter, 131–32, *132*

sitting trot, 113, 114–18, *115,* 253

sizing bits, 49, *49*

Skidmore College, 9–10

snaffle bits, 41–42, *41–42,* 45–49, *47–49,* 121

soft-tissue injuries, 278–79, *279*

soundness, horse, 13, 268–87

Spanish Riding School of Vienna, 3, *3,* 4, 5, 7, *7,* 9, 66, 97, 167, *167,* 308–9, *309*

sport horses, 273

sport of dressage and art, 5–7, *5–7*

sport-psychology, 16

spurs, 26–27, *27,* 99, 229, 236

stadium jumping (show-jumping), 293, *293*

stall etiquette at shows, 241

Steiner, Axel, *55*

Steiner, Betsy, 256, *258*

Steinkraus, William, 9

stepping-over-the-sidewalk-cracks exercise, 138, 141

stepping-stones vs. steps, training scale, 96

stiff side of horse, 145

stirrup leathers and irons, 36–38, *37–38*

stirrups, working without, 82, 86–87, *86–87,* 116, 116–17

straightness, training scale, 89, *89,* 92–95, *92–95,* 161

straps (billeting system), *33,* 33–34

strength, rider, 67

strength training, rider, 253–54, *254,* 255–60, *257–60*

stretching circle (stretchy-chewy) exercise, 122, *124,* 124–25

stretching work, 196–97, *197*

stride, 98

"strung out," 123, *123*

Sultan, *102, 157, 170, 176, 191, 194, 199, 231*

superficial digital flexor tendon, 278–79, *279*

suppleness

  horse, 196–99, *197–99*

  rider, 67

support boots, 51, *51,* 76, *76*

suspension, 98, *98,* 99, 113, *113,* 130, 131, *131*

suspensory ligament, 279, *279*

Swift, Sally, 71, 125

Sydnor, Eliza, *211*

synthetic vs. leather tack, 35

Tack and equipment, 28–51

  lunge lessons, 76–81, *76–81*

  showing, 229–35, *231–34,* 236

tails, grooming, 232–33, *232–33*

"taking," 92

teamwork, dressage, 15–16, *16*

teeth and bitting problems, *282,* 282–84

Tempel Lipizzans, 309

tempo, 103, 104, 153

test, riding a, 244–48, *245–47*

"test of choice," 212

tests (patterns), 6, 7, 208

tests, show, *219–21,* 219–23, *223*

therapeutic options, 280, 284–87, *286–87*

Third Level, 206, **206,** 207, 219

Thoroughbreds, 271, 272, 273

three-beat gait (canter), 130–31, *131,* 136, 271

three-day eventing, 5

three-loop serpentine, arena exercise, 166, *166*

"through," 276, *276*

tights vs. breeches, 23–25, *24,* 115

timing of aids, 135, 149

"together, bringing him" (half-halts), 74, 122, 125–26, *126*

tracking up, 105, *105*

"tracks," 178

trailering-in for lessons, 63

trail rides, 193–94

training, basic, 53–199

Training Hunters, Jumpers and Hacks (Chamberlin), 8

Training Level, 206, **206,** 207, 208, 219, 220, *220,* 221

training scale

  horse, 46, 57, 88–96

  rider, 118

transitions, 147, 152–56, *154–55,* 191

traveling for lessons, 63–64

travers (haunches-in), 182, *182,* 183–84, *184*

Traurig, Christine, 306

Travolta M, *288*

trimming horse for show, 233

trot, 112–29

trot half-pass right, 167, *167*

trot leg-yield, 172, *172*

trot to halt, 104

trot-to-walk transition, 154, *154–55*

tummy tuck by horse, 277

turn on the forehand, 169–70, *169–70*

turn on the haunches, 184–88, *185–87*

turnout of horse, 198–99, *199*

Tuttle, Capt. Hiram, *8*

two-beat gait (trot), 112–13, *113*, 128, 271

two-loop serpentine, 161

two-point (half-seat), 195, *195*

types vs. breeds of horses, 273

Udon, 271

ultrasound (therapeutic), 287

Under Foot (USDF), 281

underwear, padded, 26, 115

uneven gaits, 278

United States, dressage, 8–13, *8–13*

unmounted rehearsal of test, 222

uphill balance of horse, 270

"up" transitions, 153, 154, *154–55*

U.S. Army Olympic Equestrian Team (1932), *6*

U.S. Dressage Federation (USDF), 313–16

awards, 316

conferences, 303, 315–16

Under Foot, 281

founding of, *9*, 10–13

group-member organizations (GMOs), 59, 60, 212, 218–19, 302, 303, 313

instructor certification, 61–62, 88, 314–15

judge education, 211, 249, 315

memberships and fees, 214–15, **214–15**

national programs and symposia, 303

organizational structure of, *313*, 313–14

recognized shows, 213–19, **214–15** *216–17*, 225

Regional Dressage Championships, 313, *313*, 316

tests published by, 219

University, 316

USDF Connection, 58, 62, 218

USDF Directory, 160, 219, 292

Web site for, 315

U.S. Equestrian Federation (USEF), 10, 11, 12, 107, 136, 178, 206, **206,** 211, 218, 219

U.S. Equestrian Team (USET), 10, 11, 12

U.S. Pony Clubs (USPC), 208

"using your seat," 71, 74, 100, *100*, 117

Veterinarian for show, 216, *216*, 217

veterinary health certificate, 213, 215, **215**

visualization of test, 222

voice aids, 101

volunteers for show, 217, *217*

Von Rosen, Count Clarence, 5, 6

Walk, 97–111

walk-halt-repeat, 103–4, 105, 149

walk-to-canter transition, 154, *154–55*

Wanless, Mary, 117

warmbloods, 271, 272–73, *273*, 281

warm-up, 190–91, *191*, 197, *242*, 242–44

water drinking, rider, 266–67

"way of going," 268–70, *269*

Weebles and balanced seat, 117

weight aids, 71, 101–2, 133–35, *135*

Western-pleasure horse, 112, 269, *269,* 270

Western saddle, 29, 31, 32, *32*

whips, 26–27, *27,* 99, *99, 176,* 176–77, 229

whites (show attire), 243

"wide behind" stance, 150

Wilcox, Lisa, 97

Williams, George, *viii, 246, 291,* 309

Winsome Adante, *293*

working canter, 136–37, *137*

working gaits, 57

working trot, 119, *119*

World Equestrian Games, 7, 308

Xenophon, 2

"**Z**ipping up the abdominals," 103, 117–18, 134, 256

OTHER STOREY TITLES YOU MIGHT ENJOY

101 Dressage Exercises for Horse & Rider, by Jec Aristotle Ballou. Dressage is the ultimate achievement of oneness between horse and rider. This training manual offers tips and exercises for achieving that oneness, for both classical dressage riders and the wider audience of English and Western equestrians. 240 pages. Paper with comb binding. ISBN 1-58017-595-3.

The Horse Conformation Handbook, by Heather Smith Thomas. This comprehensive volume explains how conformation relates to structure and function and what to look for when evaluating a horse. Whether you're buying your first horse, choosing a horse for a competitive sport, selecting breeding stock, or simply want to learn more about your equine companion, ***The Horse Conformation Handbook*** is an invaluable reference. 400 pages. Paperback. ISBN 1-58017-558-9. Hardcover. ISBN 1-58017-559-7.

Storey's Horse-Lover's Encyclopedia, edited by Deborah Burns. This comprehensive, user-friendly, A-to-Z guide to all things equine covers breeds, tack, facilities, daily care, health issues, riding styles, shows, and much more. 480 pages. Paperback. ISBN 1-58017-317-9.

Horsekeeping on a Small Acreage, Second Edition, by Cherry Hill. Thoroughly updated, full-color edition of the best-selling classic details the essentials for designing safe and functional facilities whether on one acre or one hundred. Hill describes the entire process: layout design, barn construction, feed storage, fencing, equipment selection, and much more. 320 pages. Paperback. ISBN 1-58017-535-X.

Storey's Guide to Raising Horses, by Heather Smith Thomas. Whether you are an experienced horse handler or are planning to own your first horse, this complete guide to intelligent horsekeeping covers all aspects of keeping a horse fit and healthy in body and spirit. 512 pages. Paperback. ISBN 1-58017-127-3.

Storey's Guide to Training Horses, by Heather Smith Thomas. This comprehensive guide covers every aspect of the training process—from basic safety to retraining a horse that has developed a bad habit—this is an essential handbook for all horse owners. 512 pages. Paperback. ISBN 1-58017-467-1.

Easy-Gaited Horses, by Lee Ziegler. Discover the pleasures of riding a horse that is calm, obedient, relaxed, and sure-footed with this comprehensive guide to training and riding a variety of horses in specific gaits. 256 pages. Paperback. ISBN 1-58017-562-7.

The Rider's Fitness Program, by Dianna R. Dennis, John J. McCully, and Paul M. Juris. This unique, six-week workout routine is designed specifically for equestrians to help build the strength, endurance, and skills that will enhance the riding experience. 224 pages. Paperback. ISBN 1-58017-542-2.

The Horse Behavior Problem Solver, by Jessica Jahiel. Using a friendly question-and-answer format and drawing on real-life case studies, Jahiel explains how a horse thinks and learns, why it acts the way it does, and how you should respond. 352 pages. Paperback. ISBN 1-58017-524-4.